A·N·N·U·A·L EDITIONS

Adolescent Psychology

01/02

Third Edition

EDITORS

Anita M. Meehan
Kutztown University of Pennsylvania

Anita M. Meehan is professor of psychology at Kutztown University of Pennsylvania. She received a B.A. from Wilkes College with majors in psychology and elementary education and an M.A. and Ph.D in developmental psychology from Temple University. Her research interests have focused on cognitive and social development. Most recently, she published and presented work on gender schemas and sex-role development.

Eileen Astor-Stetson
Bloomsburg University of Pennsylvania

Eileen Astor-Stetson is a professor of psychology at Bloomsburg University. She received an A.B. in psychology from Douglass College, Rutgers—The State University of New Jersey, and a Ph.D. in psychology from Vanderbilt University. She has two general areas of research. One involves age-related changes in perception. The other focuses on predictors of safer sex behaviors in adolescents and young adults, including risk taking, alcohol use, and knowledge about HIV. Dr. Astor-Stetson has also presented work on techniques for teaching students about safer sex.

McGraw-Hill/Dushkin
530 Old Whitfield Street, Guilford, Connecticut 06437

Visit us on the Internet
http://www.dushkin.com

Credits

1. Perspectives on Adolescence
Unit photo—© 2000 by Cleo Freelance Photography.
2. Puberty and Biology
Unit photo—United Nations photo by John Isaac.
3. Cognitive Growth and Education
Unit photo—© 2000 by Cleo Freelance Photography.
4. Identity and Socioemotional Development
Unit photo—© 2000 by Cleo Freelance Photography.
5. Family Relationships
Unit photo—© 2000 by Cleo Freelance Photography.
6. Peers and Youth Culture
Unit photo—© 2000 by Cleo Freelance Photography.
7. Teenage Sexuality
Unit photo—United Nations photo by John Isaac.
8. Problem Behaviors and Interventions
Unit photo—© 2000 by Cleo Freelance Photography.

Copyright

Cataloging in Publication Data
Main entry under title: Annual Editions: Adolescent Psychology. 2001/2002.
1. Psychology—Periodicals. I. Meehan, Anita *comp.* II. Astor-Stetson, Eileen, *comp.* III. Title: Adolescent psychology.
155.5'05   ISBN 0–07–242572–5   82–646006   ISSN 1094-2610

Third Edition

Cover image © 2001 PhotoDisc, Inc.

Printed in the United States of America   34567890BAHBAH5432   Printed on Recycled Paper

Members of the Advisory Board are instrumental in the final selection of articles for each edition of ANNUAL EDITIONS. Their review of articles for content, level, currentness, and appropriateness provides critical direction to the editor and staff. We think that you will find their careful consideration well reflected in this volume.

Editors/Advisory Board

EDITORS

Anita M. Meehan
Kutztown University of Pennsylvania

Eileen Astor-Stetson
Bloomsburg University of Pennsylvania

ADVISORY BOARD

Lee Abbott
Cayuga Community College

Paul J. Berghoff
Pembroke State University

Christy Buchanan
Wake Forest University

John S. Dacey
Boston College

Florence L. Denmark
Pace University

Gregory T. Fouts
University of Calgary

Wyndol Furman
University of Denver

Emily J. Johnson
University of Wisconsin La Crosse

Maureen E. Kenny
Boston College

Daniel K. Lapsley
Ball State University

John Mirich
Metropolitan State College of Denver

John Mitchell
Okanagan University College

Alinde J. Moore
Ashland University

George Muugi
Kutztown University

Elizabeth B. Newell
California State University, Fresno

John W. Santrock
University of Texas, Dallas

Gail Scott
Briar Cliff College

Michael Shaughnessy
Eastern New Mexico University

Margaret B. Spencer
University of Pennsylvania

Staff

048047

To the Reader

In publishing ANNUAL EDITIONS we recognize the enormous role played by the magazines, newspapers, and journals of the public press in providing current, first-rate educational information in a broad spectrum of interest areas. Many of these articles are appropriate for students, researchers, and professionals seeking accurate, current material to help bridge the gap between principles and theories and the real world. These articles, however, become more useful for study when those of lasting value are carefully collected, organized, indexed, and reproduced in a low-cost format, which provides easy and permanent access when the material is needed. That is the role played by ANNUAL EDITIONS.

New to ANNUAL EDITIONS is the inclusion of related World Wide Web sites. These sites have been selected by our editorial staff to represent some of the best resources found on the World Wide Web today. Through our carefully developed topic guide, we have linked these Web resources to the articles covered in this ANNUAL EDITIONS reader. We think that you will find this volume useful, and we hope that you will take a moment to visit us on the Web at **http://www.dushkin.com** to tell us what you think.

No longer a child and not yet an adult, adolescents find themselves caught in the middle. Popular culture often depicts adolescence as a period of raging hormones, emotional upheaval, rejection of parents, and blind conformity to peers. One goal of this anthology is to present a more balanced picture of adolescence, including both positive and negative aspects of this developmental transition. We chose articles that address timeless adolescent issues such as puberty, the identity crisis, and establishing independence from parents. We also chose articles that discuss contemporary issues affecting adolescents, parents, and professionals who interact with adolescents. For example, articles examine violence in schools, use of the Internet, nontraditional families, working adolescents, and steroid use. We made an effort to include readings that focus on effective strategies and interventions for helping adolescents through this transition period, particularly at-risk adolescents.

We have organized this anthology into eight units. The units cover issues related to the fundamental biological, cognitive, and socioemotional changes of adolescence as well as the contexts of adolescent development (family, school, peers, work). In keeping with this perspective that the ecological context of adolescent development is crucial to understanding, we also incorporated articles that examine the impact of socioeconomic, gender, ethnic, and cultural influences on adolescent development. Unit 1 looks at adolescence in historical and contemporary perspectives. Unit 2 examines the biological and psychological impact of puberty. Unit 3 explores issues related to cognitive growth and education, and unit 4 addresses identity and socioemotional development. Unit 5 covers family relationships during adolescence, while unit 6 focuses on peers and youth culture. Teen sexuality issues are examined in unit 7. Problem behaviors like teen violence, drug use, and suicide are included in unit 8.

Many readings present controversial topics that we hope will spur classroom debate. For example, Are mandatory exit exams a good solution for ensuring that high school students have met educational standards? Do adolescents today have a harder time establishing an identity? Do we blame the media too much for the problems of today's adolescents? Should sex education programs stress abstinence or condom use?

We hope that the articles in this third edition of *Annual Editions: Adolescent Psychology* will be thought-provoking and interesting for the reader and that the readings will result in a deeper understanding of adolescent development. We would like to thank the reviewers who made comments on previous editions and we would also like to know what you think. Please take a few minutes to complete the article rating form in the back of this volume. Anything can be improved, and we need your help to improve future editions of *Annual Editions: Adolescent Psychology*.

Anita M. Meehan
Editor

Eileen Astor-Stetson
Editor

Contents

Perspectives on Adolescence

Three articles in this section examine what defines adolescence.

Puberty and Biology

Six selections in this section consider what impact puberty has on the maturing adolescent.

The concepts in bold italics are developed in the article. For further expansion please refer to the Topic Guide and the Index.

UNIT 3

Cognitive Growth and Education

The dynamics encountered by adolescents as they learn to cope with society and educational experiences are discussed in the seven articles in this section.

The concepts in bold italics are developed in the article. For further expansion please refer to the Topic Guide and the Index.

UNIT 4

Identity and Socioemotional Development

Five articles in this section look at how an adolescent copes with self-esteem, establishing a sense of identity, emotional development, and emotional intelligence.

The concepts in bold italics are developed in the article. For further expansion please refer to the Topic Guide and the Index.

UNIT 5

Family Relationships

In this section, five articles examine how much influence family life has on adolescent development.

UNIT 6

Peers and Youth Culture

Six articles in this section consider the extent that gender roles, peer group pressure, drugs, and mass media influence the socialization of an adolescent.

The concepts in bold italics are developed in the article. For further expansion please refer to the Topic Guide and the Index.

UNIT 7

Teenage Sexuality

Eight articles in this section discuss
how adolescents view sexual behavior
and the importance of sex education.

The concepts in bold italics are developed in the article. For further expansion please refer to the Topic Guide and the Index.

ix

The concepts in bold italics are developed in the article. For further expansion please refer to the Topic Guide and the Index.

UNIT 8

Problem
Behaviors and
Interventions

In this section, six articles address
some of the problems faced
by today's adolescents. These
include drug abuse, violence,
steroid use, suicide, and alienation.

The concepts in bold italics are developed in the article. For further expansion please refer to the Topic Guide and the Index.

This topic guide suggests how the selections and World Wide Web sites found in the next section of this book relate to topics of traditional concern to adolescent psychology students and professionals. It is useful for locating interrelated articles and Web sites for reading and research. The guide is arranged alphabetically according to topic.

The relevant Web sites, which are numbered and annotated on pages 4 and 5, are easily identified by the Web icon (◉) under the topic articles. By linking the articles and the Web sites by topic, this ANNUAL EDITIONS reader becomes a powerful learning and research tool.

3

DUSHKIN ONLINE

● AE: Adolescent Psychology

The following World Wide Web sites have been carefully researched and selected to support the articles found in this reader. If you are interested in learning more about specific topics found in this book, these Web sites are a good place to start. The sites are cross-referenced by number and appear in the topic guide on the previous two pages. Also, you can link to these Web sites through our DUSHKIN ONLINE support site at *http://www.dushkin.com/online/*.

The following sites were available at the time of publication. Visit our Web site—we update DUSHKIN ONLINE regularly to reflect any changes.

General Sources

1. Ask NOAH About: Mental Health
http://www.noah.cuny.edu/illness/mentalhealth/ mental.html
This enormous resource contains information about child and adolescent family problems, mental conditions and disorders, suicide prevention, and much more.

2. Health Information Resources
http://nhic-nt.health.org/Scripts/Tollfree.cfm
Here is a long list of toll-free numbers that provide health-related information.

3. Knowledge Exchange Network (KEN)
http://www.mentalhealth.org/aboutken/index.htm
The CMHS National Mental Health Services Exchange Network (KEN) provides information about mental health via toll-free telephone services.

4. Mental Health Net
http://mentalhelp.net
This is a comprehensive guide to mental health online, featuring 6,300 individual resources.

5. Psychnet
http://www.apa.org/psychnet/
Access APA Monitor, the American Psychological Association newspaper, APA Books on a wide range of topics, PsychINFO, an electronic database of abstracts on over 1,350 scholarly journals, and HelpCenter.

Perspectives on Adolescence

6. Adolescence: Change and Continuity
http://www.personal.psu.edu/faculty/n/x/ nxd10/adolesce.htm#top
At this site, students who took a course, *The Transition to Adulthood*, at Pennsylvania State University offer an excellent series of areas to explore concerning basic domains, such as biological, cognitive, and social changes; contexts, such as family changes during adolescence, family influences, school, and work; and issues, such as identity development, intimacy, psychosocial problems, and more.

7. Facts for Families
http://www.aacap.org/info_families/index.htm
The American Academy of Child and Adolescent Psychiatry provides concise, up-to-date information on issues that affect teenagers and their families. Fifty-six fact sheets include teenagers' issues, such as coping with life, sad feelings, inability to sleep, or not getting along with friends.

8. The Opportunity of Adolescence
http://www.winternet.com/~webpage/ adolescencepaper.html
This paper calls adolescence the turning point, after which the future is redirected and confirmed, and goes on to discuss the opportunities and problems of this period to the in-dividual and society, using quotations from Erik Erikson, Jean Piaget, and others.

Puberty and Biology

9. Biological Changes in Adolescence
http://www.personal.psu.edu/faculty/n/x/nxd10/ biologic2.htm
This site offers a discussion of puberty, sexuality, biological changes, cross-cultural differences, and nutrition for adolescents.

Cognitive Growth and Education

10. At-Risk Children and Youth
http://www.ncrel.org/sdrs/areas/at0cont.htm
North Central Regional Educational Laboratory (NCREL) offers this list of resources. Critical issues include rethinking learning for students at risk, linking at-risk students to integrated services, providing effective schooling for students at risk, and using technology to enhance engaged learning.

11. Cognitive Changes in Adolescence
http://www.personal.psu.edu/faculty/n/x/nxd10/ cognitiv.htm#top
Helpful articles, with related Web addresses, are available at this site. The first is "Adolescents: What Are They Thinking?" The second is "How Do Cognitive Changes during Adolescence Affect the Parent/Child Relationship?"

Identity and Socioemotional Development

12. AAUW's Initial Research
http://www.aauw.org/2000/sgsa.html
The American Association of University Women shares its research online. Abstracts include "Shortchanging Girls, Shortchanging America" and other reports that can then be ordered.

13. ADOL: Adolescence Directory On-Line
http://education.indiana.edu/cas/adol/adol.html
This is an electronic guide to information on adolescent issues. Some of the issues concern conflict and violence, peer mediation, mental health problems, and health issues.

14. CYFERNET-Youth Development
http://www.cyfernet.mes.umn.edu/youthdev.html
Excellent source of many articles on youth development, including impediments to healthy development.

15. Socioemotional Development
http://www.valdosta.peachnet.edu/~whuitt/psy702/ affsys/erikson.html
Erik Erikson's concepts are outlined here, followed by examples for the use of secondary school teachers in encouraging identity formation in their students.

Family Relationships

16. CYFERNET: Cooperative Extension System's Children, Youth, and Family Information Service
http://www.cyfernet.org
CYFERNET provides hundreds of complete online publications featuring practical, research-based information in six major areas.

17. Help for Parents of Teenagers
http://www.bygpub.com/parents/
In addition to discussing the book, *The Teenager's Guide to the Real World*, and how it can help parents, this site lists other book sources and Web sites for parents and teens.

18. Mental Health Net: Facts for Families Index
http://mentalhelp.net/factsfam/
The American Academy of Child and Adolescent Psychiatry publishes informational brochures that provide concise and up-to-date material on issues such as teen suicide, stepfamily problems, teen eating disorders, and manic-depressive illness.

19. Stepfamily Association of America
http://www.stepfam.org
The problems that surround step-parenting and stepchildren are discussed at this site. Just click on Facts and Figures and then on FAQS to reach many aspects of adolescent adjustment based on the type of family in which they live.

Peers and Youth Culture

20. Higher Education Center for Alcohol and Other Drug Prevention
http://www.edc.org/hec/
This U.S. Department of Education site has interactive discussion forums and a Just for Students section.

21. Justice Information Center (NCJRS): Drug Policy Information
http://www.ncjrs.org/drgswww.htm
This is a list of national and international World Wide Web sites on drug policy information.

22. National Clearinghouse for Alcohol and Drug Information
http://www.health.org
This is an excellent general site for information on drug and alcohol facts that might relate to adolescence.

23. Peers
http://www.personal.psu.edu/faculty/n/x/nxd10/peers2.htm#top
This paper discusses all aspects of peer relationships, including cliques and crowds, problem behavior and gangs, popularity and rejection, and issues in dating.

Teenage Sexuality

24. Adolescents and Abstinence
http://www.noah.cuny.edu/sexuality/siecus/fact2.html
The Sexuality Information and Education Council of the United States provides data on teenage sexual behavior.

25. American Sexual Behavior
http://www.icpsr.umich.edu/gss/report/t-report/topic25.htm

This article, "American Sexual Behavior," discusses trends, sociodemographics, and risky behavior.

26. CDC National AIDS Clearinghouse
http://www.cdcnpin.org
This complete source on AIDS includes "Respect Yourself, Protect Yourself," which are public service announcements.

27. Welcome to AboutHealth
http://www.abouthealth.com
This health site includes information about sexuality, HIV and AIDS, peer pressure, and other information to help adolescents. Sites include In Our Own Words: Teens & AIDS, Risky Times, and links to other sites.

Problem Behaviors and Interventions

28. Anxiety Disorders in Children and Adolescents
http://12.17.20.55/aboutanxietydisorders/childrenadolescents
On this page, the Anxiety Disorders Association of America (ADAA) discusses anxiety disorders in children and adolescents under seven headings.

29. Mental Health Net: Eating Disorder Resources
http://eatingdisorders.mentalhelp.net
This is a very complete list of Web references on eating disorders, including anorexia, bulimia, and obesity.

30. Mental Health Risk Factors for Adolescents
http://education.indiana.edu/cas/adol/mental.html
This collection of Web resources is useful for parents, educators, researchers, health practitioners, and teens. It covers abuse, conduct disorders, stress, and support.

31. Questions & Answers about Child & Adolescent Psychiatry
http://www.aacap.org/about/q&a.htm
This site of the American Academy of Child & Adolescent Psychiatry attempts to answer the questions related to feelings and behaviors that cause disruption in the lives of young adults and the people around them.

32. Suicide Awareness: Voices of Education
http://www.save.org
This is the most popular suicide site on the Internet. It has information on dealing with suicide, along with material from the organization's many education sessions.

33. Teenage Problems
http://www.bygpub.com/books/tg2rw/problems.htm
This extract on the Web from *The Teenager's Guide to the Real World* offers an abstract on teenage problems: depression, suicide, eating disorders, and other diseases. It is especially useful for its list of hotline phone numbers.

34. Youth Suicide League
http://www.unicef.org/pon96/insuicid.htm
This UNESCO Web site provides international suicide rates of young adults in selected countries.

We highly recommend that you review our Web site for expanded information and our other product lines. We are continually updating and adding links to our Web site in order to offer you the most usable and useful information that will support and expand the value of your Annual Editions. You can reach us at: http://www.dushkin.com/annualeditions/.

www.dushkin.com/online/

Unit Selections

Key Points to Consider

❖ How diverse were families throughout the history of the United States? How have families changed since colonial times? Why is it misleading and counterproductive to assume that there has been a "traditional" American family?

❖ How have economic changes through the twentieth century caused changes in the way society viewed adolescents? How have changes in society since the 1940s caused changes in the American family?

❖ In what ways is adolescence a time of great potential? What data indicate that the difficulties of adolescence are overstated?

 **Links** **www.dushkin.com/online/**

These sites are annotated on pages 4 and 5.

Meagan applies her lipstick expertly without a mirror, wears the acceptable fashions to school, and clutches her new stuffed bear as she worries that a friend may give her a Barbie doll for her birthday when she clearly has outgrown them. This 12-year old is not a young child, but neither is she an adult. She is in that stage between childhood and adulthood: adolescence.

Exactly what characterizes adolescence is not clearly established. G. Stanley Hall, who is credited with founding the scientific study of adolescence in the early part of the 1900s, saw adolescence as corresponding roughly to the teen years. He believed individuals of this age had great potential, but also experienced extreme mood swings. He labeled this a period of "storm and stress." Because of their labile emotions, he believed that adolescents were typically psychologically maladjusted. What did he believe was the cause of this storm and stress? Basically, he believed that it was biological. Hall's views had a profound effect on the subsequent study of adolescence. Biological factors that underlie adolescence and direct the transition from childhood to adulthood were studied and questioned. More modern researchers took very different views on the causes and characteristics of adolescence than those of Hall.

Erik Erikson (1902–1994), a psychologist interested in how people formed normal or abnormal personalities, believed that adolescence was a key period in development. He felt that it was during adolescence that individuals developed their identity. Like Hall, he believed that there was a biological component underlying development; unlike Hall, Erikson emphasized the role society played in the formation of the individual. Erikson proposed that adolescents must confront a number of conflicts (for example, understanding sex roles and oneself as male or female) in order to develop an identity. The form of these conflicts, and the problems the adolescent faced addressing them, were influenced by the individual's culture. If adolescents were successful in meeting the conflicts, they would develop a healthy identity; if unsuccessful, they would suffer role diffusion or a negative identity. Similar to Hall, Erikson saw adolescence as a period where the individual's sense of self is disrupted, and so it was typical for adolescents to be disturbed. Today, Erikson's ideas on identity formation are still influential. However, his stereotype of adolescents as all suffering because of psychological problems has been called into question.

Margaret Mead, an anthropologist who started studying adolescents in the 1920s, presented a perspective on adolescence that differed from both Hall's and Erikson's. She concluded that culture,

rather than biology, was the underlying cause of a transitional stage between childhood and adulthood. In cultures that held the same expectations for children as for adults, the transition from childhood to adulthood was smooth; there was no need for a clearly demarcated period where one was neither child nor adult. In addition, adolescence did not have to be a period of storm and stress or of psychological problems. Although some of Mead's work has since been criticized, many of her ideas remain influential. Today's psychologists concur with Mead in that adolescence should not be a time of psychological maladjustment. Modern anthropologists agree that biology alone does not define adolescence. Rather, the sociocultural environment in which an individual is raised will affect how adolescence is manifested and what characterizes it.

What social and cultural factors lead to the development of adolescence in our society? Modern scholars believe that adolescence as we know it did not even exist until the end of the 1800s. During the end of the nineteenth century and the beginning of the twentieth century, societal changes caused the stage of adolescence to be invented. In this period the job opportunities for young people doing either farm labor or apprenticeships in factories were decreasing. For middle-class children, the value of staying in school in order to get a good job was stressed. Since there were fewer job opportunities, young people were less likely to be financially independent and had to rely on their families. By the beginning of the twentieth century, legislation ensuring that adolescents could not assume adult status was passed, child labor laws restricted how much time young people could work, and compulsory education laws required adolescents to stay in school. In the 1930s, for the first time in this country's history, the majority of high school age individuals were enrolled in school. These teenagers were physically mature people who were dependent on their parents—they were neither children nor adults.

The articles in this unit focus on the emergence of adolescence in our culture and the characteristics of adolescents in our society. In the first essay, Thomas Hine describes the changing roles of adolescents through American history. Stephanie Coontz, in the second article, describes the various forms American families have taken from colonial times to the present, concluding with a discussion of society's influence on families and children. In the final article in this section Michael Newcomb argues that adolescence need not be seen as a difficult period. Rather, family, school, and society can create environments where adolescence can be a period of enormous potential.

Perspectives on Adolescence

THE RISE AND DECLINE
OF THE TEENAGER

THE WORD emerged during the Depression to define a new kind
of American adolescence—one that prevailed for half a century
and may now be ending

BY THOMAS HINE

WHEN THE ANTHROPOLOGIST MARGARET MEAD JOUR-
neyed to the South Pacific in 1926, she was
looking for something that experts of the
time thought didn't exist: untroubled adolescence.

Adolescence, psychologists and educators
believed, was inevitably a period of storm and
stress. It debilitated young men and women.
It made their actions unpredictable, their characters flighty and undependable. And if people who had lived through their teens didn't
remember being that unhappy, some said, it
was because it had been so traumatic that
their conscious minds had suppressed what
really happened.

At the age of twenty-five, Mead, who wasn't
all that far beyond adolescence herself, simply
couldn't believe that this picture of life's second decade expressed a necessary or universal truth. If she could find a place where social
and sexual maturity could be attained without a struggle, where adolescence was so
peaceful it scarcely seemed to exist, her point
would be made. So she went to Samoa.

There are few places left on earth remote
enough to give a contemporary observer real
perspective on how Americans think about
their young people. The teenager, with all the
ideas about adolescence that the word en-
codes, is one of our most potent cultural ex-
ports. All around the world, satellites beam
down MTV with its messages of consumption, self-indulgence, alienation, angst, and
hedonism. The American invention of youth

culture has become thoroughly international;
it causes consternation and sells products everywhere.

Still, although it is extremely difficult to
travel far enough across the earth to escape
our culture's ideas about teenagers, one can
travel in time. Youth has a history, and since
the European colonization of North America,
the second decade of life has offered a tremendous diversity of expectations and experiences. They haven't all been good
experiences; most were backbreaking, some
horrifying. One needn't be nostalgic for those
lost forms of youth in order to learn from
them. Nobody wants to send young people
off to the coal mines, as was done a century
ago, or rent them out to neighboring households as servants, as seventeenth-century
New Englanders did. Nevertheless, history
can be our Samoa, a window into very different ways of thinking and behaving that can
throw our own attitudes into sharp relief and
highlight assumptions that we don't even
know we're making.

Like Mead, who freely admitted that her
research in Samoa was shaped by what she
viewed as a problem in the American culture
of her own time, I have set out on historical
explorations spurred by a suspicion that
something is deeply wrong with the way we
think about youth. Many members of my generation, the baby boomers, have moved seam-
lessly from blaming our parents for the ills of
society to blaming our children. Teenage vil-

lains, unwed mothers, new smokers, reckless drivers, and criminal predators are familiar figures in the media, even when the problems they represent are more common among other age groups. Cities and suburbs enact curfews and other laws that only young people need obey, while Congress and state legislatures find new ways to punish young offenders as adults.

The way we think about teenagers is most contradictory. We assume that they should be somehow protected from the world of work, yet many high school students work as much as twenty hours a week. Teenagers form the core of our low-wage retail and restaurant work force, the local equivalent of the even lower-wage overseas manufacturing work force that makes the footwear and other items teens covet.

Yet at the same time as our economy depends on the young, we tend to view teenagers as less than trustworthy. This is a hangover from the attitudes Mead was trying to fight, though nowadays we're likely to ascribe young people's perceived quirks to "raging hormones." Most adults seem to view this conflicted, contradictory figure of the teenager as inevitable, part of the growth of a human being. Yet many people now living came of age before there was anything called a teenager. This creature is a mid-twentieth-century phenomenon. And almost everything has changed since the early 1940s, when it emerged. Are teenagers still necessary?

The word *teenager* initially saw print in 1941. It isn't known who thought up the word; its appearance, in an article in *Popular Science*, was not likely its first use. People had been speaking of someone in his or her teens for centuries, but that was a description of an individual. To speak of someone as a teenager is to make that person a member of a very large group, one defined only by age but presumed to have a lot in common. The word arose when it did because it described something new.

The teenager was a product of the Great Depression. Like other massive projects of the New Deal—the Hoover Dam, the TVA—it represented an immense channeling and redirection of energy. Unlike such public works, however, it was a more or less inadvertent invention. It happened in several steps.

First came the country's general economic collapse and a dramatic disappearance of jobs. As in previous panics and depressions, young people were among those thrown out of

work. What was different was that after 1933, when Franklin D. Roosevelt took office, virtually *all* young people were thrown out of work, as part of a public policy to reserve jobs for men trying to support families. Businesses could actually be fined if they kept childless young people on their payrolls. Also, for the first two years of the Depression, the Roosevelt administration essentially ignored the needs of the youths it had turned out of work, except in the effort of the Civilian Conservation Corps (CCC), which was aimed at men in their late teens and early twenties.

There was, however, one very old and established institution available to young people who wanted to do something with their time and energy: high school. The first public high school had opened in Boston in 1821, but secondary education was very slow to win acceptance among working-class families that counted on their children's incomes for survival. Not until 112 years after that first school opened were a majority of high-school-age Americans actually enrolled.

T HE DEPRESSION WAS THE WORST POSSIBLE time for high school to catch on. The American public education system was, then as now, supported primarily by local real estate taxes; these had plummeted along with real estate values. Schools were laying off teachers even as they enrolled unprecedented numbers of students. They were ill equipped to deal with their new, diverse clientele.

For many of these new students, high school was a stop-gap, something one did to weather a bad time. But by 1940 an overwhelming majority of young people were enrolled, and perhaps more important, there was a new expectation that nearly everyone would go, and even graduate.

This change in standards was a radical departure in the way society imagined itself. Before the Depression finishing high school was a clear mark that a youth, particularly a male, belonged to the middle class or above. Dropping out in the first or second year indicated membership in the working class. Once a large majority started going to high school, all of them, regardless of their economic or social status, began to be seen as members of a single group. The word *teenager* appeared precisely at the moment that it seemed to be needed.

Not long before, many young people in their mid-teens had been considered virtually grown up. Now that they were students rather than workers, they came to seem younger than before. During the 1920s "youth" in the movies had meant sexually mature figures, such as Joan Crawford, whom F. Scott Fitzgerald himself called the definitive flapper. Late in the 1930s a new kind of youth emerged in the movies, personified above all by the bizarre boy-man Mickey Rooney and the Andy Hardy movies he began to make in 1937. His frequent co-star Judy Garland was part of the phenomenon too. As Dorothy, in *The Wizard of Oz*, Garland was clearly a woman, not the girl everyone pretended she was. The tension between the maturity she feels and the childishness others see in her helps make the film more than a children's fantasy. It is an early, piquant expression of the predicament of the teenager.

Another less profound but amazingly enduring model for the emerging idea of the teenager was that perennial high schooler Archie, who first appeared in a comic book in 1941. He was drawn by Bob Montana, a teenager himself, who was working for a living as a staff artist at a comic book company. For the last half-century Archie, Jughead, Betty, Veronica, and their circle have appealed more to youngsters aspiring to become teenagers than to teenagers themselves.

Nevertheless, the early popularity of characters like Andy Hardy and Archie indicated that the view of high school students as essentially juvenile was catching on. A far stronger signal came when the draft was revived, shortly before the United States entered World War II. Although married men with families were eligible for induction, in many cases up to the age of forty, high school students were automatically deferred. Young men of seventeen, sixteen, and younger had been soldiers in all of America's previous wars and, more than likely, in every war that had ever been fought. By 1941 they had come to seem too young.

Having identified the teenager as a Frankenstein monster formed in the thirties by high school, Mickey Rooney movies, child psychology, mass manufacturing, and the New Deal, I might well have traced the story through bobbysoxers, drive-in movies, Holden Caulfield, Elvis, the civil rights martyr Emmett Till, top-forty radio, Gidget, the Mustang, heavy metal, Nirvana. Instead I found myself draw farther into the past. While the teenager was a new thing in 1940, it nevertheless was an idea with deep roots in our culture.

AT THE VERY DAWN OF ENGLISH SETTLEment in North America, Puritan elders were declaring that they had come to this savage continent for the sake of their children, who did not seem sufficiently grateful. (Like latter-day suburbanites, they had made the move for the sake of the kids.) They were also shocked by the sheer size of their children. Better nutrition caused Americans of European background to reach physical and sexual maturity sooner than their parents had and to grow larger than their parents. No wonder some early settlers fretted that their children were different from them and at risk of going native.

By the middle of the eighteenth century, there was a whole literature of complaint against both apprentices who affected expensive and exotic costumes and licentious young people given to nighttime "frolicks." Jonathan Edwards gave one of the most vivid descriptions of moral decline and then proceeded to deal with it by mobilizing youthful enthusiasm within the church. By the time of the American Revolution, half the population was under sixteen. Young women over eighteen were hard to marry off, as one upper-class observer noted, because their teeth were starting to rot. (Seemingly unrelated issues like dental hygiene have always played an unsung role in the way we define the ages of man and woman.)

Yet as youthful as the American population was, young people stood in the mainstream of social and economic life. They were not the discrete group that today's teenagers are. "In America," wrote Alexis de Tocqueville in 1835, "there is in truth no adolescence. At the close of boyhood, he is a man and begins to trace out his own path."

Things were beginning to change, however. High school, the institution that would eventually define the teenager, had already been invented. By the second quarter of the nineteenth century, it was becoming clear that rapid changes in manufacturing, transport, and marketing meant that the children of merchants, skilled artisans, and professionals would live in a very different world from that of their parents. Adults could no longer rely on passing on their businesses or imparting their skills to their children, who would probably need formal schooling. Increasingly, prosperous Americans were having fewer children and investing more in their education.

At the time, most secondary schooling took place in privately operated academies. These varied widely in nature and quality, and for the most part students went to them only when they had both a need and the time. These schools didn't have fixed curricula, and students and teachers were constantly coming and going, since being a student was not yet a primary job. Students most often stayed at boardinghouses near the academies; they rarely lived at home.

The tax-supported high school, which by the 1860s had displaced the private academy, was based on a different set of assumptions. Attendance at it was a full-time activity, in which the student adjusted to the school's schedule, not vice versa. Whereas academies had been the product of a society in which most economic activity happened in the home, high school evolved in tandem with the ideal of the bourgeois home, protected from the world of work and presided over by a mother who was also the primary moral teacher. High school students, by definition, led privileged, sheltered lives.

Most academies had enrolled only males, but nearly all high schools were from the outset coeducational. There was some public consternation over mixing the sexes at so volatile an age, but most cities decided that providing separate schools was too costly. High schools were acceptable places to send one's daughter because they were close to home. Moreover, their graduates were qualified to teach elementary school, a major employment opportunity for young women. The result was that females constituted a majority of the high school population. Moreover, male graduates were likely to be upper class, since they included only those who didn't have to drop out to work, while female graduates represented a wider social range.

Some of the early high schools were conceived as more practical and accessible alternatives to college. In a relatively short time, however, high school curricula became dominated by Latin and algebra, the courses required by the most selective colleges. Parents looked to win advantage for their children, so a "good" high school became one whose students went on to top colleges.

The earliest high schools treated their students almost as adults and allowed them to make decisions about their social lives. Students organized their own extracurricular ac-

tivities and played on athletic teams with older men and workers. Toward the end of the nineteenth century, however, high schools increasingly sought to protect their charges from the dangers of the larger world. They organized dances so that their students wouldn't go to dance halls. They organized

UPI/CORBIS-BETTMANN

Prom night in Maryland, 1953.

sports so that students would compete with others their own age. They created cheerleading squads, in the hope that the presence of females would make boys play less violently. They discovered and promoted that ineffable quality "school spirit," which was supposed to promote loyalty, patriotism, and social control. By the turn of the twentieth century, the football captain could escort the chief cheerleader to the senior prom.

This all sounds familiar, but this high school crowd still accounted for less than 10 percent of the secondary-school-age population. Nearly all the rest were working, most of them with their families on farms, but also in factories, mines, and department stores, in the "street trades" (as newspaper hawkers or delivery boys), in the home doing piecework, or even as prostitutes. If early high school students are obvious predecessors to today's teenagers, their working contemporaries also helped create the youth culture.

ONE THING THE WORKING-CLASS YOUNG shared with high school students and with today's teenagers is that they were emissaries of the new. Parents wanted their children to be prepared for the future. Among the working class, a substantially immigrant population, newness was America itself. Throughout the nineteenth century settlement workers and journalists repeatedly observed the way immigrant parents depended on their children to teach them the way things worked in their new country. They also noted a generation gap, as parents tried to cling to traditions and values from the old country while their children learned and invented other ways to live. Parents both applauded and deplored their children's participation in a new world. Youth became, in itself, a source of authority. When contemporary parents look to their children to fix the computer, program the VCR, or tell them what's new in the culture, they continue a long American tradition.

For laboring purposes one ceased to be a child no later than the age of ten. In many states schooling was required until twelve or thirteen, but compulsory attendance laws were rarely strictly enforced. In Philadelphia in the 1880s the standard bribe to free one's child from schooling was twenty-five cents. This was an excellent investment, considering how dependent many families were on their children. In Fall River, Massachusetts, some mill owners hired only men who had able-bodied sons who could also work. In Scranton, Pennsylvania, children's incomes usually added up to more than their fathers'.

The working teenager is, of course, hardly extinct. American high school students are far more likely to have part-time jobs than are their counterparts in other developed countries and their work hours are on average substantially longer. The difference is that families don't often depend on their wages for their livelihood. Teenagers today spend most of what they earn on their own cars, clothing, and amusement. Indeed, they largely carry such industries as music, film, and footwear, in which the United States is a world leader. Their economic might sustains the powerful youth culture that so many find threatening, violent, and crude.

WE CAN SEE THE ORIGINS OF THIS YOUTH culture and of its ability to horrify in the young urban workers of the late nineteenth century. Young people, especially the rootless entrepreneurs of the street trades, were among the chief patrons of cheap theaters featuring music and melodrama that sprang up by the hundreds in the largest cities. (In Horatio Alger's hugely popular novels, the first stage of the hero's reform is often the decision to stay away from the theater and use the admission price to open a savings account.) They also helped support public dance halls, which promoted wild new forms of dancing and, many thought, easy virtue.

Adults are perennially shocked by the sexuality and the physical vitality of the young. There is nevertheless a real difference between the surprise and fear parents feel when they see their babies grow strong and independent and the mistrust of young people as a class. One is timeless. The other dates from 1904 and the publication of G. Stanley Hall's fourteen-hundred-page *Adolescence: Its Psychology and Its Relations to Physiology, Anthropology, Sociology, Sex, Crime, Religion and Education.*

With this book Hall, a psychologist and the president of Clark University, invented the field of adolescent psychology. He defined adolescence as a universal, unavoidable, and extremely precarious stage of human development. He asserted that behavior that would indicate insanity in an adult should be considered normal in an adolescent. (This has long since been proved untrue, but it is still widely believed.) He provided a basis for dealing with adolescents as neither children nor adults but as distinctive, beautiful, dangerous creatures. That people in their teens should be considered separately from others, which seems obvious to us today, was Hall's boldest, most original, and most influential idea.

The physical and sexual development of young people was not, he argued, evidence of maturity. Their body changes were merely armaments in a struggle to achieve a higher state of being. "Youth awakes to a new world," he wrote, "and understands neither it nor himself." People in their teens were, he thought, recapitulating the stage of human evolution in which people ceased to be savages and became civilized. He worried that young people were growing up too quickly, and he blamed it on "our urbanized hothouse life that tends to ripen everything before its time." He believed it was necessary to fight this growing precocity by giving young people the time, space, and guidance to help them weather the tumult and pain of adolescence.

It is hard to believe that a book so unreadable could be so influential, but the size and comprehensiveness of Hall's discussion of adolescents lent weight and authority to other social movements whose common aim was to treat people in their teens differently from adults and children. Among the book's supporters were secondary school educators who found

Teenagers and Crime

FROM PURITAN NEW ENGLAND TO LITTLETON in 1999, youth violence has been a fact of American life and a frequent national preoccupation

THEY ARE ARMED. THEY ARE DANGEROUS. They are our children.

These sentiments sound chillingly up-to-date, as current as the latest suburban high school massacre or big-city gang killing. In fact, youth crime—and especially adult fear of youth crime—has been a perennial American concern. An apprentice rapes his master's ten-year-old daughter in seventeenth-century Massachusetts. A son shoots his father and mother with a rifle on the Kentucky frontier. Street gangs terrorize neighborhoods in nineteenth-century New York, Philadelphia, Boston, and Baltimore. Indeed, though the word *teenager* is about sixty years old, and *adolescent* has been used in its current sense for about ninety-five years, Americans have been speaking of and fretting about "juvenile delinquents" for nearly two centuries.

Throughout our history young Americans have shocked their elders by the callousness and brutality of their crimes and prompted worries that violence is an outgrowth of our national character. "Their crimes have the unrestrained and sanguinary character of a race accustomed to overcoming all obstacles," wrote the social reformer Charles Loring Brace in his celebrated 1872 book *The Dangerous Classes of New York.* "They rifle a bank, where English thieves pick a pocket; they murder where European proletaires cudgel or fight with fists. . . . The murder of an unoffending old man is nothing to them."

Young people's bloody deeds seem perpetually unprecedented. "Younger and younger children commit more and more serious and violent acts," wrote Dr. Fredric Wertham in his sensational 1953 bestseller *The Seduction of the Innocent.* "Even psychotic children did not act like this fifteen years ago." Wertham blamed gory, sadistic comic books. Among the criminals he cited was a fourteen-year-old who in 1950 fired a rifle from the window of a New York apartment house, shooting to death a man watching the Giants play baseball at the Polo Grounds. Such acts of apparently random violence often have a strong impact on public opinion, touching off, as they did in the 1950s, panic over juvenile crime.

IN FACT, THE POST-WORLD WAR II ERA WAS A time of declining youth crime. The same is true of the 1990s, another period in which teenage violence has been an important public issue. Statistics never galvanize attention as powerfully as do two or three horrible incidents. There are, unfortunately, always plenty of these. What seems to vary is the amount of attention Americans choose to pay. So one must track two separate histories. One concerns crimes committed by young people; the other deals with popular concern over juvenile crime.

While the first of these seems to rest on a solid factual ground, different definitions of crime and of youth and changing standards of enforcement make long-term comparisons difficult. For example, most nineteenth-century records deal with urban crime. Street gangs, such as New York City's notorious Dead Rabbits and Plug Uglies, sprang up in most major cities during the second third of the nineteenth century. Like today's youth gangs, they had members who ranged in age from the barely pubescent to men in their mid-twenties, with the majority in their teens. (In Philadelphia, some volunteer fire brigades were in effect youth gangs, and they sometimes set fire to buildings that their rivals had contracted to protect.) Gangs were so closely associated with massive immigration and explosive urbanization that the most popular solution was to get their members off the streets by sending those who didn't yet appear to be hardened criminals out of the cities to what was assumed to be the purifying atmosphere of the countryside or wilderness.

Although such banishment cut down on urban crime, the country wasn't exactly peaceful either. While the urban gangs fought with rocks and clubs and knives, young people on the frontier were armed from an early age. There are no good records on the subject, but personal memoirs of life in the West recount an enormous amount of casual, gun-related mayhem.

One such account, by Miguel Angel Otero, who became territorial governor of New Mexico, is a sentimental, nostalgic recollection of youth in Kansas, Colorado, and New Mexico during the 1870s, but with a formidable body count. Many of Otero's young friends were killed or injured in gunfights, hunting accidents, range wars, battles with Indians, and even suicides. This youthful carnage has not been counted as or considered part of the problem of juvenile delinquency but rather is seen as part of the general lawlessness of the frontier, where young people had little choice but to grow up quickly.

In America, as nearly everywhere, the overwhelming majority of violent crimes are committed by young men from about fifteen to thirty years of age. This is the period during which males reach physical and sexual maturity. They feel confident. They take risks. They are also susceptible to being influenced by others. (Not coincidentally this is the age group from which soldiers have traditionally been drawn.)

IF ADOLESCENCE IS A CONSPIRACY BY CULTURE to deny the evidence of physical and sexual maturity, crime is one of the few ways available for young people to assert the power they feel. While young criminals use up-to-date technologies such as automatic weapons and computers, crime remains one of the few pursuits that operate on the pre-industrial idea that you're grown up when your body is.

Thus crime rises when the number of people in the prime criminal age group rises. It happened in the 1960s, when the baby boomers became old enough to commit crimes, and it will very likely happen during the next decade or more as the number of Americans in their teens and twenties surges.

(Continued)

The second history, that of American parents frightened of their unruly young, began early. Few laws have been tougher on youth crime than this 1656 New Haven-colony statute: "If any man have a stubborn, rebellious son, of sufficient age and understanding, namely sixteen years and upward, which will not obey the voyce of his father, or the voyce of his mother; and that when they have chastened him, will not hearken unto them, then shall his father and his mother (being his natural parents) lay hold on him, and bring him to the magistrates assembled in court, and testifie unto them that their son is stubborn and rebellious, and will not obey their voyce and chastisement, but lives in sundry notorious crimes; such a son shall be put to death."

W E DON'T KNOW OF ANY CRIME WAVE ALONG Long Island Sound in the mid-seventeenth century, and in fact this law seems not to have led to any executions. Nevertheless, its passage shows that these Puritan pioneers were extremely anxious about the behavior of their sons.

This early document in the history of Americans' fear of young people's transgressions is revealing. It defines the problem not in terms of any specific crime but rather in the fear that young men will fail to respect their parents' authority from the time they are physically mature to the time they will be legally emancipated and able to keep the money they earn, at twenty-one.

It is tempting to see this law, passed eighteen years after the colony was founded, as a reflection of parents' fears that growing up in the New World was producing a new, uncontrollable kind of person. A century later observers such as Benjamin Franklin took it for granted that American young people were less patient and more impetuous than their European counterparts. Franklin himself was what we would now call a teenage runaway, a fugitive apprentice who ran far enough to be free of his obligations to a master who was also his older brother.

American youths seemed to be naturally rebellious because they had so many possibilities and so little need to depend on their families. In 1776, a time when half the colonial population was under twenty, Thomas Paine compared England to a parent who wasn't able to acknowledge that its child was fully grown. For two generations after the revolution, young people celebrated the Fourth of July by getting drunk and shooting off guns and explosives, a display of patriotism that often led to serious injuries.

Concern about "juvenile delinquency" began in the 1820s, about the same time the first high schools opened. The social reformers who founded the earliest houses of refuge and reformatories believed that the character of young people up to age sixteen or so was still malleable. Rather than send the young to prisons, where they would learn to be criminals, they sought to separate them and inculcate the values they would receive in a sound, middle-class Protestant home. The leaders of what became known as the child-saving movement saw youthful rebellion against parents as both a problem and an opportunity. Defiant young people threatened the social order, but placed in special institutions and schools, they could be perfected into better Americans. This issue became particularly urgent with the explosive immigration that began in the 1840s.

The American-born children of immigrants were soon being identified as the most dangerous of the dangerous classes because, the argument went, they had jettisoned many of the social and moral values their parents had brought from the old country while not adopting the distinctive American Protestant mores that still dominated the culture. These first-generation Americans were said to dominate the emerging city youth gangs, stealing goods off piers and filling the streets with prostitutes. Immigrant children were often forced into activities that led to crime, as when their destitute parents sent them out to scavenge for wood, coal, and other useful items. There was a fine line between such foraging and outright thievery, and other people's children are perennially scarier than one's own. Many of the most prominent youth gangs were made up of immigrants' children, but others had members of English-American ancestry who also lived in poor neighborhoods.

Immigrant parents, shocked by their children's behavior, sometimes committed their own young to institutions for juvenile delinquents, little realizing that those who wanted to reform the children saw the parents as the biggest problem. They viewed their houses of refuge as an opportunity to free the young from their parents' drunkenness, irresponsibility, and disorder and from the superstitious influence of priests and other immigrant-community leaders. Reformatories took on the molding of good citizens long before that task was assumed by high schools.

Social reformers hoped these institutions would reproduce some of the values of the newly emergent middle-class family, in which domestic life was separated from work, children were presumed innocent, and the mother would be at home as the chief moral teacher. This paradigm has survived to the present, even though now, as in 1850, only a minority of families truly achieve it.

I T HAS BECOME THE CENTERPIECE OF OUR common vision of a proper, wholesome life, and we still believe so fully in its efficacy that despite our national traditions of violence and rebelliousness, when a young person emerges from such a home to do something atrocious, we believe his deed should have been absolutely impossible.

—T. H.

in Hall's writing a justification for their new enthusiasm about moving beyond academic training to shape the whole person. They also found in it a justification for raising the age for ending compulsory school attendance.

Hall's book coincided as well with the rise of the juvenile-court movement, whose goal was to treat youth crime as a problem of personal development rather than as a transgression against society. This view encouraged legislatures and city councils to enact laws creating curfews and other "status offenses"—acts affecting only young people. (A decade earlier women's organizations had successfully campaigned to raise the age of consent for sex in most states, which greatly increased the number of statutory-rape prosecutions.)

Hall's findings also gave ammunition to advocates of child-labor laws. Their campaigns were for the most part unsuccessful, but employment of children and teens dropped during the first two decades of the twentieth century anyway, as machines replaced unskilled manufacturing jobs in many industries. In the years after Hall's book came out, manufacturers increasingly spoke of workers in their teens as unreliable, irresponsible, and even disruptive. They had stopped thinking of fourteen-year-olds as young ordinary workers and begun to view them as adolescents.

Each of these movements was seen as a progressive attempt to reform American society, and their advocates certainly had their hearts in the right place. But the price for young people was a stigma of incompetence, instability, and even insanity. Adolescents couldn't be counted on. Hall even argued that female adolescents be "put to grass" for a few years and not allowed to work or attend school until the crisis had passed.

This was the orthodoxy Mead was trying to combat when she wrote *Coming of Age in Samoa*. She wanted to disprove Hall's psychoanalytic assertion that adolescence is inherent to all human development and replace it with the anthropological view that cultures invent the adolescence they need. Maturity, she argued, is at least as much a matter of social acceptance as it is of an individual's physical and mental development. In Samoa, she said, adolescence was relatively untroubled, because it didn't have to accomplish very much. The society changed little from generation to generation. Roles were more or less fixed. Young people knew from childhood what they should expect. American adolescence was more difficult because it had to achieve more, although she clearly didn't believe it had to be quite so horrible as Hall and his followers thought.

Serious questions have been raised about some of Mead's methods and findings in Samoa, and Hall's theories have been thoroughly discredited. These two seminal thinkers on adolescence represented extreme views, and adolescence is of course both biological and cultural. The changes it brings are unmistakable, but countless external factors shape what it means to be a grown-up in a particular place and time. In a dynamic society like that of the United States, the nature of adolescence must inevitably shift over time.

Jailed for robbery in 1945, these two Iowa boys, fourteen and seventeen, escaped with the help of girlfriends.

Indeed, Mead's research, which concentrated on young women, was a product of the sexual revolution of the 1920s, in which female sexuality was widely acknowledged for the first time. Prostitution was on the decrease, and the sexual activity of "respectable" young women was rising. In *This Side of Paradise* F. Scott Fitzgerald's young Princetonians were amazed at how easy it was to be kissed. But the protagonist in the novel gives what proved to be an accurate account of what was going on. "Just as a cooling pot gives off heat," she says, "so all through youth and adolescence we give off calories of virtue. That's what's called ingenuousness." Short skirts, bobbed hair, corset checkrooms at dances, and petting parties were seen by people at the time as symptoms of libertinism among the "flaming youth," but when Kinsey interviewed members of this generation three decades later, he learned that the heat had been more finely calibrated than it appeared. Young women had been making their chastity last as long as they needed it to. It turned out that while 40 percent of females in their teens and 50 percent of males petted to orgasm in the 1920s—nearly twice the pre-war rate—petting was most common among those who had had the most schooling. While commentators focused on the antics of the upper classes, working-class young people, who were closer to marriage, were twice as likely to have gone beyond and had sexual intercourse.

DESPITE ENDURING POPULAR INTEREST IN Mead's findings, Hall's notion that adolescence is an inevitable crisis of the individual has, over the years, been more potent. (Perhaps it speaks more forcefully to our individualistic culture than does Mead's emphasis on shared challenges and values.) Certainly, during the post-World War II era, when the teenager grew to be a major cultural and economic phenomenon, the psychoanalytic approach dominated. J. D. Salinger's Holden Caulfield, literature's most famous teenager, has an unforgettable voice and great charm, but it is difficult to read *Catcher in the Rye* today without feeling that Holden's problems are not, as he hopes, a phase he's going through but truly pathological. While Salinger doesn't make a judgment in the book, 1950s readers would most likely have thought Holden just another troubled adolescent, albeit an uncommonly interesting one.

When Hall was writing, at the turn of the twentieth century, he generalized about adolescents from a group that was still a small minority, middle-class youths whose main occupation was schooling. In all of his fourteen hundred pages, he never mentioned the large number of young people who still had to work to help support their families. Half a century later American society was more or less as Hall had described it, and just about everyone could afford to have an adolescence.

The twenty-five-year period following the end of World War II was the classic era of the teenager. Family incomes were growing, which meant that more could be spent on each child and educational aspirations could rise. Declining industries, such as radio and the movies, both of which were threatened by television, remade themselves to appeal to the youth market. Teenage culture gave rise to rock 'n' roll. Young people acquired automobiles of their own and invented a whole new car culture.

At the same time, though, teenagers were provoking a lot of anxiety. Congressional committees investigated juvenile delinquency for a decade. High schools and police forces took action against a rising wave of youth crime, a phenomenon that really didn't exist. Moreover, there were indications that not all teenagers were happy in their presumed immaturity. Many, if not most, of the pop icons of the time, from Elvis on down, were working-class outsiders who embodied a style very different from that of the suburban teen.

And many teenagers were escaping from their status in a more substantive way, by getting married. The general prosperity meant that there were jobs available in which the high school dropout or graduate could make enough to support a family. In 1960 about half of all brides were under twenty. In 1959 teenage pregnancy reached its all-time peak, but nearly all the mothers were married.

This post-World War II era brought forth the third key thinker on American adolescence, the psychologist Erik Erikson. He assumed, like Hall, that adolescence was inherent to human development and that an identity crisis, a term he invented, was necessarily a part of it. But he also acknowledged that this identity must be found in the context of a culture and of history. He argued that not only does adolescence change over the course of history but it also is the time when individuals learn to adapt themselves to their historical moment. "The identity problem changes with the historical period," he wrote. "That is, in fact, its job." While earlier thinkers on adolescence had made much of youthful idealism, Erikson argued that one of the tasks of adolescence was to be fiercely realistic about one's society and time.

He did not think that forging an identity in such a complex and confusing society as ours was easy for most people. He wanted adolescence to be what he termed "a psycho-social moratorium," to allow people the time and space to get a sense of how they would deal with the world of which they would be a part. Among the results would be an occupational identity, a sense of how one would support and express oneself.

And so ideas about the nature of adolescence have shaped our image of teenagers. Reclassifying all people of secondary school age as teenagers wasn't possible until nearly all had some period of adolescence before entering adult life. Still, *teenager* isn't just another word for *adolescent*. Indeed, the teenager may be, as Edgar Z. Friedenberg argued in a 1959 book, a failed adolescent. Being a teenager is, he said, a false identity, meant to short-circuit the quest for a real one. By giving people superficial roles to play, advertising, the mass media, and even the schools confuse young people and leave them dissatisfied and thus open to sales pitches that promise a deepening of identity.

Whether you agree with that argument or not, it does seem evident that the challenges of adolescence have been changing rapidly in the last several decades, leaving the label "teenager" as little more than a lazy way of talking about young people. The term encompasses a contradictory grab bag of beliefs, prejudices, and expectations. It can allow us to build a wall around an age group and to assume that its members' problems can safely be ignored.

The generation entering its teens today will be in sheer number, if not as a percentage of the population, the largest in our history. The people in this age group have already emerged as the most significant marketing phenomenon since the baby boom. They have spurred the opening of new teen-oriented clothing stores in malls and the launching of successful new magazines. They are helping make the Internet grow. They even have their own television network, the WB. They have their own money to spend, and they spend a lot of their families' income too, partly because their mothers are too busy to shop.

BUT THEY DO NOT REPRESENT ANY RETURN TO the teenage golden age of the 1950s and 1960s. This generation has grown up in a period of declining personal income and increasing inequality. A sizable percentage consists of the children of immigrants. Educational aspirations are very high, and no wonder: You need a college education today to make a salary equivalent to that of a high school graduate in 1970. The permanent occupational identity that was available in the post-World War II society of which Erikson wrote, one in which lifelong work for large corporations was the norm, has all but disappeared. Many see their parents still striving for the sort of stable identity Erikson thought could be resolved in youth. While it appears to be a great time to be a teenager, it seems a difficult one to be an adolescent.

Throughout history Americans in their teens have often played highly responsible roles in their society. They have helped their families survive. They have worked with new technologies and hastened their adoption. Young people became teenagers because we had nothing better for them to do. High schools became custodial institutions for the young. We stopped expecting young people to be productive members of the society and began to think of them as gullible consumers. We defined maturity primarily in terms of being permitted adult vices, and then were surprised when teenagers drank, smoked, or had promiscuous sex.

We can no longer go to Samoa to gain perspective on the shape of our lives at the dawn of the third millennium, nor can we go back in time to find a model for the future. What we learn from looking at the past is that there are many different ways in which Americans have been young. Young people and adults need to keep reinventing adolescence so that it serves us all. Sometimes what we think we know about teenagers gets in our way. But just as there was a time, not long ago, before there were teenagers, perhaps we will live to see a day when teenagers themselves will be history.

Thomas Hine's book The Rise and Fall of the American Teenager *was published September 1999 by Bard.*

The Way We Weren't

The Myth and Reality of the "Traditional" Family

Stephanie Coontz

Families face serious problems today, but proposals to solve them by reviving "traditional" family forms and values miss two points. First, no single traditional family existed to which we could return, and none of the many varieties of families in our past has had any magic formula for protecting its members from the vicissitudes of socioeconomic change, the inequities of class, race, and gender, or the consequences of interpersonal conflict. Violence, child abuse, poverty, and the unequal distribution of resources to women and children have occurred in every period and every type of family.

Second, the strengths that we also find in many families of the past were rooted in different social, cultural, and economic circumstances from those that prevail today. Attempts to reproduce any type of family outside of its original socio-economic context are doomed to fail.

Colonial Families

American families always have been diverse, and the male breadwinner-female homemaker, nuclear ideal that most people associate with "the" traditional family has predominated for only a small portion of our history. In colonial America, several types of families coexisted or competed. Native American kinship systems subordinated the nuclear family to a much larger network of marital alliances and kin obligations, ensuring that no single family was forced to go it alone. Wealthy settler families from Europe, by contrast, formed independent households that pulled in labor from poorer neighbors and relatives, building their extended family solidarities on the backs of truncated families among indentured servants, slaves, and the poor. Even wealthy families, though, often were disrupted by death; a majority of colonial Americans probably spent some time in a step-family. Meanwhile, African Americans, denied the legal protection of marriage and parenthood, built extensive kinship networks and obligations through fictive kin ties, ritual co-parenting or godparenting, adoption of orphans, and complex naming patterns designed to preserve family links across space and time.

The dominant family values of colonial days left no room for sentimentalizing childhood. Colonial mothers, for example, spent far less time doing child care than do modern working women, typically delegating this task to servants or older siblings. Among white families, patriarchal authority was so absolute that disobedience by wife or child was seen as a small form of treason, theoretically punishable by death, and family relations were based on power, not love.

The Nineteenth-Century Family

With the emergence of a wage-labor system and a national market in the first third of the nineteenth century, white middle-class families became less patriarchal and more child-centered. The ideal of the male breadwinner and the nurturing mother now appeared. But the emergence of domesticity for middle-class women and children depended on its absence among the immigrant, working class, and African American women or children who worked as servants, grew the cotton, or toiled in the textile mills to free middle-class wives from the chores that had occupied their time previously.

Even in the minority of nineteenth-century families who could afford do-

From *National Forum: The Phi Kappa Phi Journal*, Summer 1995, pp. 11–14. © 1995 by Stephanie Coontz. Reprinted by permission of the publisher.

mesticity, though, emotional arrangements were quite different from nostalgic images of "traditional" families. Rigid insistence on separate spheres for men and women made male-female relations extremely stilted, so that women commonly turned to other women, not their husbands, for their most intimate relations. The idea that all of one's passionate feelings should go toward a member of the opposite sex was a twentieth-century invention—closely associated with the emergence of a mass consumer society and promulgated by the very film industry that "traditionalists" now blame for undermining such values.

Early Twentieth-Century Families

Throughout the nineteenth century, at least as much divergence and disruption in the experience of family life existed as does today, even though divorce and unwed motherhood were less common. Indeed, couples who marry today have a better chance of celebrating a fortieth wedding anniversary than at any previous time in history. The life cycles of nineteenth-century youth (in job entry, completion of schooling, age at marriage, and establishment of separate residence) were far more diverse than they became in the early twentieth-century. At the turn of the century a higher proportion of people remained single for their entire lives than at any period since. Not until the 1920s did a bare majority of children come to live in a male breadwinner-female homemaker family, and even at the height of this family form in the 1950s, only 60 percent of American children spent their entire childhoods in such a family.

From about 1900 to the 1920s, the growth of mass production and emergence of a public policy aimed at establishing a family wage led to new ideas about family self-sufficiency, especially in the white middle class and a privileged sector of the working class. The resulting families lost their organic connection to intermediary units in society such as local shops,

neighborhood work cultures and churches, ethnic associations, and mutual-aid organizations.

As families related more directly to the state, the market, and the mass media, they also developed a new cult of privacy, along with heightened expectations about the family's role in fostering individual fulfillment. New family values stressed the early independence of children and the roman-

tic coupling of husband and wife, repudiating the intense same-sex ties and mother-infant bonding of earlier years as unhealthy. From this family we get the idea that women are sexual, that youth is attractive, and that marriage should be the center of our emotional fulfillment.

Even aside from its lack of relevance to the lives of most immigrants, Mexican Americans, African Americans, rural families, and the urban poor, big contradictions existed between image and reality in the middle-class family ideal of the early twentieth century. This is the period when many Americans first accepted the idea that the family should be sacred from outside intervention; yet the development of the private, self-sufficient family depended on state intervention in the economy, government regulation of parent-child relations, and state-directed destruction of class and community institutions that hindered the development of family privacy. Acceptance of a youth and leisure culture sanctioned early marriage and raised expectations about the quality of married life, but also introduced new tensions between the generations and new conflicts between husband and wife over what were adequate levels of financial and emotional support.

The nineteenth-century middle-class ideal of the family as a refuge from the world of work was surprisingly modest compared with emerging

twentieth-century demands that the family provide a whole alternative world of satisfaction and intimacy to that of work and neighborhood. Where a family succeeded in doing so, people might find pleasures in the home never before imagined. But the new ideals also increased the possibilities for failure: America has had the highest divorce rate in the world since the turn of the century.

Not until the 1920s did a bare majority of children come to live in a male breadwinner-female homemaker family. . . .

In the 1920s, these contradictions created a sense of foreboding about "the future of the family" that was every bit as widespread and intense as today's. Social scientists and popular commentators of the time hearkened back to the "good old days," bemoaning the sexual revolution, the fragility of nuclear family ties, the cult of youthful romance, the decline of respect for grandparents, and the threat of the "New Woman." But such criticism was sidetracked by the stock-market crash, the Great Depression of the 1930s, and the advent of World War II.

Domestic violence escalated during the Depression, while murder rates were as high in the 1930s as in the 1980s. Divorce rates fell, but desertion increased and fertility plummeted. The war stimulated a marriage boom, but by the late 1940s one in every three marriages was ending in divorce.

The 1950s Family

At the end of the 1940s, after the hardships of the Depression and war, many Americans revived the nuclear family ideals that had so disturbed commentators during the 1920s. The unprecedented post-war prosperity allowed young families to achieve consumer satisfactions and socioeconomic mobility that would have been inconceivable in earlier days. The 1950s family that resulted from these economic and cultural trends, however, was hardly "traditional." Indeed it is best seen as a historical aberration. For the first time in 100 years, divorce rates dropped, fertility soared, the gap between men's and women's job and educational prospects widened (making middle-class women more dependent on marriage), and the age of marriage fell—to the point that teenage birth rates were almost double what they are today.

Admirers of these very *nontraditional* 1950s family forms and values point out that household arrangements and gender roles were less diverse in the 1950s than today, and marriages more stable. But this was partly because diversity was ruthlessly suppressed and partly because economic and political support systems for socially-sanctioned families were far more generous than they are today. Real wages rose more in any single year of the 1950s than they did in the entire decade of the 1980s; the average thirty-year-old man could buy a median-priced home on 15 to 18 percent of his income. The government funded public investment, home ownership, and job creation at a rate more than triple that of the past two decades, while 40 percent of young men were eligible for veteran's benefits. Forming and maintaining families was far easier than it is today.

Yet the stability of these 1950s families did not guarantee good outcomes for their members. Even though most births occurred within wedlock, almost a third of American children lived in poverty during the 1950s, a higher figure than today. More than 50 percent of black married-couple families were poor. Women were often refused the right to serve on juries, sign contracts, take out credit cards in their own names, or establish legal residence. Wife-battering rates were low, but that was because wife-beating was seldom counted as a crime. Most victims of incest, such as Miss America of 1958, kept the secret of their fathers' abuse

until the 1970s or 1980s, when the women's movement became powerful enough to offer them the support denied them in the 1950s.

The Post-1950s Family

In the 1960s, the civil rights, antiwar, and women's liberation movements exposed the racial, economic, and sexual injustices that had been papered over by the Ozzie and Harriet images on television. Their activism made older kinds of public and private oppression unacceptable and helped create the incomplete, flawed, but much-needed reforms of the Great Society. Contrary to the big lie of the past decade that such programs caused our current family dilemmas, those antipoverty and social justice reforms helped overcome many of the family problems that prevailed in the 1950s.

In 1964, after fourteen years of unrivaled family stability and economic prosperity, the poverty rate was still 19 percent; in 1969, after five years of civil rights activism, the rebirth of feminism, and the institution of nontraditional if relatively modest government welfare programs, it was down to 12 percent, a low that has not been

below the poverty line had *never* been examined by a physician; by 1970 this was true of only 8 percent of the poor.

Since 1973, however, real wages have been falling for most Americans. Attempts to counter this through tax revolts and spending freezes have led to drastic cutbacks in government investment programs. Corporations also spend far less on research and job creation than they did in the 1950s and 1960s, though the average compensation to executives has soared. The gap between rich and poor, according to the April 17, 1995, *New York Times*, is higher in the United States than in any other industrial nation.

Family Stress

These inequities are *not* driven by changes in family forms, contrary to ideologues who persist in confusing correlations with causes; but they certainly exacerbate such changes, and they tend to bring out the worst in *all* families. The result has been an accumulation of stresses on families, alongside some important expansions of personal options. Working couples with children try to balance three full-

. . . romanticizing "traditional" families and gender roles will not produce the changes . . . that would permit families to develop moral and ethical systems relevant to 1990s realities.

seen again since the social welfare cutbacks began in the late 1970s. In 1965, 20 percent of American children still lived in poverty; within five years, that had fallen to 15 percent. Infant mortality was cut in half between 1965 and 1980. The gap in nutrition between low-income Americans and other Americans narrowed significantly, as a direct result of food stamp and school lunch programs. In 1963, 20 percent of Americans living

time jobs, as employers and schools cling to policies that assume every employee has a "wife" at home to take care of family matters. Divorce and remarriage have allowed many adults and children to escape from toxic family environments, yet our lack of social support networks and failure to forge new values for sustaining intergenerational obligations have let many children fall through the cracks in the process.

Meanwhile, young people find it harder and harder to form or sustain families. According to an Associated Press report of April 25, 1995, the median income of men aged twenty-five to thirty-four fell by 26 percent between 1972 and 1994, while the proportion of such men with earnings below the poverty level for a family of four more than doubled to 32 percent. The figures are even worse for African American and Latino men. Poor individuals are twice as likely to divorce as more affluent ones, three to four times less likely to marry in the first place, and five to seven times more likely to have a child out of wedlock.

As conservatives insist, there is a moral crisis as well as an economic one in modern America: a pervasive sense of social alienation, new levels of violence, and a decreasing willingness to make sacrifices for others. But romanticizing "traditional" fami-lies and gender roles will not produce the changes in job structures, work policies, child care, medical practice, educational preparation, political discourse, and gender inequities that would permit families to develop moral and ethical systems relevant to 1990s realities.

America needs more than a revival of the narrow family obligations of the 1950s, whose (greatly exaggerated) protection for white, middle-class children was achieved only at tremendous cost to the women in those families and to all those who could not or would not aspire to the Ozzie and Harriet ideal. We need a concern for children that goes beyond the question of whether a mother is waiting with cookies when her kids come home from school. We need a moral language that allows us to address something besides people's sexual habits. We need to build values and social institutions that can recon-cile people's needs for independence with their equally important rights to dependence, and surely we must reject older solutions that involved balancing these needs on the backs of women. We will not find our answers in nostalgia for a mythical "traditional family."

Stephanie Coontz teaches history and family studies at The Evergreen State College in Olympia, Washington. Her publications include *The Way We Never Were: American Families and the Nostalgia Trap* **and** *The Way We Really Are: Coming to Terms with America's Changing Families* **(both published by Basic Books). She is a recipient of the Washington Governor's Writer's Award and the Dale Richmond Award of the American Academy of Pediatrics.**

Adolescence: Pathologizing a Normal Process

Michael D. Newcomb
University of Southern California

> It was the best of times, it was the worst of times.
>
> (Dickens, 1859, p. 1)

Dickens was referring to a historical period of fervor, instability, crisis, and promise. So too is adolescence.

We have far too long focused on adolescence as the worst of times, emphasizing the stressful and disruptive life changes that occur during this developmental period (e.g., Newcomb & Harlow, 1986; Newcomb, Huba, & Bentler, 1981, 1986). Little attention has been devoted to understanding adolescence as the potential best of times. The three feature articles [in *The Counseling Psychologist*, July 1996] underscore this by considering the optimal development of adolescents in terms of a biopsychosocial perspective (Wagner, 1996), conflict resolution (Van Slyck, Stern, & Zak-Place, 1996), and training of counselors to deal with this special population (Kaczmarek & Riva, 1996). Each of these articles makes important claims about the positive aspects and optimal functioning potential of adolescents.

This research was supported by grant DA 01070 from the National Institute on Drug Abuse. I thank Rod Goodyear for his comments on a draft of this article.

Address correspondence and reprint requests to Dr. Michael D. Newcomb, Division of Counseling Psychology, University of Southern California, Los Angeles, CA 90089-0031.

However, I do not feel they have gone far enough to challenge effectively, let alone change, our pervasive belief that adolescence is by and large a bummer experience. I will not deal directly with these three articles but rather struggle with the questions of why we pathologize adolescence and what are the forces that make us focus on the teenage years as the worst of times and not the best of times.

After many years of research on adolescence and young adulthood, I have come to believe that much of what we consider as adolescence is a social construct (e.g., Blumer, 1971; Spector & Kitsuse, 1987) based on selective memory, unresolved conflicts, and thinly veiled social agendas. Henley (1986) has noted that "adding a psychological dimension to traditional sociological approaches has tremendous potential to add understanding of how individuals perceive issues, how definitions change, and under what circumstances they do" (p. 76). The social construct of adolescence is more than a subjective response to a social problem or condition but rather sets the tone, focus, and agenda for studying this particular stage of life. This characterization of adolescence emphasizes the worst of times by focusing on the high risks (e.g., Dryfoos, 1990; Newcomb, 1995), problem behaviors (e.g., Jessor & Jessor, 1997; McGee & Newcomb, 1992), and serious consequences (Newcomb & Bentler, 1988a, 1988b) of things that can go wrong during this developmental period. This perspective has been the dominant one in defining adolescence, with little attention devoted ro resilience, potential for growth, and optimal functioning, which are equally, if not more, likely during this critical transition (e.g., Blechman, 1996; Blechman, Prinz, & Dumas, 1995; McCarthy, Newcomb, & Bentler, 1994; Newcomb & Feliz-Ortiz, 1992).

Although not wholly unrelated to reality or the objectivist approach (e.g., Best, 1989b), social constructs are largely shaped and molded by claims makers who typify specific problems in particular sorts of ways. For instance, when studying the developmental periods of childhood and adolescence, several specific problems come to mind, which have been shaped by claims makers into social constructs reflecting these developmental periods of life. For instance, problems with crack cocaine and other drugs are readily prominent (e.g., Humphreys & Rappaport, 1993; Reinarman & Levine, 1989) as well as child abuse and child victims (e.g., Best, 1989a; Johnson 1989), the pernicious influence of rock-and-roll and popular music (e.g., Gray, 1989; Newcomb, 1996), the prevalence of drug use on the job or at school (e.g., Newcomb, 1994; Staudenmeier, 1989), and learning disabilities and medicalization of the classroom (e.g., Erchak & Rosenfeld, 1989).

Who are these claims makers, and why do they do this? Some are politically motivated and hope to design and establish social policy and funding priorities in line with a particular ideology that creates a specific conceptualization of the problem (e.g., Humphreys & Rappaport, 1993). Many others are social scientists, like each of us. These include well-meaning researchers and practitioners who may be emphasizing the negativity and adversity of adolescence for more unconscious and unresolved aspects of this critical life period in their own lives. Although this is speculative and may seem extreme, we all must ask why we study and research the topics we choose. Part of the answer to this question may lie in our own development and unresolved conflicts and issues of our pasts and how we make sense of (construct) them. Few would argue that how each of us views adolescence as adults is largely a result of our personal experience of this life period.

At the risk of reifying another social construction of adolescence, I would like to offer an alternate conceptualization of this developmental period that does not focus on the worst of times but rather on the most powerful of times. Adolescence is a time of birth, preparation, independence, and evolvement; it is exciting and stressful (Erikson, 1968). It can be filled with hope and aspiration at the same time as fear, dread, and uncertainty; the extremes of emotion and demands are vast and generate equally powerful responses that reverberate throughout our lives (e.g., Franz, McClelland, & Weinberger, 1991; Newcomb & Bentler, 1988a, 1988b).

For most of us, our first experience of sexual intercourse occurred during late adolescence (e.g., Newcomb, in press; Udry & Billy, 1987). It is also the age for beginning paying jobs, becoming financially autonomous, establishing our identity and existence separate from our families, developing intimate and supportive relationships of all sorts, and forging our own individual identity and life goals (e.g., Erikson, 1968; Newcomb, in press). These are sensitive and provocative issues and experiences that imbue and pervade our entire existence. We are never at peace with them, and they arouse strong, emotional, and value-laden responses throughout life. Because these vital issues of adolescence (i.e., sex, drugs, independence, intimacy, self-support [financial, emotional, and physical]) are ones that we live with the remainder of our lives, some suggest that we all continue to reprocess these events, traumas, and experiences of adolescents. Do we as researchers and counselors perpetuate this in our professional pursuits? Moreover, in so doing, do we become claims makers for the sturm and drang of adolescence? Perhaps it is a psychodynamic cathartic experience for us to emphasize and thereby continue to reprocess the negative aspects of being a teenager. Perhaps we are even drawn to this profession for this very reason.

Other claims makers may feel threatened by the necessary risk taking and experimentation that are typical features of adolescence. To create and forge a solid individual identity, teenagers must explore available options and potential ways of being. What could be considered normal development has become problems and pathology. Shedler and Block (1990) found a curvilinear relationship between drug use and psychological health of teenagers. Those who did not use any drugs as a teenager were rigid, inflexible, "anxious, emotionally constricted, and lacking in social skills" (p. 612). Teenagers who used drugs frequently had the most psychological and interpersonal problems. However, those adolescents who engaged in some drug experimentation were the most well adjusted both personally and socially. Optimal development cannot be sanitized social conformity. Teenagers must break the rules to a moderate extent if they are to establish a true and effective personal identity. Too much conformity creates problems the same as too much rebelliousness. For many adults, this essential experimentation and "pushing the envelope" may be threatening and difficult. But for optimal development, it is crucial when kept in moderation.

Adolescence is a truly vital critical period; not only in the physiological sense of pubertal development (e.g., Caspi & Moffitt, 1991) but even more so as the psychosocial transition point and final training ground for young adulthood and later adult role responsibilities (e.g., Havighurst, 1972). The timing of adult transition events is pivotal to optimal development (Newcomb, in press), with those occurring too early or too late creating problems with the successful acquisition of adult roles and the skills necessary to thrive in the next life stage of young adulthood and beyond.

In the past 30 years, we have seen a dramatic shift away from the proactive, systems-oriented, and enhancement-of-life approach taken by the Community Mental Health Movement. We have moved toward a perspective that emphasizes individual remediation, personal deficits, and a problem-focused War on Drugs (e.g., Humphreys & Rappaport, 1993) and social warfare rather than social welfare (e.g., Mosher & Yanagisako, 1991; Newcomb, 1992). It is too simplistic and misleading to view drug abuse and other problems that can emerge during adolescence as only individual behavior. We must remember that all individual behavior is "embedded in a sociocultural context that strongly determines its character and manifestations" (Newcomb & Bentler, 1989, p. 242). Each individual is a product of and actor with his or her environment. We must understand and approach each person as a component of the social system within which he or she exists.

Taking an objectivist position, it is hard to justify the adversity and sturm and drang typically associated with adolescence, at least in terms of the problems regularly attributed to teenagers. For instance, Lewinsohn, Hops, Roberts, Seeley, and Andrews (1993) established prevalence rates for several diagnostic disorders among adolescents. Only 8% ever met the criteria for any type of substance use disorder, 7% met criteria for any form of disruptive behavior disorder, and less than 1% met criteria for any type of eating disorder. These three diagnostic groups reflect many of the most typically considered problems during adolescence in the categories of drug use, acting out, and eating disorders. Interestingly, the most common diagnosis was for unipolar depression, with a 20% lifetime prevalence rate. We are yet to see a national campaign, outpouring of federal funds, or federal office act to wage a War on depression among teenagers, despite the fact that suicide is the third leading cause of death among teenagers (e.g., Dorgan, 1995).

By pointing out these contrasts, I in no way want to diminish or trivialize the serious consequences of drug abuse, child abuse, eating disorders, and delinquency among teenagers. I simply want to place these problems within a more balanced conceptualization of adolescence and emphasize and question the relative lack of concern with other serious problems (i.e., depression) and, most important, the failure to focus on processes that enhance optimal development among teenagers. In other words, we seem more concerned with remediating the worst of times rather than increasing the chances for the best of times.

Stanton Peele has been a long-term opponent of the "Diseasing of America" (Peele, 1989). He has taken specific umbrage with the focus on pathologizing and excessive treatment of adolescents who use drugs (e.g., Peele, 1986, 1987). In fact, he questions the true extent of drug abuse problems during adolescence and believes we are running scared from the problem rather than dealing with the real issues (e.g., Peele, 1987) and that our cures for adolescent drug abuse may be substantially worse than the actual problem (Peele, 1986).

We have too long focused on how life stressors create problems during adolescence (Newcomb & Harlow, 1986), only recently studying the protective, buffering, and resilience factors that can prevent problems from arising even under stressful conditions. My research is certainly not immune to the focus on understanding the problems of adolescence (e.g., Newcomb, Maddahian, & Bentler, 1986) and how they are structured (i.e., general deviance) (McGee & Newcomb, 1992; Newcomb & McGee, 1991). For instance we have been quick to accept and utilize a syndrome of problem behaviors among adolescents (e.g., Jessor & Jessor, 1977) and have rarely considered or tried to develop a syndrome of healthy and adaptive behaviors.

However, if we are to see a real effect on reducing these problems, preventing them from occurring initially, and enhancing or optimizing adolescent development, we must focus on resilience, buffering factors, and mediating influences (e.g., National Advisory Mental Health Council, 1996; Newcomb & Felix-Ortiz, 1992). Many of these approaches have stubbornly broken away from the seductive individual defect models that have lately exemplified our national approach to social problems (e.g., Humphreys & Rappaport, 1993) and emphasize more complex and comprehensive models that view individual development within a larger systems perspective.

There are increasingly more examples of this more integrated approach to understanding and working with adolescents to overcome risk conditions and enhance optimal development. For instance, it has been reasonably well established that parent drug use is related to numerous problem behaviors of their children (e.g., West & Prinz, 1987). However, we have only recently addressed other mediating (e.g., Newcomb & Rickards, 1995) or moderating factors (e.g., Farrell, Barnes, & Banerjee, 1995). Franz et al. (1991) have demonstrated the long-term beneficial effects of having warm and affectionate parents on many positive social accomplishments as adults. This emphasizes the vital role of the family in optimizing development. Schulenberg, Bachman, O'Malley, and Johnston (1994) have established the crucial role of college plans and high school grade point average on later prosocial behaviors. This emphasizes the central role of education and school bonding on healthy development, and parents play a central role in this process (e.g., Wills, McNamara, & Vaccaro, 1995).

We must reject an individual deficit model and embrace a systems approach to enhance optimal development and protection from risk for teenagers. Counseling psychologists are particularly well suited for and trained in enhancing the positive rather than only remediating the negative. Yet even these three very fine articles slip into the latter rather than sticking with the former. What is the momentum that creates our myopia? Perhaps more diversified methodologies may help us break away from this stilted construct of adolescence (e.g., Hoshmand & Polkinghorne, 1992; Polkinghorne, 1988).

After all of this, I am left with a plaguing doubt that underscores the power of social constructs and individual experience. I still wonder whether I may be only fighting my own trauma of this terrible stage of life. After all, even after a couple decades, I can clearly remember my huge zits, the humiliation of communal showers, the sleepless nights of unbridled (and unfulfilled) hormones, and being called on for an answer in my French class when I could not even understand the question.

References

Best, J. (1989a). Dark figures and child victims: Statistical claims about missing children. In J. Best (Ed.), *Images of issues: Typifying contemporary social problems* (pp. 21–37). New York: Walter deGruyter.

Best, J. (1989b). Extending the constructionist perspective: A conclusion and an introduction. In J. Best (Ed.), *Images of issues: Typifying contemporary social problems* (pp. 243–253). New York: Walter deGruyter.

Blechman, E. A. (1996). Coping, competence, and aggression prevention: Part 2. Universal school-based prevention. *Applied & Preventive Psychology, 5,* 19–35.

Blechman, E. A., Prinz, R. J., & Dumas, J. (1995). Coping, competence, and aggression prevention: Part I. Developmental model. *Applied & Preventive Psychology, 4,* 211–232.

Blumer, H. (1971). Social problems as collective behavior. *Social Problems, 18,* 298–306.

Caspi, A., & Moffitt, T. E. (1991). Individual differences are accentuated during periods of social change: The sample case of girls at puberty. *Journal of Personality and Social Psychology, 61,* 157–168.

Dickens, C. (1859). *Tale of Two Cities* [Monograph]. New York and London: Dodd, Mead.

Dorgan, C. A. (1995). *Statistical record of health and medicine.* Detroit, MI: Gale Research.

Dryfoos, J. G. (1990). *Adolescents at risk: Prevalence and prevention.* New York: Oxford University Press.

Erchak, G. M., & Rosenfeld, R. (1989). Learning disabilities, dyslexia, and the medicalization of the classroom. In J. Best (Ed.), *Images of issues: Typifying contemporary social problems* (pp. 79–97). New York: Walter deGruyter.

Erikson, E. H. (1968). *Identity, youth, and crisis.* New York: Norton.

Farrell, M. P., Barnes, G. M., & Banerjee, S. (1995). Family cohesion as a buffer against the effects of problem-drinking fathers on psychological distress, deviant behavior, and heavy drinking in adolescents. *Journal of Health and Social Behavior, 36,* 377–385.

Franz, C. E., McClelland, D. C., & Weinberger, J. (1991). Childhood antecedents of conventional social accomplishment in midlife adults: A 36-year prospective study. *Journal of Personality and Social Psychology, 60,* 586–595.

Gray, H. (1989). Popular music as a social problem: A social history of claims against popular music. In J. Best (Ed.), *Images of issues: Typifying contemporary social problems* (pp. 143–158). New York: Walter deGruyter.

Havighurst, R. J. (1972). *Developmental tasks and education* (3rd ed.). New York: McKay.

Henley, N. M. (1986). Women as a social problem: Conceptual and practical issues in defining social problems. In E. Seidman & J. Rappaport (Eds.), *Redefining social problems* (pp. 65–79). New York: Plenum.

Hoshmand, L. T., & Polkinghorne, D. E. (1992). Redefining the science-practice relationship and professional training. *American Psychologist, 47,* 1–12.

Humphreys, K., & Rappaport, J. (1993). From the community mental health movement to the War on Drugs: A study in the definition of social problems. *American Psychologist, 48,* 892–901.

Jessor, R., & Jessor, S. L. (1977). *Problem behavior and psychosocial development: A longitudinal study of youth.* New York: Academic Press.

Johnson, J. M. (1989). Horror stories and the construction of child abuse. In J. Best (Ed.), *Images of issues: Typifying contemporary social problems* (pp. 5–19). New York: Walter deGruyter.

Kaczmarek, P.G. & Riva, M. T. (1996). Facilitating adolescent optimal development: Training considerations for counseling psychologists. *The Counseling Psychologist, 24,* 400–432.

Lewinsohn, P. M., Hops, H., Roberts, R. E., Seeley, J. R., & Andrews, J. A. (1993). Adolescent psychopathology: I. Prevalence and incidence of depression and other *DSM-III-R* disorders in high school students. *Journal of Abnormal Psychology, 102,* 133–144.

McCarthy, W. J., Newcomb, M. D., & Bentler, P. M. (1994). The effect of teenagers' family characteristics on the development of subsequent young adult competence. In R. D. Parke & S. G. Kellam (Eds.), *Exploring family relationships with other social contexts* (pp. 169–197). Hillsdale, NJ: Lawrence Erlbaum.

McGee, L., & Newcomb, M. D. (1992). General deviance syndrome: Expanded hierarchical evaluations at four ages from early adolescence to adulthood. *Journal of Consulting and Clinical Psychology, 60,* 766–776.

Mosher, J. F., & Yanagisako, K. L. (1991). Public health, not social warfare: A public health approach to illegal drug policy. *Journal of Public Health Policy, 12,* 278–323.

National Advisory Mental Health Council Basic Behavioral Science Task Force (1996). Basic behavioral science research for mental health. *American Psychologist, 51,* 22–28.

Newcomb, M. D. (1992). Substance abuse and control in the United States: Ethical and legal issues. *Social Science and Medicine, 35,* 471–479.

Newcomb, M. D. (1994). Prevalence of drug use in the workplace: Cause for concern or irrational hysteria? *Journal of Drug Issues, 24,* 49–82.

Newcomb, M. D. (1995). Identifying high-risk youth: Prevalence and patterns of adolescent drug abuse. In E. Rahdert, D. Czechowicz, & I. Amsel (Eds.), *Adolescent drug abuse: Clinical assessment and therapeutic intervention* (pp. 7–38). Rockville, MD: National Institute on Drug Abuse.

Newcomb, M. D. (1996). *Sex, drugs, and rock-and-roll: Fact, fantasy, or confound?* Unpublished manuscript.

Newcomb, M. D. (in press). Pseudomaturity among adolescents: Construct validation, gender differences, and associations in adulthood. *Journal of Drug Issues.*

Newcomb, M. D., & Bentler, P. M. (1988a). *Consequences of adolescent drug use: Impact on the lives of young adults.* Newbury Park, CA: Sage.

Newcomb, M. D., & Bentler, P. M. (1988b). Impact of adolescent drug use and social support on problems of young adults: A longitudinal study. *Journal of Abnormal Psychology, 97,* 64–75.

Newcomb, M. D., & Bentler, P. M. (1989). Substance use and abuse among children and teenagers. *American Psychologist, 44,* 242–248.

Newcomb, M. D., & Felix-Ortix, M. (1992). Multiple protective and risk factors for drug use and abuse: Cross-sectional and prospective findings. *Journal of Personality and Social Psychology, 63,* 280–296.

Newcomb, M. D., & Harlow, L. L. (1986). Life events and substance use among adolescents: Mediating effects of perceived loss of control and meaningless in life. *Journal of Personality and Social Psychology, 51,* 564–577.

Newcomb, M. D., Huba, G. J., & Bentler, P. M. (1981). A multidimensional assessment of stressful life events among adolescents: Derivation and correlates. *Journal of Health and Social Behavior, 22,* 400–415.

Newcomb, M. D., Huba, G. J., & Bentler, P. M. (1986). Determinants of sexual and dating behavior among adolescents. *Journal of Personality and Social Psychology, 50,* 428–438.

Newcomb, M. D., Maddahian, E., & Bentler, P. M. (1986). Risk factors for drug use among adolescents: Concurrent and longitudinal analyses. *American Journal of Public Health, 76,* 525–531.

Newcomb, M. D., & McGee, L. (1991). Influence of sensation seeking on general and specific problem behaviors from adolescence to young adulthood. *Journal of Personality and Social Psychology, 61,* 614–628.

Newcomb, M. D., & Rickards, S. (1995). Parent drug-use problems and adult intimate relations: Associations among community samples of young adult women and men. *Journal of Counseling Psychology, 42,* 141–154.

Peele, S. (1986). The "cure" for adolescent drug abuse: Worse than the problem? *Journal of Counseling and Development, 65,* 23–24.

Peele, S. (1987). Running scared: We're too frightened to deal with the real issues in adolescent substance abuse. *Health Education Research, 2,* 423–432.

Peele, S. (1989). *Diseasing of America: Addiction treatment out of control.* Lexington, MA: Lexington Books.

Polkinghorne, D. E. (1988). *Narrative knowing and the human sciences.* Albany, NY: SUNY Press.

Reinarman, C., & Levine, H. G. (1989). The crack attack: Politics and media in America's latest drug scare. In J. Best (Ed.), *Images of issues: Typifying contemporary social problems* (pp. 115–137). New York: Walter deGruyter.

Schulenberg, J., Bachman, J. G., O'Malley, P. M., & Johnston, L. D. (1994). High school educational success and subsequent substance use: A panel analysis following adolescents into young adulthood. *Journal of Health and Social Behavior, 35,* 45–62.

Shedler, J., & Block, J. (1990). Adolescent drug use and psychological health: A longitudinal inquiry. *American Psychologist, 45,* 612–630.

Spector, M., & Kitsuse, J. I. (1987). *Constructing social problems.* New York: Aldine deGrutyer.

Staudenmeier, W. J., Jr. (1989). Urine testing: The battle for privatized social control during the 1986 War on Drugs. In J. Best (Ed.), *Images of issues: Typifying contemporary social problems* (pp. 207–221). New York: Walter deGruyter.

Udry, J. R., & Billy, J. O. G. (1987). Initiation of coitus in early adolescence. *American Sociological Review, 52,* 841–855.

Van Slyck, M., Stern, M., & Zak-Place, J. (1996). Promoting optimal adolescent development through conflict resolution education, training, and practice: An innovative approach for counseling psychologists. *The Counseling Psychologist, 24,* 433–461.

Wagner, W. G. (1996). Optimal development in adolescence: What is it and how can it be encouraged? *The Counseling Psychologist, 24,* 360–399.

West, M. O., & Prinz, R. J. (1987). Parental alcoholism and childhood psychopathology. *Psychological Bulletin, 102,* 204–218.

Wills, T. A., McNamara, G., & Vaccaro, D. (1995). Parental education related to adolescent stress-coping and substance use: Development of a mediational model. *Health Psychology, 14,* 464–478.

Unit 2

Key Points to Consider

❖ What physical changes can parents and teenagers expect at adolescence? Do we adequately prepare teenagers for the physical changes of puberty? How can parents and other adults help teenagers cope with puberty? How does the timing of puberty (early, on time, or late) affect adolescents? What puberty rites exist in U.S. culture and subcultures?

❖ How does body image relate to self-esteem? How do body image concerns differ for girls and boys? How do pubertal changes affect adolescent mood and emotional state?

 **Links**   **www.dushkin.com/online/**

9. **Biological Changes in Adolescence**
   http://www.personal.psu.edu/faculty/n/x/nxd10/biologic2.htm

These sites are annotated on pages 4 and 5.

Randy, a 14-year-old, is sulking in his room after arguing with his parents. They are upset because he refuses to work on the oral report he is supposed to give in English class tomorrow. He cannot tell them the real reason why he does not want to do the assignment. He just told his parents that the report was on a stupid topic, and he refused to do it. In reality, Randy is worried that his voice will crack, and, worse yet, that he will get an erection while standing up in front of the whole class and everyone will notice.

The physical changes accompanying the onset of puberty are usually the first clear indicators that a child is entering the period of adolescence. The changes are a source of both pride and embarrassment for the developing adolescent. The physiological changes are regulated by a structure in the brain known as the hypothalamus. The hypothalamus is responsible for stimulating the increased production of hormones that control development of the primary and secondary sex characteristics. Primary sex characteristics are physical differences in the reproductive system itself. Examples include growth of the ovaries and testicles. Secondary sex characteristics are physical differences not directly involved in reproduction. Examples include voice changes, height increases, facial hair in males, and breast development in females.

The hypothalamus signals the pituitary gland, which in turn stimulates the gonads to produce sex hormones (androgens and estrogens). The hypothalamus then detects the level of sex hormones present in the bloodstream and either calls for less or more hormone production. During childhood, the hypothalamus is very sensitive to sex hormones and keeps production at a low level. For some reason that is not completely known yet, the hypothalamus changes its sensitivity to the sex hormones. Significantly greater quantities of sex hormones are needed before the hypothalamus signals the pituitary to shut down production. The thyroid and adrenal glands also play a role in the development of secondary sex characteristics.

The physiological changes themselves occur over a 5 to 6 year span. Girls generally start to undergo puberty 18 to 24 months before boys, with a typical onset at age 10 or 11. The earliest signs of pubertal changes in girls are breast budding, height spurt, and sparse pubic hair. Experiencing a first menstrual cycle is a midpubertal event, with the average age of menarche in the United States being 12 years old. For boys, initial signs are that testicles begin to increase in size, a small amount of pubic hair appears, and the height spurt begins. Facial hair, deepening voice, and first ejaculation occur later.

The sequence of pubertal changes is fairly constant across individuals; however, the timing of puberty varies greatly from one person to the next. Some adolescents are out of step with their peers because they mature early, whereas others are late

maturers. The advantages and disadvantages of early versus late maturation have been the subject of research and several readings touch on this topic. One conclusion is that early maturation is correlated with earlier involvement in risk-taking behaviors like alcohol use and sexual activity. In extreme cases, biological disorders result in delayed or precocious puberty, but there are new medications for treating these conditions.

The onset of puberty is affected by diet, exercise, and genetic history. Largely due to improved nutrition and control of illnesses, puberty occurs 3 to 4 years earlier today than it did 150 years ago. Adolescents today also grow several inches taller and weigh more. A visit to historical homes will show that the doorways and beds were much smaller in previous centuries. This trend toward earlier maturation is a worldwide phenomenon that has presumably reached a leveling off point.

As Randy's story illustrates, adolescents experience psychological and social challenges related to puberty. Sexual arousal increases and the teenager must learn how to handle sexual situations. Gender-typical behavior is more expected. The adolescent must also incorporate bodily changes into his or her self-image. Concerns about physical appearance become a major preoccupation and play a significant role in self-esteem at this time. Several articles address this issue. In particular, the readings examine body image concerns as they relate to males versus females, early versus late maturers, and whites versus blacks.

Parents and other adults are often less than forthcoming in their talks with adolescents about the changes they will be experiencing. This contributes to adolescents' anxiety about their bodies and how "normal" they are. One reading looks at boys' experience of their first ejaculation. Girls today are often prepared for their first menstrual cycle and discuss its appearance with mothers and friends. In contrast, boys' first ejaculation is largely a nonevent. Some cultures employ rites of passage to mark entrance into manhood or womanhood. Many such rites of passage involve physical markings of the adolescent, such as circumcision.

Inside the Teen Brain

Behavior can be baffling when young minds are taking shape

By Shannon Brownlee

One day, your child is a beautiful, charming 12-year-old, a kid who pops out of bed full of good cheer, clears the table without being asked, and brings home good grades from school. The next day, your child bursts into tears when you ask for the salt and listens to electronic music at maximum volume for hours on end. Chores? Forget it. Homework? There's little time, after talking to friends on the phone for five hours every night. Mornings? Your bluebird of happiness is flown, replaced by a groaning lump that can scarcely be roused for school. In short, your home is now inhabited by a teenager.

The shootings in Littleton, Colo., focused the nation's attention on aberrant adolescent behavior, but most teens never come close to committing violent acts. Still, even the most easygoing teenagers often confound their elders with behavior that seems odd by adult standards.

For most of this century, the assumption has been that teenage *sturm und drang,* the insolence and the rages, are all directed at parents. Teens turn against authority figures, went the conventional wisdom, in an effort to define who they are and to assert their independence—a view that spawned the teenage rebel, that quintessential American icon. The alternative explanation was that hormones, those glandular bringers of sexual stirrings and pimples, were to blame.

The true source of teenage behavior lies north of the gonads. It's that 3-pound blob of gray and white matter known as the brain.

Yes, teenagers do have brains, but theirs don't yet function like an adult's. With the advent of technologies such as magnetic resonance imaging, neuroscientists have discovered that the adolescent brain is far from mature. "The teenage brain is a work in progress," says Sandra Witelson, a neuroscientist at McMaster University in Ontario, and it's a work that develops in fits and starts.

Until the past decade, neuroscientists believed that the brain was fully developed by the time a child reached puberty and that the 100 billion neurons, or nerves, inside an adult's skull—the hardware of the brain—were already in place by the time pimples began to sprout. The supposition was that a teenager could think like an adult if only he or she would cram in the necessary software—a little algebra here, some Civil War history there, capped by proficiency in balancing a checkbook. But the neural circuitry, or hardware, it turns out, isn't completely installed in most people until their early 20s.

And just as a teenager is all legs one day and all nose and ears the next, different regions of his brain are developing on different timetables. For instance, one of the last parts to mature is in charge of making sound judgments and calming unruly emotions. And the emotional centers in the teenage brain have already been revving up, probably under the influence of sex hormones.

This imbalance may explain why your intelligent 16-year-old doesn't think twice about getting into a car driven by a friend who is drunk, or why your formerly equable 13-year-old can be hugging you one minute and then flying off the handle the next.

Indeed, the brain inside a teenager's skull is in some ways closer to a child's brain than to an adult's. Still being forged are the connections between neurons that affect not only emotional skills but also physical and mental abilities. That means that it might be unreasonable to expect young teenagers to organize multiple tasks or grasp abstract ideas. And these still-developing neural links leave a teenager vulnerable: Depression in adolescence may set up circuits in the brain that will make it much harder to treat the illness later in life.

But these changes aren't all for the worse. The brain's capacity for growth through adolescence may also indicate that even troubled teenagers can still learn restraint, judgment, and empathy. "Adolescence is a time of tumultuous change in the brain," says Jay Giedd, a child psychiatrist at the National Institute of Mental Health in Bethesda, Md. "Teenagers are choosing what their brains are going to be good at—learning right from wrong, responsibility or impulsiveness, thinking or video games."

If there's one thing that drives parents nuts about their teenagers, it's moodiness. "It's hot and cold, nasty and nice," says Vicki Sasso, 34, the mother of 13-year-old Angelo, a ninth grader from Staten Island, N.Y. "One minute loving me, one minute hating me." Don't blame Angelo; blame the parts of his brain that process emotions and make decisions. His prefrontal cortex, where judgments are formed, is practically asleep at the wheel. At the same time, his limbic system, where raw emotions such as anger are generated, is entering a stage of development in which it goes into hyperdrive.

Brain police. The limbic system, located deep in the brain's interior, is associated with gut reactions, sparking instant waves of fear at the sight of a large snake or elation at a high SAT score. In adults, such emotional responses are modulated by the prefrontal cortex, the part of the brain that lies just behind the forehead and that acts as a sort of mental traffic cop, keeping tabs

From *U.S. News & World Report,* August 9, 1999, pp. 44–54. © 1999 by U.S. News & World Report. Reprinted by permission.

on many other parts of the brain, including the limbic system.

Indeed, the brain works something like a loosely organized team, with various parts carrying out different tasks and more or less cooperating with one another. The prefrontal cortex, says Karl Pribram, director of the Center for Brain Research and Informational Sciences at Radford University in Virginia, is in charge of "executive functions."

These include the brain's ability to handle ambiguous information and make decisions, to coordinate signals in different regions of the brain, and to tamp down or prolong emotions generated in the limbic system. In an adult, for instance, an overheard insult might arouse a murderous rage, until the prefrontal cortex figures out that the comment was meant for somebody else and tells the limbic system to pipe down. As Pribram puts it, "The prefrontal cortex is the seat of civilization."

Something very different happens in teenagers, according to Deborah Yurgelun-Todd, a neuropsychologist at McLean Hospital in Belmont, Mass. In recent experiments, Yurgelun-Todd and graduate student Abigail Baird showed adults and teenagers photographs of people's faces contorted in fear. When the researcher asked her subjects to identify the emotion being expressed, all of the adults got it right. Many of the teens, however, were unable to correctly identify the expression.

Then the researchers used functional magnetic resonance imaging, a technology that takes a picture of brain activity every three seconds or so in order to see which parts are being used during processing. Adult brains, the scientists discovered, light up in both the limbic areas and the prefrontal cortex when looking at expressions of fright. In teenagers, however, the prefrontal cortex was almost dark while the limbic system lit up.

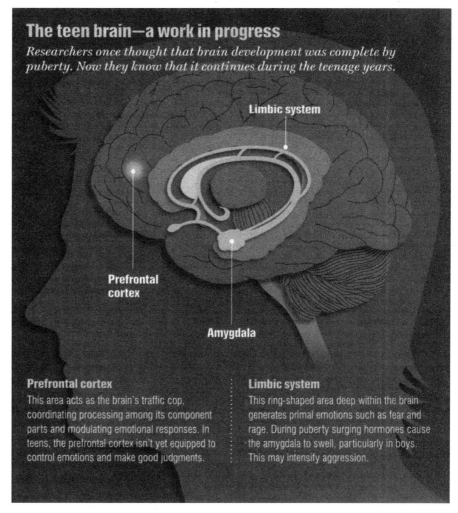

The teen brain—a work in progress

Researchers once thought that brain development was complete by puberty. Now they know that it continues during the teenage years.

Limbic system

Prefrontal cortex

Amygdala

Prefrontal cortex
This area acts as the brain's traffic cop, coordinating processing among its component parts and modulating emotional responses. In teens, the prefrontal cortex isn't yet equipped to control emotions and make good judgments.

Limbic system
This ring-shaped area deep within the brain generates primal emotions such as fear and rage. During puberty surging hormones cause the amygdala to swell, particularly in boys. This may intensify aggression.

STEPHEN ROUNTREE—*USN&WSR*

Sources: *American Medical Association Encyclopedia of Medicine, The Human Body*

These results suggest to Yurgelun-Todd that kids may not be as good as we think they are at interpreting facial expressions, in part because the prefrontal cortex is not yet lending the limbic system a hand. Teenagers are not adept readers of social signals, such as facial expressions, even if they seem to do nothing but socialize. "You have to actually learn how to read emotions," says Yurgelun-Todd. "We may think anger is pretty obvious to our kids, but they may not."

Map makers. Yurgelun-Todd's research reinforces other new findings suggesting that the average teenager's prefrontal cortex isn't ready to take on the role of brain CEO. At NIMH, Giedd and colleagues are using another type of

---

MISSED SIGNALS

You were angry?

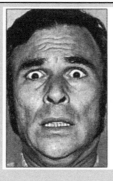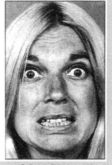

© PAUL EKMAN, 1976 (2)

When grown-ups and teens don't see eye to eye, the problem might be in the brain. Neutropsychologists studying brain development showed standardized pictures of fearful faces to 15 adults and 15 teenagers. All the adults correctly identified the emo-

tion, but 11 of the teens guessed wrong at least once, picking emotions such as anger or discomfort instead. The researchers, at McLean Hospital in Belmont, Mass., say teenagers relied more on the primitive emotion center of the brain and less on the region tied to judgment than adults did. Teens literally think differently than adults, so their baffling behavior may reflect cluelessness, not stubborness. —*Roberta Hotinski*

MRI, which captures brain structure rather than activity, to chart for the first time normal brain development from childhood through adolescence.

Since 1991, Giedd and his colleagues have mapped the brains of nearly 1,000 healthy children and adolescents ranging in age from 3 to 18. Each child must lie inside a claustrophobically narrow tube surrounded by the giant, humming machine, holding perfectly still for 10 minutes at a stretch while a computerized brain image is built.

The researchers expected to find that after puberty, the brain looks like an adult's. Instead, they found that the prefrontal cortex undergoes a growth spurt at around age 9 or 10, when neurons begin sprouting new connections, or synapses. Most of these connections subsequently die off, starting at about age 12, in a process called pruning—a sort of "use it or lose it" system for ensuring that the brain nourishes only the neurons and synapses that are useful. Pruning, which occurs in different parts of the brain at different times, also appears to allow the brain to think more efficiently.

Until the prefrontal cortex has been pruned, most young teenagers don't yet have all the brain power they need to make good judgments. Researchers suspect that the excess of synapses means the young adolescent mind can't easily keep track of multiple thoughts, and it can't gain instant access to critical memories and emotions that allow grown-ups to make judicious decisions.

"Good judgment is learned, but you can't learn it if you don't have the necessary hardware," says Yurgelun-Todd. An unfinished prefrontal cortex also means that young teenagers may also have trouble organizing several tasks, deciding, for example, which to do first: call a friend, wash the dishes, or read the book for a report that's due in the morning.

The teenage tendency to leap before looking is compounded by the fact that adolescence is a time for seeking out new experiences, including some that are dangerous. "I think all people do stupid things sometimes. It just seems like teenagers do it more often," says Rachael Fisher, an 18-year-old senior from Lakewood, Colo. That's an understatement. Driving without a seat belt, getting tattooed, smoking cigarettes, shoplifting—the list of foolish things kids do is longer than most parents really want to know.

Parents can relax a little, says Lynn Ponton, a child psychiatrist at the University of California-San Francisco and author of *The Romance of Risk.* "Risk taking is normal." But not all of it, she adds, is safe. Other research suggests that about 60 percent of a teenager's tendency to act impulsively and misjudge potential danger is genetic, a trait that is shared with other family members and is probably the result of differences in brain chemicals among individuals.

Mental mosh pit. Researchers also think that new experiences, especially those with a *frisson* of danger or the thrill of the new, tap into a teenager's so-called reward system, a set of neurons that link emotional centers to many other parts of the brain and that can produce feelings of intense pleasure. This is the same set of neurons affected by certain illicit drugs, such as cocaine, that release dopamine, one of the brain chemicals, or neurotransmitters, that are responsible for arousal and motivation.

Marvin Zuckerman, a professor of psychology at the University of Delaware, and others suspect that thrills—like sneaking out at night or jumping into the mosh pit at a heavy-metal concert—stimulate the teenage brain's dopamine system, for reasons that are not yet fully understood. The result, however, is clear: Teenagers are far

---

OBSESSED WITH FOOD

Anorexia's roots in the brain

It began innocently enough with an hour a day of exercising to a Jane Fonda workout take, but once Wendy Headrick began losing weight in eighth grade, she could not stop. Soon she quit eating candy, then fat and meat. By the end of the year, she says, "I was drinking water, eating cucumbers and other vegetables, and chewing gum to curb my appetite." Within 18 months, the 5-foot, 6-inch teen had dropped from 145 to 84 pounds.

Headrick had anorexia nervosa, the eating disorder that afflicts millions of American teenagers, most of them girls. Once thought to be entirely the result of cultural pressures on girls to be thin, anorexia and bulimia (also an eating disorder) are now thought to be related as well to changes in the brain that occur at puberty.

Headrick says the idea to lose weight occurred to her at age 13, when neighborhood children began teasing her for being overweight. Most pubescent girls find themselves gaining weight suddenly because their bodies must have a certain percentage of fat in order to mature sexually, says Sarah Leibowitz, a neurobiologist at Rockefeller University in Manhattan. As a girl enters puberty, her hypothalamus, a part of the brain that controls basic functions like sex and eating, starts churning out high levels of a neuro-chemical that stimulates appetite.

Obsessed. While all girls put on fat at puberty, only a fraction become focused on losing weight to the point of harming themselves. Headrick, now a 20-year-old junior at Ohio State, in Columbus, recalls, "I was obsessed with food. I would cook and cook and cook but not eat. I would watch what everybody else put in their months."

That obsessiveness may hold a clue to what's going on in an anorexic's brain, says Walter Kaye, director of the Eating Disorders Clinic at the University of Pittsburgh, where Headrick took part in a study. He has found that girls with eating disorders have higher than average levels of serotonin, a brain chemical that helps transmit electrical signals between neurons. People with high levels, says Kaye, "tend to be obsessive, anxious perfectionists. They are the best little girls in the world." This need to be perfect may start them on the road to starvation, but what keeps them going, Kaye suspects, is the discovery that starving themselves makes them feel better. Food contains a component of a protein that's necessary for the body to manufacture serotonin. Starving themselves may ease their anxieties by lowering the levels of serotonin in their brains. -S.B.

Why teens need more snooze time

It's only 9:30 at night, but 15-year-old Ryan O. is already snuggling into bed, pulling a quilt decorated with dolphins and killer whales up over his ears. He tosses and turns for several minutes before drifting off—possibly because there are 12 electrodes fixed to his scalp and face and an infrared video camera is recording his every move for researchers watching a video monitor in another room.

Ryan is one of several hundred teenagers who over the past decade have entered the twilight world of Brown University's Bradley Hospital sleep lab, allowing sleep physiologist Mary Carskadon to record their brain waves and eye movements in slumber and to test how lack of sleep affects their mental and physical skills. Carskadon's research has shown that teenagers who want to sleep all day are not lazy; they are simply following the dictates of their biological clocks.

Sleep is influenced by the circadian timing system, a bundle of neurons, embedded deep in the brain, that regulates production of a sleep-inducing chemical called melatonin and sets natural bedtime and rise time. Carskadon has shown that teenagers need more sleep than they did as children, and their biological clocks tell them to catch those extra winks in the morning. Most teens, she says, need 9 hours and 15 minutes of sleep a night, possibly because hormones that are critical to growth and sexual maturation are released mostly during slumber.

Cop some z's. That means that they average teenager's brain isn't ready to wake up until 8 or 9 in the morning, well past the first bell at most high schools. When Carskadon and colleagues surveyed more than 3,000 Rhode Island high school students, they found that the majority were sleeping only about seven hours a night. More than a quarter of the students averaged 6½ hours or less on school nights. In another study, when students were asked to fall asleep in the lab during the day, many conked out within three or four minutes, a sure sign they were sleep deprived. Carskadon also discovered that the students' melatonin levels were still elevated into the school day. "Their brains are telling them it's nighttime," she says, "and the rest of the world is saying it's time to go to school."

Kids who have to get up before their biological clocks have buzzed miss out on the phase of sleep that boosts memory and learning. Periodically during slumber, the brain enters rapid eye movement (REM) sleep, so called because the eyes dart back and forth under the lids. During REM sleep, the brain resets chemicals in the emotional centers and clears short-term memory banks, where they day's events are stored temporarily. Without enough REM sleep, Carskadon and others have discovered, people became cranky and depressed; their memory and judgment are impaired; and they perform poorly on tests of reaction time. Carskadon has found that teens who get the least sleep earn C's and D's, while those who get the most tend to get A's and B's.

One solution is to push back the time high schools start, something many schools are reluctant to do. Barring that, Carskadon and other experts say you should emphasize sleep's importance and help your teenager get more through biology:

■ To encourage your teen to go to bed at a reasonable hour, keep lights low in the evening and open curtains in the morning. Light absorbed through the eyes can reset the biological clock.

■ Kids can catch up on sleep on weekends—up to a point. Going to bed in the wee hours and snoozing until noon only disrupts the brain's clock further. It's better to go to bed within about an hour of usual bedtime and then sleep an hour or two later. -*S.B.*

and his colleagues recently reported for the first time that, in both sexes, surges of testosterone at puberty swell the amygdala, an almond-shaped part of the limbic system that generates feelings of fear and anger. (Girls' bodies make testosterone by breaking down estrogen, while boys' bodies transform testosterone into an estrogen-like hormone called estradiol.) This blossoming of the amygdala is especially pronounced in boys, but it may account for the rise in aggressiveness and irritability seen in both sexes at adolescence. Increased levels of estrogen at puberty are responsible for the sudden growth of the hippocampus, the part of the brain that processes memory. The larger the hippocampus, the better the memory, at least in animals. The hippocampus in girls grows proportionally larger than it does in boys, a finding that may help explain why women are better than men are at remembering complex social relationships and are likely to suffer less from the memory loss that accompanies Alzheimer's.

Estrogen and testosterone may not alter the brain at puberty so much as flip neurological switches, which were set by hormonal levels while a child was still in his mother's womb. Once flipped, these switches have a profound effect on a teenager's sex drive and moodiness.

Shifts in prenatal hormones also affect mental skills in ways that may not become apparent until later in life. Testosterone, for example, appears to shape centers in the brain that process spatial information. Evidence for this comes from a study of girls with congenital adrenal hyperplasia, or CAH, a condition that causes their adrenal glands to pump out excess androgen, a testosterone-like hormone, during prenatal development. Once the girls are born, they are given cortisone, to keep the body from producing too much androgen.

Their brains, however, have already been molded. Sheri Berenbaum, a psychologist at Southern Illinois University medical school, and others have found that as teenagers, girls with CAH report they are more aggressive than their sisters, and they have better spatial skills—the ability to rotate an object in their minds, for instance, or to imagine how pieces of a shape fit together. They are also more interested than their sisters in becoming engineers and pilots, traditionally masculine professions. But re-

more interested in novelty than children or adults are, probably because it makes them feel good. Other research has shown that at the same time, levels of another neurotransmitter, serotonin, appear to decline temporarily in most adolescents, making them more likely to act impulsively.

Added to this brew of neurotransmitters are the sex hormones, which not only turn on an interest in sex but also change the brain's architecture. Giedd

searchers don't yet know precisely how testosterone molds the brain's ability to imagine all the facets of an object, or why it would make girls (or boys, for that matter) want to become engineers.

One of the last steps in making an adult brain is the coating of nerves in white matter, fatty cells that spiral around the shaft of nerves like vines around a tree. The white matter, also known as myelin, acts like the insulation on an electric cord, allowing electrical impulses to travel down a nerve faster and more efficiently. This is one reason a toddler is less coordinated than a 10-year-old. It now appears that many of the nerves connecting different processing centers in the brain don't finish myelinating until the early 20s.

Some of the nerves that become sheathed during adolescence connect areas of the brain that regulate emotion, judgment, and impulse control. Francine Benes, a neuroscientist at McLean Hospital, says that these nerves myelinate in girls earlier than in boys, which may help explain why teenage girls seem more emotionally mature than boys, whose myelin levels may not equal girls' until age 30.

The myelination process also has been implicated in schizophrenia, which often becomes apparent in late adolescence. Benes believes the faster transmissions overload defective nerves in schizophrenics. "If the circuit starts to have too much information coming in too rapidly, it may become overwhelmed."

Laying foundations. Researchers feel they have only begun to probe the workings of the adolescent brain, but their findings already offer some new ways for parents to deal with teenagers. During adolescence, many higher mental skills will become automatic, just the way playing tennis and driving do. Kids who exercise their brains, in effect, by learning to marshal their thoughts, to measure their impulses, and to understand abstract concepts, are laying the neural foundations that will serve them for the rest of their lives.

"This argues for doing a lot of things as a teenager," says the NIMH's Giedd. "You are hard-wiring your brain in adolescence. Do you want to hard-wire it for sports and playing music and doing mathematics—or for lying on the couch in front of the television?" This hard-wiring also provides yet another reason for teens not to take drugs or alcohol, because they may permanently alter the balance of chemicals in their brains.

Parents can take comfort in knowing that searching for new experiences is a normal part of growing up. The trick, say experts, is helping kids find healthy sources of stimulation. For one child, being in the school play or volunteering in the community may provide plenty of excitement. For another, it could take hang-gliding lessons. The problem, of course, is that safe risks are not always available to the kids who need them. "Middle-class kids can go skiing and scuba diving," says the University of Delaware's Zuckerman. "But for many kids, there's just crime, sex, drugs, and rock-and-roll."

The best news for parents is that the vast majority of kids will make it through adolescence with few permanent scars, except perhaps the occasional hole through a bellybutton. New research shows that most children emerge from adolescence physically and emotionally intact—although their parents will probably never be the same. Mary Scott, 48, of Port Jefferson, N.Y., is a veteran of teenage wars: She's the mother of two adolescents and a 22-year-old. "Occasionally they do things that are so incredibly selfish, it's unbelievable," she says. On the other hand, Scott adds, "If they didn't drive you crazy, they'd never leave [the nest]." Maybe adolescence is nature's way of forcing children to grow up.

With Roberta Hotinski, Bellamy Pailthorp, Erin Ragan, and Kathleen Wong

Take a teen-brain quiz online at http://www.usnews.com

Yesterday's Precocious Puberty Is Norm Today

By JANE E. BRODY

A friend who runs the child care program at a Brooklyn high school reports that one of the newly enrolled mothers, a freshman, is 13. Her baby's father is 14. While children having children is not a new phenomenon, the ever-dropping age of puberty is.

Many parents become worried when their 7- or 8-year-old daughters begin to develop breasts or grow pubic hair. They wonder, is this normal? Will the surge of sex hormones adversely affect the girls' behavior, moods or physical growth? Can girls who are still emotionally and socially immature adjust well to early physical maturation? And when should more explicit sex education and cautions about birth control begin?

What's Normal?

Two years ago, Dr. Marcia E. Herman-Giddens and colleagues described the results of physical examinations of 17,077 American girls, which revealed that white girls were showing bodily signs of sexual maturity an average of one year earlier than previous studies had indicated, and black girls two years earlier. On the average, breast development was notable before age 10 in white girls and before age 9 in black girls, and the growth of pubic hair generally occurred about a year later. But even at age 7, 27 percent of black girls and nearly 7 percent of white girls had begun to grow breasts, pubic hair or both.

The findings, she and others suggest, should prompt a redefinition of the ages at which puberty is considered precocious. Current medical textbooks state that just 1 percent of girls younger than 8 show signs of puberty. In a new review of existing data, in the Oct. 4 issue of the journal *Pediatrics,* Dr. Paul B. Kaplowitz, Dr. Sharon E. Oberfield and members of the Lawson Wilkins Pediatric Endocrine Society concluded that "the onset of breast development between 7 and 8 years of age in white girls and between 6 and 8 years in African-American girls may be part of the normal broad variation in the timing of puberty and not, in most cases, a pathological state."

Breast development is stimulated by estrogen, which is released from the ovaries upon a hormonal signal from the pituitary gland. The growth of pubic hair, however, is a result of stimulation by androgen, the so-called male sex hormone, also produced by the ovaries.

There has been much speculation about why earlier maturation may be occurring in girls, especially because there has been no apparent advance (and no racial difference) in the onset of puberty in boys. For girls, better nutrition over all and fewer infectious diseases no doubt play a role, because these trends result in more consistent growth. The increase in childhood obesity may also be a factor, because fatty tissue is a source of the sex hormone estrogen. Another suggested possibility is increased exposure to certain plastics and insecticides that degrade into substances that have estrogenlike effects.

But whatever the reasons, the phenomenon is real and, to many parents, worrisome. The new report by Dr. Kaplowitz of the Medical College of Virginia and Virginia Commonwealth University, Dr. Oberfield of Columbia University College of Physicians and Surgeons and members of the endocrine society should prove reassuring.

Effects of Early Maturity

Parents of adolescent girls know all too well that life can be an emotional roller coaster, with unpredictable outbursts of temper and outrageous or infuriating behavior. Indeed, precocious puberty has been associated with behavioral problems. In one study of 33 early-maturing girls, as a group, they appeared to be more depressed, socially withdrawn, aggressive and moody than a comparable group of girls who had not yet entered puberty. But another study that followed girls with precocious puberty to age 17½ found that they suffered no lasting psychological effects, except a tendency toward excessive psychosomatic complaints.

Although girls undergoing early sexual maturation may be far from their teenage years, parents would probably do well to read up on how to cope with an adolescent and what is considered the range of normal behavior for this often volatile time of life.

Another common concern involves the ability of girls as young as 7 or 8 to cope with menstruation. Dr. Kaplowitz and his colleagues point out that a 7-year-old who is developing breasts will not undergo the start of menstrual cycles, or menarche, for another two years. That time gap should give parents and pediatricians enough time to prepare. Also, once a girl starts menstruating, she is potentially able to become pregnant and needs explicit sex education. Adults who wait too long end up with pregnant 13-year-old girls.

But the main concern for pediatricians and for some parents is the effect that hormones might have on the child's growth. Estrogen is known to cause the growth plates in long bones to close, which can slow or shut down linear growth. Concerned parents and pediatricians sometimes wonder whether early-maturing girls should be given a hormone that blocks the pituitary stimulus of the ovaries and would presumably allow such girls to grow taller.

Here, the new evidence is most reassuring. Dr. Kaplowitz and his co-authors point out that "the younger the age at onset of puberty, the longer the duration of puberty," meaning that the adolescent growth spurt occurs for a longer time in early-maturing girls. This in part offsets the loss of adult height that might occur when the skeleton matures earlier. Indeed, girls who undergo early menarche tend to grow somewhat more than girls whose menarche occurs later. The end result is little if any difference in adult height.

Thus, the authors state, the concern that girls who enter puberty "between 6 and 8 years of age will become very short adults without intervention is overstated, because adult height within the normal range is reached in the majority of cases." Only if the onset of puberty occurs before age 6 has hormonal therapy been shown to make a meaningful difference in a girl's height.

Who should undergo evaluation for early puberty? The authors recommend that white girls younger than 7 and black girls younger than 6 who show breast or pubic hair development should be examined to be sure they have no disorder that involves an excess production of hormones that could distort their development. Too much androgen, for example, would cause masculinization and could result in infertility. Girls who have any of the following conditions should be fully evaluated:

- An unusually rapid progression of puberty that would cause rapid skeletal maturation and a predicted height four inches less than their genes might dictate or less than 4 feet 11 inches.
- The presence of any newly developed problem involving the central nervous system, including headaches, seizures or neurological deficits.
- Behaviors suggesting that the girl's emotional state, or the family's emotional state, is being adversely affected by the progression of puberty.

Finally, the authors say, parents of boys would be wise to seek medical evaluation if evidence of excessive androgen production (other than the growth of pubic hair) occurs before age 9. Such signs might include enlargement of the penis and scrotum, acne and very rapid growth. Boys who mature too rapidly, the authors say, often have a central nervous system disorder.

The 1997 Body Image Survey Results

BY DAVID M. GARNER, PH.D.

For the past three decades, women and, increasingly men have been preoccupied with how they look. But the intense scrutiny hasn't necessarily helped us see ourselves any more clearly. While as individuals we are growing heavier, our body preferences are growing thinner. And thinness is depicted everywhere as crucial to personal happiness. Despite the concerns of feminists and other observers, body image issues seem to be only growing in importance.

When most people think of body image, they think about aspects of physical appearance, attractiveness, and beauty. But body image is so much more. It's our mental representation of ourselves; it's what allows us to contemplate ourselves. Body image isn't simply influenced by feelings, and it actively influences much of our behavior, self-esteem, and psychopathology. Our body perceptions, feelings, and beliefs govern our life plan—who we meet, who we marry, the nature of our interactions, our day-to-day comfort level. Indeed, our body is our

personal billboard, providing others with first—and sometimes only—impressions.

With that in mind, Psychology Today decided it was time for another detailed reading of the state of body image. The landmark PT national surveys of 1972 and 1985 are among the most widely cited on the subject. We wanted to try and understand the growing gulf between actual and preferred shapes—and to develop the very revealing picture that can be seen only by tracking changes over time. We asked David Garner, Ph.D., to bring his vast expertise to our project. Garner, the director of the Toledo Center for Eating Disorders, is also an adjunct professor of psychology at Bowling Green State University and of women's studies at the University of Toledo. He has been researching and treating eating disorders for 20 years, heading one of the earliest studies linking them to changes in cultural expectations for thinness. From measurements of *Playboy* centerfold models and Miss America contestants, he documented that these

Who Responded to the Survey			How You Describe Yourselves		
Some of your vital statistics:			What you have to say about yourselves		
	WOMEN	**MEN**		**%WOMEN**	**%MEN**
Total number	3,452	548	Relationship-oriented	75	63
Average age	32	35	Career-oriented	62	56
Actual weight	140	180	Happy person	69	66
Desired weight	125	175	Spiritually-oriented	66	53
Height	5'5"	5'11"	Feminist	55	20
Caucasian	87%	82%	Traditional values	44	43
College grad +	62%	54%	Athletic	33	45
Income: $50,000 +	39%	38%	Pro-choice	73	64
Heterosexual	93%	79%	Politically conservative	21	28
Bisexual	4%	8%	Strong belief in astrology	16	14
Health problems	36%	30%			

Reprinted with permission from *Psychology Today*, January/February 1997, pp. 30-36, 38-40, 42-44, 75, 76, 78, 84. © 1997 by Sussex Publishers, Inc.

A Very Revealing Picture: Psychology Today's 1997 Body Image Survey Findings

Many of our survey results astounded even us veteran observers of the body wars. Among the most important findings:

• Body image is more complex than previous research suggests. It's influenced by many factors, including interpersonal factors, individual factors such as mood, and physical factors like body weight. Cultural pressures also play their part. Which factors are most important vary from person to person.

• Body dissatisfaction is soaring among both women and men—increasing at a faster rate than ever before. This is the great paradox of body preoccupation—instead of insight, it seems to breed only discontent. But a revolution in the way women see themselves—or, more accurately, *want* to see themselves—may be brewing.

• How important is it for people to be the weight they want? Fifteen percent of women and 11 percent of men say they would sacrifice more than five years of their lives to be the weight they want. Twenty-four percent of women and 17 percent of men say they would give up more than three years.

• Among young women ages 13 to 19, a whopping 62 percent say they are dissatisfied with their weight. And it gets a bit worse with age: Sixty-seven percent of women over age 30 also say they are unhappy with how much they weigh.

• While body hatred tends to stay at about the same level as women age, today's young women may be more vulnerable to self-disparagement as they get older. They are being initiated into feelings of body dissatisfaction at a tender age, and this early programming may be difficult to undo.

• Body dissatisfaction afflicts those women who describe themselves as feminists (32 percent) as well as those who say they are more traditional (49 percent). Nevertheless, feminist beliefs seem to confer some behavioral protection: Feminists say they are less willing to use drastic measures like vomiting to control their weight.

• Physical factors, such as gaining weight, are the most common cause of negative feelings about the body. Nevertheless, relationships also have an impact. If your mate doesn't think you look great, you're likely to feel devastated.

• Pregnancy is increasingly being seen not as a normal body function but as an encumbrance to body image. And some women say they are choosing not to have children for this reason.

• More than 75 percent of women surveyed say that menstruation, another normal body function, causes them to have negative feelings about their bodies.

• Bad moods wreak havoc on women's feelings about their bodies. Women get caught in a vicious spiral: emotional distress causes body loathing; disgust with their body causes emotional distress.

• Teasing during childhood or adolescence has an indelible effect on women's feelings about their bodies. Women say that the negative fallout can last for decades—no matter what shape they're currently in.

• What's a quick way to feel good about your body? Good sex. The survey found that in general, good sexual experiences breed high levels of body satisfaction.

• Sexual abuse is an important contributor to body dissatisfaction—but only women who have been sexually abused think so. Other women don't grasp the damage abuse can do to feelings about the body. The experience of sexual abuse seems to create a divide that mirrors the general cultural debate over the validity of allegations of sexual abuse.

• What's the most reliable way to develop positive feelings about your body—to say nothing of boosting your health? Respondents say it's exercising—just for the pleasure of it.

• Curiously, most people say that when it comes to weight control, exercising does not boost body satisfaction. Only women who are very heavy disagree.

• It's no longer possible to deny the fact that images of models in the media have a terrible effect on the way women see themselves. Women who have eating disorders are most influenced by fashion models.

• A model backlash has already begun. Although images of fashion models are intended to inspire identification and emulation, more than three out of ten women say they make them feel angry and resentful. They make more than four out of ten women feel insecure. Women say they are dying to see models that are more representative of the natural range of body types.

"model women" had become significantly thinner from 1959 to 1979 and that advertising for weight-loss diets had grown correspondingly. A follow-up study showed the trend continuing through the late 1980s.

Garner, along with Cincinnati psychotherapist Ann Kearney Cooke, Ph.D., and editor at large Hara Estroff Marano, crafted five pages worth of questions and in our March/April 1996 issue we asked you how you see, feel, and are influenced by your bodies. The response was phenomenal: about 4,500 people returned questionnaires from every state, not to mention Europe, Israel, Puerto Rico, Pakistan, Saudi Arabia, South Africa, New Zealand, Peru, Australia, Japan, and China. Ten months after the questionnaire hit the newsstands, responses are still com-

Extreme Weight Control

To control my weight during the past year, once a week or more:

	%WOMEN	%MEN	EATING DISORDER*	NO EATING DISORDER
Induced vomiting	6	1	23	1.5
Abused laxatives	6	3	17	3
Took diuretics	5	4	10	4
Used diet pills	12	6	20	9

*Women identifying themselves as having a diagnosed or undiagnosed eating disorder.

ing in. Many of you supplemented your surveys with pages pouring out heart and soul. And though you could reply with complete anonymity a whopping two-thirds chose to include names, addresses, and phone numbers. Some of you even included pictures!

Our statistical analyses were conducted on the first 4,000 responses—3,452 women and 548 men (86 percent women, 14 percent men)—a much wider gender split than in our readership as a whole, which is 70 percent women and 30 percent men. (See "Who Responded to the Survey" below.) The predominantly female response clearly says something about the stake women have in this topic. Participants were primarily Caucasian, college-educated, in their early to mid thirties, middle-income, and heterosexual. Women who responded range in age from 13 to 90 and weigh between 77 and 365 pounds (89 women weigh 100 pounds or less; 82 women weigh more than 250 pounds). Men range in age from 14 to 82 and weigh between 115 and 350 pounds. You describe yourselves as relationship-oriented, pro-choice, intellectual, politically liberal, and spiritual. At the top of your worry list are financial matters and romantic relationships. A significant segment described health problems that vary from relatively minor ailments to cancer and AIDS.

Appearing to Be Dissatisfied

The 1997 Psychology Today Body Image Survey shows there's more discontent with the shape of our bodies than ever before. Okay, there are some things we like about our appearance: height, hair, face, feet, and the size of our sex organs generate the most approval. In the span between face and feet, our primary sex organs are a small oasis of favor amidst a wasteland of waist land. Apparently there's little pressure to change the things that we can't see or change. Of course, these areas tend not to be repositories for the accumulation of fat, that object of abhorrence. In contrast, the negative focus remains on our visible attributes, the ones that display fat—the ones that can presumably be controlled or corrected with enough self-discipline.

Fifty-six percent of women say they are dissatisfied with their overall appearance. Their self-disparagement is specifically directed toward their abdomens (71 percent), body weight (66 percent), hips (60 percent), and muscle tone (58 percent). Men show escalating dissatisfaction with their abdomens (63 percent), weight (52 percent), muscle tone (45 percent), overall appearance (43 percent), and chest (38 percent).

Weight dissatisfaction means one thing to men and something entirely different to women. The overwhelming majority of women—89 percent—want to lose weight. How much? The average woman's weight is 140 pounds; the preferred weight is 125 pounds. Only 3 percent of the women who say they are dissatisfied with their bodies want to gain weight; 8 percent want to stay the same. By contrast, 22 percent of the men who say they are dissatisfied with their bodies want to *gain* weight. (See "Men and Body Image.")

The survey also shows a correlation between body dissatisfaction and body weight—those who are more dissatisfied tend to be heavier. In fact, the average weight of the most dissatisfied women is about 180 pounds; the least dissatisfied weigh in at 128 pounds. Both groups have an average ideal weight that's lower than their actual weight; however, in the former group it's fifty pounds away from reality compared with three pounds for the least dissatisfied.

What Shaped Your Body Image When You Were Young?

Some of the facts that figure into body image:

	%WOMEN	%MEN
PHYSICAL		
My personal feelings about weight	58	35
INTERPERSONAL		
Being teased by others	44	35
My mother's attitude about my body	31	13
My father's attitude about my body	23	11
Positive sexual experiences	26	28
Sexual abuse	18	7
CULTURAL		
Movie or TV celebrities	23	13
Fashion magazine models	22	6
Sports figures	7	16

The Weight of Influence:
Factors Fostering
Positive Body Image

What's instrumental in making you feel
good about your body?

	%WOMEN	%MEN
PHYSICAL		
Exercising regularly	64	62
Losing weight	62	39
Feeling thin	53	24
Accepting my body the way it is	50	36
Wearing flattering clothes	46	21
INTERPERSONAL		
Compliments on my appearance	48	44
Love from another person	43	44
Positive sexual experiences	40	41
Good relationships	33	34
EMOTIONAL		
Confidence in my abilities	39	38
Feeling effective as a person	39	36
Meditating	11	9

How important is it for people to be the weight they want? We put the question in stark terms and asked, "How many years of your life would you trade to achieve your weight goals?" The findings are astounding: Fifteen percent of women and 11 percent of men say they'd sacrifice more than five years of their lives; 24 percent of women and 17 percent of men say they would give up more than three years. These answers make us regret not testing the extremes and offering 10- and 20-year options. Still, we can confidently conclude that a significant minority of you believe life is worth living only if you are thin.

A rather drastic measure of weight control is cigarette smoking. Statistics reveal that smoking is on the rise among young women. Robert Klesges, Ph.D., and colleagues at the University of Memphis have repeatedly shown that smoking is used by many women for weight control. While we didn't specifically ask whether you smoke, we did ask whether you smoke to control your weight. About 50 percent of women and 30 percent of men say they puff away to control the pounds.

Body dissatisfaction has very different implications for people depending upon how heavy they are. Among those well above normal weight, body dissatisfaction is a painful expression of despair, but understandable given the cultural stigma of being fat. However, an equivalent amount of self-loathing on the part of thin people suggests a different type of problem—distortion on top of dissatisfaction. Thin women distort reality by seeing themselves as fat. Today this type of distortion is rampant and has become the norm. It explains why so many women are susceptible to eating disorders, where the pursuit of thinness is driven by faulty perceptions rather than reality. One hundred and fifty-nine women in our sample are extremely underweight—and 40 percent of them still want to lose weight. Many have eating disorders, to be described later.

Age and Body Image

A number of national studies have shown that body weight is increasing among American adults. Moreover, epidemiologic studies find that body weight increases with age. For both men and women it tends to increase during the first five decades of life, then decline on the way to our inevitable destiny. Although the pattern of gradual weight gain during adulthood recently sparked a public health frenzy leading to such programs as C. Everett Koop's Shape Up America, an analysis of 13 major studies of weight change by Reuben Andres, M.D., of the Gerontology Research Center in Baltimore, Maryland, found that people who put on some pounds during adulthood survive longer than those who maintain or even lose weight.

The Weight of Influence:
Factors Fostering Negative
Body Image

What's instrumental in making you feel
bad about your body?

	%WOMEN	%MEN
PHYSICAL		
Gaining weight	66	37
Not exercising regularly	44	36
Looking at my stomach in the mirror	44	33
Looking at my face in the mirror	16	15
A certain time in my menstrual cycle	29	–
INTERPERSONAL		
My partner's opinion of my appearance	40	29
Being around someone critical	32	19
Someone rejecting me	26	24
Relationships not going well	24	21
Negative sexual experiences	20	16
EMOTIONAL		
Not feeling confident	22	18
Being in a bad mood	15	9

Our findings confirm that body weight usually increases with age. On average, both men and women tend to put on five to ten pounds per decade, a trend that stops between the ages of 50 and 59. Weight declines slightly after age 60.

Since satisfaction with our appearance is so closely tied to how much we weigh, particularly for women, it's logical to assume that our self-disparagement would gradually increase over a lifetime. But that's not what we found. The youngest women, ages 13 to 19, are both the thinnest and the most satisfied with their appearance, however 54 percent of them are still dissatisfied. The number barely increases to 57 percent among women ages 20 to 29. And it remains at around this level, even though women gained five to ten pounds each succeeding decade.

We can't say for sure how these young women will feel as they get older; a survey, of course, taps different women at each age, not the same women over time. Nevertheless, the magnitude of self-hatred among young women is astonishing. Despite being at a weight that most women envy they are still plagued by feelings of inadequacy. The good news is that even though women gain weight with age, they don't become more dissatisfied as they get older. In fact, there's some evidence that as they age they gain insight and appreciation of their bodies' abilities.

Induction into our culture's weight concerns is happening for women at younger ages. Girls today not only have more weight concerns when they're young, they also lack buffers to protect their psyches. Kids don't know themselves well and have not yet developed many competencies to draw on. It's easier for them to look outside themselves to discover who they are—and find themselves lacking. While we may not be able to draw conclusions about them based on the experiences of older women, we can only hope that over time they develop the insight of this 55-year-old woman from Pennsylvania: "From age 15 to 25, I was very concerned about my body image and went on many diets. As I matured, I realized that personality and morals are more important than how you look and stopped beating myself up and accepted my body. Now I don't worry about my weight but I do eat healthfully and exercise moderately."

In contrast to women, only 41 percent of young men ages 13 to 19 say they are dissatisfied with their appearance. The figures stay about the same for men ages 20 to 29 (38 percent), then spike to 48 percent among 30- to 39-year-olds. They decline again for the 40 to 49 age group (43 percent) and increase for men ages 50 to 59 (48 percent). Again, in contrast to women, a significant proportion of dissatisfied men want to *add* body mass, not lose it. But the critical point is that men as a group are more satisfied with their appearance, although the number who are tormented about their weight and shape appears to be growing.

The Locus of Focus

Because we were interested in discovering what was most instrumental in creating positive and negative feelings about your bodies, we asked how your body image is influenced by certain aspects of physical appearance: gaining weight, feeling thin, looking at your face in the mirror, looking at your stomach in the mirror. Exercise was also included, because we use it to change our body weight and shape.

Do Fashion Models Influence How You Feel About Your Appearance?

What's the media's impact on how we see ourselves?

	%WOMEN	Extremely Satisfied Women	Extremely Dissatisfied Women	%MEN
I ALWAYS OR VERY OFTEN:				
Compare myself to models in magazines	27	17	43	12
Carefully study the shapes of models	28	18	47	19
VERY THIN OR MUSCULAR MODELS MAKE ME:				
Feel insecure about my weight	29	12	67	15
Want to lose weight	30	13	67	18
Feel angry or resentful	22	9	45	8

We assumed focusing on features like the face and the stomach—the latter the bearer of fat and of children—would produce highly-charged feelings, both good and bad. However, we were specifically interested in trying to understand the relative impact of different physical features on body feeling—the locus of focus. We also wanted to measure how physical aspects of appearance stack up against interpersonal factors, such as being rejected, receiving compliments, being teased, and sexual experiences, as well as emotional components, like feeling effective as a person and over-all happiness.

When it comes to what causes negative feelings, gaining weight is at the top of the list for everyone: two-thirds of women and about a third of men say it's a very important cause of their disapproval of their bodies. And the stomach, not the face, is the prevailing locus of disapproval for both men and women. Looking at your stomach in the mirror is an extreme downer for 44 percent of women and 33 percent of men—compared to the face, which was a downer for 16 percent of women and 15 percent of men.

Women are hit with a very specific source of body antipathy: more than 75 percent say that "a certain time in the menstrual cycle" is an important cause of negative feelings about their bodies. And a fear of fatness may be perverting women's attitudes toward pregnancy and childbearing. About a third of women say that, for them, pregnancy itself is an important source of negative body feelings.

If these feelings are strong enough, it's only reasonable to assume that they may affect some women's decisions to have kids. As one 25-year-old Maryland woman offers: "I love children and would love to have one more—but only if I didn't have to gain the weight." A 43-year-old woman from Georgia proselytizes against pregnancy: "I tell every young girl that if they like the way their body looks, don't get pregnant. It messes up a woman's body."

While interpersonal factors are the cause of negative feelings about the body for fewer people, they are highly influential for a significant minority. Forty percent of women and 29 percent of men say their partner's opinion about their appearance is very important to their body image. About a quarter of all respondents say the same goes for someone rejecting them. Thus there's a major connection between the way we feel about our body and the way we perceive others feel about it. One 54-year-old New York woman says: "Since my partner sees me as beautiful, I feel beautiful." This interpersonal connection seems to take root early, as a 17-year-old woman from New York explains: "My partner's feelings about me and my looks mean everything to me. If my mate had an unfavorable opinion, that would be devastating."

What impact does our mood have on our feelings about our body? The survey, as well as other research, suggests a potentially deadly two-way self-perpetuating process. When we feel bad about anything, our body satisfaction plummets, and when we hate our body, our mood takes a dive. A 39-year-old Connecticut woman captures the vicious cycle: When I'm in a bad mood about anything, I get more critical of my body. When I am more critical of my body, I lose confidence in my abilities." A 35-year-old woman from Pennsylvania illustrates the process: "When I am in a bad mood about something else, my focus often goes right to my body weight and I either feel fat or I obsess about food."

The connection between mood and body is critical; it suggests that body dissatisfaction is not a static entity but rather is governed, at least in part, by our general emotional state. When we feel bad about something else, our bodies get dragged down in the negative tide.

Among the many aspects of body image we looked at was the role of certain life orientations. For example, we compared women who call themselves feminists with those who view themselves more traditionally. There are no differences between the groups in average body weight. But 32 percent of feminists, compared with 49 percent of traditional women, are strongly dissatisfied with their overall appearance. When asked more specifically about their weight, 24 percent of feminists and 40 percent of traditional women are extremely dissatisfied. The differences translate directly into behavior—twice as many traditionally oriented women vomit to control their weight as women claiming to be feminists. It appears that feminist beliefs confer some behavioral protection.

When we asked what leads to positive feelings about your bodies, the results generally mirrored the findings about negative feelings, but there are some interesting differences. Weight-related factors tended to top the list of sources of positive feelings, paralleling the results for negative feelings. Exercise generated the greatest source

The Big Bad Body

The dissatisfaction we feel toward our bodies has not only risen since 1972, the rate at which it's rising is accelerating:

	1972 Survey%		1985 Survey%		1997 Survey%	
	WOMEN	MEN	WOMEN	MEN	WOMEN	MEN
Overall appearance	25	15	38	34	56	43
Weight	48	35	55	41	66	52
Height	13	13	17	20	16	16
Muscle tone	30	25	45	32	57	45
Breasts/chest	26	18	32	28	34	38
Abdomen	50	36	57	50	71	63
Hips or upper thighs	49	12	50	21	61	29

of positive feelings. But moderate exercise, we found, goes a long way. People who exercise a lot do not seem to feel any better than those who exercise moderately.

And while both men and women identify a few circumstances that could crash their feelings about their bodies, you point out more factors that bolster it. About twice as many people judge sexual experiences as a source of good feelings rather than bad. For both sexes, interpersonal and emotional factors more often serve to reinforce, not punish. This is encouraging news; it implies that there are many avenues for us to improve our feelings about our bodies.

When we asked what shaped your body image during childhood and adolescence, most women and a significant minority of men reiterate the cultural theme that thinness is the key to happiness. But interpersonal factors also weigh heavily on most of us during development, and women rank them more important than men.

For many, teasing during childhood or adolescence had a crushing effect on body image. So much so that the extent of the damage can't be captured by a questionnaire. The narratives paint a graphic picture of the pain. As one 59-year-old Illinois man recounts: "Being teased when I was a child made me feel bad about my body for years and years." A 37-year-old woman from Ohio admits: "No matter how thin I become, I always feel like the fat kid everyone made fun of." An 18-year-old Iowa woman says: "The memories absolutely haunt me and make me feel like something is wrong with me."

By far, however, the dominant factor that regulates our feelings about our appearance is our body weight—actual body weight as well as attitudes about it. The weight of this influence is staggering compared to other factors. Body weight alone accounts for 60 percent of our overall satisfaction with our appearance; all other physical features combined add only 10 percent more to our level of satisfaction. This suggests a simple solution—just change your weight and happy times will follow. Unfortunately, it's not that simple.

Exercise: The New Holy Grail?

Virtually everyone surveyed says they exercised during the past year—97 percent of both sexes. And exercise gets high marks when it comes to breeding positive body feelings (by a narrow margin for women, a substantial majority for men). Seventy-six percent of women and 86 percent of men report exercising at least two hours a week; 20 percent of women and 27 percent of men exercise five or more times a week for at least 30 minutes. There's a modest relationship between the amount of time spent exercising and satisfaction with appearance, and this is stronger for men than women.

On the surface, it appears that exercise is an uncomplicated remedy for achieving harmony with our bodies. But a closer look at our findings tempers this conclusion. More than 60 percent of women and 40 percent of men indicate that at least half of their workout time is spent exercising to control their weight. And for a significant proportion of both sexes—18 percent of women, 12 percent of men—all exercise is aimed at weight control.

But all that exercise is not leading to body satisfaction, since 88 percent of these women and 79 percent of these men say they are dissatisfied with their appearance. By contrast, among those who exercise for weight control less than 25 percent of the time, only a third are dissatisfied with their appearance. For many women, exercise is simply one more weapon in the weight-control war, a practice that mutes its ability to boost body satisfaction.

However, heavier women say the more they exercise, the bigger the boost to body satisfaction. Among women who weigh more than average, 30 percent of those who exercise more than five times a week are satisfied, compared to 20 percent who exercise less than once a week.

Whether or not exercise is effective as a method of weight control, it does tend to make us feel better about our appearance. It also improves both health and mood.

Men and Body Image

In general, men say they are more satisfied with their bodies than women. And weight plays a less important role in shaping their feelings about their bodies. A little over 12 percent of the men who responded to our survey say they're gay. In general, gay men are more concerned about their weight and have more eating concerns.

	%ALL MEN	%GAY MEN	% WOMEN
I am extremely or somewhat satisfied with my body	57	44	44
Gaining weight is very important in making me feel bad about my body	37	46	66
Feeling thin goes a long way toward making me feel good about my body	24	34	53
Do you ever diet?	58	70	84
Have you ever been diagnosed with an eating disorder?	3	9	14
Do you think you have an eating disorder but haven't been treated?	5	17	14
DO YOU USE:			
Diet pills	5	12	10
Laxatives	2	6	4
Diuretics	3	8	4
Vomiting	1	3	4

Sex and Body Image

Sexual experiences affect our body image, and our body image affects our sexual liaisons. You describe this reciprocal relationship poignantly. Body image affects sexual experiences: "The less attractive I feel, the less I desire sex," says a 31-year-old woman from Louisiana. "If at all possible I avoid sex; however, if it should happen, I am unwilling to let go. I have the feeling I may be vulgar to my partner."

Sexual experiences affect body image: "A bad sexual experience makes me feel embarrassed about my body," admits a 19-year-old Texas woman. Sexual abuse amplifies this self-abasement: "Having been sexually assaulted brought a lot of body hatred, and a desire to not have a body," a 24-year-old woman from Illinois says.

As has been the case for so many other variables in the 1997 Survey, weight gets in the middle of the picture. One 20-year-old Missouri woman states: "I try to lose weight for boyfriends. When I am fat, I know that no one wants to be with me. I feel like unless I have a good body, no decent guy wants me!"

The connection between sexual experiences and body image is affirmed in our overall findings. More than a third of all men (40 percent) and women (36 percent) say that unpleasant sexual experiences are moderately to very important in causing negative feelings of their body. But an even greater percentage—70 percent of men and 67 percent of women—feel that good sexual experiences contribute to satisfactory feelings about their bodies. Few believe they are irrelevant (6 percent of men and 7 percent of women).

Twenty-three percent of women consider sexual abuse moderately to very important in having shaped their body image in childhood or adolescence. That's twice the number of men—10 percent—who think so, perhaps reflecting the difference in rates of abuse between men and women. But the vast majority of men (85 percent) and women (74 percent) declare that it's almost or completely irrelevant, no doubt indicating their lack of personal experience.

The personal accounts of some respondents leave no doubt as to the devastating effects of sexual abuse. An 18-year-old woman says: "As a young child, I was sexually abused by my father. I grew up feeling as though there was something inherently dirty and evil about my body." Abuse is clearly a dominant factor in body image for members of both sexes, but it's not ubiquitous, unlike such factors as teasing by others (73 percent of women and 57 of percent men) and personal feelings about weight (79 percent of women and 56 percent of men).

Intriguingly, those who are dissatisfied with their bodies are much more inclined to view negative sexual experiences as important than those who are body-satisfied. Only 15 percent of women who are extremely satisfied with their bodies say that negative sexual experiences are very important in determining their body image (42 percent say that negative sexual experiences are completely irrelevant). In contrast, 41 percent of body-dissatisfied women regard negative sexual experiences as very important (only 16 percent say they are completely irrelevant). The same is true for men.

Sexual and physical abuse are important contributors to body dissatisfaction—but again primarily it's women who have been sexually abused who think so. Sexual abuse is judged very important by 30 percent of women who are extremely body-dissatisfied, versus 13 percent of the extremely body-satisfied group. Women who feel good about their bodies and have not been victims of abuse just don't grasp the damage abuse can do to feelings about the body.

EXTREME WEIGHT CONTROL

Eating disorders occur when a person's intense preoccupation with their "fatness leads them to extreme measures to control their weight. Considerable research indicates that anorexia and bulimia are outgrowths of a negative body image and, further, that today's epidemic increase in eating disorders is related to the intense pressure put on women to conform to ultraslender role models of feminine beauty.

A remarkable 84 percent of women and 58 percent of men report having dieted to lose weight. A sizable proportion of respondents say they have resorted to extreme and dangerous weight-control methods in the last year: 445 women (13 percent) and 22 men (4 percent) say they induce vomiting; more than a third of each of these groups vomit once a week or more. Fourteen percent of women (480) and 3 percent of men (16) say they have actually been diagnosed with eating disorders. Among the very underweight women in our survey, 31 percent (49) indicate they have been diagnosed with an eating disorder. And 11.5 percent of women and 2 percent of men say they have an eating disorder but have never received treatment, although the type of eating disorder was not specified.

Vomiting was more common among those who say they have been diagnosed (23 percent), less common among those who identify themselves as having untreated eating disorders (11 percent). Perhaps most surprising is that 1.5 percent of women (38) vomit for weight control and don't feel they have an eating disorder!

Laxative abuse for weight control is common among those diagnosed with eating disorders (17 percent) and those self-identified (9 percent). It is also reported by 3 percent of women (72) who don't feel they have eating disorders.

Vomiting and laxative abuse seem to be increasingly accepted as "normal" methods of weight control. And eating disorders themselves have become the object of envy gaining celebrity status with each new high-profile victim. There's even evidence that eating disorders acquire a positive patina with media exposure—even it it's

Altering Your Image: Strategies from the Trenches

One of the major goals of the 1997 Body Image Survey was to learn more about how people have remade their image. Though we anticipated receiving a few brief suggestions, we were inundated with your personal accounts of change. We have summarized your suggestions but kept your words. Try and discover what factors play a role in your struggle with your body. And be deliberate about creating a lifestyle that increases your chances for ending the war with your body.

1. Develop criteria for self-esteem that go beyond appearance. One way to make appearance less important is to develop other benchmarks for self-evaluation. A 51-year-old woman from California summarizes the approach: "By achieving in other areas, balancing successes and failures, searching where positives are possible." A 53-year-old Washington man says, "focusing on succeeding at work, participating in sports, and friendships have helped me overcome my negative body feelings."

2. Cultivate the ability to appreciate your body, especially how it functions. One middle-aged woman writes: "I have often wanted to write an article called 'I Have a Beautiful Body.' No, I don't look like Jane Fonda. I look like a normal 46-year-old woman who has had three children. But my body is beautiful because of all it does for me. I have two eyes that can see, a large nose for smelling, a large mouth for eating and smiling, two hands that can hold and hug, two breasts that have nursed three sons, an abdomen that was home to three babies, two legs that can walk everywhere I want to go, and two feet to take me there."

"I have extremely red hair and as a child I hated it because it was so different," says a 20-year-old woman from California. "I have come to realize that my hair is a beautiful and exotic part of me. Now I cherish it."

3. Engage in behavior that makes you feel good about yourself. "When I have negative thoughts and feelings about my physical appearance, I try to behave in ways that will turn them around, like exercise and buying a piece of clothing that enhances my appearance," says a 30-year-old Missouri woman.

"Although Rubenesque at age 54, I currently model nude for a local university art school, meditate daily to focus inward, and enjoy dancing, swimming, archery, art, and my writing projects," says a Georgia woman.

4. Reduce your exposure to noxious images. "I stopped buying fashion magazines completely when I was about 24," says a 30-year-old woman from Michigan. "Comparing myself to the models had a very strong and negative impact."

"One of the things that helped me become more accepting of my body was the realization that it was okay to be female," says a 67-year-old woman from Ohio. "It sounds hokey, but watching old movies starring Sophia Loren and Ava Gardner helped. These women had shoulders, and breasts, and hips, and are some of the sexiest women I have ever seen."

5. Exercise for strength, fitness, and health, not just weight control. "When I was able to stop focusing on how my body looked and began experiencing what it could help me accomplish—climbing, swimming, cycling, surviving in the wilderness—it made me feel extremely satisfied," says a 28-year-old woman from Louisiana.

"About a year ago I started walking every day for about an hour," says a 22-year-old woman from New York. "Because I was walking I felt so good. I also lost 10 pounds, but that didn't matter. My attitude changed because I cared about my health."

6. Seek out others who respect and care about your body; teach them how to talk about and touch your body. "The most recent experience that has helped has been a lover," says a 67-year-old Ohio woman. "He makes me glad to be in this body with this shape and these dimensions."

7. Get out of abusive relationships. "If my partner didn't like my appearance, he would no longer be my partner," says a 31-year-old woman from Alabama. "I eliminate the negative."

8. Identify and change habitual negative thoughts about your body. "I constructed a tape of positive self-talk with personal goals and feelings I want to achieve," says a 25-year-old Washington woman. "When I have a bad attitude about my body, I pop in my tape. It really helps improve my self-image."

"When I look in the mirror at my body I always try to say nice things rather than cringe," continues the wise-beyond-her-years 25-year-old.

9. Decode more complicated thoughts about the body. Are negative thoughts and feelings about your body distracting you from other issues that are really bothering you? A 60-year-old woman writes: "A factor that has helped me come to terms with my body was recognizing that much of my relationship problems had more to do with shyness and lack of social skills than physical appearance. Once I worked on my people skills, I found that I worried less about my appearance."

10. If you can't get over your bad body image, consider seeking professional help. "I was bulimic for 12 years," says a 36-year-old woman from Oregon. "My recovery was based on individual counseling, support from friends, and a hell of a lot of hard work on my part."

11. Control what you can, forget about what you can't. "As far as negativity about my physical appearance," says a 33-year-old woman from Michigan, "I've had one simple rule: work on improving what you can realistically change, and don't spend time worrying about the rest."

negative—and that actually helps spread them by social contagion. This was driven home by a patient I recently saw. When told she really didn't meet the diagnostic criteria for an eating disorder, she burst into tears. "I tried so hard to get an eating disorder, to be like [a high profile gymnast]," she lamented, "but I guess I can't even get this right."

Not surprisingly, one of the keys to helping people overcome eating disorders is fostering the development of a positive body image. Unfortunately, this means swimming against the cultural stream, as it's extremely hard to avoid ubiquitous thin-is-beautiful messages. Studies of prime-time television indicate that programs are dominated by people with thin body types and thinness is consistently associated with favorable personality traits. But one of the most interesting aspects of the psychology of appearance is that not everyone succumbs to the same pressures.

MEDIATING SELF-PERCEPTION

The media play an important role as a cultural gatekeeper, framing standards of beauty for all of us by the models they choose. Many observers, including eating-disorder specialists, have encouraged producers and editors to widen the range of beauty standards by including models more representative of real women. But often they respond by saying that more diversity will weaken sales; recently *Vogue* magazine acknowledged the outrage toward gaunt fashion models—but denied there's any evidence linking images of models to eating disorders.

The 1997 Body Image Survey gathered direct information on this issue and more generally on the media's impact on self-perception. The results are nothing short of fascinating. Forty-three percent of women report that "very thin or muscular models" make them feel insecure about their weight. This is true for only 28 percent of men. Just under half of women (48 percent) indicate very thin models make them want to lose weight to look like them; 34 percent of men agree. Though drawn to and driven by the image of fashion models, 34 percent of women declare they are angry and resentful at these presumed paragons of beauty, as are 15 percent of men.

The impact of the media, however, is somewhat selective, affecting most strongly those who are dissatisfied with their shape, and who are generally heavier and farther away from the cultural ideal. Women who are extremely satisfied with their weight compare themselves to and study the shapes of models less than half as often as women who are body-dissatisfied.

Even more striking, 76 percent of the women who are dissatisfied with their bodies say that very thin or muscular models make them feel insecure about their weight very often or always (versus 12 percent of body-satisfied women). Sixty-seven percent also say models make them want to lose weight (versus 13 percent of body-satisfied

women), and 45 percent say models make them angry or resentful (versus 9 percent of body-satisfied women).

Similarly, those who say they've been diagnosed with an eating disorder report being highly influenced by fashion models. Forty-three percent compare themselves to models in magazines; 45 percent scrutinize the shapes of models. Forty-nine percent say very thin models make them feel insecure about themselves, and 48 percent say they "make me want to lose weight to be like them."

Clearly, body satisfaction, a rather rare commodity, confers relative immunity to media influence. But the existence of a large number of women who are drawn to media imagery but resent the unreality of those images is cause for concern. It suggests they are experiencing an uncomfortable level of entrapment. We wonder how long it will take for their resentment to be unleashed full force on the fashion industry and/or the media—and in what form.

Women and, to a lesser degree, men are not only affected by images in the media, they also want to see themselves represented differently. They're clamoring for change and willing to put their money on their predilections. The overwhelming majority of all respondents—93 percent of women, 89 percent of men—want models in magazines to represent the natural range of body shapes; 82 percent of women assert they are willing to buy magazines containing heavier models, as do 53 percent of men, even though most still believe that clothes look better on thin models.

One 30-year-old woman captures the feeling: "The media portray an image of the perfect woman that is unattainable for somewhere between 98 to 99 percent of the female population. How are we supposed to live up to that standard that is shoved in our faces constantly—I hate it."

THE SHAPE OF THINGS TO COME

More than ever before, women are dissatisfied with their weight and are fighting it with relentless dieting and exercise. Thinness has become the preeminent yardstick for success or failure, a constant against which every woman can be measured, a gauge that has slowly permeated the male mentality. Yet the actual body weight of women in the U.S. has increased over the last 30 years, and consumer pressure for weight-loss products is surging.

Research shows that dieting to lose weight and fear of fatness are now common in girls as young as nine years old—and escalate dramatically during adolescence, particularly among those at the heavier end of the spectrum. The risk of developing an eating disorder is eight times higher in dieting 15-year-old girls than in nondieting 15-year-old girls.

The 1997 Body Image Survey results and cumulative clinical experience suggest there is merit to becoming comfortable with yourself even if you don't conform to current cultural body-size ideals. Some people are naturally fatter, just as others are naturally thinner. Despite a $50 billion-a-year diet industry; conventional treatments for obesity are an abysmal failure. Traditional dietary and behavioral treatments may have an effect in the short term, but they do not produce lasting and clinically significant amounts of weight loss. They are no match for the genetic and biological factors that regulate body weight. They certainly reinforce the myth that weight loss is the preferred route to improve self-esteem. Perhaps the wisest course is to get plenty of exercise—and accept yourself the way you are rather than try to mold yourself into a narrowly defined and arbitrary ideal, no matter how widely pictured it is.

Preoccupation with body image is undoubtedly not good for our mental health, but it also seems to be a metaphor for something larger in the culture—if we could only figure out what. Over a decade ago, the late social critic Christopher Lasch argued that our culture of mass consumption encourages narcissism, a new kind of self-consciousness or vanity through which people have learned to judge themselves not merely *against* others but *through* others' eyes. The "image" projected by possessions, physical attractiveness, clothes, and "personality" replace experience, skills, and character as gauges of personal identity, health, and happiness. We are thrown into a chronic state of unease, perfect prey for an array of commercial "solutions."

Psychiatrists and psychologists have also weighed in on the meaning of body image issues. At the 1996 meeting of the American Psychological Association, Yale psychiatrist Alan Feingold, M.D., received an award for detailing differences in body-image pressures on men and women. Dr. Feingold contends that pressure on women to look good is not only growing but reflects intensified competition for dwindling resources; after all, looks confer a kind of status to women. Others point to role conflicts for women; power issues; a mother-daughter generational rift; and the possibility that in a world of rapidly shifting realities, we seize on the body as an island of certainty—numbers on a scale represent quantifiable accomplishment. Perhaps it's all of these; the body is a big screen on which we now project all of our anxieties.

ADOLESCENT MALE ATHLETES: BODY IMAGE, DIET, AND EXERCISE

Pamela S. McKay Parks and Marsha H. Read

ABSTRACT

The purpose of this study was to investigate and compare body image concerns, attitudes toward eating/weight control, and reasons for exercising between two groups of adolescent male athletes—football players ($N = 44$) and cross-country runners ($N = 30$). Subjects responded to surveys covering eating attitudes, weight concerns, physical traits, perceived and ideal body shape/size, and reasons for exercising. Significant differences were noted; Football players reported a more positive body image; cross-country runners indicated a greater degree of body dissatisfaction, more disordered eating patterns, and a greater degree of concern for weight control which identified this group as one in need of increased health education.

INTRODUCTION

Body image is a complex phenomenon that includes physiological, psychological, and sociological components. Research has indicated that the degree of satisfaction with one's body image is related to one's self-esteem (Becker, 1981; Grodner, 1991; Ham, Easton, Himburg, & Greenburg, 1983; Hendry & Gillies, 1978; Mishkin et al., 1986; Richards, Casper, & Larson, 1990; Rosen, Gross, & Vara, 1987). Body image perception is thought to consist of both "body percept—accuracy of body size estimation" and "body concept—degree of body dissatisfaction or disparagement" (Casper & Offer, 1990; Loosemoore, Mable, & Galgan, 1989; Mishkin et al., 1986; Silberstein, Striegel-Moore, Timko, & Redin, 1988). Additionally, distortions of body image have been reported not only in populations with eating disorders such as anorexia nervosa and bulimia, but in nonclinical samples. Within nonclinical samples, body image distortions have been associated with lowered self-esteem, depression, and chronic dieting (Cash, Counts, & Huffine, 1990; Mishkind et al., 1986; Wardle & Beales, 1986).

Concerns about body image has traditionally been thought to be a female preoccupation (Cash, Counts, & Huffine, 1990; Dwyer, Feldman, & Mayer, 1967; Grodner, 1991; Loosemoore, Mable, & Galgan, 1989; Striegel-Moore & Silberstein, 1985). However, societal and cultural trends suggest that body image concerns also may affect males. The adolescent male is vulnerable to the pressure to attain the "ideal" male body (Ham et al., 1983; Hendry & Gilles, 1978). This ideal includes a masculine physique (V-shaped), tallness, and muscularity (mesomorphic body build) (Damhorst,

Reprint requests to Marsha H. Read, Ph.D., R.D., Dept. of Nutrition, University of Nevada, Reno, Nevada 89557.

Littrell, & Littrell, 1987; Koff & Rierdan, 1990; Mishkind et al., 1986). The desire to achieve this image may induce some adolescents to participate in athletics in general, while the individual's body type may provide the impetus for selection of a particular sport (e.g., mesomorphs may tend to select football). Regardless of whether a sport is selected as a result of a natural body type or as a way to achieve a desired body type, there are apt to be cases where the "ideal" and the "actual" body types will not or cannot coincide. This raises the resultant question of body image concerns. Most data on this subject has been obtained from college- and adult-aged populations. There is limited information regarding younger male athletes. This study was undertaken to investigate and compare body image concerns between two groups of adolescent male athletes—football players and cross-country runners. In addition, since modification of body build is often attempted via diet and exercise, data were also gathered on attitudes toward eating and weight control and reasons for exercising.

METHOD

Sample Selection

A convenience sample of adolescent male football players and cross-country runners were chosen because of the contrasts in body size (i.e., the larger, more muscular physique for football players and the leaner physique of cross-country runners).

Subjects consisted of seventy-four male athletes, ranging in age from 14 to 18 years (30 cross-country runners and 44 football players). Contacts with the athletes were made through the coaching staffs of high schools in the local area. Each coach was given information on the purpose of the study and the instruments to be administered. Because of the varied scheduling and team meetings, each coach had to find an appropriate time to administer the questionnaire. Coaches emphasized the need to take the questionnaires seriously and provided clarification to the participants. The questionnaires were completed and returned immediately to the coaches. The researchers then collected the questionnaires.

Questionnaires

Each athlete completed a packet of questionnaires which consisted of the Body Esteem Scale (BES) (Franzoi & Shields, 1984), the Body Size Drawings (BSD) (Fallon & Rossen, 1985), the Eating Attitudes Test (EAT) (Garner, Olmsted, Bohr, & Garfinkel, 1982), and the Reasons for Ex-

ercise Inventory (Siberstein et al., 1988). The BES and BSD were used as measures of self-esteem. The BES consists of three dimensions—physical attraction, upper body, and condition. The EAT has three sub-scales: Factor I (dieting), Factor II (bulimia and preoccupation with food), and Factor III (oral control). There are seven dimensions to the Reasons for Exercise Inventory: weight control, fitness, mood, health, attractiveness, enjoyment, and tone.

In addition to the information gathered from the various scales, a personal information form provided data on current (self-reported) and desired weight, sport (in the case of football, player position and conditioning activities; and in the case of cross-country runners, miles run per week) and age. Self-reported rather than actual weights were utilized due to constraints the process would have placed on practice time, which coaches were reluctant to concede.

Completion of the questionnaires and the personal information form took 15–20 minutes. All surveys were completed confidentially.

Statistical Analyses

A repeated measure of ANOVA was used to test for differences between the football players and the cross-country runners with respect to actual and desired weights and heights. Repeated measure of ANOVA was also used to examine differences in perceived actual and ideal body size drawings (BSDs) between the two groups. Independent t-tests assessed differences between the groups on the three dimensions (attraction, upper body, and condition) of the BES, differences in Factor I, II, and II of the EAT test, and on the seven domains of the Reasons for Exercise Inventory. A 0.05 level of significance was employed.

RESULTS

Characteristics of the Sample

Among the cross-country runners, 50% ran between 40 and 50 miles per week; 30% ran 20–49 miles per week, and 20% ran between 60 and 80 miles per week. Among the cross-country runners, 67% ran 6 to 7 days per week, 6% ran twice a day, and 4% failed to report the number of days. Among the cross-country runners, 3.3% did not report participation in any other athletic endeavor, 3.3% reported engaging in wrestling, 3.3% in baseball, and 6.7% in basketball. Forty percent of the cross-country runners also reported participating in track, but none reported participating in football.

Table 1: Current and Desired Heights and Weights of a sample of High School Athletes. N = 74

Football Players (n=44)

	Mean	SD	Range
Current weight (lbs)	181.09	29.21	135–265
Desired weight (lbs)	202.18	31.02	135–275
Current height (ins)	67.86	22.17	66–77
Desired height (ins)	73.71	2.00	68–77

Cross Country Runners (n=30)

	Mean	SD	Range
Current weight (lbs)	143.96	19.82	96–190
Desired weight (lbs)	146.40	22.21	90–210
Current height (ins)	70.40	3.71	60–76
Desired height (ins)	74.14	3.81	69–84

Combined Total Sample

	Mean	SD	Range
Current weight (lbs)	166.34	31.58	96–265
Desired weight (lbs)	183.60	38.71	90–275
Current height (ins)	68.89	17.22	60–76
Desired height (ins)	73.86	2.72	66–84

Of the football players, 48% did not report a specific position. For those who did: linebacker—16%, fullback—5%, tackle—7%, defensive end—2%, flanker—2%, nose guard—2%, wide receiver—5%, lineman—9%, center—2%, and punter—2%. Thirty-eight percent reported running long distances (mean = 12.7 miles per week), and 86% reported running short distances or sprints. Sprinters indicated that they ran an average of 3.3 days per week. Other athletic activities reported by football players included 2.3% rugby, 4.5% wrestling, 22.7% baseball, 9.1% basketball, 2.3% mountain biking, and 6.8% track; 11.4% did not report participation in another athletic activity. The athletes were queried as to "reasons for exercise" via the Reasons for Exercise Inventory (Silberstein et al., 1988). Among the reasons given were: weight control, fitness, mood, health, attractiveness, tone, and enjoyment. Football players rated fitness, mood, health, and attractiveness as more important reasons for exercise than did runners.

Satisfaction/dissatisfaction with Height and Weight

The current and desired weights and heights of the sample are presented in Table 1. It should be noted that there may be an outlier in each group. In the football group, one individual reported a weight of 135 pounds. In the cross-country group, three individuals reported somewhat higher weight than is usually anticipated for this sport—170, 180, and 190 pounds, respectively. Of the total sample, 61 (83%) were dissatisfied with their current weight, and 52 (71%) wanted to be taller.

Of the football players, 35 (80%) desired an increase in body weight, (15%) wanted to lose weight, and the remaining (5%) were satisfied with their current weight. This contrasts with 11 (37%) of the cross-country runners who were satisfied with their current weight; 21 (43%) of the cross-country runners expressed a desire to gain weight, whereas 6 (20%) wanted to lose weight. A comparison of the desired weight gain/loss between football players and cross-country runners is presented in Figures 1 and 2.

A repeated measure of ANOVA was used to test for differences in actual and desired weight and height among the athletes. Significant differences were found in the main effect of group (football players vs. cross-country runners) ($F = 59.33$, $p = .0001$), and in the main effect of current vs. desired weight ($F = 12.738$, $p = .008$). There was also a significant difference between football players and cross-country runners with respect to current and desired weight ($F = 4.85$, $p = .0134$). Tests of simple main effects were utilized to investigate this interaction. The alpha level was set at .01 to minimize Type I error. The re sults indicated no significant difference in runners' current weight and desired weight ($F = 24.97$, $p = .4053$), whereas there was a significant difference in football players' current and desired weights ($F = 24.97$, $p = .001$). Most football players desired to weigh more; only 9% desired to weigh less.

No significant differences were found between groups regarding current and desired height. However, there was a significant difference in the main effect for both groups with respect to current and desired height ($F = 60.453$, $p = .0001$). Both groups wanted to be taller.

Body Esteem Scale (BES)

Significant differences were found between groups on the physical attraction dimension of the BES. There were also significant differences in the upper body dimension of the BES, but not on the condition dimension of the BES (Table 2). Football players scored higher on the physical attraction and upper body dimensions, indicating a higher degree of body esteem for these factors.

Body Size Drawings (BSD)

A significant difference was found with respect to perceived actual and perceived ideal body shape ($F = 7.99$, $p = .0062$). Tests of simple main effects were utilized to determine that the differences originated primarily with the cross-country runners ($F = 25.158$, $p < .0001$). To display the gap between perceived and actual desired BSDs, frequency data is presented in Table 3. The range was from a "gap" of minus four (indicating individuals who desired a BSD four sizes less than perceived actual) to a "gap" of plus 3 (indicating individuals who desired a BSD three sizes greater than their perceived actual). Forty percent of the runners had a gap of + 2, indicating those who desired a BSD two sizes greater than their perceived actual BSD. This compared to 18% of the football players who indicated a + 2 gap. Additionally, 21% of the football players were happy with their perceived actual weight (i.e., did not desire a change in BSD), whereas only 3% of the runners were happy with their perceived actual weight.

Eating Attitudes Test (EAT)

No significant differences were found in Factor I (dieting), but there were significant differences in Factor II (bulimia and food preoccupation) and Factor III (oral control) between the groups. Cross-country runners scored higher on Factors II (bulimia) and Factor III (oral control). Higher scores suggest more disturbed attitudes toward food and eating.

DISCUSSION AND IMPLICATIONS

For cross-country runners and football players a significant relationship was found between scores on the BES and the BSD. Also, differences were found between groups with respect to body image, attitudes, and behaviors toward eating/dieting and reasons for exercising.

Even though a large percentage (83%) of football players desire the weight gain, they still reported more positive responses for body satisfaction and more positive attitudes/behaviors toward eating/weight control. As noted, football players scored higher on the BES. This may reflect the fact that their reported current average weight was approximately 37 pounds greater than that of the cross-country runners. This greater weight suggests a greater "mesomorphic" profile, which is generally perceived as the male ideal body type. Harmatz, Gronendyke, and Thomas (1985) reported that males who perceive themselves as thinner than average are more likely to have a negative self-view and hence, lower self-esteem. The runners as a group did perceive themselves as being thinner and did exhibit more negative responses to the BES. Last, it should be recognized that many football players are attracted to and have chosen a sport that tends to conform

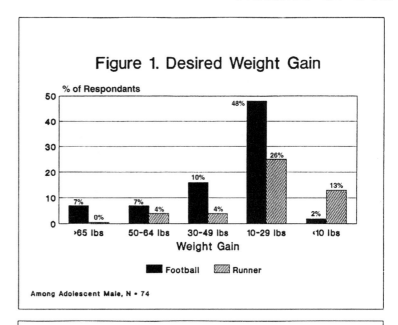

Figure 1. Desired Weight Gain

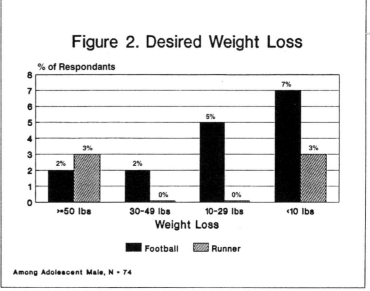

Figure 2. Desired Weight Loss

Table 2: Comparison of adolescent male football players and cross country runners on the three dimensions of the Body Esteem Scale (BES). N = 74

Dimension	Football Players (n=44)		Cross Country Runners (n=30)	
	Mean	SD	Mean	SD
Attraction	40.81	6.33	36.70	5.60*
Upper Body	32.50	5.49	29.70	4.89*
Condition	53.67	7.62	52.56	5.48

*Significant at P = .05

Table 3: Differences in desired and perceived actual Body Size Drawings (BSD) of adolescent male football players (N=44) and cross country runners (N=30).

Difference between desired and perceived actual BSD	football		runners	
	n	**% of N**	**n**	**% of N**
−4.00 size difference	1	2	0	0
−3.00 size difference	0	0	0	0
−2.00 size difference	4	9	0	0
−1.00 size difference	8	18	4	13
0.00 size difference	9	21	1	3
+1.00 size difference	12	27	11	37
+2.00 size difference	8	18	12	40
+3.00 size difference	2	5	2	7
+4.00 size difference	0	0	0	0

to the general physical criteria for masculinity, including greater upper body size and a mesomorphic body build. The football players in this study expressed satisfaction with their upper body dimensions, whereas an increase in upper body size was the predominate change sought by runners.

Although cross-country running requires a leaner physique, the cultural belief that males should possess a muscular body, places the runner in conflict. Also, in recent years a number of Olympic cross-country and track stars have exhibited a very lean, yet very mesomorphic body type. This desire for a very lean, yet muscular body type is also prevalent in gymnastics which, interestingly, is a sport noted for a high incidence of eating disorders such as anorexia and bulimia. There is some evidence (Burekes-Miller & Black, 1988; Yates, Leehey, & Shisslak, 1983) that runners may also be more prone to disordered eating behaviors, and the data from the present study indeed show that they scored higher on the bulimia and oral control portions of the EAT instrument. Thus it appears that education is needed to help runners both accept and value their particular body build and to avoid disordered eating as a response to body dissatisfaction.

REFERENCES

Becker, R. D. (1981). Insight body-image problems. *Journal of Canadian Adolescent Medicine*, March, 36–41.

Burckes-Miller, M. E., & Black, D. R. (1988). Behaviors and attitudes associated with eating disorders: Perceptions of college athletes about food and weight. *Health Education Research*, 3(2), 203–208.

Cash, T. F., Counts, B., & Huffine, C. E. (1990). Current and vestigial effects of overweight among women: Fear of fat, attitudinal body image, and eating behaviors. *Journal of Psychopathology and Behavioral Assessment*, 12(2), 157–167.

Casper, R. C., & Offer, D. (1990). Weight and dieting concerns in adolescents: Fashion or symptom? *Pediatrics*, 86(3), 384–390.

Damhorst, M. L., Littrell, J. M, & Littrell, M. A. (1987). Age differences in adolescent body satisfaction. *Journal of Psychology*, 121(6), 553–562.

Dwyer, J. T., Feldman, J. J., & Mayer, J. (1967). Adolescent dieters: Who are they? *American Journal of Clinical Nutrition*, 24(10), 1045–1056.

Fallon, A. C., & Rosen, P. (1985). Sex differences in perceptions of body shape. *Journal of Abnormal Psychology*, 94, 102–105.

Franzoi, S. L., & Shields, S. A. (1984). The body esteem scale: Multidimensional structure and sex differences in a college population. *Journal of Personality Assessment*, 48(2), 173–178.

Garner, D. M., Olmsted, M.P., Bohr, Y., & Garfinkel, P. E. (1982). The eating attitudes test: Psychometric features and clinical correlates. *Psychological Medicine*, 12, 871–878.

Grodner, M. (1991). The psychology of eating disorders. *Nutri-News*, August.

Ham, G. L., Easton, P. S., Himburg, S. P., & Greenburg, B. (1983). Body image perception of children and adolescents with psychiatric disorders. *International Journal of Obesity*, 7, 321–326.

Harmatz, M. G, Gronendyke, B. A., & Thomas, T. (1985). The underweight male: The unrecognized problem group of body image research. *Journal of Obesity and Weight Reduction*, 4(4), 258–267.

Hendry, L. B, & Gillies, P. (1978). Body type, body esteem, school, and leisure: A study of overweight, average, and underweight adolescents. *Journal of Youth and Adolescence*, 7(2), 181–193.

Koff, E., & Rierdan, J. (1990). Gender, body image, and self-concept in early adolescence. *Journal of Early Adolescence*, 10(1), 56–58.

Loosemoore, D. J., Mable, H. M., & Galgan, W. D. (1989). Body image disturbance in selected groups of men. *Psychology: A Journal of Human Behavior*, 26(2/3), 56–58.

Mishkind, M. E., Rodin, J., Silberstein, L. R., & Striegel-Moore, R. H. (1986). The embodiment of masculinity. *American Behavioral Scientist*, 29(5), 545–562.

Richards, M. H., Casper, R. C., & Larson, R. (1990). Weight and eating concerns among pre- and young adolescent boys and girls. *Journal of Adolescent Health Care*, 11, 203–209.

Rosen, J., Gross, J, & Vara, L. (1987). Psychological adjustment of adolescents attempting to lose or gain weight. *Journal of Consulting and Clinical Psychology*, 55(5), 742–747.

Silberstein, L. R., Striegel-Moore, R. H., Timko, C., & Rodin, J. (1988). Behavioral and psychological implications of body dissatisfaction: Do men and women differ? *Sex Roles*, 19(3&4), 219–232.

Striegel–Moore, R. H., & Silberstein, L. (1985). Toward an understanding of risk factors for bulimia. *American Psychologist*, 41(3), 246–263.

Wardle, J., & Beales, S. (1986). Restraint, body image and food attitudes in children from 12—8 years. *Appetite*, 7, 209–217.

Yates, A., Leehey, K., & Shisslak, C. M. (1983). Running—An analog of anorexia? *New England Journal of Medicine*, 308, 251–255.

A Study of White Middle-Class Adolescent Boys' Responses to "Semenarche" (The First Ejaculation)

James H. Stein and Lynn Whisnant Reiser

James H. Stein, Instructor, Department of Medicine, Rush-Presbyterian-St. Luke's Medical Center, Chicago, Illinois. Received M.D. from Yale School of Medicine.

Lynn Whisnant Reiser, Clinical Professor, Department of Psychiatry, Yale University School of Medicine, New Haven, Connecticut. Received M.D. from Yale School of Medicine.

Received September 4, 1992; accepted August 18, 1993

Few empirical studies focus on how boys respond to puberty. This paper presents the results of a questionnaire and interview survey of 36 white middle-class adolescent male camp counselors (mean age, 18.4 years) that addressed pubertal changes and first ejaculation ("semenarche"). It is a descriptive and hypothesis-generating study. The first ejaculation, biologically significant in sexual and reproductive functioning, was found to be psychologically meaningful but socially invisible. The mean age at semenarche was 12.9 years. All of the boys in the group had sex education in school, yet many felt unprepared for their first ejaculation, which occurred earlier than they expected and before formal education. Those who felt prepared expressed more positive feelings and coped better. Common responses to semenarche included surprise, curiosity, pleasure, and confusion. Most subjects did not tell anyone that this event occurred and many boys initially confused ejaculation and urination. The association of the first ejaculation with sexuality makes it a charged event. Psychosocial and developmental difficulties in sexual education for young males are noted.

INTRODUCTION

The male experience of the first ejaculation has received little research attention. This invisibility is reflected in the lack of a generally accepted term in the English language for the event. "Semenarche"—a word meaning the beginning of semen—is a logical term for the first ejaculation (Sarrel, personal communication, 1987).[1] This paper uses this designation and suggests the common adoption of this term as a name for the first ejaculation.

Research interest in male puberty and the significance of the first ejaculation has focused on biology (Kinsey, 1948; Tanner, 1971; Richardson and Short, 1978; Hirsch, 1988)—the psychological and social components of this phenomena have not been adequately addressed. This deficiency is found both in standard textbooks of psychiatry (Kaplan and Saddock, 1989) and pediatrics (Behrman, 1992) and in the psychoanalytic literature. Yet there are indications that semenarche is an important event.

Kinsey *et al.* (1948) concluded from his retrospective study of 4590 men that the first ejaculation was "the most significant of all adolescent developments" and stated that "the newly adolescent boy's capacity to ejaculate, [and] his newly acquired physical characteristics of other sorts, do something to him which brings child play to an end and leaves him awkward about making further socio-sexual contacts." A questionnaire study of 146 male college students (Shipman, 1968) suggested that semenarche was an important and frightening experience because sex education for boys was inadequate. In contrast, Gaddis and Brooks-Gunn (1985) concluded from a small interview study of 13 adolescent boys that the first ejaculation was not as traumatic as previously reported.

This paper presents a descriptive and hypothesis-generating study of adolescent male camp counselors to determine how they remembered the experience of semenarche and other changes of puberty, and how their education and interaction with family and peers contributed to their understanding pubertal changes.

Table I. Experience of Positive and Negative Feelings at Semenarche (Interview Data)[a]

Feeling	Mean	Percentage		
		Not at all	A little	A lot
Positive feeling				
Positive	2.4	28	14	58
Prepared	2.6	17	25	58
Pleasurable	2.4	36	8	56
Grown up	2.2	39	17	45
Excited	2.1	33	31	36
Glad	2.0	39	28	34
Relieved	1.9	42	25	34
Happy	1.8	44	33	22
Proud	1.5	61	28	11
Negative feeling				
Surprised	3.0	14	11	75
Confused	2.4	33	14	52
Embarrassed	2.0	47	25	27
Out of control	1.7	64	14	22
Upset	1.4	75	11	14
Dirty	1.4	81	6	14
Scared	1.5	64	25	12
Disgusted	1.5	67	22	12
Unhappy	1.3	78	17	6
Painful	1.1	92	6	3
Angry	1.1	94	6	0
Ripped off	1.0	97	3	0
Neutral feeling				
Curious	2.9	8	25	67

[a]$N = 36$. A 4-point scale was used, including (1) *not at all*, (2) *a little*, (3) *somewhat*, and (4) *a lot*. The percentage of subjects who responded "somewhat" are included above in "a lot."

METHOD

Thirty-six white, middle-class, Jewish male camp counselors ranging in age from 15.7 to 21.5 years (average age of 18.4 years) enrolled in this study. This corresponds to 98% participation by the male counseling staff at this private camp. A written questionnaire was followed by a 45-minute audiotaped semistructured interview (with JS). The questionnaire served as an introduction to the topics that were more explicitly discussed in the interview. Using both research tools provided a measure of intrasubject reliability—questions in the questionnaire and interview were parallel and responses were consistent when compared (except for one exception described below). The research tools included questions regarding physical changes that accompanied puberty, education and sources of information about puberty, and psychological and social responses to these changes. Fearing that parents might consider this an explicit introduction of sexual topics, camp officials excluded campers age 10–14 years from the study. Subjects

were informed about the study by the camp director who presented it as a survey study of how boys experience the changes of puberty. They were interviewed individually in a private setting by a researcher who had been a former camper and counselor at the camp. Each discussant signed a release assuring confidentially.

RESULTS

Age at Semenarche

When asked how old they were when they had their first ejaculation, most subjects initially claimed not to remember (responded "don't know" on the questionnaire, or answered "I don't know" in the interview). Five subjects left the question blank on the questionnaire. When restated in the interview as "What grade were you in?" and when more specific questions about context were asked, *all* remembered the circumstances of this event (although 2 still did not remember their age). The average age was 12.9 ± 1.5 years.

Context of Semenarche

Semenarche occurs in a number of different contexts—such as during sleep (nocturnal emission), masturbation, or in sexual activity with another person. In interview data, a wet dream was the most common context for semenarche (20 boys) and masturbation was the next (13 boys). In contrast to the agreement on other questions, there was a discrepancy between 4 subjects' answers to this in the interview and on the questionnaire. These subjects reported on the questionnaire that semenarche occurred during masturbation, but in the interview as a nocturnal emission. These subjects' discomfort during the interview as rated high by self-report and by the interviewer, and these subjects provided few descriptive details. This suggests that masturbation may be a more common context for semenarche than is reflected in the interview data. Three subjects experienced semenarche during heterosexual activity—2 having intercourse, one engaging in petting. No subjects reported that their first ejaculation occurred during homosexual activity.

Response to Semenarche

Subjects were asked to rate the extent to which they experienced 22 feelings at semenarche (Table 1). A 4-point scale (*not at all, a little, somewhat, a lot*) was adapted from Gaddis and Brooks-Gunn (1985). The final two categories (*somewhat* and *a lot*) were reported as "a lot" to facilitate comparison with Gaddis and Brooks-Gunn, who did the same. In the interview, subjects were encouraged to elaborate on any strong feelings that they may have had. Representative and interesting anecdotes are presented below. Many reported having had strong feelings (rarely negative) at their first ejaculation. The qualitative aspect of their response and conflict was more evident in the interviews:

My wet dream was kind of an experience that I didn't experience. It had nothing to do with my mental attitude. I was sound asleep, I woke up the next morning and my sheets were pasty—I slept through it—After you wake up your mind is kind of happy and then you realize 'oh my god, this is my wet dream.' (Emphasis added)

Seventy-five percent of the subjects reported feeling surprised that they were so young when their first ejaculation took place and at the physical intensity of the first ejaculation. The extent to which a subject felt "surprised" was strongly correlated with feeling confused (Pearson $r > 0.60$, $p < 0.001$), embarrassed ($r > 0.52$, $p < 0.001$), scared ($r > 0.61$, $p < 0.001$), and out of control ($r > 0.68$, $p > 0.001$). Many of those who felt "surprised" also felt unprepared ($r > 0.52$, $p < 0.001$). "Surprised did not correlate with "pleasure" or "happiness."

Subjects whose semenarche was a wet dream were more likely to initially confuse semen with urine. Eleven subjects (31%) reported that their first ejaculation reminded them of "urinating" or "wetting the bed."

It took kind of awhile to click in—later in the day I finally figured out what the hell was going on. I thought I had pissed in my pants at first! It reminded me of peeing in my pants—that was my first reaction even thought I'd never done it.

Subjects whose first ejaculation was during masturbation remembered more pleasure (two-tailed $t = 3.71$, $df = 31$, $p < 0.05$) and happiness (two-tailed $t = 2.08$, $df = 31$, $p < 0.05$) than did subjects whose first ejaculation was during a nocturnal emission. The latter, however, did not express more negative feelings. The data suggest that the source of difference was the conscious experience of an orgasm that accompanied masturbation.

Boys who experienced their first ejaculation while masturbating commented:

My parents had these videotapes. I knew they were X-rated and I really wanted to see them. My parents were out of town. I knew they were hidden in their closet. I threw them in, I thought 'this is very interesting' and the next thing I knew—Bam!—I honestly didn't know what I was doing.

I think I was trying to masturbate—I didn't really—it was—the actual ejaculation came as a surprise—I knew what I was doing but didn't know what would happen—I—I remember—I remember—realizing what had happened but not really knowing exactly until later.

The only common negative feeling was confused (50%):

I was in my bed—I really didn't know what I was doing—just touching myself. I was at the point where I knew it would happen but I was confused—I really didn't know what was going on and was embarrassed because of it.

A boy who woke up after a nocturnal emission remembered:

I didn't know what it was so I blew off, since the rest of the mornings I woke up normal. I thought I was just nervous or something.

Sixty-seven percent of the subjects remembered feeling curious, wondering how they could make the ejaculation happen again, when it would happen again, and if it would be different with a girl. This boy expresses that sense of wonder:

I was curious to see—I wasn't expecting to have sex or anything. It was just generally—I didn't know exactly how—would it happen again? It had never happened before.

In interviews, the strongest negative responses were related to embarrassment and feeling out of control, especially to less prepared subjects.

I was alone but I was very embarrassed because I was *out of control*. That was my major feeling—I was worried it would happen again. I put it together about a week later when I did it again. Then I figured it out. (Emphasis added)

The association with urination may also contribute to the sense of being out of control—some boys had expected ejaculation, like urination, to be under voluntary sphincter control. "I thought it was just like peeing."

I thought it would happen when I wanted it to, that I'd have control over it. I was scared about the *loss of control*. (Emphasis added)

The most stressful experience of semenarche, and the only one that was described as "painful," was that of a boy whose first ejaculation (at age 17) was with a woman. He was embarrassed about not having control over his body in the presence of another person.

It was a lot painful. It hurt. I don't know why. That's what I remember. It was enjoyable to have it done, not physically. I was just glad I got it over. The pain was indescribable.

In contrast to that subject's experience, many of the subjects described the experience as pleasurable:

Well at first I felt really—like it was weird cuz I had never felt that way before. But after a little bit it was—pleasurable. It was good—It felt good—You just have to feel it for yourself.

Some subjects, however, reported feeling uncomfortable with the unexpected intensity of the pleasure that they felt at the first ejaculation.

Education

Classes at school were the most common source of information about puberty in general. Nearly all of the subjects completed "health education" courses in fifth or sixth grade, and continued their education about physical development and human sexuality well into high school. In spite of having an extensive health and sex education curriculum, more than one-quarter of the boys recalled that classes failed to explain ejaculation. In the classes that did discuss ejaculation, the topic was postponed until the eighth grade, after many boys had already experienced their first ejaculation. The boys remembered that teachers put emphasis on informing students that pubertal changes were "normal" and "healthy." The subjects' responses reflected this focus, as many subjects described their first pubertal changes as a signal that they were "normal."

One boy whose semenarche was during masturbation at age 12 expressed these complicated feelings:

It didn't make me feel proud. It made me feel guilty, like I'd done something wrong. Those kind of feelings—The class didn't say anything. I still think it's something I shouldn't do— My only relief was that I was *normal*. (Emphasis added)

Another boy whose semenarche was a nocturnal emission described a predominant sense of relief at being normal:

I woke up the next morning and noticed the wetness. I felt relieved. I expected it. I mean, people talked about it and the classes—sex ed—told about what happens and it happened. *It's a normal thing*—I didn't have much emotion attached to it. I felt prepared for it, but I never expected it—I didn't want anyone to know—I was glad that it happened. (Emphasis added)

The only late-maturer in the study expressed this sentiment (relief at being normal) most strongly.

Forty-two percent of the subjects felt unprepared for semenarche. "Prepared" subjects reported feeling more "proud" and "positive" (two-tailed $t = 3.02$, $df = 34$, $p < 0.005$); "Unprepared" subjects, stronger negative feelings—more "confused" (3.87, 34, $p < 0.001$, "upset" (4.87, 34, $p < 0.001$), "scared" (3.18, 34, $p < 0.005$), "disgusted" (3.34, 34, $p < 0.002$), "out of control" (2.70, 34, $p < 0.02$).

For example, one boy stated:

I'm almost positive that it was a wet dream. The problem was that I didn't know what it was. It was just so—I never knew what it was. I was surprised I wet my bed—what did I do? I only found out a year later what it was.

Only one-third of the boys considered parents important sources of information about ejaculation. For those, this topic was usually discussed by a father alone or both parents together—in one case information about ejaculation was provided by a mother alone. Conversations about semenarche *after* it happened were rare. Only 2 subjects told their mother or father that their first ejaculation had occurred. Most boys were very secretive:

For the first time I knew something that they [parents] didn't— it was a private thing that nobody else knew.

Boys often hid the evidence of a nocturnal emission by changing the sheets themselves (some even performed midnight laundering). Others assumed their parents knew but did not mention it directly:

My mom, she knew I had them. It was all over my sheets, and bedspread and stuff, but she didn't say anything, didn't tease me and stuff. I was kind of glad. She never asked if I wanted to talk about it—I'm glad. I never could have said anything to my mom.
    I don't remember when it happened or how old I was, but

I didn't tell anyone. My friends, we didn't talk about it, but if it came up, you know we always played these games—'So have you done this, so have you done this, so have you done this'—I would say I had. But I didn't say 'by the way mom, my bed is wet.' I mean, I knew what an ejaculation was, and I knew that I hadn't wet my bed.

When a boy did tell someone, it was usually a friend. The boy's descriptions reveal more about the fragmentary quality of this kind of discussion with friends:

Before it I remember being in the boy's locker room at school and my friend telling me about having a wet dream and he said 'Oh, everyone has it' and I remember thinking and I remember lying and I remember experimenting with masturbation after that.
    While it was going on no one wanted to say anything about it. We all kind of left it alone—After it happened and we knew what was going on, we laughed about it with friends. Laughed at guy's penises, you know.
    I had no idea what—I had no idea what was happening—It just hurt and I said 'I gotta go,' so I found my friend and said 'I gotta talk to you' and it just went from there. He made me feel better—I was embarrassed about telling my friend—it just really hit me. I just told him. I didn't hold back cuz I wanted to know what was happening. I said 'I wanna know what happened.' He said 'Oh yeah, you came,' and I felt happy after that, glad it happened.

Pubertal Events

Seventy-eight percent of the subjects stated that the appearance of pubic hair was a memorable signal that puberty had started.[2] However, as a group they felt that neither this biological change nor any other was in itself a symbol for their change in status and self-perception. A few boys like this one did assert the importance of the first ejaculation:

The next morning I felt really gross—I knew what it was. I don't think it was pleasurable—I was embarrassed. I don't know, I just remember being in my bed and feeling that I had just—I knew I didn't wet my bed. I mean, I felt weird that this change had just happened—*it was pretty major*. (Emphasis added)

Less than 40% felt that the first ejaculation was important. More often they asserted, like this boy, that

The things that I really remember are the things that I did sexually.

The events (Table II) that were most meaningful for this group were social—"making out" was very meaningful for 89%, "dating" for 83%, and "Bar Mitzvah" for 72%.

Only 10 subjects (28%) felt it was noteworthy that after the first ejaculation they were physically able to "get a girl pregnant." Most reported that they rarely considered the possibility that they could father a child. Their confusion is evident in their words:

I never thought about getting a girl pregnant. I knew biologically that I could father a child.

DISCUSSION

The subjects comprised a homogeneous sample of boys with similar religious, educational, and socio-economic backgrounds. They were socially well adjusted enough to be chosen as camp counselors. Because participation was high, this well-defined population can be *compared* to others, but cannot be used to generalize about other demographic groups. As in all retrospective studies, experiences subsequent to target events may have influenced memories of the event in an unquantifiable manner (recall bias). The average time since semenarche for our subjects was 5.5 ± 0.9 years, so it relied more on memory than the study of young adolescent boys conducted by Gaddis and Brooks-Gunn (1985). Although both of these study samples were small, the higher participation rate (90%) and larger sample size (36) suggest that this study had less selection bias than the study by Gaddis and Brooks-Gunn (1985, 62% participation, 13 subjects). Given these limitations, the study is meant to be descriptive and hypothesis-generating.

The results were consistent with the descriptions of the events that signaled pubertal onset in the populations studied by Kinsey *et al.* (1948) and Tanner (1971). The average age of semenarche in Kinsey's study was about a year older, 13.88 years. Adolescent boys experience strong, but rarely negative feelings at semenarche, including surprise, confusion, curiosity, and pleasure. The conscious experience of orgasm allows those who experience their first ejaculation by masturbation to feel more "pleasure" and "happiness." Although boys whose first ejaculation is during a wet dream do not report more negative feelings, they more often confuse semen with urine, at least initially. Boys rarely discuss their first ejaculation and usually hide the evidence. Semenarche is not a socially recognized event and adolescent boys deny attaching much significance to it, especially in light of later sexual experiences.

The first ejaculation, biologically significant in sexual and reproductive functioning, is socially invisible. Thus, semenarche is not comparable to menarche as a significant symbolic developmental milestone. The lack of a name for the first ejaculation contributes to making this an invisible event and parallels the failure to label adequately the female external genitalia (especially sexual structures) in the education of girls (Lerner, 1976). The connection of the first ejaculation with sexuality makes it a charged event.

Despite sex education and hygiene classes at school and some parental input, many of the boys in this group felt unprepared for their first ejaculation, which occurred earlier than they expected. Education, including a specific discussion about ejaculation before semenarche occurs, can positively influence how boys experience pubertal transformation. Those who were prepared coped better, in contrast to the subjects interviewed by Gaddis and Brooks-Gunn (1985) and in agreement with Shipman's study (1968).

In view of the current crisis in the prevention of AIDS and unwanted pregnancies, the data from this study raise many questions about how best to educate boys about puberty and when to provide information. Education regarding semenarche frequently occurred *after* the boys had already experienced the

Table II. The Significance of Social and Physical Events (Interview Data)[a]

Feeling	Mean	Percentage		
		Not at all	A little	A lot
Physical event				
Develop pubic hair	2.9	8	14	78
Growth spurt	2.8	8	31	61
Growth of penis	2.5	11	28	61
Develop facial hair	2.5	19	25	56
Develop acne	2.3	33	22	45
Voice change	2.3	25	33	42
First ejaculation	2.3	19	42	39
Develop axillary hair	2.1	22	44	34
Growth of testes	1.9	31	44	25
Social event				
Making out	3.3	8	3	89
Dating	3.2	6	11	83
Bar Mitzvah	3.0	14	14	72
Shaving	2.7	17	17	66
Using cologne	2.2	25	39	36
Change nudity practice	2.1	31	36	33
Showering	1.9	44	28	28
Using deodorant	1.9	39	36	25
Wearing jockstrap	1.8	50	28	22

[a] $N = $ A 4-point scale was used, such that (1) *not at all,* (2) *a little,* (3) *somewhat,* and (4) *a lot.* The percentage of subjects who responded "somewhat" are included above in "a lot."

event, so earlier sex education is clearly needed. In addition, emphasis should be placed on the fact that many boys are fertile at or before semenarche (Richardson and Short, 1978; Hirsch, 1988).

The difficulties in sexual education for preadolescents are many:

Frequently, newly provided sexual information seems to be promptly forgotten. At times this rather amazing phenomenon may be due to a feigned ignorance in the service of secrecy, out of uneasiness with the subject matter or compliance with the cultural double standard. Frequently, thought, it represents a genuine, unconscious denial of anxiety-producing knowledge. ("Normal Adolescence," 1968, p. 792)

In addition, a boy's ability to understand the physical changes of puberty is limited by his cognitive ability, which is usually still at the concrete or early formal operations stage (Piaget, 1972) when he experiences his first ejaculation. Sigmund Freud (1895/1959a, 1895/1959b) pointed out how persistently adults, particularly parents, avoided acknowledging childhood (and adolescent) sexuality. This observation is still accurate and is reflected in the boy's reports and in the paucity of empirical studies of childhood sexuality.

One boy suggested an approach to this problem in terms of a favorite series of childhood picture books:

> I would describe it [puberty] as 'Curious George.'[3] *Because you really don't know what's going on unless you really get it explained by somebody who doesn't have a bias on it.* I always really liked Curious George—he always wants to find out more about things he shouldn't, and that's what puberty is. (Emphasis added)

This empirical survey study of a well-defined population of normal adolescent boys suggests that although the first ejaculation is not traumatic for the majority of boys, it is a memorable, highly charged event that is less anxiety producing if there has been prior education. There is a need for both prospective and retrospective studies documenting the experience of semenarche in other ethnic and socioeconomic groups in order to delineate the impact of this event upon subsequent psychosocial development and to clarify how best to respond to boys' curiosity in preparing them for puberty.

REFERENCES

Behrman, R. E. (1992). *Nelson's Textbook of Pediatrics* (14th ed.). W. B. Saunders, Philadelphia, PA.

Freud. S. (1959a). The Sexual Enlightenment of Children—an Open Letter to Dr. M. Furst, 1907. In *Standard Education* (Vol. 9). London: Hogarth Press. (Originally published 1895).

Freud. S. (1959b). On the Sexual Theories of Children, 1908. In *Standard Edition* (Vol. 9). London: Hogarth Press. (Originally published 1895).

Gaddis, A., and Brooks-Gunn, J. (1985). The male experience of pubertal change. *J. Youth Adolesc.* 14: 61–69.

Hirsch, M., Lunenfeld, B., Modan, M., Ovadia, J., and Shemesh, J. (1988). Spermarche—The age of onset of sperm emission. *Sex. Active Teen.* 2: 34–38.

Kaplan, H., and Saddock, B. J. (1989). *Comprehensive Textbook of Psychiatry* (5th ed.). Williams & Wilkins, Baltimore, MD.

Kinsey, A. C., Pomeroy, W. B., and Martin, C. E. (1948). *Sexual Behavior in the Human Male.* W. B. Saunders, Philadelphia, PA.

Lerner, H. (1976). Parental mislabeling of female genitals as a determinant of penis envy and learning inhibitions in women. In *Female Psychology—Contemporary Psychoanalytic View,* ed. H. Blum. International Universities Press, New York.

Normal Adolescence: Its dynamics and impact. (1968). In Group for the Advancement of Psychiatry (Volume VI, Report No. 68).

Piaget, P. (1972). *The Child's Conception of the World.* Littlefield Adams, Totowa, NJ.

Rey, H. A. (1941). *Curious George.* Houghton Mifflin, Boston.

Richardson, D. W., and Short, R. V. (1978). Time of onset of sperm production in boys. *J. Biosocial Sci. Suppl. 5,* 15–25.

Sarrel, P. M. (1987). Personal communication.

Shipman, G. (1968). The psychodynamics of sex education. *Family Coord. 7,* 3–12.

Tanner, J. M. (1971). Sequence, tempo, and individual variation in growth and development of boys and girls aged twelve to sixteen. *Daedalus* 100, 907–930.

NOTES

1. Shipman (1968) proposed that the first ejaculation be named either "primus ejaculatus" from the Latin or "spermarche" from the Greek. The latter term is used most commonly but is inaccurate, since spermarche—the appearance of sperm (using spermaturia as a marker)—occurs *before* the first ejaculation (Richardson and Short, 1978; Hirsch *et al.,* 1988).

2. This is in accordance with Tanner's Development Stage 2, when pubic hair first appears (Tanner, 1971). Reddening of the scrotum and enlargement of testes and scrotum, also occurring in Stage 2, were not mentioned by any subject.

3. *Curious George* refers to a series of children's picture books (Rey, 1941) that recount the adventures of a "good little monkey" who is "always very curious."

The Consequences of Insufficient Sleep for Adolescents

Links Between Sleep and Emotional Regulation

Any review of adolescent lifestyles in our society will reveal more than a dozen forces converging to push the sleep/arousal balance away from sleep and toward ever-higher arousal. What harm could there be in trying to push back a little toward valuing sleep? The potential benefits, according to Dr. Dahl, seem enormous.

BY RONALD E. DAHL

ADOLESCENTS often "get by" with relatively little sleep, but it may be far less than they need. The observations of many parents, educators, and clinicians are in close agreement with a wealth of scientific data about the growing frequency of this worrisome pattern of behavior. As discussed in other articles in this special section, there has been recent progress in understanding many of the factors that contribute to adolescent sleep loss, including the role of early school starting times and the role of various biological and social influences on adolescents' self-selected bedtimes.

The increasing evidence that teenagers seem to be getting less sleep leads inevitably to the pragmatic question "How much sleep do adolescents really need?" Unfortunately, the medical/scientific answer to this question seems tautological. Sufficient sleep is defined as "the amount necessary to permit optimal daytime functioning."

As impractical as that answer may appear, there are two important rea-

RONALD E. DAHL, M.D., is an associate professor of psychiatry and pediatrics at the University of Pittsburgh Medical Center, Pittsburgh, Pa.

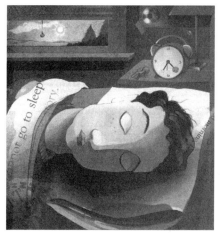

Illustration by Brenda Grannan

sons for such a definition. First, sleep requirements can be remarkably different across individuals. Second, at a physiological level, sleep and waking states are closely intertwined aspects of a larger system of arousal regulation. (Sleep researchers often use the Chinese symbol of yin/yang to designate the interrelationship of sleep/wake states.)

At the center of this discussion is a critical and pragmatic point: any evaluation of the sleep habits of adolescents must include a careful consideration of the *waking consequences* of sleep loss. The question becomes, in essence,

"What are the daytime signs of diminished functioning that indicate insufficient sleep?" While there is a shortage of well-controlled research studies that seek to answer this question, this article focuses on the convergence of evidence suggesting that *changes in mood and motivation are among the most important effects of sleep loss*. Thus an important place to begin looking for evidence of insufficient sleep among adolescents is in the area of emotional or behavioral difficulties.

There is no shortage of epidemiological and clinical studies documenting recent increases in the rates of many psychiatric disorders among adolescents. Certainly many complex factors are likely to have contributed to the emotional and behavioral problems of teenagers, but the possible link to adolescent sleep patterns bears some scrutiny. There is clear evidence that sleep loss *can* lead to the development or exacerbation of behavioral and emotional problems.[1] The key question is "How great is the contribution of sleep deprivation to these problems?" The magnitude of this link remains an open question that can only be answered through careful empirical research.

In the meantime, these issues have enormous ramifications for the fields of medicine and education with regard both to the physical and mental health of adolescents and to detriments to effective learning and social development. Many policy decisions will be influenced by our understanding and interpretation of the importance of sleep in these areas.

In this article I provide an overview of current scientific and clinical information regarding the consequences of insufficient sleep in adolescents. I pay particular attention to links between sleep and emotional regulation. The following is a brief outline of the main points to be presented:

1. *Sleepiness.* This is the most direct consequence of adolescent sleep loss, and it manifests itself most significantly in difficulty getting up on time for school and in falling asleep in school. These problems can further contribute to conflicts with parents and teachers and to poor self-esteem. Sleepiness is also associated with a strong tendency toward brief mental lapses (or microsleeps) that greatly increase the risk of motor vehicle and other kinds of accidents.

2. *Tiredness.* This is a symptom of sleep loss and includes changes in motivation—particularly difficulty initiating behaviors related to long-term or abstract goals and decreased persistence in working toward goals.

3. *Mood, attention, and behavior.* Sleep loss can have negative effects on the control of mood, attention, and behavior. Irritability, moodiness, and low tolerance for frustration are the most frequently described symptoms in sleep-deprived adolescents. However, in some situations, sleepy teenagers are more likely to appear silly, impulsive, or sad.

4. *Impact of emotional and behavioral problems.* Emotional arousal and distress can cause both difficulty falling asleep and sleep disruptions. Behavioral problems and family chaos can contribute to even later bedtimes and to sleep schedules that are ever more incompatible with school schedules.

5. *Bi-directional effects.* There are bi-directional effects between sleep and behavioral/emotional problems. It can be difficult at times to identify the causal links. For example, a depressed adolescent with severe sleep problems may be showing sleep disturbances that stem from depression or mood problems that stem from sleep disruption. Sleep loss can also contribute to a negative spiral or vicious cycle of deterioration. That is, sleep loss can have a negative effect on mood and behavior, which leads to subsequent emotional/behavioral difficulties that further interfere with sleep. This produces a sequence of negative effects in both domains. In some clinical cases, such negative spirals appear to be a pathway to withdrawal from school or serious psychiatric problems.

The Need for Sleep: An Overview

Before discussing the specific consequences of insufficient sleep in adolescents, it is necessary to begin with a general overview on what sleep is and why it is necessary at all.

Sleep is *not* simply rest. Mere rest does not create the restorative state of having slept. (Anyone who doubts this should try the following experiment tonight: spend eight hours resting in bed, with eyes closed, body relaxed, mind floating, in a deeply tranquil state, but without ever going to sleep; then keep track of your mood and performance tomorrow.) The fundamental difference between sleep and a deeply relaxed wakefulness is that sleep involves dropping into a state with a relative *loss of awareness of and responsiveness to the external world.* This state of unresponsiveness appears to be necessary for the restorative processes that occur during sleep to take place.

Furthermore, sleep itself is an *active* process. Sleep involves dynamically changing patterns and progressive stages, with some brain regions showing a great deal of activity in some sleep stages. Moreover, there are several aspects of sleep necessary for full restoration, including the continuity, timing, and patterning of different stages of sleep, as well as the timing of the sleep in relation to other biological rhythms.

For example, if subjects are permitted a full night's sleep but are awakened every 15 minutes for brief periods, on the following day they will report tiredness, fatigue, and emotional changes similar to having obtained insufficient amounts of sleep. Similarly, if subjects are permitted as much sleep as they need but are selectively deprived of one sleep stage—such as REM (rapid eye movement) sleep or delta sleep—they also report daytime consequences. And, as anyone who has experienced jet lag can attest, sleep that occurs at the wrong circadian phase is often fragmented and inefficient at restoration.

Sleep is not some biological luxury. Sleep is essential for basic survival, occurring in every species of living creature that has ever been studied. Animals deprived of sleep die. (Experiments with rats show that they can survive without sleep for about as long as they can survive without food.) Yet the specific function of sleep—*why* it is necessary for survival—remains a scientific mystery and the focus of a great deal of investigation.

Within this scientific mystery, however, are two important clues that are relevant to discussions of sleep and adolescent health. First, sleep seems to be particularly important during periods of brain maturation. (Across species, maturing individuals sleep more than fully mature individuals.) Second, sleep is naturally restricted to times and places that feel safe. Most species have evolved mechanisms to ensure that sleep is limited to such safe places as burrows and nests and to times of relative safety from predators. In humans, there is a similar tendency for safe feelings to promote sleep while feelings of threat or stress tend to inhibit sleep.

These links between sleep and stress are an important source of sleep disruption among adolescents. A key point can be best illustrated by a brief consideration of the evolutionary underpinnings of these biological links between sleep and emotion. For most of early human history, large nocturnal-hunting carnivores surrounded our ancestors, who had no access to physically safe sleep sites. (Humans cannot sleep in trees or on cliff edges, because we lose all muscle tone during REM sleep.) In the human ancestral environment, the main protection against predators was a close-knit social group. The human brain evolved under conditions that made this sense of social belonging and social connectedness the basis for feelings of relative safety. Natural tendencies in the human brain continue to reflect these links, so that fears of social rejection can evoke powerful feelings of threat and so lead to sleep disruption, while feelings of love, caring, and social connection create a feeling of safety and so promote sleep.

Finally, it is important to consider the ways in which the sleep and vigilance systems change during adolescent development. The maturation of humans during puberty includes physical and mental changes in preparation for taking on adult roles (with increased demands for threat appraisal and response). Changes in the vigilance system include a greater capacity for sleep disruptions from social stresses, including fears, anxieties, and emotional arousal.[2] Thus adolescent sleep systems appear to become more vulnerable to stress at a time when social turmoil and difficulties are often increasing.

Consequences of Insufficient Sleep In Adolescents

There is a surprising lack of controlled studies examining the effects of sleep deprivation or insufficient sleep among adolescents. However, there is extensive circumstantial evidence, clinical evidence, and research in adults that is relevant to these questions. While there is a general convergence of these findings, one important caveat is that we need a greater number of direct investigations. A second note of caution is that we lack information about *long-term* or *chronic* effects of insufficient sleep, since the limited data available have addressed only the immediate and short-term effects of sleep loss.

In brief, there are four main effects of acute sleep loss: 1) sleepiness, 2) motivational aspects of tiredness, 3) emotional changes, and 4) alterations in attention and performance. Before discussing each of these briefly, I wish to stress one general principle that applies across categories: the influence of *effort*. That is, the effects of sleep deprivation can be offset or even overridden for *short* periods of time by increased effort (or by increasing the external motivation to perform through rewards or punishments). The good news here is that most capabilities can be maintained over a short interval if necessary, while the bad news is that everything is harder to do. In some ways this is the cardinal feature of sleep deprivation: it takes increased effort to perform the same cognitive, emotional, or physical tasks.

1. *Sleepiness*. The most obvious and direct effect of inadequate sleep is a feeling of sleepiness. Sleepiness is most problematic during periods of low stimulation, such as in the classroom, when reading or driving, or when doing repetitive activities. Highly stimulating activities—particularly those involving physical activity or emotional arousal—can often mask moderate levels of sleepiness. Thus many sleep- deprived adolescents report that they can stay out very late at night and not feel tired, whereas if they were to lie quietly reading a book, they would fall asleep in minutes.

Another important aspect of sleepiness is the tendency toward brief mental lapses or micro-sleeps. Often, an individual is not even aware of these short gaps in awareness and responsiveness. However, such a lapse in the midst of driving, operating machinery, or doing anything else that requires vigilance can have dire consequences.

Several indirect consequences of sleepiness are also worth mentioning. These include adolescent conflicts with parents and teachers that arise from the difficulty of getting up in the morning or the ease of falling asleep in class; increased use of stimulants (particularly caffeine and nicotine); and synergistic effects with alcohol (the impairments from a combination of alcohol and sleepiness appear to be more than additive, resulting in a deadly combination of influences).

2. *Tiredness*. A separate symptom of sleep loss that can be defined as a feeling of fatigue or decreased motivation is tiredness. Tiredness makes it difficult to initiate (and persist at) certain types of behavior (especially tasks deemed boring or tedious). The effects of tiredness are less apparent when performing tasks that are naturally engaging, exciting, or threatening— perhaps because it is easier to recruit extra effort to offset tiredness. Conversely, the effects of tiredness are more pronounced for tasks that require motivation to be derived from abstract goals or consequences (e.g., reading or studying uninteresting material in order to increase the chances of attaining some future reward).

Tedious tasks without the imminent prospect of reward (or fear of immediate consequences) are much more difficult to initiate and complete when one has been deprived of sleep. Similarly, tasks that require planning, strategy, or a complex sequence of steps to complete are more difficult when one is tired. This general category of tasks (requiring motivation linked to abstract goals, delayed rewards/consequences, planning, strategy, and so on) involves abstract processing areas in the front of the brain (regions of the prefrontal cortex) that appear to be particularly sensitive to sleep deprivation.[3] The potential relevance of these types of motivational changes to educational goals and processes seems obvious.

3. *Emotional changes*. The emotional changes that are secondary effects of sleep loss are very important but very complex. There are at least three factors that make this a complicated area for investigators: 1) the emotional effects of sleep deprivation appear to be highly variable across individuals and across situations, 2) emotion and emotional regulation are very hard to measure accurately, and 3) there are bi-directional interactions between mood and sleep disturbances (this third aspect was noted above and will be addressed separately below).

One of the main sources of information in this area comes from clinical descriptions of children and adolescents with various sorts of sleep disorders or transient sleep disruptions. There are also a few studies (including ongoing research in our laboratory) that obtain measures of emotion before, during, and after a single night of sleep deprivation, and then again following a recovery sleep.

The major theme across these studies is evidence suggesting *mood lability*. Not only does there appear to be greater variability in emotional states following sleep loss, but there also appears to be less control over emotional responses in many adolescents. For example, if faced with a frustrating task, a sleep-deprived teenager is more likely to become angry or aggressive. Yet, in response to something humorous, the same subject might act more silly or inane. Several adolescents reported increased crying reactions during sad scenes in videotaped movies when they were sleep-deprived. Many subjects reported increased irritability, impatience, and low tolerance for frustration when asked to perform tedious computer tasks. In general, these findings often looked like a decrease in inhibition or conscious control over emotions following sleep loss. It is also important to point out that some subjects seemed to show no measurable changes in any emotion when sleep-deprived.

These results are quite preliminary, include a high degree of variability across individuals, and will require replication with larger samples to establish statistical significance. However, these findings fit very well within a general pattern of similar observations regarding *effortful control*. That is, the primary emotional changes following sleep loss suggest a decrease in the ability to control, inhibit, or modify emotional responses to bring them into line with long-term goals, social rules, or other learned principles. Effortful control over emotion involves regions of the prefrontal cortex of the brain that are similar to those discussed previously with regard to abstract goals.

Changes in emotional regulation that result in decreased control following sleep loss could have serious consequences in terms of many high-risk behaviors among adolescents. The inability to control emotional responses could influence aggression, sexual behavior, the use of alcohol and drugs, and risky driving. Clearly, additional research will be needed to better delineate these complex but important issues relevant to adolescent health.

4. *Changes in attention and performance.* Following sleep loss, changes in attention and performance also represent a complex area of investigation in children and adolescents. There are three main points. First, sleep loss is associated with brief mental lapses in attention during simple tasks that can be partially offset by increased effort or motivation. Second, sleep deprivation can sometimes mimic or exacerbate symptoms of ADHD (attention deficit/hyperactivity disorder), including distractibility, impulsivity, and difficulty with effortful control of attention. Third, there is also emerging evidence that sleep deprivation has marked influences on the ability to perform complex tasks or tasks that require attention in two or more areas at the same time.

While the first point about brief mental lapses has already been addressed, the latter two points warrant some discussion. A potential link between ADHD symptoms and sleep deprivation has received considerable discussion from several investigators.[4] Both ADHD and sleep deprivation are associated with difficulty with self-control of behavior, attention, and impulses. Both ADHD and the daytime symptoms of sleep deprivation will often respond to stimulant medication. Furthermore, ADHD symptoms are more frequent in children with sleep disorders, and there has been some reported improvement in ADHD symptoms in children following treatment of sleep problems. Finally, other studies have reported increased rates of sleep complaints and disorders in children diagnosed with ADHD. This is a very complex area, and disentangling the connections and relative contributions across these domains will require additional careful studies.

One pragmatic recommendation, however, is quite simple. For any child or adolescent who exhibits symptoms of ADHD, the importance of a good night's sleep and a regular sleep/wake schedule should be emphasized to avoid the consequences of sleep loss that could exacerbate symptoms.

One of the most interesting areas of study is evidence that some types of complex tasks may be particularly sensitive to the effects of sleep deprivation. James Horne has presented extensive evidence showing that dual tasks and tasks that require creative or flexible thinking are sensitive to sleep loss.[5] (These tasks all require abstract processing in areas of the prefrontal cortex.) Our own research group has generated similar findings in its examination of dual tasks following sleep deprivation in adolescents and young adults. For example, students with one night of sleep deprivation exhibited no significant changes in performance on a difficult computer task and showed no effect on postural balance. However, when the students performed both tasks simultaneously, sleep deprivation had a marked effect on balance.[6] In recent pilot studies we have also found the same pattern of results in adolescents performing cognitive and emotional tasks. Performance at either task could be maintained following sleep deprivation—but not both.

On one hand, detriments in performing a dual task (like controlling thoughts and feelings at the same time) might sound like an esoteric or subtle effect of sleep deprivation; on the other hand, it is important to point out that fluency in such dual tasks is the foundation of social competence. These are the daily challenges that must be balanced in the everyday life of adolescents: thinking and solving problems while navigating the emotional reactions of complex social situations, using self-control over impulses and emotions while pursuing goals, experiencing anger yet weighing the long-term consequences of actions. If further research substantiates the marked effects of insufficient sleep on these types of complex tasks in adolescents, then we should have significant concerns about the importance of sleep patterns in the normal development of social competence.

Sleep and Emotional Disorders in Adolescents

It is essential to underscore the complex intersection between sleep regulation and behavioral and emotional problems in adolescents. Clearly, there are two-way interactions between these systems. The regulation and timing of sleep can be altered by behavioral or emotional disorders, while cognitive, behavioral, and emotional control during daytime hours can be influenced by the way adolescents sleep. Furthermore, daytime activities, changes in the environment, and stressful events can have profound transient effects on sleeping patterns in the absence of any clear-cut psychopathology. In addition, medications used to treat psychiatric disorders often affect sleep, and sleep loss can exacerbate mood and behavioral symptoms.

Perhaps the best-studied example of such interactions is the relationship between sleep and depression. Subjective sleep complaints are very common in children and adolescents who have been diagnosed with Major Depressive Disorder (MDD). Symptoms include insomnia (75% of cases) and hypersomnia (25%). Hypersomnia difficulties are reported more frequently after puberty. Insomnia symptoms usually include difficulty falling asleep and a subjective sense of not having slept deeply all night.

Recently, clinicians and researchers have seen increasing numbers of adolescents with overlapping phase delay disorders or other sleep/wake schedule disorders associated with depression. Depressed adolescents frequently have difficulty falling asleep, are unable to get up or refuse to go to school, sleep until late in the day, complain of extreme daytime fatigue, and, over time, shift to increasingly more delayed sleep/wake schedules. Likewise, surveys reveal that adolescents who get less than 6 3/4 hours of sleep each school night or report more than a two-hour difference between school night and weekend bedtimes have a higher level of complaints of depressed mood than adolescents who get more sleep or who sleep on more regular sleep/wake schedules.

Clinicians who are experienced with these problems have pointed out that in many cases it is difficult to differentiate decreased motivation, school refusal/anxiety, delayed circadian phase, attention difficulties, and depressive symptomatology. Clearly, both sleep patterns and behavioral symptoms must be carefully assessed in an effort to prevent the problems, diagnose them accurately, and plan successful treatment.

There is also evidence of changes in the sleeping electroencephalograms (EEGs) of depressed adolescents, including increased time to fall asleep and altered patterns of REM sleep. Furthermore, changes in EEG measures of sleep predicted an increased recurrence of depressive episodes during longitudinal follow-ups in early adulthood.[7]

In some cases, treatment of sleep complaints and problems—including regularizing the sleep/wake schedule, cognitive behavioral therapy for insomnia, and short-term treatment with medication for severe insomnia—can have a positive impact on depressive symptoms.[8] On the other hand, effective treatment of depression can also be a critical aspect of improving sleep.

Negative Spirals?

As I described above, one area of concern with regard to the interconnections between sleep and emotional disturbances is the potential for a progressive sequence or spiral of negative effects. Insufficient sleep can amplify emotional difficulties, which can then produce further sources of distress and increased disruption of sleep. The reason for this concern arises more from clinical experience than from any controlled studies, and so the concern is perhaps best illustrated by describing a case.

Jay had a history of poor sleep habits (e.g., bedtimes past midnight, erratic sleep/wake schedule) beginning in about seventh grade. In ninth grade the problems became worse as he struggled to get to sleep at night (usually falling asleep at 1 a.m.) and to wake up in the morning and then had problems with distractibility and behavior at school. He also reported some symptoms of depression, including loss of interest in some activities, daytime fatigue, and worsening performance at school. His symptoms improved transiently in the summer, when he slept from 3 a.m. until noon.

In 10th grade Jay began attending a high school that started at 7:30 a.m., which required him to wake up at 6 a.m. to meet the school bus at 6:30 a.m. He had a very difficult time getting up for school at that hour because his average bedtime was 2 a.m. He made several attempts to go to bed earlier but found himself unable to fall asleep. He was never able to follow through in a way that would permit him to establish an earlier pattern of bedtime, and he quickly reverted to his 3 a.m.-to- noon sleep schedule on all weekends and holidays. Jay sometimes stayed up working at his computer or watching television—he says this was because he hated the feeling of lying in bed trying unsuccessfully to fall asleep. Before long, he was regularly missing school or arriving late and falling asleep in class.

Jay, who had at one time been identified as a gifted student, was failing most of his classes and appeared increasingly lethargic, subdued, and uninterested in school. His school counselor referred him to a mental health clinic. Over the course of several months, he was diagnosed as having depression with some ADHD symptoms (e.g., difficulty finishing tasks, distractibility). Trials of antidepressants and stimulant medication resulted in small transient improvements in some symptoms, but Jay was never able to reestablish good sleep patterns that were compatible with his school schedule. Eventually he withdrew from school, became increasingly depressed and withdrawn, and was hospitalized after a serious suicide attempt.

At the time of hospitalization, Jay had severe chronic insomnia and a major depressive disorder. Despite multiple interventions, these problems persisted. He showed very little motivation to return to school and appeared to have chronic depressive symptoms. At discharge his long- term prognosis was not promising.

In a case such as Jay's, it is impossible to disentangle the relative contributions of the sleep and mood dysregulations. While no general conclusions can be drawn from this single case, it does illustrate the complexity of these interactions and the importance of obtaining a better understanding in these areas.

Policy Decisions for Today and Direction For the Future

Frequently in this article I have cautioned readers about the need for additional research to improve our understanding of the complex issues arising from the consequences of insufficient sleep among adolescents. Our current knowledge is preliminary and based on a paucity of controlled data. Furthermore, we are probably at an equally early stage in our understanding of the behavioral and emotional problems of adolescents. Nonetheless, behavioral and emotional difficulties are currently the largest source of morbidity and mortality among adolescents. While it is possible that sleep loss makes only a minuscule contribution to adolescents' problems with emotional regulation, it is extremely likely that it plays some role. It is also quite possible that insufficient sleep plays a significant role in leading up to some of these problems in a vulnerable set of individuals.

Identifying vulnerability to sleep loss may represent an important future direction for research, since there appear to be such large individual differences in the effects of acute sleep loss. Such vulnerability could be related to a tendency to need more sleep, to being a "night owl," or to a biological vulnerability toward emotional disorders.

Clearly, more research is needed to help inform policy makers, whose decisions will further affect adolescent sleep patterns. Cost-benefit analyses regarding the relative importance of sleep will require more precise quantification in these areas. In the meantime, one might make a reasonable case that the odds are heavily in favor of sleep as an increasingly important health concern among adolescents.

To reiterate the main point with which I began, adequate sleep is defined as the amount necessary for optimal daytime functioning. It appears that the potentially fragile underpinnings of adolescent social competence (controlling thoughts and feelings at the same time) may be most sensitive to the effects of inadequate sleep. Any review of adolescent lifestyles in our society will reveal more than a dozen forces converging to push the sleep/arousal balance away from sleep and toward ever-higher arousal. What harm could there be in trying to push back a little toward valuing sleep? The potential benefits seem enormous.

1. Ronald E. Dahl, "The Regulation of Sleep and Arousal: Development and Psychopathology," *Development and Psychopathology*, vol. 8, 1996, pp. 3-27.

2. Ronald E. Dahl et al., "Sleep Onset Abnormalities in Depressed Adolescents," *Biological Psychiatry*, vol. 39, 1996, pp. 400-410.

3. James A. Horne, "Human Sleep, Sleep Loss, and Behaviour Implications for the Prefrontal Cortex and Psychiatric Disorder," *British Journal of Psychiatry*, vol. 162, 1993, pp. 413-19.

4. Ronald D. Chervin et al., "Symptoms of Sleep Disorders, Inattention, and Hyperactivity in Children," *Sleep*, vol. 20, 1997, pp. 1185-92.

5. Horne, op. cit.

6. Abigail Schlesinger, Mark S. Redfern, Ronald E. Dahl, and J. Richard Jennings, "Postural Control, Attention and Sleep Deprivation," *Neuroreport*, vol. 9, 1998, pp. 49-52.

7. Uma Rao et al., "The Relationship Between Longitudinal Clinical Course and Sleep and Cortisol Changes in Adolescent Depression," *Biological Psychiatry*, vol. 40, 1996, pp. 474-84.

8. Ronald E. Dahl, "Child and Adolescent Sleep Disorders," in idem, ed., *Child and Adolescent Psychiatric Clinics of North America: Sleep Disorder* (Philadelphia: W. B. Saunders, 1996).

Unit Selections

Key Points to Consider

❖ What impact does the school environment have on the academic and social development of boys and girls? How can we curb the recent rash of school violence such as the shootings at Columbine High School? Are single-sex schools a better environment for development than coed schools? Do adolescents who are schooled at home have sufficient opportunities to interact with peers?

❖ Should high schools institute exit exams for graduation? Does today's emphasis on outcomes assessment encourage cheating? What does the LD label really mean and do we overuse the diagnosis of learning disabled?

❖ What roles do heredity and environment play in intelligence? Why does it matter? What about racial, gender, and cultural differences in IQ scores? in mathematics achievement?

 **Links** | **www.dushkin.com/online/**

These sites are annotated on pages 4 and 5.

Adolescence entails changes in cognitive capacities that are just as monumental as the biological changes. Whereas the thinking of children tends to be more literal, more tied to reality and to what is familiar, the thought processes of adolescents are more abstract, systematic, and logical. Adolescents can appreciate metaphor and sarcasm, they can easily think about things that do not exist, they can test ideas against reality, and they can readily conceive of multiple possibilities. Many of these improvements in thinking abilities contribute to conflict with adults as adolescents become much better able to argue a point or take a stand. They are better at planning out their case and at anticipating counterarguments. They are also more likely to question the way things are because they can now conceive of other possibilities.

Study of the cognitive changes that occur in adolescence has largely been based on the work of the Swiss psychologist, Jean Piaget, and his colleague Barbel Inhelder. Piaget and Inhelder described the adolescent as reasoning at what they called the "formal operational" stage. Children from the approximate ages of 7 to 11 years old were described as being in the "concrete operational" stage. Although not all researchers agree with Piaget and Inhelder that these adolescent cognitive abilities represent true stage-like changes, all agree that adolescent thought is characteristically more logical, abstract, and hypothetical than the thought of children. Having certain mental capacities does not mean that adolescents, or even adults for that matter, will always reason at their rational best!

Indeed, building on the work of Piaget and Inhelder, David Elkind has argued that the newly emerging formal operational cognitive abilities lead to some troublesome consequences for adolescents. For one thing, adolescents tend to overintellectualize. They often make things too complex and fail to see the obvious, a phenomenon that Elkind calls pseudostupidity. Teachers often experience this as adolescents overanalyze every word of a multiple-choice question. Elkind also maintains that much of the extreme self-consciousness of adolescents occurs because they construct an imaginary audience. Formal operations make it possible for adolescents to think about other people's thoughts. Adolescents lose perspective and think that others are constantly watching them and thinking about them. A related mistake is that adolescents are likely to believe that everyone shares their concerns and knows their thoughts. This belief that one is at the center of attention further leads to the development of what Elkind calls the personal fable. Namely: If everyone is paying so much attention to me I must be special and invulnerable. Bad things won't happen to me. I won't get in a car crash. I won't get pregnant. Pseudo-stupidity, the imaginary audience, and the personal fable diminish as adolescents' cognitive abilities mature and as they develop friendships in which intimacies are shared. Peer interaction helps adolescents see that they are not as unique as they thought, nor are they such a focus of everyone else's attention.

Piaget's views on cognitive development have been quite influential, particularly in the field of education. The general philosophy is that learning must be active and that the curriculum needs to be tied to the student's cognitive level. Also, as Elkind points out, awareness of the cognitive abilities and shortcomings of adolescents can make their behaviors more comprehensible to parents, teachers, counselors, and other professionals who work with adolescents.

While developmentalists in the Piaget tradition focus on the ways in which the thought processes of children and adolescents differ, other researchers have taken a different turn. In the psychometric approach the emphasis is on quantifying cognitive abilities such as verbal ability, mathematical ability, and performance on general intelligence (IQ) tests. Adolescents clearly have more vocabulary, more mathematical knowledge, more spatial ability, etc., than children. Their memories are better as they process information more efficiently and use memory strategies more effectively. They have a greater knowledge base, which enables them to link new concepts to existing ideas. Psychometric intelligence, in other words, increases with age. Because of comparison to age peers though, relative performance on aptitude tests remains fairly stable. A 9-year-old child's performance on an IQ test, for example, is fairly predictive of that same adolescent's IQ score at age 15. Performance on standardized tests is often used to place junior high and high school students in ability tracks, a practice that is increasingly being questioned.

The measurement of intelligence, as well as the very definition of intelligence, has been controversial for decades. A classic question is whether intelligence is best conceptualized as a general capacity that underlies many diverse abilities or as a set of specific abilities. Traditional IQ tests focus on abilities that relate to success in school and ignore abilities such as those that tap creativity, mechanical aptitude, or practical intelligence. The role of genetic versus environmental contributions to intelligence has been hotly debated. At the turn of the century the predominant view was that intelligence was essentially inherited and little influenced by experience. Today, the consensus is that an individual's intelligence is very much a product of both nature and nurture. Greater controversy centers on the role that heredity versus the environment plays in explaining racial, ethnic, and gender differences in performance on various cognitive tests. A subsection of this unit explores current issues in measuring and explaining cognitive performance.

Issues about cognitive abilities are important for education. Schools need to take the developmental abilities and needs of adolescents into account in planning programs. Moreover, we have a high dropout rate and need to examine alternatives for keeping youth in school. Several articles discuss ideas for improving the educational climate and experience for all students, including women and minorities.

Cognitive Growth and Education

Musings in the Wake of Columbine

What Can Schools Do?

Until we make schools engaging learning communities whose members value those communities and feel welcome within them, we are right to think that the next Columbine could happen anywhere, Ms. Raywid and Ms. Oshiyama point out.

BY MARY ANNE RAYWID AND LIBBY OSHIYAMA

THERE HAVE BEEN multiple attempts to figure out the reasons for the Columbine High School tragedy. The availability of guns has been widely blamed, as has the violence depicted in films and videos. Some analysts have turned their sights on parental failure. Others have looked to deep-seated personality problems within the young assassins, while still others have focused on the seductive power of hate groups. There is probably some truth in most of these explanations, plus others, with the choice among them being largely a matter of individual perspective.

"The truth" lends itself to many interpretations. We know that if we look to psychologists for explanations of human behavior, we characteristically get different answers from what sociologists would offer and different answers from what anthropologists would offer. Educators venture answers, too. But unless they are going to content themselves with mere hand wringing, they must look to explanations that schools

MARY ANNE RAYWID is professor emerita, Hofstra University, Hempstead, N.Y., and currently a member of the Graduate Affiliate Faculty, University of Hawaii, Manoa. LIBBY OSHIYAMA is an international educational consultant whose home is in Hawaii.

can do something about. Otherwise they are simply placing the problem beyond their control.

Actually, there is a good bit of knowledge suggesting directions that schools can take in order to avoid more tragedies like Columbine. It is also knowledge about which we can be fairly confident. In this article we will be reflecting on the broad strategies that strike us as most promising. They pertain to school size and organization, as well as to what we teach—both deliberately and inadvertently.

There is overwhelming evidence that violence is much less likely to occur in small schools than in large ones. In fact, not surprisingly, students behave better generally in schools where they are known. It is in large schools, where alienation often goes hand in hand with anonymity, that the danger comes. As James Garbarino of Cornell University, one of the nation's top scholars on juvenile delinquency, has put it, "If I could do one single thing [to stop the scourge of violence among juveniles], it would be to ensure that teenagers are not in high schools bigger than 400 to 500 students."[1]

As suggested by all the standard indicators—truancy, dropout rates, involvement rates, graffiti, vandalism, violence—youngsters in small schools rarely display the anger at the institution and the people in it that was so

blatant at Columbine and is evident in many high schools elsewhere as well. The evidence regarding school size and risk comes not only from individual school studies but also from research syntheses—analyses of relevant studies undertaken across the country. Here are claims from three such syntheses:

> Larger school size is related to . . . higher levels of disorder and violence, student alienation, and teacher dissatisfaction.[2]

* * *

> Student social behavior—as measured by truancy, discipline problems, violence, theft, substance abuse, and gang participation—is more positive in small schools.[3]

* * *

> Research has consistently found that students at small schools are less alienated than students in large schools—and this positive effect is especially strong for students labeled "at risk."[4]

* * *

> Behavior problems are so much greater in larger schools . . . that any possible virtue of larger size is canceled out by the difficulties of maintaining an orderly learning environment.[5]

The reason why size is important is because the first lesson Columbine seems to urge for schools is the need to make them genuinely user-friendly places for all students—places where everyone is welcomed into a genuine community and each student is known well by at least one adult staff member who assumes responsibility for his or her positive growth and success. The student assassins of Columbine, by contrast, were outcasts who banded together after repeated acts of rejection and humiliation by two high-status campus groups, the "jocks" and the "preps."[6] And although they and others paraded around the campus in identifiable dress (black trench coats), gave one another Nazi salutes, and submitted assignments that should have spelled danger (videos on killing, poetry about death, violence-filled essays), no single faculty member was in a position to put the picture together, and evidently none felt a personal responsibility to address these particular aberrations. Indeed, with no one responsible for seeing and acting on the whole picture with regard to these boys, the multiple signs of trouble couldn't even be tallied. And the principal could report that he had actually never heard of the "trench coat mafia" in his school.[7]

This situation is not atypical of comprehensive high schools of nearly 2,000 youngsters. In such schools, many students remain virtually anonymous for their entire stay. Others are singled out by their peers for harassment and humiliation, which teachers typically find beyond their province—if they become aware of it at all. It is a mistake to assume that teachers in such schools don't care or that they are indifferent to students. We are reaping the results of the way we have organized schools and divided up staff responsibilities. We have apportioned things so that teachers' primary responsibility is not for youngsters but for content and grade levels. (Only the guidance counselors could be thought to be more responsibile for individuals than for content—but they too must focus primarily on accomplishing specific duties, like programming and college admissions, and with such large numbers of students that it is ludicrous to think they have time to find out what's on an individual youngster's mind.) No matter what we choose to focus on in articulating school organization—content or something else—it means that other things become less visible and may be obscured. Sometimes they are things that are centrally related to the kinds of human beings we are creating.

Yet there are schools today in which *students* are the focus and these human requirements are being met. Such schools are largely to be found in cities—which have been far more alert to potential crises than have suburbs and rural areas. But obviously, one of the clearest lessons of suburban Columbine High School is that violence is not confined to the inner city or to disadvantaged youngsters. Indeed, both at Columbine and at other schools in which multiple killings have occurred, the assassins have come from middle-class families.

The first requirement for making schools into communities where all youngsters are known is the one with which we began, the obvious need to make them smaller. You simply can't

You simply can't have much by way of genuine community in a school of several thousand.

have much by way of genuine community in a school of several thousand. There are just too many logistical obstacles for community to emerge in schools of such scale. And so subcommunities of various sorts develop there instead—cliques, including the jocks and the nerds. In most high schools, the cliques, plus the gangs formed outside school, are left to fulfill the human need—peaking at adolescence—for close ties and peer recognition. Our failure to acknowledge and respond to this need in school organizational design is strange: we know the "herding" instinct is strongest during adolescence. Never before or afterward does it seem more important to people. Yet most schools just leave fulfillment of that instinct to chance. Columbine suggests that if we fail to acknowledge and deliberately nurture human connection in schools, youngsters will find it for themselves. And it will not always be the kind of connection and connecting that we would want for the young.

There is another strange feature about the way we have organized high schools. We are quite aware that adolescents are not adults—and that adolescence can be the most difficult and painful stage of growing up. Yet we defer little if at all to the immaturity of the school's "clients," placing them in the most unpleasant and demanding circumstances they may ever have to

encounter: they are moved every 45 minutes all day long and are expected to shift attention and mental gears at the ringing of a bell. They can find themselves in seven or eight entirely different groupings during the day, with seven or eight different bosses (teachers—who may not know one another, either). And rules regarding their dress, speech, and comportment may be rigid in an effort to exert control over the nameless faces. As the principal of one famous high school has put it, "If God knew what high schools were going to be like, He'd have made kids differently."

What do high schools need to be instead? Small enough so that people can know one another. Small enough so that individuals are missed when they are absent. Small enough so that the participation of all students is needed. Small enough to permit considerable overlap in the rosters from one class to another. Small enough so that the full faculty can sit around a table together and discuss serious questions. Small enough to permit the flexibility essential to institutional responsiveness—to the special needs of individuals and to the diverse ways teachers want to teach. (In large schools, instruction must always bow to the schedule, which controls everyone's time impartially. Small schools can simply suspend customary arrangements for a day or rewrite the weekly schedule as the need arises.)

As we analyze and reanalyze the tragedy at Columbine High School, many people identify it as a series of events crying out for education in tolerance. They seem both right and wrong. Certainly they are correct in the notion that youngsters must be taught how to relate to others—to groups as well as to individuals. The famous line from a song in *South Pacific*, "You have to be taught to hate and fear," may be half right. But you also have to be taught to appreciate. Thus positive lessons on how to see and treat others must be included in formal education. But to the extent that aims determine our strategy for reaching them, it might be well to examine whether "tolerance" is really sufficient. Tolerance, after all, is the parallel in human affairs of the laws we have established to bring "justice" to the public sector. They are parallel in that both are intended to apply not primarily to friends but to strangers.

Toward individuals for whom we lack the personal feelings we have for friends, tolerance is supposed to be the broad general attitude. And it is an attitude of neutrality or benign indifference: you live your way, and I'll live mine. We are really just beginning to sense that it is not enough. There is much to recommend it as legal policy, but there seems less to be said for it as a general principle of living to be taught the young. There are other approaches that would probably have a lot more psychological validity. In the first place, it would help if schools *modeled* respect for individuals—that is, if all coming in contact with the school—students, parents, visitors—were consistently treated with courtesy and in such a fashion that their dignity remained intact. This is a broader demand than we often construe it. It shows a lack of respect, for instance, says former resident principal at the U.S. Department of Education, Paul Schwarz, for school officials to fail to learn the names of students enrolled in a given school. It shows a lack of respect for schools to repeatedly assign youngsters to groups widely recognized to consist of "dummies" or "losers." It telegraphs another sort of lack of respect when lavatory doors can't be closed or locked—or when there is no toilet paper.

Somewhat more directly, youngsters must be taught about and held responsible for respecting their classmates. This is a matter first just of physical respect. Although we may think of this point as too obvious to deserve mention, a survey of one college class revealed that every single student in the class had been physically threatened by others in high school![8] But what is also necessary is respect for the individual's *persona*. It would be surprising if the ridiculing and the repeated rejections of the Columbine boys who became assassins were unrelated to their rage. But the kind of respect indicated will probably have to go well beyond the tolerance that schools typically state as their official position.

We need to deliberately cultivate in schools the qualities associated with *acceptance,* such as empathy and compassion. This is not to say that we want youngsters to find acceptable any behavior that a schoolmate exhibits. But it is reasonable to ask them to accept that even behaviors we might abhor are motivated by the same needs that motivate our own behavior—and that the needs, if not the manner in which we fulfill them, define the commonality among human beings.

Again, these traits must be both modeled by staff members and deliberately cultivated among students. The major ways of cultivating them are, first, through the personal relationships that constitute school communities, but also through what is taught—certainly in the humanities. Literature can instruct eloquently in kinship, empathy, and compassion, as can people's history, to cite just two examples. Over the years, schools have tended to focus on making youngsters more informed, more rigorously trained, more skilled. Perhaps we had better begin focusing on also making them more humane. The tragedy at Columbine would certainly recommend it.

We need to deliberately cultivate in schools the qualities associated with acceptance.

As is the case with respect, there are other ways than the curriculum in which schools teach tolerance or acceptance—or their opposites. Just as it is possible for institutions to operate in ways that make them, in effect, racist or ethnically biased, sexist or homophobic, they can also operate in ways that make plain their rejection of such stances. Some small schools guard against negative institutional bias—and against the stinging comments youngsters can deliver to their peers—by deliberately generating bonds among students. Other schools content themselves with having strictly enforced rules against malicious statements. (At one small high school, for instance, one of the very few rules to which there can be no exceptions is "No dissing"—no slurs, no taunts, no jabs.) And at another institution, the discovery of humiliating graffiti on a wall of the school prompted a three-stage response: first, indignation; then a student-led march through the campus; and then the establishment of "Acceptance Month."[9]

In addition to teaching respect and tolerance or acceptance, high schools must figure out ways to meet another adolescent need: young people need contact and interaction with adults—and we seem to have forgotten how central such contact is to the purposes of education. A goodly part of what we are trying to do in educating, after all, is to sell youngsters the adult world—to initiate them into its perspectives

and cultivate appreciation for what it values. But we've been trying to do so on an absolute minimum of personal contact. And as sociologist James Coleman pointed out, while so-called disadvantaged youngsters may be deprived of this "social capital" because their parents lack it, middle-class and affluent youngsters are often just as deprived of it because their parents don't spend the time to share it with them.[10]

In high schools we try to dole out this precious capital in packages called "courses." And we do so in ways that reduce interaction demands on adults: one teacher is expected to lay it out for 30 students at a time, with minimal or no out-of-class interaction with most of them. But youngsters need to talk to adults, and education might work a lot more effectively for many more of them if we built more interaction into the equation. You simply can't manage it when a teacher is responsible for 150 students. This hardly suffices for knowledge transmission, let alone individualized instruction. Small schools manage to build in interaction in a number of ways—for example, with the advisories described below; in assessment procedures wherein a group of adults confer with a student over his or her work; in mentorship programs that strive to generate long-term, significant connections between one adult and one youngster; and in joint-inquiry projects that cast students and teachers as co-researchers.[11]

Even socially adept adolescents are often lonely. They need adults who will talk and listen to them. Moreover, they need to feel that they are being taken seriously by an adult. Today's circumstances honor well adolescents' desire to establish distance between themselves and those adults to whom they've always been closest. It fails the paradoxical need, however, to interact with other adults, to test ideas on them, to see what earns the approval of a respected adult confidante and what doesn't fly.

So how can we accommodate all of these needs and imperatives? What must we do to shift the sights of comprehensive high schools so that concerns such as these—the teaching of acceptance and respect, the provision of cross-generational interaction—can become prominent in their organization and programs? Some changes will certainly be required. First, we would have to set out to make high schools much smaller. Enrollments would not exceed 700 or 800 if we were serious. It wouldn't have to mean new buildings. But it would have to mean reorganization to the extent of breaking down an existing high school of 3,000 into perhaps five or six separate, autonomous schools, each with its own faculty and students and its own separate program. It's not impossible, and in fact it is being done in a number of cities. But it takes some venturesome and courageous leadership to redefine school organization this way.

But small is not enough. It is possible to cut high schools down to enrollments of 400 or 500 and then try to operate mini-comprehensive high schools! To avoid this, schools must be reorganized to display alternative priorities and virtues. If the school is to be arranged to make the positive development of each youngster paramount, quite a reshuffling of roles and responsibilities will be necessary.

The second requirement for making schools into communities is to find some equitable way to assemble students (and teachers) into groups in which genuine community can be launched and sustained. Routine assignment practices won't work because they don't produce groupings in which people have enough in common to generate community. We've tried age grouping in schools and ability grouping. Neither of these has yielded enough commonality for community, and ability grouping has proved highly inequitable as well. So why not try *interests* as the basis for grouping? Why not let teachers who share an interest—in the arts, or in the sea, or in sports, or in critical thinking—band together to offer a program that will attract students with similar interests? It doesn't mean that the school will teach only the content connected with the arts or the sea or with sports or thinking. Every youngster needs and should have a full curriculum. But it does mean that the sea or sports will provide the context in which as much of the rest of the curriculum as possible is presented.

This way, what calls the group into being—on the part of teachers as well as students—is a shared interest or concern. This interest becomes the nucleus around which a school community can be based. It's not enough to ground a community, but it's a start— as well as an acknowledgment of the obvious truth that a real community is unlikely to emerge from just any collection of human beings that chance brings together. For instance, teachers who disagree fundamentally on what

education is about and what its top priorities should be cannot arrive at a very viable professional community. Youngsters who share few common interests or concerns aren't very likely to bond into a community of learners. To fail to acknowledge this (as we schoolpeople often do) is to close one's eyes to the way the world is.

The third requirement for making schools into communities is the recognition that it takes deliberate effort. It won't just happen by itself, even in a small school. In addition to encouraging common and generally shared pursuits, effective small schools accomplish this goal by organizing carefully hewn cooperative learning activities, community-building activities involving self-disclosure, and—especially for severely alienated students—collective problem-solving events.

A concern to establish community also requires seeing students quite differently. Teachers cannot be content with dealing with their students as one-dimensional, exclusively academic creatures. They must be concerned with them as multifaceted human beings. They must commit to aiding development of multiple sorts—cognitive, social, emotional, moral, as well as academic—and this requires close-up knowledge of individuals. There are a number of approaches that can be used to stimulate the sharing among students that community must involve. For instance, students might remain with a single group for most of their classes and perhaps for several years. Arrangements are needed to generate close ties with at least one adult and one group of peers. In many schools, the practice chosen consists of advisory groups of perhaps 12 to 15 youngsters who may meet daily with the same advisor over a period of several years. There may also be out-of-school, weekend advisory activities, such as visits to college campuses. The advisor is charged with becoming a source of assistance and advice, an advocate, an adult friend, and a liaison between home and school.

Successful small schools conceive of and pursue community in a variety of ways. One principal summarizes his school's philosophy as "There are no strangers here."[12] Another educator casts the ideal climate in terms of the "four R's": mutual *respect* among all the school's constituents, *reciprocity* among students and between them and adults, *responsibility* to self and the greater community, and a *reverence* for place and its connections.[13] And as still others see it, establishing school community is a matter of deliberately

fostering interdependence and interconnectedness among and between faculty members and students.[14] But despite the different ways of expressing it, what lies at the core for all is a "personalization" that large schools, and even some small ones, lack—an awareness of, and willingness to acknowledge and work with, human beings in full dimension, not just as students perceived in cohorts or batches to be processed (e.g., sophomores, the second-period German 2 class, gifted and talented, hyperactive). Shifting to this perspective is not easy. But unless and until we do, we may well be headed for more tragedy and heartbreak. Until we make schools engaging learning communities whose members value those communities and feel welcome within them, we are right to think that the next Columbine could happen anywhere.

1. Quoted in Robert M. Gladden, "The Small School Movement: A Review of the Literature," in Michelle Fine and Janis I. Somerville, eds., *Small Schools, Big Imaginations* (Chicago: Cross City Campaign for Urban School Reform, May 1998), p. 116.
2. Ibid., p. 113.
3. Kathleen Cushman, "Why Small Schools Are Essential," *Horace,* January 1997, p. 3.
4. Gladden, p. 114.
5. Kathleen Cotton, "Affective and Social Benefits of Small-Scale Schooling," *ERIC Digest,* Clearinghouse on Rural Education and Small Schools, Charleston, W.Va., December 1996.
6. Bruce Shapiro, "The Guns of Littleton," *The Nation,* 17 May 1999, p. 4.
7. David Von Drehle, "A Model School for Some, Cliques and Taunts for Others," *Washington Post National Weekly Edition,* 3 May 1999, pp. 7–8.
8. Barbara Kantrowitz and Pat Wingert, "Beyond Littleton: How Well Do You Know Your Kid?," *Newsweek,* 10 May 1999, pp. 36–40.
9. "A Response to Hate," *Franklin and Marshall,* Spring 1999, p. 7.
10. James S. Coleman and Thomas Hoffer, *Public and Private High Schools: The Impact of Communities* (New York: Basic Books, 1987).
11. See, for example, Mary Anne Raywid, "Central Park East Secondary School: The Anatomy of Success," *Journal of Education for Students Placed at Risk,* April 1999, pp. 131–51; and idem, "A School That Really Works: Urban Academy," *Journal of Negro Education,* Winter 1994, pp. 93–110.
12. Paul Schwarz, "New Models of Educational Leadership," speech presented at the Outreach College, University of Honolulu, 30 July 1998.
13. Libby Oshiyama, "A Response to Columbine: What We Must Do," speech presented to the Rotary Club of Honolulu, 3 May 1999.
14. Gregory A. Smith, ed., *Public Schools That Work: Creating Community* (New York: Routledge, 1993).

Mommy, What's a Classroom?

It's not only Christian fundamentalists anymore: now hundreds of thousands of parents are teaching their own kids at home. Just what the unschooled are learning—or aren't—is a subject of much debate.

By Bill Roorbach

I LOVED GRADE SCHOOL. I MEAN, EVERY SEPtember I just loved getting back to it. I loved sharpening those pencils and putting grocery-bag covers on my textbooks. I loved my teachers unquestioningly—those towering, unbenign presences—and shrank before them. I loved the games at recess, the bullying danger of the blacktop, the qualmy allure of the off-limits forest at the far end of the playground. I loved the checker games in the back of the classroom when recess got rained out. I loved snow days, because then there was time to play at home and time to read whatever grown-up book I wanted to read. Best of all, I loved staring out the schoolroom windows in spring, watching the maples bud and leaf and fill out. And man, come to think of it, there was nothing—nothing—like the last day of school when you roared off the bus and leapt on your bike and rode away into summer. Even if you loved school, there was nothing better than not going, nothing better in the world.

THIS AFTERNOON, THE PLAN IS A FIELD TRIP TO THE science museum downtown, so Janet Rhodes is going easy—no need for a highly structured morning. There's always tomorrow,

or the day after, plenty of time for the formal stuff when you're teaching at home. Her husband, Kevin, a lawyer, is already on his way to the upscale firm in Columbus where he works.

Janet is in the kitchen of the family's modest town house in suburban Powell, Ohio, sipping coffee, making plans for the rest of the week: Darcy's first Girl Scout outing, Hilary's choir rehearsals, Gillian's skating lessons. A little math every day for each, a lot of quiet reading, essays for Darcy and Hilary, handwriting practice for all. On Thursday, it's the library, then over to see Connie, a good old friend, to borrow a book of science experiments and make plans for group Spanish and French lessons with Connie's kids, who are also taught at home.

"Where's my book!" Hilary shouts. She's 8 and imperious, and expects that book to appear, right now. No mystery why a book might go missing in this house, though. Books are everywhere: in the bedrooms, in the bathroom, stacked under Mom's desk, piled around the armchair Hilly regally occupies, her fingerprinted eyeglasses high on her nose.

Gillian, 6, springs downstairs from the bedroom, hesitates long enough to see what her sisters are up to, blitzes the basement playroom and the jazzy new computer: math drills from CD shareware.

"Your book is in Mom and Dad's room," she calls up. Hilary groans, but deigns to rise.

The oldest daughter, Darcy, 10, sits at the dining-room table, ignoring all the bustle around her; she hasn't once looked

Bill Roorbach teaches in the graduate writing program at Ohio State University. He is the author of "Summers With Juliet," a memoir.

'Until recently, I was also paranoid about the level of education I was receiving,' says Peter Kowalke, 17, home-schooled his entire life. 'I mean, I thought I was smart, but what was really going on behind the doors of the school? Was I missing anything?'

up from her book about Harriet Tubman. She has books to read, essays to write.

Not much after 9, Mom comes into the living room, drying her hands. Her voice is a bell: "Who wants to sing?" She sits easily on the floor in front of the natty little couch. Gillian pops up the stairs, somersaults dramatically across the living-room carpet, arranges herself between Mom's outstretched legs. Darcy marks her page, rises deep in thought, shuffles over. Hilary, not to be hurried, comes to sit at last. She and Darcy each throw an arm around Mom's neck.

"Yankee Doodle," says Janet Rhodes. She opens "Hear the Wind Blow: American Folksongs Retold," by Scott Russell Sanders, hot from the library. And they begin. Mom's voice is full and strong. Hilary kids around, singing loud like an opera diva. Darcy is very serious, reading along, singing softly. Gillian partly sings and partly listens, rolls her head, pats Mom's knees. They take the song to six obscure verses, then Mom reads Sanders's text, explaining big words, making connections to other lessons. The girls titter at Doodle's feisty independence.

FORGET VOUCHERS AND CHARTER SCHOOLS, forget private or parochial. To a rapidly growing number of parents, school choice means no school at all. This new breed includes not only religious fundamentalists hoping to avoid profane teaching but also all kinds of parents concerned about the method and quality of their children's education. They have done some serious research, found support groups, ransacked libraries, availed themselves of computer and Internet resources and have taken their kids out of school. Or never enrolled them.

Peter Kowalke, 17, lives in a woodsy suburb of Cleveland and hasn't attended a single day of school, at least not until now. He's taking math and science at the local community college, filling in gaps before he applies to a university, getting the first grades of his life: two A's and one B. Peter's father teaches electronics and television production at nearby Mentor High School; his mother used to teach English and is now studying to become a paralegal.

"The highs of home schooling are pretty obvious," Peter says. "Better education, personalized education, strong family influence, better understanding of self, an ardent desire to learn, exposure to the possibilities. Some of the lows? Alienation, horrible spelling, horrible handwriting. The most negative thing is the life style. Personally, I often feel separated from others. Until recently, I was also paranoid about the level of

education I was receiving. I mean, I thought I was smart, but what was really going on behind the doors of the school? Was I missing anything?"

The decision to home-school is problematic, not often supported by family and friends and only recently finding any approval at all from the culture at large. The very mention of home schooling excites distrust: What about the kids' socialization? Are parents competent to teach? Does home schooling even work?

A spoof by three home-schooling mothers from Lexington, N.C. (to the tune of "The Twelve Days of Christmas"), asks the rest:

"On the 12th day of home school my neighbor said to me: 'Can they go to college? What about graduation? They'll miss the prom! I could never do this! Look at what they're missing! How long will you home-school? Why do you do this? [Here comes the "five golden rings" part] You *are* so strange! What about P.E.? Do you give them tests? Are they socialized? And can you home-school legally?' "

The answer to the last question is perhaps the only easy one. After more than two decades of court battles, home schooling is now legal in every state, subject to various restrictions and reporting requirements. For home schoolers in Ohio, like the Rhodeses and the Kowalkes, the regulations are fairly simple. A family must notify the school district superintendent of its intention to home-school and promise to provide 900 hours of instruction per year covering fine arts, language arts, math, science, social studies, geography, fire safety, physical education and health. At the end of the school year, each child must submit to standardized achievement exams or have a portfolio of his or her work evaluated by a certified teacher. If a child's progress doesn't satisfy the evaluator—which is rare—it might be back to school.

Though home schooling clearly means sacrifice for parents (loss of income and the death of free time, for two examples; "You *are* so strange," for a third), thousands are opting in. Their reasons range over an enormous spectrum, from religious to pedagogical, from political to entirely personal. Libertarians see home schooling as a basic gesture of freedom. Deinstitutionalizers think of it as the natural next step after home birthing. Some progressive educators see in home schooling an inexhaustible laboratory in which their ideas can be observed at work. Certain conservatives consider home schooling the last, best hope for the three R's. And of course there's the protective impulse: many parents cite what they call negative socialization—school violence, rampant sex, illegal drugs—as prime incentives for teaching their own kids.

'I wouldn't want my child educated like that,' says a spokeswoman for the National Education Association. 'Or to grow up in a society where the majority were educated like that. Our society is loose enough as it is. The thing that binds us together in this country is public education.'

Because of the diffuse nature of the movement, a dependable count of home schoolers is hard to come by. Patricia Lines, senior research associate with the United States Department of Education in Washington, calculates that 500,000 to 700,000 American children are now taught at home, up from just 10,000 to 15,000 in 1970. Brian Ray, president of the National Home Education Research Institute in Salem, Ore., estimates that 700,000 to 1.15 million kids learn at home; other sources put the number as high as 2.5 million. According to Ray's figures, 50,000 children are taught at home in Ohio, making it the third-largest home-schooling state, after Texas and California (New York is seventh, with about 35,000.)

Ray teaches his own seven children at home, so it may be difficult to see him as a disinterested researcher. But his studies about the efficacy of home schooling seem solid enough to warrant examination. In one, 16,311 home-schooled students from around the country took the nationally calibrated Iowa Test of Basic Skills; their average placed them in the 79th percentile in reading, the 73d in language and math. Ray cites other studies asserting that home-schooled children have "lower problem behavior scores" and "significantly higher self-concepts" than children in public schools.

Ronald Areglado, the associate executive director of programs with the National Association of Elementary School Principals, is not persuaded by Ray's findings. "There's too much emphasis on test scores as the evidence that home schooling is successful," he says. "My worry is that these children become isolated and fragmented; their world is cut up into pieces; there's no interaction with school kids; they may not play as much. If you think about your own elementary school experience, one of the main things was that you hung around with other kids. It's going to take a kid with a lot of resiliency to keep up friendships without school."

Peter Kowalke shrugs off such suggestions. "Last year, I went to two homecoming dances," he says. "Two different girls, two different school systems. Girls? I've met some through the mail, through the Internet, met some at various functions. One time I was volunteering at a senior-citizen's dance, hit it off with another volunteer. You know, you're out and doing things and one friend leads to another and it snowballs. It's the way any adult makes friends."

THE LEADING VOICE OF THE SECULAR HOME-schooling movement continues to be the education theorist John Holt, despite his death in 1985. Holt believed that experts are of little use, that "credentialism" is at the heart of the sickness of American education. After years spent trying to reform schools, he finally came to believe that school itself was the problem. In "Teach Your Own" (1981), he recommended "unschooling"—child-led, interest-based learning—whose fundamental belief is that kids are great learners and don't need to be told how or when to do it. Holt felt that testing and ranking and sorting, even teachers themselves, are schoolish ideas that are harmful and inhibitive and unnecessary.

Away from schools, especially public schools, Holt's argument goes, kids keep their naturally intense love of learning and get a better, less fractured education. Kids don't learn that adults are the enemy, so they can develop real relationships with the adults around them; kids don't learn to taunt and fear each other, so they can develop real relationships with each other as well. In the end, parents and kids grow closer as education becomes indistinguishable from daily family life, and kids and parents get to know each other as people, even as friends.

"People say to us, 'Oh, I'd never have the patience to home-school,' " Janet Rhodes says. "But it's not patience. You've just got to like your kids. Which isn't so hard. When they're with you all the time, you know them better. They're not coming home stressed out about something that happened at school that you don't know about."

When I described unschooling, or at least my understanding of it, to Kathleen Lyons, a spokeswoman for the National Education Association, she didn't pause. "I wouldn't want my child educated like that," she said. "Or to grow up in a society where the majority were educated like that. Our society is loose enough as it is. The thing that binds us together in this country is public education."

Holt wrote that schools don't really provide that kind of glue, and can't, "Not as long as they also have the job of sorting out the young into winners and losers, and preparing the losers for a lifetime of losing."

At the other end of the vast home-schooling movement from Holt and the unschoolers are what one home-schooling researcher calls "the essentialists," many of them religious, who feel that schools have collapsed from listening to too many ideas like Holt's. For them, it's back to the basics of education, which often include the Bible. This is home schooling with the trappings of the classroom intact: maps and blackboards, tests and grades, corporal punishment and detention,

'In school, a kid like Darcy is road kill,' says Darcy's mother. Kids who are different really get it from other kids. And teachers, even the best teachers, don't have time to protect a more tender child. Sometimes they're as mean as the kids.'

old-fashioned values and school prayer. Mom is called Mrs. Whomever, and it's definitely Mom doing the teaching.

The Home School Legal Defense Association is the primary organization at the Christian end of the spectrum and easily the largest home schooling organization of any kind. Its president, Michael Farris, is a lawyer, a former co-chairman of Pat Buchanan's Presidential campaign and the father of nine children, all of whom have been or will be taught at home. For Farris, home schooling fits into a package of familiar fundamentalist Christian issues, including creationism. But he respects unschoolers, sees them as allies. "I like that the unschoolers reject textbooks and embrace real books," he says. "The thing I don't care to follow myself is the 'let my kid do his own thing' philosophy. I think you need to offer more parenting and leadership, more skills. But the unschoolers' results are really good, and we'll defend them to the hilt. There's not one right way to do it."

BACK WHEN SHE WAS IN COLLEGE, PAULA KOWALKE began thinking she would find an alternative to school for her future children. "I read A. S. Neill's 'Summerhill' and then John Holt," she recalls. "I just got fascinated." And when the other 5-year-olds got on the bus for kindergarten, her son Peter stayed home.

For Kevin and Janet Rhodes, the route to home schooling was different, less planned. During Darcy's first year at a progressive Montessori preschool, her teachers noticed she couldn't concentrate in a roomful of kids. Her parents were unhappy with the changes they saw in her: she was coming home agitated, stressed out. She developed nervous habits and slept poorly. Her parents launched an exhaustive search of alternative schools and private programs, hoping to find schooling that would allow their daughter to learn and concentrate in her own way.

They ran across books by John Holt and other home-schooling advocates. Janet had never seen herself as an education experimenter, but the example of a home-schooling friend convinced her to try it. Kevin was cautious but willing.

"We gave ourselves a year," Janet says. She had already quit her job as the executive secretary to the president of a small oil company (the work that put Kevin through law school), had already decided she would dedicate herself to her kids' lives. Kevin had started his own law practice and was sometimes able to come home at lunchtime and lend a hand. They began.

"We knew home school was working right away as we watched Darcy's agitation diminish," Kevin says. "Suddenly this frustrated child could learn. One by one, her nervous habits dropped away." Kevin and Janet continued their reading and planning, attended the meetings of a home-schooling support group, inspected (and for the most part rejected as too inhibiting) prepackaged curriculums, grew more confident.

"In school, a kid like Darcy is road kill," Janet says. "Kids who are different really get it from other kids. And teachers, even the best teachers, don't have time to protect a more tender child. Sometimes they're as mean as the kids. Darcy is a very deliberate child; she speaks slowly, she learns methodically, she's sensitive. Even her sisters are tough on her."

Hilary and Gillian, Darcy's younger sisters, are pretty standard learners, if there are such things. Why not send them to school, make life easier for Mom?

"We just started to see Hilary engaged in the learning process, Kevin says. "Then Gillian too. Everything was working beautifully. There was no incentive to do anything different—though my older sister, Kathy, is quite skeptical."

Kathy Chase lives in Spokane, Wash., where her own two children go to public school. "I wasn't surprised that Kevin and Janet would home-school," she says. "They're very closely knit, very within themselves. They don't feel the need to have huge social interactions. They're content with the five of them. Very protective. I worry they get a little isolated." Long pause. "But I'm sure their kids are well ahead of mine, just because of the one-on-one time working with them. Home schooling is for a certain kind of parent—not me.

Janet's father, too, is ambivalent. "He thinks they'd be better off in school," Janet says. "I think I've finally convinced him, though. My mom worries about them not getting socialized."

Kevin looks pained. "The 'S' word," he says.

When I ask if he's worried about isolation, it's clear he has heard the question before. "A complete nonissue!" he says, rising in his seat. "Define the context in which you fear there may be isolation. Is the concern that somehow if you home-school you're never going to let your kids go out and play with the neighbors, or attend Brownies, or take skating lessons? Is it that somehow you won't be part of the community, won't go to church or concerts or museums or the mall? Which is more isolating, to be with the same 30 other kids and teacher in a building with 500 kids and other teachers, day after day, month after month, or to be out in the larger community several times every week, nearly every day, with people of all ages and races and socio-economic backgrounds?"

The Rhodeses spend about $700 a year directly on home schooling: museum and historical society memberships, gas money for two or three field trips a week, whatever books they can't get out of the library, models, kits, workbooks, the required yearly evaluation ($45 per child). Last year, they spent an additional $893 on music classes, but the girls have moved on to cheaper pursuits—Girl Scouts and Brownies, history club, choir, swimming lessons, skating, ballet.

"People ask, 'How long are you going to do this?' " Kevin says. "I tell them, 'As long as it's working.' "

But if the Rhodeses object to any form of standardized testing, how do they know it's working?

"It's not a mystery—I compare my kids to other kids, of course," Kevin says. "You know, at a birthday party, I hear someone Gillian's age read her birthday card aloud, and I realize, well, we're doing pretty well here."

Last year, the family even brought in Linda Campbell, their Ohio-certified evaluator, for a voluntary midyear visit. "I was having a confidence crisis," Janet says. "And we got some reassurance. A reality check. When you're home-schooling, the responsibility is on *you*. And you feel it."

Campbell has made a business of advising parents and evaluating home-schooled children, whether by administering achievement tests or, for families who shun testing, assessing portfolios. "Some people come to me all nervous, like I'm going to have my hair in a bun, look down my nose through my glasses at them," Campbell says. "But I just try to guide them through the areas the state requires: math, science, reading, all of it. My standards are high. When I sign on the line, I'm saying the child is learning and growing at an appropriate level. In more than 600 evaluations, I've had to decline only 3—all of them teens. They basically spent their year getting up late, turning on the tube. Then when school gets out, they're out the door to see friends. Sometimes they *want* to do poorly. They *want* to be in school, and it's the only way their parents are going to let it happen."

The Rhodeses say it's up to their girls, one by one, whether or not they go into the public schools for junior high or high school. Janet suspects the girls will opt to stay at home. "From what I hear, the teen years are when home schooling really takes off," Janet says. "It becomes theirs; they begin to own it."

PETER KOWALKE HAS ALWAYS PLANNED ON COLLEGE. "In my family, there's the idea that successful people go to college," he says. "I could do a home-school college thing—there would certainly be benefits—but there are trials to both ways. The way I figure, I'm so tired of the trials of home schooling that I want to sample the trials of college."

He shows me around his house. There's a cozy sunken living room, a spare bedroom made over into a packed computer command post. Peter is at once confident and self-conscious, part boy, part man, awkward yet assured. He is close to his brother, Adam, 15, also 100 percent home-schooled. ("Adam's very sharp, very likely my best friend.") Their bedroom is super tidy, carefully arranged: fancy cantilevered bunks built by their father for littler boys, two small desks tucked in, a packed shelf of books. Peter's favorites: "How to Win Friends and Influence People," "Awaken the Giant Within" and, of course, "The Teen-Age Liberation Handbook," by Grace Llewellyn, who advises teens not to drop out of high school but to "rise out."

Sitting at the kitchen table, Peter recalls younger days: "When I first started home schooling, people hadn't heard of it. Clerks at stores would comment, 'Aren't you supposed to be at school?' I'd launch into my speech, how I don't go to school. I didn't feel like some weirdo, though I was aware that certain people were thinking, 'This is this really strange kid, he's got all these weird beliefs.'

"Junior-high age was a hard time. I stayed at home a lot more. Young teens are often known for having these delusions of grandeur, and I had the biggest. Because I didn't go to school, a lot of people thought I was this genius, too good for the schools, and I kind of played that up, started to believe it. Not the geek-genius thing. I mean, I was a football player, too. The image I promoted was the football star who walked around reading Shakespeare at practice."

Peter played football in a youth football league until he was 15. He broke both wrists (separately), played anyway, became a kind of local hero. The next step should have been the high-school team, but the Ohio High School Athletic Association wouldn't—and won't—let unenrolled kids play. No classes, no sports. Peter turned down one solution: partial enrollment, in which a class or two gets you on the team. (Nationally, access to sports and other extracurricular activities is shaping up as the next legal battle for home schoolers.)

His mother looked into fighting the ruling, but Peter asked her not to bother. "I decided to bow out at my glory," he says, "rather than go to a mediocre high school to play on a team that wasn't very good and probably have my delusions about my own ability shattered, all after turning my back on home schooling, which I really valued."

The next year he got himself certified as a coach, which kept him in the game. "Coaching lessened the pain of quitting," he says. "But those first few hits as the other kids started the game were always hard on me. And at the banquets, they wouldn't talk about my playing ability or even my coaching ability but about my intellectual ability, how I was always reading."

Peter played softball for a while, then got seriously interested in weight lifting. And more and more he spent his time publishing a desktop zine called Nation ("Not *The* Nation," he says, anticipating a complaint). Nation is filled with the voices of, among others, scores of Peter's pen pals and E-mail friends; he's got 100 subscribers by now and puts out an issue every other month.

One regular contributor is Amy Tavormina, 16, who attends the private Notre Dame Academy in Toledo, several hours from the Kowalkes' Cleveland suburb. She and Peter started as pen pals three years ago, wrote back and forth daily, then actually met. They dated in a long-distance way for a year, but now they are back to being buddies and pen pals. "Peter has as many friends as I do, but not the close personal contact all the time," Tavormina says. "A lot of his communication is via E-mail and letters. But my friendships are face to face. Home-schooled kids miss other stuff, too, the fine moments, like the victory of finishing a paper. And I've got wonderful teachers. That's another person, another adult you can get an opinion from. Me, I need the pressure and the competition. I would hate to home-school."

Peter became obsessed with charting his home-schooling progress, fastidiously documenting his studies for the Clonlara School, a private school based in Ann Arbor, Mich., that also works with home schoolers. The Kowalkes, like many home-schooling families, use Clonlara not only for the academic help (including the company's Compuhigh, which offers high school courses over the Internet) but for the credentials it can supply: transcripts, documentation of study and a functional high-school diploma, which helps home schoolers avoid the stigma of a G.E.D. (General Educational Development) diploma.

"I went from just living to living with a purpose," Peter says. "I took it very literally, that I had to keep all these records for Clonlara. I had the dream of graduating in three years. I had to prove myself, show that I was as good as schooled kids. I worried. There were moments of fear. Those young teen years you don't realize that all kids have these doubts about themselves. You think it's about home schooling.

"So I did five hours of academic work a day. I obsessively kept track to the minute. On reflection, I'm really sad I did that. My mom, of course, was letting me follow my interests. There was this horrible weakness in math and science. I spent my time publishing, writing, weight lifting, thinking about football. At that age, you're pretty stubborn. You know the best way. I should have asked for more help. Finally, I just got into a crisis stage, a panic: 'I'm not going to make the three years! I'm not a super-genius!' It was a big crash. I was the lowest of the low."

As it turns out, Peter's A.C.T., or American College Test, score of 27 puts him in the 91st percentile; he won't tell me his S.A.T. scores, which disappointed him. One of his goals in taking math and science at Lakeland Community College is to complete his Clonlara program; another goal is to get used to classrooms, to ease into an alien world.

His first pick for a university (he'll apply when he finishes up at Lakeland) is Case Western Reserve in Cleveland, a respected private school, comfortably close to home. His second pick is Miami University (known nationally as Miami of Ohio), a less expensive, less selective public university, just a little farther away. His A.C.T. score easily puts him in the running at Case and is well above the mean at Miami.

"We've actually developed a specific policy on home-schooled applicants in the last two or three years," says William T. Conley, the dean of undergraduate admissions at Case. "College admissions is all about the pipeline, and the home schooling numbers are growing rapidly, so we better be ready."

Still, Conley has some personal reservations about home schooling. "My wife and I have said to each other that people must be out of their minds to want to spend that much time with their kids," he says. "And the academics! It's hard enough just worrying that your kid has got his poem written for class the next day. I'm skeptical, concerned for the kids—there's a lot to be said for suffering the fools in their local high schools."

Eric J. Furda, director of undergraduate admissions at Columbia University (whose nieces, coincidentally, are home-schooled), says that the admissions process for home schoolers isn't unlike that for the graduates of progressive or experimental private schools. But Furda admits that he needs plenty of background information to compare home-schooled applicants with applicants from known high schools: What curriculum was used? How was it decided that the student was ready to move on to the next level in, say, math? How significant are the transcripts when they are provided by parents? "We need some national comparison," Furda says, recommending that home schoolers take five S.A.T.-II subject tests: writing, math, history, science and a language.

How will Peter Kowalke's application to Case be evaluated?

"We are looking at these students in a very specific light," Conley says. "Are they prepared for the intellectual, academic and social environment here at Case Western Reserve? The S.A.T.-II subject tests give us a handle on how much French or calculus or history the home-schooled kid has actually learned. Then, once the kid's in our pool, we look for the subtleties. In some cases, the home schoolers are very limited in nonacademic involvement. There won't be the traditional marching band, tennis 1, 2, 3, 4. One automatically assumes that a home-schooled kid will be limited socially. So we look closely: Do they work at the local McDonald's? Do they volunteer with Habitat for Humanity, have a paper route, work with the town theater company?"

Then there's the interview, required for home schoolers. "We feel that if they've been pursuing their education at 31 Walnut Lane, we need to get them on the academic plant, see if they feel comfortable," Conley says.

When I describe Peter Kowalke—test scores, community involvement, independent projects, college-level math and science—Conley says: "What's his name? Can you tell me his name? He sounds good."

O.K. for Peter, but (assuming they would even be interested in college) what about the purest unschoolers, who often refuse to take tests, refuse to create schoolish transcripts, refuse to use grades?

"I don't think so," Conley says. "We just don't know how to look at that."

I'M A COLLEGE PROFESSOR; I HAVE DEGREES; I'm a product of public schooling from Grade 1 to Grade 12. It's all but impossible for me to see learning in any light but the fluorescent blare of the classroom, with testing and grades and grade levels, with layers of experts in control, with winners and losers, standards, norms, averages against which to judge the efforts and abilities of every kid you send up.

It's tough to let go of all that, maybe impossible. My American sense of the rightness of school, the inevitability of school, the hegemony of school, is akin to my sense of the rightness of the oceans, of rivers, of rain. God made them, right?

Still, there's something noble—if perhaps quixotic—in refusing the culture's assumptions about school, in marching into the fray alone, an individualism distinctly American.

The Rhodeses carry on, cheerfully stressed, caught up in their commitment, intrepidly facing the future and its unknown challenges, alone.

For Peter Kowalke, the deed is done. Twelve years ago, his folks marched him off in his own direction, and there's general agreement—from friends, from teachers, from standardized tests—that he has come out fine. Perhaps it does no good to wonder how it would have been for Peter in school. Would he have starred in sports? Would he have suffered his crisis? Would he have published Nation and made so many friends so far from home? Would he have handled the pressures of the cliques? Or got in with the wrong crowd? Would he have found mentors among his teachers? Or would he have remained too proud to ask for help?

All moot. Now it's off to college. "This is the time when most kids become individuals," he says. "But I've always been an individual. My friends and I are finally all getting on the same wavelength. I've proved I can do well academically. I know I can interact well with the other kids. I can do well in college. I'm O.K."

Peter has become so interested in science that he plans to major in it. And eventually, college behind him, he wants to mix emerging computer technologies with his publishing experience in some way no one has yet dreamed of. "The biggest benefit of home schooling is that it chops away the barriers, opens up all the limits in life. Even with its trials, home schooling shows you there are alternatives. You think: Could I do it a different way? You have confidence."

He looks around his mother's kitchen, shakes his head, gives me a hard look. His assurance seems to flicker, then blazes.

The LD Label for Relatively Well-Functioning Students:

A Critical Analysis

Michael Gordon, Lawrence Lewandowski, and Shelby Keiser

Abstract

The number of students identified since the mid-1970s as having learning disabilities has produced a corresponding increase in the population of such individuals in postsecondary programs. The Americans with Disabilities Act, along with Section 504 of the Vocational Rehabilitation Act of 1973, provide the basis for civil rights for students in higher education. These laws protect individuals who have a substantial limitation in a major life activity when compared with the general population. A disparity between the legal definition and the clinical definition of learning disabilities, which can encompass those identified on the basis of academic underachievement relative to intellectual potential, has stimulated debate about the fairest, most appropriate standard for declaring a student functionally impaired. Extending services to individuals without significant academic impairment may tax or even deplete scarce resources for others in greater needs, distort the normal processes by which individuals select careers, and diminish the credibility of the diagnosis itself.

The years following the passage of P.L. 94–142 have witnessed a growing number of students being identified as learning disabled. As of 1996, the prevalence of school-age youngsters identified in the learning disability (LD) classification was 5.4% (U.S. Office of Education, 1997). In some states and school districts, the LD designation is even more common (Silver, 1988). This rise in the number of students so identified has generated widespread concern about the possibility of misclassification (Gottlieb, Alter, Gottlieb, & Wishner, 1994).

One segment of the LD population that seems to be growing rapidly is individuals who are relative, not absolute, underachievers. Often categorized as "gifted" LD or "high functioning" LD, these students have received services because certain areas of their learning, although at least average, nonetheless are deficient relative either to

other, more advanced skills or to a generally more superior IQ. This conceptualization of a learning disability has justified special educational consideration for students with uneven but at least average abilities. Despite its popularity, it is also a notion that may be hard to justify. We intend this comment to provoke discussion about the viability of the LD label for students who essentially function normally in comparison with most other students.

Definitions of learning disabilities have generally rested on the shoulders of relative discrepancies (Frankenberger & Harper, 1987; Stanovich, 1991). Individuals are considered to have LD when a substantial difference exists between their expected abilities (as estimated by intellectual performance) and their actual academic performance in one or more specific areas of functioning. Although dissatisfaction reigns on many fronts with this method of

identification (Algozzine & Ysseldyke, 1986; Gregg, Hoy, & Gay, 1996; Siegel, 1999; Stanovich, 1999), it nonetheless remains at the heart of both the *Diagnostic and Statistical Manual of Mental Disorders, fourth edition (DSM-IV)* criteria (which require functioning "below that expected given the person's chronological age, measured intelligence, and age-appropriate education") and definitions based on special education laws (which typically specify some metric for judging the extent of discrepancy required to allow for the provision of services).

Traditionally, the focus of LD identification has been on students with average to low-average intellectual abilities whose academic achievement in at least one area (e.g., math, reading, writing) do not measure up to expectation. Based on a discrepancy model of disability, the definition has broadened to include individuals in the high-average to superior range of intellectual ability who perform *relatively* poorly in one or more academic areas. However, in most cases, even these individuals' lowest academic performance is still average when compared with norms for the general population. A typical scenario might involve a student with a full scale IQ of 135 but a standard score in reading comprehension of 100. Such a discrepancy between the two standard scores would, for some, justify an LD label.

Until recently, this definitional expansion gained easy acceptance because it was used to facilitate learning for generally capable students who nonetheless were not "achieving to what was considered to be their full potential." After all, the special education laws for elementary and secondary students were designed to identify educational problems and maximize outcome. Surely a compassionate and well-intentioned society aims to help all of its children achieve to the fullest. If assigning an LD label will heighten the chances of success for any child who could do better, why not?

Two factors, however, have brought some to reconsider the broadening of the LD definition (Lorry, 1998; Smith, 1998). The first is economic: Tighter school budgets and the soaring costs of providing special education services have forced communities to prioritize their expenditures. Part of that analysis has, for many school districts, involved determining whether special services should be provided for students who have only relative (intraindividual) weaknesses, not absolute abnormalities, when compared to others.

Second, passage of antidiscrimination laws, especially the Americans with Disabilities Act (ADA), has caused some to ask serious questions about the fundamental nature of a disability within an educational context (Kelman & Lester, 1997; Spear-Swerling & Sternberg, 1998). Even though the ADA was primarily drafted to protect the rights of individuals with disabilities in the workplace, it has been used increasingly to justify the provision of accommodations to students in higher education (Gordon & Keiser, 1998). For example, students can petition for special test accommodations on the various entrance exams (e.g., the SAT, MCAT, and GRE), or even on tests required for professional licensure (e.g., the medical or law boards). Many students requesting such accommodations will likely fall within the gifted or high-functioning LD category because someone with truly abnormal abilities, especially in language, would not likely gain admission to competitive institutions of higher learning.

LD evaluations that students submit to document a claim of disability will, therefore, usually rely upon a relative discrepancy model to justify the diagnosis. Although such students may not perform below the 10th percentile for the nondisabled population on accepted clinical measures, they may have certain abilities that fall more than a standard deviation below their Full Scale IQ estimate or estimates from other test indices.

Parenthetically, justification of special accommodations based on this construal of a learning disability often runs afoul of definitions of disability emanating from the ADA, attendant case law, and regulatory guidelines. According to the law, individuals can be qualified as disabled only if they suffer from "substantial impairment in a major life activity." "Substantial impairment" has generally been defined across the full range of physical and psychiatric disabilities via comparisons to the general population. In other words, individuals are disabled if their functional impairment limits them relative to most people.

The ADA's "average person" standard is thus at odds with assumptions underlying identifications of high-functioning LD, at least for individuals whose weakest abilities are still average or above. Strictly speaking, this legislation recognizes only learning disabilities that cause an individual to function abnormally relative to the general population, and not to some educational cohort (e.g., other college students) or an intraindividual profile. This standard has been central to the ADA's definition of disability from the law's inception. In fact, the report of the Senate Committee on Labor and Human Resources (the congressional committee that developed much of the ADA) indicated from the outset that "substantially limiting impairments" cannot be minor or trivial; rather, they must restrict an individual's major life activity as to the "conditions, manner, or duration under which [the activity] can be performed in comparison to most people" (S.REP. No. 101–116).

This approach to disabilities determination is embodied in the Department of Justice and EEOC regulations for compliance (Fed. Register, Vol 56, No. 144, p. 35549; EEOC Directives Transmittal No. 915.002, March 14, 1995). Moreover, courts have consistently applied this standard and have developed a body of supporting case law. For example, *Roth v. Lutheran General Hospital*, 57 F.3d 1446, 1454 (7th Cir. 1995) affirmed this principle, stating, "The term 'substantially limits' means that the individual is either unable to perform, or significantly restricted as to the condition, manner or duration under which the individual can perform, a major life activity as compared to an average person in the general population." The fact that someone may have difficulty with certain tasks, such as test taking, does not constitute the proper definition of a disability. Similarly,

the inability to achieve goals one sets for oneself, in spite of hard work, cannot be the proper definition of a disability. Thus, the court noted in *Pazer v. New York State Bd. of Law Examiners*, 849 F.Supp. 284 (S.D.N.Y. 1994), that "to hold otherwise would compel the conclusion that any underachiever would by definition be learning disabled as a matter of law" (*Id* at 287). Likewise, in *Price v. National Bd. of Medical Examiners*, 966 F.Supp. 419 (S.D.W.Va. 1997), the court stated:

> Accordingly, to determine whether an individual is substantially limited in performing a major life activity, Congress would have this Court measure the extent to which the alleged impairment limits the individual against the abilities of most unimpaired persons. (966 F. supp. at 425)

The Supreme Court has recently affirmed this construal of disability in four separate cases.

In light of the average-person standard, a conservation application of the law would likely exclude special accommodations for most college and graduate students. Furthermore, institutions that for whatever reason choose to adhere closely to ADA guidelines will often invoke the ire of students and advocates. Individuals who, thanks to the more liberal definitions of disability inherent in special education laws, received accommodations in high school may now find their college-level requests denied (Gordon & Keiser, 1998).

At first blush, the ADA's definition of disability may seem unduly restrictive and, more importantly, a potential springboard for discrimination against individuals with learning problems. If the average-person standard were to become the basis for LD determinations in the postsecondary population, many colleges, especially those serving high achievers, would not be *legally required* to provide services (although they might well find it justifiable to help their students informally and voluntarily). This prospect understandably generates intense concern within the special education community.

Although we share reservations about any overly restrictive application of an ADA-type definition of disability, we feel it only fair to ask the following admittedly provocative question: Is the average-person standard really such a bad yardstick for judging disability, even for the clinical diagnosis of LD? Asked another way, Might not the concept of "gifted or high-functioning LD" ultimately cause more harm than good in both a legal and an educational context?

In answering those questions, we think that the following points should be considered:

1. *Only in the LD arena are intraindividual discrepancies considered sufficient for the identification of a disability.* A purely relativistic approach to disability determination is indeed unique to learning disabilities (with the possible exception of speech and language disorders). For example, no physician would ever consider declaring an individual physically disabled if the patient were an unusually fast runner but only an average thrower. Nor would any doctor take seriously someone of average height who claimed a disability because he was shorter than others on a college basketball team. Similarly, vision specialists would not certify a visual handicap for an individual with only normal near vision but superior distance vision. Even other psychiatric disorders require "clinically significant impairment" before a diagnosis is deemed appropriate. All of these determinations hinge on demonstration of actual abnormality. Yet, somehow it is acceptable to identify a learning disability in individuals who are not functionally impaired relative to most people. It has become sufficient to simply establish that a student is not equally talented across the broad spectrum of cognitive and academic abilities. The LD label will often be assigned to bright and capable individuals who may not be achieving quite as well (or as easily) as some other bright and capable individuals. In fact, a bright, unmotivated student will qualify for LD classification more easily than a hardworking student with generally below-average capabilities.

2. *Superior intelligence is not necessarily a ticket to superior achievement.* A fundamental assumption underlying assignment of the LD label to relative underperformers is that someone with a high IQ should be a high achiever. According to this notion, IQ scores reflect innate ability that should allow for commensurate performance. If an individual fails to achieve at a level equal to his or her measured IQ, it must be due to a disorder or disability. This assumption is almost impossible to justify. IQ measures are poor predictors of ultimate achievement or outcome (Neisser et al., 1996; Smith, 1998). Although they may show fair correlation with concurrent achievement, they typically account for less than half of the variance in predictions of performance in college, training programs, or actual employment. Other factors, such as social judgment, impulse control, motivation, and what Goleman (1995) popularized under the rubric of "emotional intelligence" also contribute significantly to ultimate attainment. Simply put, high intelligence is never a guarantee of success, nor is it a birthright to superior achievement. It is therefore hard to rationalize the following type of statement we clinicians are apt to make in reports: "The LD diagnosis is justified because this very intelligent student is not achieving to potential." We can find no empirical justification for claiming that IQ alone somehow determines a set point for an individual's expected level of achievement. We also question the oft-stated view that IQ tests measure innate potential, whereas achievement tests assess current functioning (See Siegel, 1999). Too much academic ability is required for performance on IQ tests to allow for such a pure distinction to be drawn.

3. *Intraindividual discrepancies are common.* Another IQ-related assumption underlying relativistic determinations of disability is that discrepancies among skills almost necessarily reflect pathology. For example, diagnosticians will often justify an LD designation for students who demonstrate significant differences between their verbal and nonverbal abilities. Some clinicians are also apt to invoke a learning disability when certain IQ or achievement subtests, although still average, fall below more superior abilities. The implied assumption in this approach to diagnosis is that someone who is very good in one area should be very good in all. Conversely, any intraindividual differences must be pathognomonic. However, empirical data simply do not support this. Ysseldyke, Algozzine, and Epps (1983) noted that up to 25% of normal achievers would be classified as LD according to one or another discrepancy formula. Furthermore, Kavale and Forness (1984) reviewed 94 studies of students with LD and found no discernible IQ profiles or patterns that differentiated children with LD from those without LD. It has also been suggested that some students with relatively high IQ scores (greater than 120) will record lower achievement tests scores merely because of regression effects (Spear-Swerling & Sternberg, 1998). Many of us (although some more than others) have areas of significant strengths and weaknesses. Is it sensible to characterize normal variations in talents as necessarily pathological?

4. *The cognitive glass may be half full (as opposed to half empty).* A common practice in LD diagnosis is to establish the highest scores on testing as the indication of aptitude. If a student has exceptional skills in one or more domains of functioning, that level of ability is often considered to reflect "innate potential." Any areas that are merely average are therefore considered to reflect a relative deficit compared to that benchmark. But why is someone who is average in spelling but outstanding in reading comprehension and math considered disabled in spelling—why is he or she not just considered to be unusually good at math and reading comprehension? Are all relative *inabilities* properly characterized as *disabilities*?

5. *Etiology does not determine disability.* Research on the neuropsychological underpinnings of reading disorders has received considerable attention both within professional journals and from the national media. Many point to these findings, especially in the realm of phonological awareness, as evidence of the legitimacy and persistence of learning disabilities (Blackman, 1997). Although such data are exciting and may illuminate certain factors that contribute to reading problems, they are largely irrelevant to determinations of disability. Unfortunately, group differences on neuroimaging, electrophysiological, or neuropsychological measures do not translate into predictors of group status for individual cases, nor do they serve as markers for severity of impairment. Indeed, the predictive validity of such variables is extremely limited. Therefore, what must qualify an individual as disabled is evidence of *functional impairment*. Why someone is impaired, although certainly important for other considerations, is less pertinent to these disability-related decisions. For example, whether an individual is blind because of an inherited disorder or an industrial accident is of little concern to the ophthalmologist charged with certifying the disability. The central consideration is always the degree of functional impairment.

6. *Developmental disorders should arise during development.* A learning disability is a developmental disorder that, by definition, should become manifest during childhood. Any neuropsychological deficits underlying these disorders should therefore have their impact at the point when the associated skills are typically acquired and mastered. Individuals with deficits in phonological awareness, for example,

will likely manifest problems between preschool and second grade, when they are first taught to read. Although other sorts of processing problems may have a somewhat later impact (depending on the rate of instruction and the nature of the skill), most should, theoretically, have a relatively early onset. With the mantle of disability being extended to include those with only relative discrepancies, however, standards for age of onset are creeping upward. Diagnosticians are now routinely identifying learning disabilities in postsecondary students who never encountered meaningful impairment during high school or, in many cases, even college. Those professionals justify this by claiming that the affected individual, although able to compensate in the past through hard work and high intelligence, eventually reached an educational level that prompted the appearance of symptoms. By this logic, of course, human nature is a disability waiting to happen. Accordingly, all of us are potentially disabled if we pursue educational options that eventually outstrip our particular array of abilities. But if an individual is basically able to manage all the academic demands of a typical high school program, isn't he or she likely to be neuropsychologically intact? Might not any educational setbacks be better attributed to other factors?

7. *Diagnoses based on comparisons to an educational cohort can create a slippery slope.* One argument against the ADA's average-person standard is that it establishes an unfair comparison group. To qualify as disabled, why should a law student have to perform abnormally compared to the general population? Shouldn't it be enough that certain scores fall below what is typical of other law students? As we see it, the problem with this logic is that it essentially leads to the conclusion that you are disabled relative to the company you keep. If the comparison sample is others of similar occupational aspirations, then the concept of disability becomes wildly distorted. Conceivably, any one of us might be considered nondisabled in one educational program (e.g., respiratory therapy) but find ourselves disabled in another, perhaps more competitive academic setting (e.g., medical school). Under such a metric, poor matches between individual abilities and career choice can quickly rise to the level of a disability. A struggling law student might not be disabled, she might just have made a poor choice of program or career. However, under a cohort-based comparison, she could be considered disabled.

8. *A relativistic LD definition heightens the chances that consistently average individuals will be treated unfairly.* A serious problem with assigning an LD label to students who in absolute terms function normally is that it opens the door to discrimination against others. Consider two students, Joe and Fred, who are both enrolled in a college English course. Joe, who has generally average abilities across the board, would never qualify for an LD label. Fred, on the other hand, was identified as LD because his average scores in reading comprehension compared poorly to his other, more exceptional skills and to his high IQ. On the basis of this designation, the university granted Fred extra time for examinations. Even though both Joe and Fred are average in reading comprehension, Fred gets a clear advantage on timed tests simply because he is *even better* in other academic domains. It would be easy to understand why Joe might feel that he is being treated unfairly. From his viewpoint, the playing field is tilted in Fred's favor because professionals and administrators want to make sure that the brighter student has the best chance of performing above average. And, because accommodations are often unrestricted, Joe might also be upset to learn that Fred probably gets extra time on *all* tests, not just those that have a heavy demand for reading comprehension. Why should Fred get extra time even on a calculus test, which involves little reading? And, to add the proverbial insult to injury, how fair is it that Fred will likely get extra time on important tests such as the LSAT, GRE, or MCAT, even though Joe would certainly also benefit from such an accommodation?

9. *Liberal assignment of the LD label diminishes resources available to the more impaired.* One of the risks inherent in broad definitions of disability is that monies, energies, and services will be spread too thin. A segment of the population that surely suffers from a dilution of resources includes individuals with frank abnormalities. Schools have limited numbers of resource rooms, special education personnel, and psychologists available to assist individuals in need. In the zero-sum world of school budgets, already scarce services rendered to a high-functioning student with relative discrepancies will diminish remedial opportunities for those with absolute impairments. In fact, the group that may suffer the most from the current system are students with low-average cognitive abilities whose academic performance, while poor, is not sufficiently discrepant from measured IQ to qualify as a disability. Such students are less apt to produce a significant cognitive/academic discrepancy because there is less statistical room along the normal curve for the academic scores to fall. Therefore, students with low-average IQs will likely be most neglected by a discrepancy model. This practice serves to delimit LD classifications for students from culturally diverse backgrounds (McLeskey, Waldron, & Wornhoff, 1990).

10. *It is not necessarily a boon to students with uneven abilities to be designated as disabled.* The common justification for granting accommodations to students with at least average abilities is that they should have every chance of fulfilling their potential and aspirations. To deny these individuals that extra time or special note taker is therefore viewed as a needless impediment to a successful career. (Incidentally, this assumption runs into headlong conflict with the aim of the ADA, which was to promote equal access and opportunity, not maximize outcome or guarantee success.) It may be, however, that addressing the academic problems of these students with "high functioning LD" through legal accommodations can be counterproductive. Resorting too quickly to LD-based explanations for failure or perceived underachievement often distracts students and educators from exploring other explanations for academic difficulties: inadequate instruction, limited motivation, poor study habits, ill-advised course selection, psychiatric factors, or inappropriate expectations. Another concern is that, especially in higher education, problem solving through declarations of disability can distort the process by which individuals normally find their way to a suitable career. An example: Casey wants to become a doctor but finds college calculus and organic chemistry daunting. Before the advent of legal accommodations, he might have responded to his low grades in these courses by rethinking his career plans. He might have transferred to a program that better fit his own particular matrix of abilities. However, nowadays he has the option of trying to gain accommodation through being identified as learning disabled. Implementation of accommodations may postpone what perhaps is the inevitable—that a career in medicine is not for him. Meanwhile, precious time and money are lost.

We hope that the points we have made here raise legitimate questions about the practice of assigning LD labels to individuals whose worst functioning is still average. For legal determinations, the ADA generally casts a dim view on this approach to qualifying an individual as disabled. However, it might also be that an ADA-style average-person standard for judgments of impairment should serve as a rough guideline for clinical assessment, even when formal accommodations are not germane. In many respects, such a model is easiest to justify on conceptual, empirical, and administrative grounds. This stance is in keeping with models of LD championed by Siegel (1999), Stanovich (1999), and other experts, all of whom are calling for a new approach to LD identification based on actual and substantial academic impairment.

An entirely fair rejoinder to this position is as follows: If an LD label required absolute impairment, then we would be denying special help for all those individuals who, despite normal functioning, still struggle in one or more areas. In so doing, we would eliminate the means by which parents and postsecondary students can force educational institutions to tailor programming for individuals who, although not grossly impaired, could do better. Although these institutions should, without legal requirement, make reasonable accommodations, they often do not. Tampering with the LD label may risk the integrity of an important force for good.

The issue, therefore, turns on whether it is justified to blur definitions of disability and lower diagnostic standards to effect changes in educational policy and practice. Should the LD label serve as a tool for improving our school systems and advocating for students who do not meet strict diagnostic criteria, but who require somewhat more attention or flexibility in their programming? But might such use of diagnosis drain resources from efforts to improve education generally and provide services for those who are more seriously impaired?

Our questioning of the assumptions underlying a relativistic LD label, particularly when it is applied to those seeking legal accommodations, is not intended as a broadside against the field. We simply worry that theoretical and operational definitions of LD have been twisted, stretched, and battered beyond recognition. It certainly is a different set of concepts from the ones introduced by Werner, Strauss, Kirk, Cruikshank, Myklebust, and other pioneers of the LD field, all of whom worked more with moderately to severely impaired learners than with bright, advantaged weak readers. Professionals, parents, and policymakers may want to reconsider who truly warrants an LD label, special education services, and legal accommodations. Unless such issues are examined forthrightly, the LD arena will become increasingly vulnerable to public skepticism and budgetary axes.

ABOUT THE AUTHORS

Michael Gordon, PhD, is a professor of psychiatry and director of the ADHD program at SUNY Health Science Center in Syracuse, New York. His interests include the assessment of externalizing disorders, concepts underlying disability determinations, and community-oriented parenting programs. Lawrence Lewandowski, PhD, is a professor of psychology and director of the Clinical Neuropsychological Laboratory at Syracuse University. His research and writing activities cover neuropsychological, cognitive, psychosocial, and developmental aspects of learning disabilities and related disorders. Shelby Keiser is manager of the Office of Test Accommodations at the National Board of Medical Examiners. She is a member of the AHEAD Ad Hoc Committee on Documentation of Learning Disabilities and the Consortium on Documentation of ADHD. Address: Michael Gordon, SUNY Health Science Center, 750 East Adams St., Syracuse, NY 13210.

REFERENCES

Algozzine, B., & Ysseldyke, J. E. (1986). The future of the LD field: Screening and diagnosis. *Journal of Learning Disabilities, 19,* 394–398.

American Psychiatric Association. (1994). *Diagnostic and statistical manual of mental disorders* (4th ed.). Washington, DC: Author.

Blachman, B. (1997). *Foundations of reading acquisition and dyslexia.* Mahwah, NJ: Erlbaum.

Frankenberger, W., & Harper, J. (1987). States' criteria and procedures for identifying learning disabilities in children: A comparison of 1981/82 and 1985/86 guidelines. *Journal of Learning Disabilities, 20,* 118–121.

Goleman, D. (1995). *Emotional intelligence: Why it can matter more than IQ.* New York: Bantam Books.

Gordon, M., & Keiser, S. (Eds.). (1998). *Accommodations in higher education under the Americans with Disabilities Act (ADA): A nonsense guide for clinicians, educators, administrators, and lawyers.* New York: Guilford Publications.

Gottlieb, J., Alter, M., Gottlieb, B. W., & Wishner, J. (1994). Special education in urban America: It's not justifiable for many. *The Journal of Special Education, 27,* 453–465.

Gregg, N., Hoy, C., & Gay, A. F. (Eds.). (1996). *Adults with learning disabilities: Theoretical and practical perspectives* (pp. 66–84). New York: Guilford Press.

Kavale, K. A., & Forness, S. R. (1984). A meta-analysis of the validity of Wechsler Scale profiles and recategorizations: Patterns or parodies? *Learning Disability Quarterly, 7,* 136–156.

Kelman, M., & Lester, G. (1997). *Jumping the queue.* Cambridge, MA: Harvard University Press.

Lorry, B. (1998). Learning disabilities. In M. Gordon & S. Keiser (Eds.), *Accommodations in higher education under the Americans with Disabilities Act (ADA): A no-nonsense guide for clinicians, educators, administrators, and lawyers* (pp. 130–153). New York: Guilford Publications.

Neisser, U., Boodoo, G., Bouchaard, T. J., Boykin, A. S., Brody, N., Ceci, S. J., Halpern, D. F., Loehlin, J. C., Perloff, R., Sternberg, R. J., & Urbina, S. (1996). Intelligence: Knowns and unknowns. *American Psychologist, 51,* 77–101.

Roth v. Lutheran General Hospital, 57 F.3d 1446 (7th Cir. 1995).

Pazer v. New York State Bd. of Law Examiners, 849 F.Supp. 284 (S.D.N.Y. 1994).

Price v. National Bd. of Medical Examiners, 966 F.Supp. 419 (S.D.W.Va. 1997).

Siegel, L. S. (1999). Issues in the definition of and diagnosis of learning disabilities: A perspective on Guckenberger v. Boston University. *Journal of Learning Disabilities, 32*(4), 304–319.

Silver, L. B. (1988). A review of the federal government's Interagency Committee of Learning Disabilities Report to the U.S. Congress. *Learning Disabilities Focus, 3,* 73–80.

Smith, C. R. (1998). *Learning disabilities: The interaction of learner, task, and setting* (4th ed.). Needham Heights, MA: Allyn & Bacon.

Spear-Swerling, L., & Sternberg, R. J. (1998). Curing our "epidemic" of learning disabilities. *Phi Delta Kappan, 79,* 397–401.

Stanovich, K. E. (1991). Discrepancy definitions of learning disability: Has intelligence led us astray? *Reading Research Quarterly, 26,* 7–29.

Stanovich, K. E. (1999). The sociopsychometrics of learning disabilities. *Journal of Learning Disabilities, 32*(4), 350–361.

U.S. Office of Education. (1997). *Nineteenth annual report to Congress on the implementation of the Individuals with Disabilities Education Act.* Washington, DC: U.S. Department of Education.

Ysseldyke, J. E., Algozzine, B., & Epps, S. (1983). A logical and empirical analysis of current practice in classifying students as handicapped. *Exceptional Children, 50,* 160–166.

Good Mentoring Keeps At-Risk Youth in School

*Psychologists develop mentoring programs that encourage students
to stay in school and improve their performance.*

Bridget Murray

Monitor staff

Sandra Castellanos, a Houston community activist, wasn't surprised when officials at a local high school expelled Crystal, a young girl she was mentoring. She knew Crystal had been skipping school and blamed her behavior on "a bad crowd" Crystal had become friendly with.

On Castellanos's suggestion, Crystal apologized to the school principal and was allowed back. Now Castellanos is helping Crystal pay more attention to the consequences of her actions, encouraging her to run with a tamer crowd and concentrate on her schoolwork.

Instances like this and research by psychologists prove that mentoring relationships keep kids in school. Mentors give kids a sense of personal connection and encouragement to function well, academically and socially.

As an added bonus, mentors sometimes boost students' academic performance by providing tutoring. In fact, psychologist Ellen Slicker, PhD, of Middle Tennessee State University, found a 100 percent retention rate for well-mentored sophomores in a study she conduced in Houston's Spring High School in the late 1980s. Every student who had a positive mentoring experience returned to school in the fall after the mentoring intervention.

MENTORS GIVE KIDS A SENSE OF PERSONAL CONNECTION AND ENOURAGEMENT TO FUNCTION WELL, BOTH ACADEMICALLY AND SOCIALLY.

Mentoring programs for 12- to 17-year olds gained popularity after 1990 U.S. Census figures showed a national high school dropout rate averaging 12 percent. Some urban areas battle dropout rates of up to 50 percent.

Dropout prevention is among several objectives in the federal government's National Education Goals. Psychologists have played an important role in coordinating and evaluating mentoring programs that bring these rates down, said Ronda C. Tally, PhD, director of the APA Center for Psychology in School and Education.

A Sense of Belonging

Slicker and her then-colleague at Texas A & M University, Douglas Palmer, PhD, studied how well Spring High School's mentoring program kept its dropout rate in check.

"Kids need to feel a sense of belonging and mentors help give them that," said Slicker. "A good mentor is someone who cares, someone who helps them feel a part of the school."

The relationship needn't be extensive, just consistent, said Rick Short, PhD, head of the APA Education Directorate's Center of Education and Training in Psychology.

"What's important is that the mentor stop by regularly, just to make sure the kid's in school and to see how things are going," said Short, who helped run mentoring programs in Kentucky schools.

In their study, Slicker and Palmer monitored mentors assigned to 86 students identified as high risk for dropping out due to low skills, bad grades and poor behavior records. Mentors were volunteer school personnel, including teachers, secretaries and teacher aides. They received special training and instructions.

During school, the mentors talked with students at their lockers between classes and met them for lunch. They kept records of the level and consistency of their mentoring activities.

The results indicated that poorly mentored students dropped out more than controls who received no mentoring at all. The poorer mentors failed to keep a stable relationship with their students. They met with the kids irregularly if at all, which caused students to lose faith in them and feel abandoned. The research suggests that at-risk kids want an adult to be available, supportive and trustworthy, said Slicker. The mentor has to keep regular appointments and show confidence in the student's abilities.

'Check and Connect'

The Partnership for School Success, a school dropout prevention project run by the University of Minnesota and the Minneapolis Public Schools, relies heavily on a mentoring component. Funded by the U.S. Department of Education, the program seeks to keep seventh- and eighth- graders with learning and emotional/behavioral disabilities from leaving school.

Using a "check-and-connect" procedure, mentors monitor students regularly for signs of truancy, acting out or academic failure, and work to connect them with services that address risk factors, said school psychologist Sandra Christenson, PhD, one of the program's principal investigators. Mentors solicit teachers, parents, administrators and community outreach workers to provide help to kids. They link students with academic supports, community service projects and recreational activities.

Mentors meet with youth at least once a week. They establish a friendship with the youth, talk to them about the economic costs of dropping out and prepare them to deal with potential challenges through social problem-solving. The mentor works through attendance problems with the child, for instance, using a five-step strategy:

- What are some choices?
- Choose one.
- Do it.
- How did it work?

The project extends traditional mentoring to include checking on students' behaviors consistently over time and immediately connecting students with pertinent interventions, said Christenson.

Nontraditional Models

Some schools, like Canton Middle School in east Baltimore, encourage mentoring relationships among students themselves.

In the early 1990s Canton paired up sixth- and eighth-graders, assigned them to work on arts-and-crafts projects and encouraged them to volunteer for philanthropic activities. Although older eighth-graders played more of a mentor role as they oriented incoming sixth-graders to the school, the general idea was to improve social skills and establish ties across grades, said an investigating psychologist, Kenneth Maton, PhD, of the University of Maryland-Baltimore County.

Other programs pair students with members of the community. Besides bad grades, a lack of friends and low participation in extracurricular activities predict dropout, Short says. Mentoring programs involve kids in the community to help build their commitment to school.

In Chicago's inner city, for example, psychologist Jean Rhodes, PhD, recruits volunteers to mentor pregnant African-American teenagers at the Simpson Alternative School. Many of the mentors are Simpson graduates who have established careers in the community.

"Mentors show the teens how successful you can be if you finish school and don't get pregnant again," said Rhodes.

A psychology professor at the University of Illinois, Rhodes is principal investigator in the five-year mentoring project, which is partially funded by the National Institute of Children's Health and Human Development.

In Washington, D.C., the Capital Partners for Education program pairs at-risk kids from inner-city schools with community leaders. Local lawyers, government officials and bankers take students to dinners and baseball games, help them with homework and call them regularly to check on their progress.

Whether mentors are parents, teachers, community leaders or older schoolmates, they may provide youths with the best incentive to get an education, Short says.

"There's nothing like a relationship to get someone to do something," he said.

Schools the source of rough transitions

Psychologists study the difficulties children face when they move from elementary school to middle school.

By Beth Azar
Monitor staff

In September, thousands of 10- to 12-year-old children will face one of the most critical transitions of their lives—the move from elementary school to middle school. For some, it sparks a downward spiral that can lead to school failure and withdrawal.

The switch from elementary school to junior high school coincides with several major changes for young adolescents. Most are in the throes of puberty; they're becoming more self-aware and self-conscious, and their thinking is growing more critical and complex. At the same time, parents and junior high teachers and parents complain that their students are flagging both in motivation and performance.

Traditionally, parents, teachers and even researchers blamed puberty alone for what they branded as inevitable declines in academic drive and achievement. But research psychologists are amassing evidence which shows that the environment and philosophy of middle schools often conflict with the needs of young adolescents. Researchers are using developmental theories of motivation to explain this conflict and to show how children can avoid failure in middle school.

ADOLESCENTS

Developmental mismatch

Since the early 1980s, psychologist Jacqueline Eccles, PhD, of the University of Michigan, and her colleagues, have collected data on the transition from elementary school to middle school. They've found that:

• On average, children's grades drop dramatically during the first year of middle school, compared to grades in elementary school.

• After moving to junior high, children become less interested in school and less self-assured about their abilities.

• Compared to elementary schools, middle schools are more controlling, less cognitively challenging, and focus more on competition and comparing students' ability.

The differences between elementary schools and middle schools cause what Eccles and her University of Michigan colleague Carol Midgely, PhD, call "developmental mismatch." They've found that middle school children report fewer opportunities for decision-making and lower levels of cognitive involvement than they had in elementary school, said Eccles' colleague, Eric Anderman, PhD, of the University of Kentucky.

At the same time, children must contend with a more complex social environment. They switch from a single teacher who knows their academic and social strengths to brief contact with many teachers. And they often face larger classes with a new group of peers.

These variables interact to make the transition to middle school challenging, said Anderman. Studies find that decreased motivation and self-assuredness contribute to poor academic performance. They have also found that drops in grades triggered by the transition can alter self-assuredness and motivation.

Goal setting

To better explain how these environmental changes affect students, some researchers have turned to goal-orientation theory, developed by Carol Ames, PhD, and her colleagues at Michigan State University. The theory identifies two types of goals that motivate people to achieve in school.

Task goals encourage learning for learning's sake—people concentrate on mastering a task, rather than striving for an expected grade. Performance goals favor learning for performance's sake—people desire a good grade to prove their competence to others or to achieve a particular end, such as parental approval.

Everyone subscribes to both types of goals, said Midgely. We want to expand our knowledge base *and* get

---

"For the low achievers, the transition to the new environment sparks a downward spiral that they can't seem to recover from."

Eric Anderman, PhD
University of Kentucky

---

good grades. But most people lean more toward one than the other. Transition researchers speculate that elementary schools are more task-focused and middle schools are more performance-focused.

This shift may throw children off balance during the transition. Indeed, several studies find that students become less task-oriented and more performance-oriented as they move from elementary to middle school, and students believe their middle-school teachers focus more on performance than tasks. At the same time, their belief in their own academic ability decreases dramatically, the studies find.

A study by Anderman and Midgely found that grades decreased more for middle-school students who had been low achievers in elementary school than for those who had been high-achieving students at the elementary level. By the year after the transition, high achievers seemed to have bounced back from first-year grade

declines while low achievers failed to rebound.

"For the low achievers, the transition to the new environment sparks a downward spiral that they can't seem to recover from," said Anderman.

These longitudinal studies suggest that changes in a child's goal orientation occur during the transition and these changes correlate with declines in motivation and performance, said Midgely. However, they don't prove that one causes the other. It's important to look beyond mean changes across big groups of students, she admits.

Carole Dweck, PhD, of Columbia University, agrees. She's found that some children thrive after the transition to middle school while others are particularly prone to failure.

The key is how they think about intelligence, she asserts. She found that children who think about intelligence as fixed—known as entity theorists—avoid tasks that challenge their ability or that risk failure. They instead choose to work on problems they know how to solve. Dweck calls this response pattern maladaptive or helpless. She believes it coincides with performance goals because the children prefer performing well to mastering something new.

Children who think about intelligence as malleable—known as incremental theorists—embrace challenging tasks and look at failure as a way to learn and improve. They tend to blame their failures on a lack of effort rather than a lack of ability. Dweck calls this response pattern mastery-oriented and believes it coincides with task goals.

Because elementary schools don't emphasize performance or failure vs. success, the differences between the two types of theorists should not show up until after the transition to junior high school, said Dweck.

In a study of 165 seventh-grade students, one year after the transition to junior high, she found an overall decline in academic achievement, compared with scores from sixth grade.

But not all students' grades declined. Indeed, while confidence in one's ability seemed to predict grades in elementary school—high confidence children had the highest grades—intelligence theory took over in junior high. The grades of high-confidence incremental theorists stayed level but those of high-confidence entity theorists sank. Also, the grades of low-confidence incremental theorists soared while those of low-confidence entity theorists remained as low as in sixth grade.

"These high-confidence kids who think intelligence is fixed, think that you should be able to do well without a lot of effort if you're smart," said Dweck. That strategy didn't work in the more challenging middle school, where teachers judged performance not based on general knowledge but on task performance.

Meanwhile, the low-confidence incremental theorists blossomed in their new environment. They were more willing to face the challenge, said Dweck.

These studies imply that not all children will suffer a drop in academic performance when they enter middle school. However, both the school environment and children's goals and attitudes about learning and intelligence need to be re-evaluated, the researchers agree.

During the school-reform boom of the 1980s, middle schools were largely ignored, according to the final report of the Carnegie Council on Adolescent Development, released last year. That omission needs to be addressed and the research on adolescent motivation and school environment included in reform efforts, the report says.

The Cheating Game

'Everyone's doing it,' from grade school to graduate school

BY CAROLYN KLEINER AND MARY LORD

Umpteen pages to plow through for honors English, anatomy, and U.S. history. . . . Geometry problems galore. . . . It was a typical weeknight for high school sophomore Leah Solowsky. Before tackling her first assignment—a Spanish essay on healthy eating—the honor-roll student logged on to her computer to chat with pals. Suddenly, it hit her: Perhaps she could download some of her workload.

Solowsky cruised to the AltaVista search engine, clicked on "Spanish," and typed in *"la dieta."* Fifteen minutes later, she had everything she needed to know about fruits, vegetables, and grains—all in flawless *español*. She quickly retyped the information and handed in her paper the next day. "I had a ton of homework, I wasn't doing that well in the class, and I felt, hey, this is one way to boost my grade," explains Solowsky, now a junior with a B-plus average at the highly competitive Gul-

D FOR DECEIT

Academic dishonesty is as much a part of school as blackboards and backpacks. The vast majority of students say they believe you must cheat to get ahead.

liver Preparatory School in Miami. "I didn't think it was cheating because I didn't even stop to think about it."

Every day across America, millions of students from middle school to medical school face similar ethical quandaries—and research indicates that most choose to cheat. In a recent survey conducted by *Who's Who Among American High School Students*, 80 percent of high-achieving high schoolers admitted to having cheated at least once; half said they did not believe cheating was necessarily wrong—and 95 percent of the cheaters said they have never been

caught. According to the Center for Academic Integrity at Duke University, three quarters of college students confess to cheating at least once. And a new *U.S. News* poll found 90 percent of college kids believe cheaters never pay the price.*

Crib sheets and copying answers are nothing new, of course. What's changed, experts maintain, is the scope of the problem: the technology that opens new avenues to cheat, students' boldness in using it, and the erosion of conscience at every level of education. "I'm scared to death," says Emporia State University psychology Prof. Stephen Davis, who recently expanded his study of cheating to graduate students—including those in

*U.S. News poll of 1,000 adults (including an over-sample of 200 college students) conducted by Celinda Lake of Lake Snell Perry & Associates and Ed Goeas of the Tarrance Group, Oct. 18–23, 1999. Margin of error: plus or minus 3.5 percent.

According to an exclusive *U.S. News* poll, **84%** of college students believe they need to cheat to get ahead in the world today.

medical school. "I hope I never get a brain disease."

Cheating arts. Academic fraud has never been easier. Students can tamper electronically with grade records, transmit quiz answers via pager or cell phone, and lift term papers from hundreds of Web sites. At the same time, an overload of homework combined with intense pressure to excel in school, from hard-driving peers and parents, makes cheating easy to justify—and hard to resist. Valedictorians are as likely to cheat as laggards, and girls have closed the gap with boys. In fact, the only thing that makes Leah Solowsky's case unusual is that she got caught—earning a zero on her Spanish paper and getting barred from the National Honor Society.

Sissela Bok, author of *Lying: Moral Choice in Public and Private Life,* suspects part of the problem may be that "people are very confused [about] what is meant by cheating." When does taking information off the Internet constitute research, and when is it plagiarism? Where does collaboration end and collusion begin? The rules just aren't that clear, particularly given the growing number of schools that stress teamwork. The result: widespread homework copying among students and a proliferation of sophisticated sixth-grade science projects and exquisitely crafted college applications that bear the distinct stamp of parental "involvement."

Most alarming to researchers is the pervasiveness of cheating among adolescents. What begins as penny-ante dishonesty in elementary school—stealing Pokémon cards or glancing at a neighbor's spelling test—snowballs into more serious cheating in middle and high school, as enrollments swell and students start moving from class to class, teacher to teacher. Professor Davis, who has gathered data on more than 17,000 students, notes that 50 years ago, only about 1 in 5 college students admitted to having cheated in high school. Today, a range of studies shows that figure has exploded, to anywhere from three quarters of students to an astonishing 98 percent.

SAM, A JUNIOR AT THE UNIVERSITY OF ALA-bama, can barely recall the first time he cheated. He thinks it must have started back in middle school, copying the occasional math assignment or printing a key formula on his forearm. (Like other current cheaters quoted in this article, Sam asked that his real name be withheld.) A decade later he is still at it, most recently lifting a paper on post-Civil War racism off the Internet. "I realize that it's wrong, but I don't feel bad about it, either, partly because I know everyone else is doing it," says Sam in a deep Southern drawl. "If I ever stole a test or something to that degree, I'd feel guilty. But just getting a couple of answers here and there doesn't bother me."

Competition for admission to elite colleges has transformed the high school years into a high-stakes race where top students compete for a spot on the sweet end of the curve. It has also spawned a new breed of perpetrator: the smart cheater. In the *Who's Who* survey, the country's top juniors and seniors talked about copying homework, plagiarizing, or otherwise cheating their way to the head of the class. "Grades are so important to these kids," sighs RevaBeth Russell, an advanced-placement biology teacher at Lehi High School in Utah, who has seen copying incidents skyrocket as collegebound students from prosperous families settle in the rural area.

CANDID CAMERA
A few test takers each year use video cameras hidden in, say, ties, to broadcast questions to an outside ringer, who calls the answers into a silent pager.

What's going on. The notion that schools are awash with cheaters doesn't always square with what administrators say goes on in their classrooms and corridors. "My goodness, the students are 12-, 13-, 14-year-old kids, and sometimes they make a bad decision," says Gary McGuigan, principal of the H. E. Huntington Middle School in San Marino, Calif. "But [cheating] isn't rampant." Sunny Hills High School in nearby Fullerton weathered two major cheating scandals in two years involving more than a dozen honor-roll students, yet principal Loring Davies insists these are "isolated" incidents.

But in scores of interviews in a cross section of communities nationwide, students gave *U.S. News* a strikingly different reading of the situation. "We all know that cheating is cheating, and we shouldn't do it," says Melissa, a student at Duke University. "But there are times that you cheat because there aren't enough hours in the day." Case in point: last month, Melissa found herself with a computer programming assignment due in a few hours—and several hours of driving to do at the same time. So she had a friend copy his program and turn it in for her. "It's not a big deal because it's just a mindless assignment," rationalizes Melissa. "It's not a final or a midterm. I mean, I understood how to do it; I just didn't have the time."

Most distressing to teachers is the way plagiarism, copying, and similar deceits devalue learning. "We're somehow not able to convince them of the importance of the process," laments Connie Eberly, an English teacher at J. I. Case High School in Racine, Wis. "It's the product that counts." For too many students and their parents, getting that diploma—that scholarship, that grant—is more important than acquiring knowledge. "I'm just trying to do everything I can do to get through this school," acknowledges Brad, a junior at an exclusive Northeastern boarding school and a veritable encyclopedia of cheating tips. (Feign illness on test days and get the questions from classmates before taking a makeup exam. Answer multiple-choice questions with 'c'—a letter that can easily be altered and submitted for a regrade.) "If this is the only way to do it, so be it," he says.

The pressure to succeed, particularly on high-stakes tests, can drive students to consider extreme measures. Two months ago, nothing mattered more to Manuel than doing well on the SAT. "If your score is high, then you get into [a good school] and scholarships come to you," explains the high school senior

90% of college students say cheaters never pay the price; 90% say when people see someone cheating, they don't turn him in.

from Houston, who is going to have to cover half of his college expenses himself. "If not, then you go to some community college, make little money, and end up doing nothing important the rest of your life." Desperate for a competitive edge, he started poking around the Net and soon stumbled upon an out-of-the-way message board where students bragged about snagging copies of the test. Manuel posted his own note, begging for help; he says he got a reply offering a faxed copy of the exam for $150 but ultimately chickened out.

While crib notes and other time-honored techniques have yet to go out of style, advanced technology is giving slackers a new edge. The Internet provides seemingly endless opportunities for cheating, from online term-paper mills to chat rooms where students can swap science projects and math solutions. They also share test questions via E-mail between classes and hack into school mainframes to alter transcripts; they use cell phones to dial multiple-choice answers into alphanumeric pagers (1C2A3D) and store everything from algebra formulas to notes on *Jane Eyre* in cutting-edge calculators. Some devices even have infrared capabilities, allowing students to zap information across a classroom. "I get the sense there's a thrill to it, that 'my teachers are too dumb to catch me,'" says English teacher Eberly.

Cram artists. As the stakes rise—from acing spelling tests, say, to slam-dunking the *SAT*—so does the complexity of the scam. "It's a constant race to keep up with what people are doing," says Gregg Colton, a Florida private investigator who serves as a security consultant for a dozen licensure and testing organizations. His biggest concern is "cram schools" that charge test takers hundreds to thousands of dollars for the chance to study a dubiously obtained copy of an exam in advance. In one notorious case, a California man sold answer-encoded pencils to hundreds of students taking graduate school entrance exams for up to $9,000 a pop; ringers had sat for the test in New York, then phoned the results across the coun-

SIGN LANGUAGE

Who needs technology? At one school in Florida, seventh graders learned sign language so they could signal test answers across crowded classrooms.

try, aided by a three-hour time difference.

Reasonably priced surveillance equipment, including hidden cameras and tape recorders, is taking cheating to a whole new level. Colton cites numerous cases in which video cameras roughly the size of a quarter were hidden in a test taker's tie (or watch or jacket) and used to send information to an outside expert, who quickly compiled answers and called them back into a silent pager. "If [students] spent as much time on their studies as they do on cheating, we'd be graduating rocket scientists all over the place," says Larry McCandless, a science teacher at Hardee Junior High in Wauchula, Fla., who recently caught his students using sign language to signal test answers to each other.

If students do spend homeroom copying assignments from one another, it may be because schools send such mixed messages about what, exactly, constitutes crossing the line. Mark, a senior at a Northeastern boarding school, doesn't believe that doing homework with a friend—or a family member—is

HIGH-TECH

Graphing calculators are often allowed in tests, but they can be programmed to store crib notes and formulas. Some can also send infrared messages.

ever dishonest and blames the people at the head of the classroom for any confusion over collaboration. "I mean, some of my teachers say you can't do it, some say two minds are greater than one," he explains, breaking into a laugh. "I obviously agree with the latter."

He isn't the only one. In a new study of 500 middle and high school students, Rutgers University management Prof. Donald McCabe, a leading authority on academic dishonesty, found that only one third said doing work with classmates was cheating, and just half thought it was wrong for parents to do their homework. So where, exactly, does teamwork end and cheating begin? It's not always that clear, even for grown-ups. According to the *U.S. News* poll, 20 percent of adults thought that doing homework for a child was fair. It's no wonder that teachers see students of every age handing in essays that contain words they can't pronounce, much less define.

Sue Bigg, a college consultant outside Chicago, often sees the hand of pushy parents. "I am beginning to think of myself in the role of 'integrity police'," she says, relating countless stories of college application essays that have been "edited" by Mom or Dad—and often for the worse, as big words replace any shred of youthful personality. "I'm afraid a lot of this cheating comes from home, where the parents' modus operandi is success at any cost." Edit-happy adults are part of the reason why schools across the country are having students do much of their writing in class nowadays. (It also prevents them from pulling papers off the Web.)

Parents who complete the bulk of their children's work often frustrate those with a more hands-off approach. "It all begins with the Pinewood Derby," grumbles Christopher Hardwick, a father of four from Philadelphia, who confesses to doing his "fair share of putting toothpicks into Styrofoam" for soap-box derbies and science projects. But Margaret Sagarese understands why parents are tempted to meddle. "You do feel caught between a rock and a hard place," says Sagarese, who lives in Islip, N.Y. "You're trying to do the right thing, and yet you know your child is going to lose, because [other classmates'] parents are doing the work."

The *U.S. News* poll found that 1 in 4 adults believes he has to lie and cheat to get ahead, and it seems this mentality is communicated to children. "Students

63% of college students say it's fair for parents to help with their kids' homework; 20% of adults think it's fair to *do* it.

see adults—parents, businessmen, lawyers—violating ethical standards and receiving a slap on the wrist, if anything, and quickly conclude that if that's acceptable behavior in the larger society, what's wrong with a little cheating in high school or college?" says Rutgers Professor McCabe. "Too often the messages from parents and teachers come off as, 'You need to do everything you can, at all costs, to get to the top.' You never see any gratification for being a good person anymore," says Audrey James, a senior at the North Carolina School of Science and Mathematics in Durham. "Once you get to high school, it's all about who has the grades and who's going to get the most scholarships."

Teaching cheating? Some blame schools, not parents or students, for the

cheating epidemic. "We should look at the way we run our institutions and the way those institutions tolerate, or at the very least, make cheating easy," says Theodore Sizer, a longtime educator and coauthor of *The Students Are Watching: Schools and the Moral Contract,* citing teachers with too large classes and too little time to get to know students or to create new assignments that cannot be pulled off the Internet.

Sometimes the schools are directly responsible. In the midst of March Madness last spring, a former tutor for the University of Minnesota revealed that she had written 400 papers for 20 basketball players between 1993 and 1998; four athletes were suspended, and the team was upset in the first round of the NCAA tournament. "You can talk to any

academic adviser [for a sports program], and they will tell you that there have been times when coaches have put pressure on them to do anything it takes to keep an athlete eligible," says Richard Lapchick, director of the Center for the Study of Sport in Society at Northeastern University. He claims that in the past year alone, he has counseled tutors and former players at six different schools to report cheating, only to have every athletic director—and one college president—investigate and deny there was a problem.

It's clear that when students really care about learning, they're much less likely to cheat. Take Bob Corbett, for example. Though he details his years of making cheat sheets and paying people to take his AP exams in *The Cheater's*

HOW THEY DO IT
The great term-paper buying caper

Click, click, cut, paste. That's all it takes to write a term paper in the information age.

The Internet has revolutionized the way students do research—and made plagiarism a breeze. Procrastinators can lift whole paragraphs from online encyclopedias or download essays from dozens of free paper mills (which purport to be for "research purposes only") like *schoolsucks.com* and Cheaters Always Win. Those willing to pay have more options: For as little as $5 a page, scores of Web sites will supply stock papers in an hour or two via fax or E-mail. Big spenders can get an original piece of work for $17.95 and up per page.

Buying papers may be easy, but is the product any good? *U.S. News* enlisted the help of a college senior to order customized and stock essays on two topics: an investigation of women in Islam and a reaction to

Chaucer's *The book of the Duchesse,* both assigned in real college courses.

The purchase was completely businesslike: All but one of the four essays arrived on time, and all were the correct length. but one company immediately posted our 15-page custom paper on its Web site, making it available to the world—even to classmates working on the same assignment—at less than half the $354 we paid.

Quality turned out to be more of a crapshoot. While free paper mills are known to subsist on poor student submissions (with such gems as "From his contradictions and defecting his principles, [Thomas] Jefferson destroyed the political precedent and is an exemplary hypocrite"), it turns out that paying top dollar for a paper is no guarantee that it's going to get an A—or even a C. Shiva Balaghi, associate director of the Hagop Kevordian Center for Near Eastern Studies at

New York University, found both women-in-Islam papers (from the site Academic Term Papers and Thousands of Papers) to be "formulistic and awkward sounding," with several misspellings. David Wallace, an English professor at the University of Pennsylvania currently teaching Chaucer, assessed our *Duchesse* offerings. He called the stock essay from Thousands of Papers "stilted and old-fashioned" but found the custom paper, from the Collegiate Care site, more convincing. Both experts pointed out that the larger and more impersonal the class, the greater the chance such essays have of succeeding as original work.

As teachers also get their hands on new technology, the balance of power may shift. Most promising are detection systems that operate like search engines, scouring the Web for passages that match portions of student essays. Berkeley neurobiologist

David Presti used a program developed by graduate student John Barrie called plagiarism.org on 320 student papers and nailed 45 cheaters who ignored warnings their work would be screened.

While plagiarism.org blew the whistle on the free papers we lifted, it failed to detect problems in paragraphs with even the slightest amount of rewriting. Both the standard and custom-ordered papers on Chaucer and women in Islam drew clean slates, too.

Meanwhile, the paper mills are keeping customers happy. Tim, a University of Arizona senior who buys around four papers a semester, recalls ordering an essay on Louis Armstrong last year. Five minutes later, he got a call from the company urging him to reconsider: One of his schoolmates had already ordered the same paper.-*C.K. and M.L. with Lindsay Faber*

Over 90% of college students say politicians cheat often. Who else do 90% think are cheaters? The media—and high schoolers.

Handbook: The Naughty Student's Bible, Corbett insists that he never cheated in any subject he really cared about or in classes with inspiring instructors. In fact, he dedicated his book to the 11th-grade teacher who "did such a wonderfully *engaging* job that he destroyed any shred of desire I may ever have had to cheat in English thereafter. . . ."

Still, the temptation is great. Prof. Gregory Cizek was inspired to write *Cheating on Tests: How to Do It, Detect It, and Prevent It,* after he caught three of his education graduate students in a clear-cut case of academic fraud a few years back; the would-be teachers apparently broke into his office, stole a copy of a final exam, collaborated, and then subbed pages of prewritten work into their tests.

The same standardized exams that drive students to do whatever it takes to gain an edge also push teachers—whose job security or salary can be linked to student performance—to do the unthinkable. This summer, for example, the Houston Independent School District demanded the resignations of a principal and three teachers after a nine-month probe turned up evidence of instructors giving oral prompting during the state achievement test and then using answer keys to correct students' responses, among other offenses.

Most cheaters don't get caught. In fact, perhaps the major reason students cheat is that they get away with it, time and time again. Numerous studies say that students almost never squeal on a classmate who cheats. And most instructors just don't want to play cop. "I'm not here to prevent students from cheating," says Robert Corless, an applied mathematics professor at the University of Western Ontario who eliminated take-home exams a few years ago after he caught students collaborating on them. "I'm here to help the genuine learners catch fire." He'll close off the easy routes, but that's about it. "Spending my time listening to appeals or accusations of cheating is not my idea of spending it well."

Procedures are the least of the hassles encountered by those who pursue cheating cases. It can be complicated, time consuming, futile, and—in the worst-case scenario—litigious. Science teacher McCandless says he feared a lawsuit when one mother berated him for damaging her daughter's self-esteem; she felt he should have waited until after a test to chastise the girl for cheating. And although legal action is rare, teachers at both the K-12 and higher-education lev-

CHEAT SHEETS

Some things never change: Scrawling formulas and important dates everywhere from wrists to baseball-cap brims is still a popular way to gain an edge.

els say it makes them wary about pursuing cheaters. John Hill, a professor of law at St. Thomas University in Florida, actually landed in court. His house was egged and his students hissed at him. And all because he charged a student whose brilliant report for a course on legal ethics was practically identical to a *Stanford Law Review* article. (She contends she mistakenly turned in an early draft.) The university honor society narrowly convicted her and meted out a token punishment. Now graduated, she is suing Hill and the university for "loss of ability to obtain a job as an attorney," among other complaints.

IT'S EARLY ON NOVEMBER 6, SAT DAY, AND RAY Nicosia is on the prowl. The director of test security for the Educational Testing Service, Nicosia is making the rounds at a high school test center that has had a string of recent security problems, to guarantee things go smoothly this time—or take steps to shut the site down. He cruises the corridors, a vision of calm amid the throngs of edgy students, and runs through a mental checklist: He verifies that test booklets are kept in a secure storage area, far away from the probing eyes—and fingers—of students, until the very last minute. He glances in classrooms, making sure that proctors follow the rules, checking and double-checking valid forms of identification, randomly assigning students to desks at least 4 feet apart, filling out a seating chart (a permanent record of who sat next to whom), and then strolling about the room during the exam, searching out wandering eyes and other suspicious activity.

To combat a scourge some deem as pernicious as underage drinking, educators are implementing such countermeasures as character education programs, honor codes, and strict academic integrity policies. "I'm not saying it's impossible to cheat, but we're taking a lot of steps to secure our tests," says Nicosia. In recent years, ETS, which administers some 11 million standardized tests a year and questions less than 1 percent of scores, has boosted prevention efforts, aiming to thwart impersonators, thieves, and copycats either before or during the act. Even the simplest precautions, from better training for proctors to a free hotline for reporting shady activity, can make a huge difference. In 1996, for example, ETS began shrink-wrapping the essay section of Advanced Placement exams, to stop students from sneaking a look during the first part of the test; peeking is now virtually non-existent.

Fighting back. Low-tech tactics work in the classroom, too. In a 1998 study conducted at two public colleges, Oregon State University economics Prof. Joe Kerkvliet found that students were 31 percent more likely to cheat in courses taught by teaching assistants—graduate students or adjunct professors—than those taught by tenured or tenure-track faculty. (Typically, 1 in 8 students will cheat on at least one exam in any given class.) By offering multiple versions of the same test, so students can't share answers with friends in different sections, adding extra proctors, and giving verbal warnings that cheaters will be punished, Kerkvliet has reduced cheating in his classes to practically zero.

Just talking about the problem can be enough to stop it. Sohair Ahmadi used to regularly cut corners back in the ninth and 10th grades—trading test answers in biology, copying homework like mad—and no one seemed to care. In her junior year, she switched schools, to the North Carolina School of Science and Mathematics, where teachers discuss academic integrity from the outset, outlining why it's important and detailing a laundry list of unacceptable behaviors. "They make it clear that cheating will not be tolerated," says Ahmadi, 18, who not only shed her habit but now heads a committee dedicated to starting a school honor code.

High-tech countermeasures are also on the rise. From the moment a student walks into ETS'S computer-based testing center at George Mason University in Fairfax, Va., for example, it's clear that Big Brother is watching. A digital camera stands in one corner, ready to snap a test-day photo for posterity; five video cameras record each student's every move; the 15 computers run customized exams, with the order and type of questions determined by a test taker's previous answers. At the moment, ETS is working toward adding a biometric scan (using, say, thumbprints to identify students) to the check-in process.

Make 'em pay. The biggest stumbling block, however, may be that when cheaters do get busted the penalties are rarely harsh. Last year, for instance, the valedictorian at Brea Olinda High School in Southern California was caught electronically altering a course grade. His punishment: being banned from the graduation ceremony. Cheat on the SAT and your score will be canceled; but you can take a retest. It's often true that getting caught cheating "doesn't have the terrifically terrible college ramifications you might think," says Don Firke, academic dean at Choate Rosemary Hall, a boarding school in Wallingford, Conn. "If a college really wants a kid, they're going to find a way to take him." Once on campus, a cheater is apt to find similarly lax discipline. With the exception of a handful of schools like the University of Virginia, which have one-strike-and-you're-out honor-code policies, the vast majority simply dole out zeros for an assignment or course in which a student has been found cheating.

Still, a growing number of institutions are trying to turn discipline into a

ADULTS CHEAT TOO
What started in elementary school...

Why bother hacking into your high school's computer system to revise your transcript when you can simply lie about having a Wharton M.B.A.? Studies show that students who cheat are likely to make it a way of life. So it's no surprise that today's workplace is full of adults who lie about everything from job experience to company earnings.

Nearly three quarters of job seekers admitted lying on their résumés in a recent survey by SelectJOBS.com, a high-tech industry employment site. Offenses ranged from omitting past jobs (40 percent) to padding education credentials (12 percent). Recruiters blame the Web, where unsavory applicants can crib from 5 million résumés currently online. John Challenger, CEO of Chicago-based recruiting firm Challenger, Gray & Christmas, says the hot job market isn't helping: In the race to find qualified candidates, "many companies have to cut back . . . on screening."

And little lies can become big problems. Take Jeffrey Grade, the flamboyant CEO for Harnischfeger, a Milwaukee mining-equipment firm named in 1997 by *Fortune* as the second-fastest-growing company in the United States. Grade boasted of his exploits as a Navy pilot in Vietnam. But *Barron*'s reported Grade was never a top gun—his military career consisted of one year in Reserve Officer Candidate School. Grade may have gone further: A class action suit brought against him and the company alleged exaggeration of earnings, among other violations of securities laws. (The suit is currently on hold.) After Harnischfeger filed for bankruptcy in June, some colleagues speculated that Grade's problems discouraged banks from giving the company credit that would have allowed it to avert filing for Chapter 11 protection.

Upping the ante. In today's stock market, companies feel more pressure than ever to deliver bigger profits, faster-growing sales, and, of course, higher stock prices. The pressure has led to some large-scale dissembling of a different sort: An increasing number of companies have begun to "manage" their earnings numbers, forming, in the words of Securities and Exchange Commission Chairman Arthur Levitt, "a web of dysfunctional relationships" to do so. Analysts gauge a company's earnings prospects, relying heavily on company guidance. Companies, in turn, take liberties where they can to meet analysts' forecasts. "Independent" auditors, who naturally want to retain clients, don't stand in the way.

Are investors cheated when companies "manage" their earnings? Maybe not. Are they misled? "Absolutely," says Charles Hill of the investment research firm First Call. As more Americans save for retirement in the stock market, a culture of gamesmanship over the numbers is weaving itself into the fabric of accepted conduct, Levitt says.—*Margaret Loftus and Anne Kates Smith*

teachable moment. At the University of Maryland-College Park, for example, students caught cheating must attend a seven-week ethics seminar. "We're not trying to mar someone's life, but we are saying, 'You're going to have to think about this behavior and what danger it poses to you and the larger society,'" says Gary Pavela, director of judicial programs and—a recent addendum—student ethical development.

Do the cheaters actually mend their ways? Leah Solowsky isn't glad she was caught plagiarizing last year, but she acknowledges that the experience did teach her a thing or two. "I learned that teachers aren't as stupid as some people think they are," she says with just a hint of humor. Pausing to think for a moment, she adds: "I mean, cheating should affect your conscience, because you are doing something wrong." Solowsky vows she's sworn off cheating for good—no matter how much loathsome Spanish homework piles up every night. *Buena suerte.*

Gender Gap in Math Scores Is Closing

Girls still avoid math in school, but new research challenges the notion that they have less mathematical ability than boys.

Bridget Murray
Monitor staff

Boys have historically outscored girls on the mathematical sections of national achievement tests, fueling the age-old debate about whether socialization or biology accounts for the performance difference.

But, except at the highest levels of analytical thinking, the gender gap in mathematical performance is narrowing, according to psychologists and testing experts.

Thirteen-year-old girls have practically caught up to boys in their adeptness at intermediate math involving moderately complex procedures and reasoning, such as geometry and simple algebra, according to a recent report from the Educational Testing Service, the nation's largest private educational measurement institution.

In 1992, 59 percent of girls vs. 60 percent of boys had reached that intermediate level, compared with 48 percent of girls vs. 55 percent of boys in 1973.

During the same period, 9-year-old boys and girls exhibited equal ability to solve basic problems.

But at age 17, boys remained ahead of girls in their ability to solve complex algebraic and precalculus problems. Roughly 10 percent of

> "GIRLS ARE DOING BETTER AT MATH [THAN BEFORE], BUT BOYS ARE STILL AIMING HIGHER BECAUSE MORE OF THEM WANT TO MAKE A CAREER OF IT. AS A RESULT, WE'RE STILL SEEING A CAREER GAP FOR MEN AND WOMEN."
>
> INA MULLIS, PHD
> BOSTON COLLEGE

boys reach the most complex level compared with 5 percent of girls.

The findings derive from testing by the government-based National Assessment of Educational Progress, also known as America's Report Card, which has tracked trends in students' academic achievement for the National Center for Education Statistics since 1973.

"Girls are doing better at math [than before], but boys are still aiming higher because more of them want to make a career of it," said Ina Mullis, PhD, an education professor at Boston College and a co-author of the ETS report. "As a result, we're still seeing a career gap for men and women."

A 1990 meta-analysis of gender differences in math performance backs the Report Card findings. Psychologist Janet Hyde, PhD, and math education professor Elizabeth Fennema, PhD, of the University of Wisconsin-Madison, examined 100 studies covering national achievement testing of 3 million people and found that males barely outperformed females at math.

A similar meta-analysis released this year by Larry Hedges, PhD, and his student Amy Nowell, of the University of Chicago, also showed boys with an unremarkable mathematical edge on girls.

Moreover, Hyde's analysis suggests that at all ages and levels, girls and boys showed similar understanding of math concepts, and that girls actually surpass boys in computation before high school. But in high school, boys show more skill at solving complex problems.

"Some people think boys are better at math at all levels," Hyde said. "We found no evidence of that. It's not until high school that boys pull ahead."

In debating reasons for the disparity at the top, psychologists and educators have offered myriad nature-vs.-nurture explanations.

Is It Variability?

Some psychologists propose a score-variability hypothesis. They contend that a greater disparity in math ability among boys compared with girls explains boys' higher scores on complex problems.

They note that more boys score higher as well as lower in math than girls and that there are more male geniuses *and* more males with developmental disabilities in the general population.

More boys than girls consistently show up in the Iowa State precocious youth study, which selects 13- to 15-year-olds with high math SAT scores.

Also, Hedges and Nowell found more male variance in their meta-analysis of six large data sets collected from tests of adolescents' cognitive abilities.

Males generally scored higher than females in all areas except reading comprehension, perceptual speed and associative memory. More males scored lower than females, as well. For instance, on the analytic reasoning section of one national test, almost twice as many males as females were in the bottom 10 percent.

. . . Or Biology?

Psychologist Doreen Kimura, PhD, at the University of Western Ontario, attributes much of the difference to biology. Men are, on average, better at math reasoning, she argues.

Her research suggests a hormonal contribution to math ability, she says. Her 1991 study on 88 college students, for example, suggests that women with high testosterone levels and men with low testosterone levels have higher spatial and mathematical ability than low testosterone women and high testosterone men. She has also found differences in the way men and women think. In a 1993 study of nearly 100 undergraduates' map-route learning, for example, men took more direct routes and made fewer errors, while women relied more on landmarks and made more errors.

Brainwaves, rather than hormones, could cause men to dominate the higher end of the math spectrum, some speculate. Based on her findings in an ongoing study of mathematically precocious youth, Iowa State University psychologist Camilla Benbow, PhD, suggests that highly intelligent boys and girls differ in the way their brains approach spatial activities.

In the study of 40 youth, researchers asked boys and girls to perform a specified spatial task—judging such facial expressions as happy, sad, angry or perplexed. The researchers found that boys had higher activity in the right hemisphere of their brains than girls. The study results are now in press.

But Hyde discounts both biological and variability hypotheses, faulting the biological explanations for being unreplicable, and the variability hypothesis for being purely descriptive and failing to describe the causes of the variability. In keeping with Hyde's meta-analysis, Benbow notes an important distinction between math performance and reasoning: Girls usually *perform* better than boys, often earning higher grades, while boys *reason* better than girls at the highest mathematical levels. Nature and nurture work together to produce this pattern.

"We need to work on nurturing girls' reasoning skills," said Benbow, noting that girls in high school select fewer math courses than boys.

. . . or course choice?

The real issue is gender differences in course choice, not math ability, said Hyde. Girls opt out of tougher high-school math courses, which explains their lower scores on standardized tests, she believes.

While Benbow links girls' math avoidance with a dislike for math, Hyde and other psychologists view gender conditioning by parents, teachers and society as the real culprit.

"Girls hear a message that math won't be as valuable for their futures as boys' and they have lower expectations for success than boys," said Hyde.

Psychologist Jacquelynne Eccles, PhD, has seen strong parental influences as she's tracked students from more than 2,000 families in southeastern Michigan schools. In a 1990 finding, she noted that parents' gender stereotyping influenced kids' own self-perceptions. This in turn influenced students' course selection. By high school, more boys participated in sports, and made honors in math and physics than girls. Some of this sex-typing was even evident by the second and third grades.

Girls are also more likely than boys to view themselves as unskilled at math and, as a result, avoid it, said Eccles, who is based at the University of Michigan Institute for Social Research. Because girls place a low value on math, they avoid optional math courses in high school, she asserted.

Gender stereotypes lead more girls to view English and other verbal courses as more important than math and science courses for their future careers. Schools can help change those preconceived notions, pointing out that even careers in the social sciences require solid math knowledge, Hyde said.

"Schools need to give girls a broader view of the careers they can choose," she said. "Once girls avoid high school math, they close themselves out of fields like engineering and other fields they didn't realize involve math, and it's a shame."

Unit 4

Key Points to Consider

❖ What is your portrait of a "normal" adolescent? What about an "abnormal" adolescent? When you were a teenager, did you worry about whether you were "normal"? How should parents handle adolescents' identity exploration?

❖ How is self-esteem affected at adolescence? Do you think girls have lower self-esteem than boys? Why or why not? How can self-concepts be improved?

❖ How can we encourage prosocial values and strong moral development? How does our culture encourage violence, especially in boys, and what can be done about it?

❖ Why is ethnic identity important? Can fostering ethnic identity help reduce risk-taking behavior? Why? How are identity and social development compounded for adolescents from multiracial backgrounds?

❖ Should we worry more about a child's emotional intelligence and less about academic intelligence? Defend your answer.

 **Links**   **www.dushkin.com/online/**

These sites are annotated on pages 4 and 5.

Each age period is associated with developmental tasks. A major aspect of psychosocial development for adolescents is the formation of a coherent personal identity. Erik Erikson referred to this as the adolescent identity crisis. Identity formation is a normative event, but it represents a turning point in development that will have consequences for later psychosocial tasks.

Children's identities often represent an identification with parents and significant others. Adolescents reflect on their identity and come to some sense of who they are and who they are not. Identity formation involves an examination of personal likes and dislikes, political, religious, and moral values, occupational interests, and gender roles and sexual behaviors. Adolescents must also form an integrated sense of their own personality across the various roles they engage in (e.g., son or daughter, student, boyfriend or girlfriend, part-time worker).

To aid in the identity formation process, Erikson advocated that adolescents be given license to explore alternative roles and values. He believed that such a moratorium period would allow adolescents to make commitments that reflect true personal choices. James Marcia elaborated on Erikson's ideas about identity formation. He described four identity statuses that depend on the degree of exploration an adolescent has engaged in and whether the adolescent has made choices or commitments to certain paths. Adolescents who are actively searching and evaluating options are said to be in moratorium, as Erikson described. An identity-achieved status is expected to follow this moratorium period eventually. Other adolescents adopt values and life roles without experiencing a period of questioning. These adolescents are called identity-foreclosed as they essentially conform to parental expectations for themselves. Conformity to parents is not automatically a sign of identity foreclosure, however. Identity-achieved individuals often make choices that fit parental values and expectations, but they do so after reflection. As a result, they are more invested in their choices and more self-confident. Finally, Marcia describes some adolescents as identity-diffused. These adolescents have not undergone a period of questioning and exploration, nor have they made clear ideological, occupational, or personal commitments. Identity-diffusion is expected for early adolescents, but it is seen as developmentally immature in college-age adolescents.

Formulating his ideas in the 1950s, Erikson proposed some differences in male and female identity development. Females were presumed to delay full identity development until the formation of an intimate relationship (that is, marriage). Interpersonal issues were seen as more paramount in female identity development with the occupational domain being more relevant to male identity development. Recent research indicates that there are fewer gender differences in identity development than may have been true of earlier generations. Carol Gilligan maintains that moral decision making is another area of gender differences. She argues that females' moral values and moral judgments reflect more concern for interpersonal relationships and caring. Males are said to have more of a legalistic outlook, which is less compassionate and more focused on the abstract application of rules. Gilligan's ideas have not been well tested to date.

An area that has received recent attention is how identity development may differ for minority individuals. In addition to exploring ideological, occupational, sexual, and interpersonal commitments, ethnicity is a salient component that must be integrated into the person's identity. Adolescents may or may not identify with an ethnic group and may either value or reject their ethnicity. Jean Phinney has articulated several phases characteristic of ethnic identity development. The stages parallel Marcia's identity statuses. Similar to identity foreclosure, some minority adolescents simply adopt the values of the dominant culture and have an unexamined ethnic identity. Others are in moratorium and are wrestling with conflicts between the values of the dominant culture and their own culture. Finally, adolescents with an achieved ethnic identity feel an emotional attachment to their ethnic group and have come to some resolution integrating ethnic group values with the dominant culture's values.

Whether male or female, minority or majority, identity issues have implications for the adolescent's emotional health, self-concept, and self-esteem. Adolescents' self-concepts become more differentiated and abstract as they think of themselves in terms of personality traits. They compare themselves to others in order to evaluate their own characteristics and abilities. They often construct an ideal self that is difficult to live up to. The abstract nature of their self-concept also means that self-evaluation is more removed from concrete, observable behaviors and is, therefore, more subject to distortion. Adolescents who are struggling with identity issues are also likely to undergo fluctuations in their self-concept as they explore alternative roles, values, and personalities.

Self-esteem reflects how good one feels about the self. The essential question is: Am I okay? Self-esteem is at a low point in early adolescence relative to other age periods. More dimensions contribute to adolescent self-esteem than is the case for children. Global self-esteem measures are often less informative as adolescents' self-esteem varies in different domains (e.g., physical attractiveness, peer acceptance, academic competence, athletic competence). Research by Susan Harter and her colleagues indicates that feeling good about one's physical appearance is the number one predictor of overall self-esteem for adolescents. The pubertal changes heighten concerns about body image and appearance. Females are even more concerned about their looks and are much more likely to have a negative body image than males are. Contrary to most expectations, recent studies show that self-esteem in African Americans is comparable to that of Caucasian Americans. Little work on self-esteem has been done in other minority populations.

The articles in this unit elaborate on the concepts discussed in this overview. Readings relate to identity formation, ethnic identity, moral values, self-esteem, and emotional functioning.

Identity and Socioemotional Development

The Moral Development of Children

It is not enough for kids to tell right from wrong. They must develop a commitment to acting on their ideals. Enlightened parenting can help

by William Damon

With unsettling regularity, news reports tell us of children wreaking havoc on their schools and communities: attacking teachers and classmates, murdering parents, persecuting others out of viciousness, avarice or spite. We hear about feral gangs of children running drugs or numbers, about teenage date rape, about youthful vandalism, about epidemics of cheating even in academically elite schools. Not long ago a middle-class gang of youths terrorized an affluent California suburb through menacing threats and extortion, proudly awarding themselves points for each antisocial act. Such stories make *Lord of the Flies* seem eerily prophetic.

What many people forget in the face of this grim news is that most children most of the time do follow the rules of their society, act fairly, treat friends kindly, tell the truth and respect their elders. Many young-

sters do even more. A large portion of young Americans volunteer in community service—according to one survey, between 22 and 45 percent, depending on the location. Young people have also been leaders in social causes. Harvard University psychiatrist Robert Coles has written about children such as Ruby, an African-American girl who broke the color barrier in her school during the 1960s. Ruby's daily walk into the all-white school demonstrated a brave sense of moral purpose. When taunted by classmates, Ruby prayed for their redemption rather than cursing them. "Ruby," Coles observed, "had a will and used it to make an ethical choice; she demonstrated moral stamina; she possessed honor, courage."

All children are born with a running start on the path to moral development. A number of inborn responses predispose them to act in ethical ways. For example, empa-

thy—the capacity to experience another person's pleasure or pain vicariously—is part of our native endowment as humans. Newborns cry when they hear others cry and show signs of pleasure at happy sounds such as cooing and laughter. By the second year of life, children commonly console peers or parents in distress.

Sometimes, of course, they do not quite know what comfort to provide. Psychologist Martin L. Hoffman of New York University once saw a toddler offering his mother his security blanket when he perceived she was upset. Although the emotional disposition to help is present, the means of helping others effectively must be learned and refined through social experience. Moreover, in many people the capacity for empathy stagnates or even diminishes. People can act cruelly to those they refuse to empathize with. A New York police officer once asked a teenage thug how he could have crippled an 83-year-old woman during a mugging. The boy replied, "What do I care? I'm not her."

A scientific account of moral growth must explain both the good and the bad. Why do most children act in reasonably—sometimes exceptionally—moral ways, even when it flies in the face of their immediate self-interest? Why do some children depart from accepted standards, often to the great harm of themselves and others? How does a child acquire mores and develop a lifelong commitment to moral behavior, or not?

Psychologists do not have definitive answers to these questions, and often their studies seem merely to confirm parents' observations and intuition. But parents, like all people, can be led astray by subjective biases, incomplete information and media sensationalism. They may blame a relatively trivial event—say, a music concert—for a deep-seated problem such as drug dependency. They may incorrectly attribute their own problems to a strict upbringing and then try to compensate by raising their children in an overly permissive way. In such a hotly contested area as children's moral values, a systematic, scientific approach is the only way to avoid wild swings of emotional reaction that end up repeating the same mistakes.

The Genealogy of Morals

The study of moral development has become a lively growth industry within the social sciences. Journals are full of new findings and competing models. Some theories focus on natural biological forces; others stress social influence and experience; still others, the judgment that results from children's intellectual development. Although each theory has a different emphasis, all recognize that no single cause can account for either moral or immoral behavior. Watching violent videos or

The Six Stages of Moral Judgment

Growing up, children and young adults come to rely less on external discipline and more on deeply held beliefs. They go through as many as six stages (grouped into three levels) of moral reasoning, as first argued by psychologist Lawrence Kohlberg in the late 1950s (*below*). The evidence includes a long-term study of 58 young men interviewed periodically over two decades. Their moral maturity was judged by how they analyzed hypothetical dilemmas, such as whether a husband should steal a drug for his dying wife. Either yes or no was a valid answer; what mattered was how the men justified it. As they grew up, they passed through the stages in succession, albeit at different rates (*bar graph*). The sixth stage remained elusive. Despite the general success of this model for describing intellectual growth, it does not explain people's actual behavior. Two people at the same stage may act differently.   —*W.D.*

LEVEL 1: SELF-INTEREST

▢ STAGE 1   PUNISHMENT "I won't do it, because I don't want to get punished."

▨ STAGE 2   REWARD "I won't do it, because I want the reward."

LEVEL 2: SOCIAL APPROVAL

■ STAGE 3   INTERPERSONAL RELATIONS "I won't do it, because I want people to like me."

■ STAGE 4   SOCIAL ORDER "I won't do it, because it would break the law."

LEVEL 3: ABSTRACT IDEALS

■ STAGE 5   SOCIAL CONTRACT "I won't do it, because I'm obliged not to."

▨ STAGE 6   UNIVERSAL RIGHTS "I won't do it, because it's not right, no matter what others say."

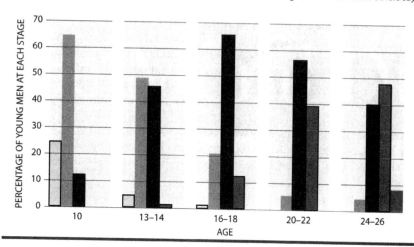

EDWARD BELL; SOURCE: ANNE COLBY *Carnegie Foundation for the Advancement of Teaching*

playing shoot-'em-up computer games may push some children over the edge and leave others unaffected. Conventional wisdom dwells on lone silver bullets, but scientific understanding must be built on an appreciation of the complexity and variety of children's lives.

Biologically oriented, or "nativist," theories maintain that human morality springs from emotional dispositions that are hardwired into our species. Hoffman, Colwyn Trevarthen of the University of Edinburgh and Nancy Eisenberg of Arizona State University have established

that babies can feel empathy as soon as they recognize the existence of others—sometimes in the first week after birth. Other moral emotions that make an early appearance include shame, guilt and indignation. As Harvard child psychologist Jerome S. Kagan has described, young children can be outraged by the violation of social expectations, such as a breach in the rules of a favorite game or rearranged buttons on a piece of familiar clothing.

Nearly everybody, in every culture, inherits these dispositions. Mary D. Ainsworth of the University of Virginia reported empathy among Ugandan and American infants; Norma Feshbach of the University of California at Los Angeles conducted a similar comparison of newborns in Europe, Israel and the U.S.; Millard C. Madsen of U.C.L.A. studied sharing by preschool children in nine cultures. As far as psychologists know, children everywhere start life with caring feelings toward those close to them and adverse reactions to inhumane or unjust behavior. Differences in how these reactions are triggered and expressed emerge only later, once children have been exposed to the particular value systems of their cultures.

In contrast, the learning theories concentrate on children's acquisition of behavioral norms and values through observation, imitation and reward. Research in this tradition has concluded that moral behavior is context-bound, varying from situation to situation almost independently of stated beliefs. Landmark studies in the 1920s, still frequently cited, include Hugh Hartshorne and Mark May's survey of how children reacted when given the chance to cheat. The children's behavior depended largely on whether they thought they would be caught. It could be predicted neither from their conduct in previous situations nor from their knowledge of common moral rules, such as the Ten Commandments and the Boy Scout's code.

Later reanalyses of Hartshorne and May's data, performed by Roger Burton of the State University of New York at Buffalo, discovered at least one general trend: younger children were more likely to cheat than adolescents. Perhaps socialization or mental growth can restrain dishonest behavior after all. But the effect was not a large one.

The third basic theory of moral development puts the emphasis on intellectual growth, arguing that virtue and vice are ultimately a matter of conscious choice. The best-known cognitive theories are those of psy-

"Could You Live with Yourself?"

In a distressed neighborhood in Camden, N.J., social psychologist Daniel Hart of Rutgers University interviewed an African-American teenager who was active in community service:

How would you describe yourself?
I am the kind of person who wants to get involved, who believes in getting involved. I just had this complex, I call it, where people think of Camden as being a bad place, which bothered me. Every city has its own bad places, you know. I just want to work with people, work to change that image that people have of Camden. You can't start with adults, because they don't change. But if you can get into the minds of young children, show them what's wrong and let them know that you don't want them to be this way, then it could work, because they're more persuadable.

Is there really one correct solution to moral problems like this one?
Basically, it's like I said before. You're supposed to try to help save a life.

How do you know?
Well, it's just—how could you live with yourself? Say that I could help save this person's life—could I just let that person die? I mean, I couldn't live with myself if that happened. A few years ago my sister was killed, and . . . the night she was killed I was over at her house, earlier that day. Maybe if I had spent the night at her house that day, maybe this wouldn't have happened.

You said that you're not a bad influence on others. Why is that important?
Well, I try not to be a bad role model. All of us have bad qualities, of course; still, you have to be a role model even if you're a person walking down the street. You know, we have a society today where there are criminals and crooks. There are drug users. Kids look to those people. If they see a drug dealer with a lot of money, they want money, too, and then they're going to do drugs. So it's important that you try not to be a bad influence, because that can go a long way. Even if you say, oh, wow, you tell your little sister or brother to be quiet so Mom and Dad won't wake so you won't have to go to school. And they get in the habit of being quiet [laughs], you're not going to school, things like that. So when you're a bad influence, it always travels very far.

Why don't you want that to happen?
Because in today's society there's just really too much crime, too much violence. I mean everywhere. And I've even experienced violence, because my sister was murdered. You know, we need not to have that in future years, so we need to teach our children otherwise.

chologists Jean Piaget and Lawrence Kohlberg. Both described children's early moral beliefs as oriented toward power and authority. For young children, might makes right, literally. Over time they come to understand that social rules are made by people and thus can be renegotiated and that reciprocity in relationships is more fair than unilateral obedience. Kohlberg identified a six-stage sequence in the maturation of moral judgment [*see box*, "The Six Stages of Moral Judgment"]. Several thousand studies have used it as a measure of how advanced a person's moral reasoning is.

Conscience versus Chocolate

Although the main parts of Kohlberg's sequence have been confirmed, notable exceptions stand out. Few if any people reach the sixth and most advanced stage, in which their moral view is based purely on abstract principles. As for the early stages in the sequence, many studies (including ones from my own laboratory) have found that young children have a far richer sense of positive morality than the model indicates. In other words, they do not act simply out of fear of punishment. When a playmate hogs a plate of cookies or refuses to relinquish a swing, the protest "That's not fair!" is common. At the same time, young children realize that they have an obligation to share with others—even when their parents say not to. Preschool children generally believe in an equal distribution of goods and back up their beliefs with reasons such as empathy ("I want my friend to feel nice"), reciprocity ("She shares her toys with me") and egalitarianism ("We should all get the same"). All this they figure out through confrontation with peers at play. Without fairness, they learn, there will be trouble.

In fact, none of the three traditional theories is sufficient to explain children's moral growth and behavior. None captures the most essential dimensions of moral life: character and commitment. Regardless of how children develop their initial system of values, the key question is: What makes them live up to their ideals or not? This issue is the focus of recent scientific thinking.

Like adults, children struggle with temptation. To see how this tug of war plays itself out in the world of small children, my colleagues and I (then at Clark University) devised

How Universal Are Values?

The observed importance of shared values in children's moral development raises some of the most hotly debated questions in philosophy and the social sciences today. Do values vary from place to place, or is there a set of universal values that guides moral development everywhere? Do children growing up in different cultures or at different times acquire fundamentally different mores?

Some light was shed on the cultural issue by Richard A. Shweder of the University of Chicago and his colleagues in a study of Hindu-Brahmin children in India and children from Judeo-Christian backgrounds in the U.S. The study revealed striking contrasts between the two groups. From an early age, the Indian children learned to maintain tradition, to respect defined rules of interpersonal relationships and to help people in need. American children, in comparison, were oriented toward autonomy, liberty and personal rights. The Indian children said that breaches of tradition, such as eating beef or addressing one's father by his first name, were particularly reprehensible. They saw nothing wrong with a man caning his errant son or a husband beating his wife when she went to the movies without his permission. The American children were appalled by all physically punitive behavior but indifferent to infractions such as eating forbidden foods or using improper forms of address.

Moreover, the Indians and Americans moved in opposite directions as they matured. Whereas Indian children restricted value judgments to situations with which they were directly familiar, Indian adults generalized their values to a broad range of social conditions. American children said that moral standards should apply to everyone always; American adults modified values in the face of changing circumstances. In short, the Indians began life as relativists and ended up an universalists, whereas the Americans went precisely the other way.

It would be overstating matters, however, to say that children from different cultures adopt completely different moral codes. In Schweder's study, both groups of children thought that deceitful acts (a father breaking a promise to a child) and uncharitable acts (ignoring a beggar with a sick child) were wrong. They also shared a repugnance toward theft, vandalism and harming innocent victims, although there was some disagreement on what constitutes innocence. Among these judgments may be found a universal moral sense, based on common human aversions. It reflects core values—benevolence, fairness, honesty—that may be necessary for sustaining human relationships in all but the most dysfunctional societies.

A parallel line of research has studied gender differences, arguing that girls learn to emphasize caring, whereas boys incline toward rules and justice. Unlike the predictions made by culture theory, however, these gender claims have not held up. The original research that claimed to find gender differences lacked proper control groups. Well-designed studies of American children—for example, those by Lawrence Walker of the University of British Columbia—rarely detect differences between boys' and girls' ideals. Even for adults, when educational or occupational levels are controlled, the differences disappear. Female lawyers have almost the same moral orientations as their male counterparts; the same can be said for male and female nurses, homemakers, scientists, high school dropouts and so on. As cultural theorists point out, there is far more similarity between male and female moral orientations within any given culture than between male and female orientations across cultures.

Generational differences are also of interest, especially to people who bemoan what they see as declining morality. Such complaints, of course, are nothing new [see "Teenage Attitudes,"by H. H. Remmers and D. H. Radler; SCIENTIFIC AMERICAN, June 1958; and "The Origins of Alienation," by Urie Bronfenbrenner; SCIENTIFIC AMERICAN, August 1974]. Nevertheless, there is some evidence that young people today are more likely to engage in antisocial behavior than those a generation ago were. According to a survey by Thomas M. Achenbach and Catherine T. Howell of the University of Vermont, parents and teachers reported more behavioral problems (lying, cheating) and other threats to healthy development (depression, withdrawal) in 1989 than in 1976 (above). (The researchers are now updating their survey.) But in the long sweep of human history, 13 years is merely an eye blink. The changes could reflect a passing problem, such as overly permissive fashions in child rearing, rather than a permanent trend.

—W.D.

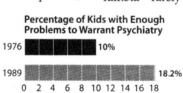

Percentage of Kids with Enough Problems to Warrant Psychiatry

1976	10%
1989	18.2%

0 2 4 6 8 10 12 14 16 18

KIDS THESE DAYS are likelier to need mental health services, judging from parents' reports of behavioral and emotional problems.

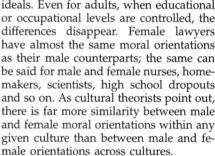

EDWARD BELL; SOURCE; THOMAS M. ACHENBACH AND CATHERINE T. HOWELL

the following experiment. We brought groups, each of four children, into our lab, gave them string and beads, and asked them to make bracelets and necklaces for us. We then thanked them profusely for their splendid work and rewarded them, as a group, with 10 candy bars. Then the real experiment began: we told each group that it would need to decide the best way to divide up the reward. We left the room and watched through a one-way mirror.

Before the experiment, we had interviewed participants about the concept of fairness. We were curious, of course, to find out whether the prospect of gobbling up real chocolate would overwhelm their abstract sense of right and wrong. To test this thoroughly, we gave one unfortunate control group an almost identical conundrum, using cardboard rectangles rather than real chocolate—a not so subtle way of defusing their self-interest. We observed groups of four-, six-, eight- and 10-year-old children to see whether the relationship between situational and hypothetical morality changed with age.

The children's ideals did make a difference but within limits circumscribed by narrow self-interest. Children given cardboard acted almost three times more generously toward one another than did children given chocolate. Yet moral beliefs still held some sway. For example, children who had earlier expressed a belief in merit-based solutions ("The one who did the best job should get more of the candy") were the ones most likely to advocate for merit in the real situation. But they did so most avidly when they themselves could claim to have done more than their peers. Without such a claim, they were easily persuaded to drop meritocracy for an equal division.

Even so, these children seldom abandoned fairness entirely. They may have switched from one idea of justice to another—say, from merit to equality—but they did not resort to egoistic justifications such as "I should get more because I'm big" or

"Boys like candy more than girls, and I'm a boy." Such rationales generally came from children who had declared no belief in either equality or meritocracy. Older children were more likely to believe in fairness and to act accordingly, even when such action favored others. This finding was evidence for the reassuring proposition that ideals can have an increasing influence on conduct as a child matures.

Do the Right Thing

But this process is not automatic. A person must adopt those beliefs as a central part of his or her personal identity. When a person moves from saying "People should be honest" to "I want to be honest," he or she becomes more likely to tell the truth in everyday interactions. A person's use of moral principles to define the self is called the person's moral identity. Moral identity determines not merely what the person considers to be the right course of action but also why he or she would decide: "I myself must take this course." This distinction is crucial to understanding the variety of moral behavior. The same basic ideals are widely shared by even the youngest members of society; the difference is the resolve to act on those ideals.

Most children and adults will express the belief that it is wrong to allow others to suffer, but only a subset of them will conclude that they themselves must do something about, say, ethnic cleansing in Kosovo. Those are the ones who are most likely to donate money or fly to the Balkans to help. Their concerns about human suffering are central to the way they think about themselves and their life goals, and so they feel a responsibility to take action, even at great personal cost.

In a study of moral exemplars—people with long, publicly documented histories of charity and civil-rights work—psychologist Anne Colby of the Carnegie Foundation and I en-

countered a high level of integration between self-identity and moral concerns. "People who define themselves in terms of their moral goals are likely to see moral problems in everyday events, and they are also likely to see themselves as necessarily implicated in these problems," we wrote. Yet the exemplars showed no signs of more insightful moral reasoning. Their ideals and Kohlberg levels were much the same as everyone else's.

Conversely, many people are equally aware of moral problems, but to them the issues seem remote from their own lives and their senses of self. Kosovo and Rwanda sound far away and insignificant; they are easily put out of mind. Even issues closer to home—say, a maniacal clique of peers who threaten a classmate—may seem like someone else's problem. For people who feel this way, inaction does not strike at their self-conception. Therefore, despite commonplace assumptions to the contrary, their moral knowledge will not be enough to impel moral action.

The development of a moral identity follows a general pattern. It normally takes shape in late childhood, when children acquire the capacity to analyze people—including themselves—in terms of stable character traits. In childhood, self-identifying traits usually consist of action-related skills and interests ("I'm smart" or "I love music"). With age, children start to use moral terms to define themselves. By the onset of puberty, they typically invoke adjectives such as "fairminded," "generous" and "honest."

Some adolescents go so far as to describe themselves primarily in terms of moral goals. They speak of noble purposes, such as caring for others or improving their communities, as missions that give meaning to their lives. Working in Camden, N.J., Daniel Hart and his colleagues at Rutgers University found that a high proportion of so-called care exemplars—teenagers identified by teachers and peers as highly committed to volunteering—had self-identities that were based on moral belief systems. Yet they scored no higher than their peers on the standard psychological tests of moral judgment. The study is noteworthy because it was conducted in an economically deprived urban setting among an adolescent population often stereotyped as high risk and criminally inclined [*see box,* "Could You Live with Yourself?"].

At the other end of the moral spectrum, further evidence indicates that moral identity drives behavior. Social psychologists Hazel Markus of Stanford University and Daphne Oyserman of the University of Michigan have observed that delinquent youths have immature senses of self, especially when talking about their future selves (a critical part of adolescent identity). These troubled teenagers do not imagine themselves as doctors, husbands, voting citizens, church members—any social role that embodies a positive value commitment.

How does a young person acquire, or not acquire, a moral identity? It is an incremental process, occurring gradually in thousands of small ways: feedback from others; observations of actions by others that either inspire or appall; reflections on one's own experience; cultural influences such as family, school, religious institutions and the mass media. The relative importance of these factors varies from child to child.

Teach Your Children Well

For most children, parents are the original source of moral guidance. Psychologists such as Diana Baumrind of the University of California at Berkeley have shown that "authoritative" parenting facilitates children's moral growth more surely than either "permissive" or "authoritarian" parenting. The authoritative mode establishes consistent family rules and firm limits but also en-courages open discussion and clear communication to explain and, when justified, revise the rules. In contrast, the permissive mode avoids rules entirely; the authoritarian mode irregularly enforces rules at the parent's whim—the "because I said so" approach.

Although permissive and authoritarian parenting seem like opposites, they actually tend to produce similar patterns of poor self-control and low social responsibility in children. Neither mode presents children with the realistic expectations and structured guidance that challenge them to expand their moral horizons. Both can foster habits—such as feeling that mores come from the outside—that could inhibit the development of a moral identity. In this way, moral or immoral conduct during adulthood often has roots in childhood experience.

As children grow, they are increasingly exposed to influences beyond the family. In most families, however, the parent-child relationship remains primary as long as the child lives at home. A parent's comment on a raunchy music lyric or a blood-drenched video usually will stick with a child long after the media experience has faded. In fact, if salacious or violent media programming opens the door to responsible parental feedback, the benefits can far outweigh the harm.

One of the most influential things parents can do is to encourage the right kinds of peer relations. Interactions with peers can spur moral growth by showing children the conflict between their preconceptions and social reality. During the debates about dividing the chocolate, some of our subjects seemed to pick up new—and more informed—ideas about justice. In a follow-up study, we confirmed that the peer debate had heightened their awareness of the rights of others. Children who participated actively in the debate, both expressing their opinions and listening to the viewpoints of others, were especially likely to benefit.

In adolescence, peer interactions are crucial in forging a self-identity. To be sure, this process often plays out in cliquish social behavior: as a means of defining and shoring up the sense of self, kids will seek out like-minded peers and spurn others who seem foreign. But when kept within reasonable bounds, the in-group clustering generally evolves into a more mature friendship pattern. What can parents do in the meantime to fortify a teenager who is bearing the brunt of isolation or persecution? The most important message they can give is that cruel behavior reveals something about the perpetrator rather than about the victim. If this advice helps the youngster resist taking the treatment personally, the period of persecution will pass without leaving any psychological scars.

Some psychologists, taking a sociological approach, are examining community-level variables, such as whether various moral influences—parents, teachers, mass media and so on—are consistent with one another. In a study of 311 adolescents from 10 American towns and cities, Francis A. J. Ianni of the Columbia University Teachers College noticed high degrees of altruistic behavior and low degrees of antisocial behavior among youngsters from communities where there was consensus in expectations for young people.

Everyone in these places agreed that honesty, for instance, is a fundamental value. Teachers did not tolerate cheating on exams, parents did not let their children lie and get away with it, sports coaches did not encourage teams to bend the rules for the sake of a win, and people of all ages expected openness from their friends. But many communities were divided along such lines. Coaches espoused winning above all else, and parents protested when teachers reprimanded their children for cheating or shoddy schoolwork. Under such circumstances, children learned not to take moral messages seriously.

Ianni named the set of shared standards in harmonious communities a "youth charter." Ethnicity, cultural diversity, socioeconomic status, geographic location and population size had nothing to do with whether a town offered its young people a steady moral compass. The notion of a youth charter is being explored in social interventions that foster communication among children, parents, teachers and other influential adults. Meanwhile other researchers have sought to understand whether the specific values depend on cultural, gender or generational background [see box, "How Universal Are Values?"].

Unfortunately, the concepts embodied in youth charters seem ever rarer in American society. Even when adults spot trouble, they may fail to step in. Parents are busy and often out of touch with the peer life of their children; they give kids more autonomy than ever before, and kids expect it—indeed, demand it. Teachers, for their part, feel that a child's nonacademic life is none of their business and that they could be censured, even sued, if they intervened in a student's personal or moral problem. And neighbors feel the same way: that they have no business interfering with another family's business, even if they see a child headed for trouble.

Everything that psychologists know from the study of children's moral development indicates that moral identity—the key source of moral commitment throughout life—is fostered by multiple social influences that guide a child in the same general direction. Children must hear the message enough for it to stick. The challenge for pluralistic societies will be to find enough common ground to communicate the shared standards that the young need.

The Author

WILLIAM DAMON remembers being in an eighth-grade clique that tormented an unpopular kid. After describing his acts in the school newspaper, he was told by his English teacher, "I give you an A for the writing, but what you're doing is really shameful." That moral feedback has stayed with him. Damon is now director of the Center on Adolescence at Stanford University, an interdisciplinary program that specializes in what he has called "the least understood, the least trusted, the most feared and most neglected period of development." A developmental psychologist, he has studied intellectual and moral growth, educational methods, and peer and cultural influences on children. He is the author of numerous books and the father of three children, the youngest now in high school.

Further Reading

THE MEANING AND MEASUREMENT OF MORAL DEVELOPMENT. Lawrence Kohlberg. Clark University, Heinz Werner Institute, 1981.

THE EMERGENCE OF MORALITY IN YOUNG CHILDREN. Edited by Jerome Kagan and Sharon Lamb. University of Chicago Press, 1987.

THE MORAL CHILD: NURTURING CHILDREN'S NATURAL MORAL GROWTH. William Damon. Free Press, 1990.

ARE AMERICAN CHILDREN'S PROBLEMS GETTING WORSE? A 13-YEAR COMPARISON. Thomas M. Achenbach and Catherine T. Howell in Journal of the American Academy of Child and Adolescent Psychiatry, Vol. 32, No. 6, pages 1145–1154; November 1993.

SOME DO CARE: CONTEMPORARY LIVES OF MORAL COMMITMENT. Anne Colby. Free Press, 1994.

THE YOUTH CHARTER: HOW COMMUNITIES CAN WORK TOGETHER TO RAISE STANDARDS FOR ALL OUR CHILDREN. William Damon. Free Press, 1997.

Raising Better Boys

Boys today face overwhelming challenges—from negative media images to epidemics of violence. But with family and community support, our boys can learn about responsibility, healing, and self-respect.

Geoffrey Canada

I had just come back to my office from a meeting when I was told that a reporter was on the phone. When I answered the call, the reporter asked what by now has become a familiar question: "Did you hear about the shooting?"

Because the reporter called me, I knew several things right away. First, whoever was shot was a child. Second, the victim was not a child with whom I work. When one of my children from Harlem is shot and killed, nobody calls; death by handgun is so common that it is no longer considered news. This shooting must have taken place in a nice, middle-class suburban or rural community. Third, I knew that more than one child was shot. Today in the United States, the shooting of one child, even in affluent

communities, is not considered newsworthy. And fourth, I knew that the shooter was a boy. In this country, our girls surely have their problems, but our boys are the ones who kill.

Boys in Trouble

At a time when we have made incredible advances in technology and medicine, we have managed to create a generation of boys who are more in trouble than ever before. The signs ought to be clear, but we are not heeding the warnings. The shootings in Paducah, Jonesboro, and Littleton might seem, by themselves, like isolated tragic incidents, but collectively they form a familiar pattern.

I saw a similar pattern begin in 1985, although I must admit that with

all my years of working with children, I didn't have a clue about what I was witnessing. In 1985, one boy with whom I worked at the Rheedlen Centers for Children and Families was shot and killed. In 1986, two more of our boys were shot and killed. In 1987, four of our boys were shot and killed. This pattern continued until, in 1989, seven boys were shot and killed. Even then I didn't recognize the killings for what they were. I tried to understand each killing as the separate act of a violent perpetrator against an innocent (and sometimes not so innocent) victim. Not until 1990 did I realize that what was happening in my New York City community, Harlem, was happening in communities in Chicago, Detroit, Kansas City, Los Angeles, Boston—

indeed, in cities and towns across the United States. We had not a series of individual violent acts, but evidence of a full-scale epidemic of violence.

In my first book, *Fist Stick Knife Gun, A Personal History of Violence in America* (1994), I wrote about the escalating violence in poor communities. By then, we had lost more than 60,000 children to handgun violence in less than 10 years. My purpose for the book was not just to recite the facts and horrors that poor children grow up with during conditions of war, but also to serve as a warning. This epidemic would spread out of the ghettos and into our middle-class enclaves if we didn't do something about it.

We haven't done much, and the killings have not abated. The Children's Defense Fund reports that between 1979 and 1996, more than 75,000 U.S. children and teens were killed by firearms and a staggering 375,000 were wounded. And we see the first signs of the same pattern of epidemic violence in communities that are not poor, not minority, not urban.

In 1996, after taking a closer look at children and violence, I realized that boys seem particularly susceptible to the most virulent form of the epidemic. The more research I did, the worse the news seemed—not just in terms of violence, but within a whole range of categories. I found a disturbing pattern among people ages 15 to 25. Three out of four deaths are of males. Males are five times more likely to die from homicide than females are. Six out of seven suicides in this age range are by males. Nine out of 10 arrests are of males. My research led to a shocking conclusion: Not just a small sample, but a huge number of boys are doing poorly.

My second book, *Reaching Up for Manhood* (1998), focused on the troubling social and environmental conditions that boys face today. On the basis of my research, I suggested what we can do to raise better boys.

During soccer season, some of my white friends and I went to 7-Eleven to buy soda. And as soon as I walked in with them, I was followed all the way around the store. Meanwhile, my white friends were stealing soda. People think that racism is gone, but it's still there.

—10th grade boy

Healing

Boys are in pain. Years of conditioning starting when boys are toddlers teach them to deny their pain, that "boys don't cry." But boys should cry. It is a natural reaction and a way to acknowledge and release pain, both physical and emotional. Denying emotions not only represses and stunts emotional growth, but it also masks our hurt from others so that they don't know that we need help.

We have to reach out to our boys early on and get them to talk about their feelings. This is easier when boys are young, but somewhere between 10 and 13, boys begin to resist talking. When they hit puberty, boys feel that it is taboo to talk about shame and inadequacy, especially with their parents. How do we get boys to remain in touch with their feelings? How can we ensure that adults in their lives are compassionate and skilled at talking with them and listening to them during this crucial period? For every boy we work with, we must ask, With whom does he talk? When the answer is no one, we must find the right people to fill that void.

Risk

Boys are encouraged to take risks very early in life. We think it natural for boys to jump off steps, climb trees, jump puddles. Adults, including parents, often consciously or unconsciously reinforce this risk-taking behavior, and boys confuse taking risks with being male and masculine. This prepares our boys for dangerous risk taking when they become adolescents. Boys often break the laws (both legal and parental) when peers challenge

them. The words "I dare you" or "What's the matter; you scared?" have ruined the life of many a boy.

We must make sure that our boys can take risks in safe environments. There are plenty of risky things for boys to do that challenge them, but in a healthy and developmentally appropriate way. Some boys play sports, some dance, some ride bikes or horses. We must offer a full menu of choices. All boys don't like basketball; some get a thrill from facing an opponent one-on-one in a game of chess; others find that nothing short of jumping into the air on a skateboard and doing a 360-degree turn will do. But one thing is certain: If we don't provide safe risks for boys, they will engage in dangerous activities that can leave scars more damaging than scraped knees and wounded egos.

Self-Worth

Our boys are the target of successful sales and marketing strategies by large and sophisticated retailers. They connect our boys' sense of self-worth to how they look and what they wear, eat, or drink. Boys get the message that they are what they look like and what they consume. Vulnerable boys are taught to focus less on their internal development than on the external world. Parents and teachers struggle to get boys to pay attention to such values as cooperation, kindness, and service. We think our boys are shallow and lack values, but we fail to realize that their minds are influenced by the smartest and most savvy advertisers in the world.

We must recognize that our boys are brainwashed by the sneaker companies, the fast food industry, the soft drink industry, and others too numerous to name. Remember Joe Camel? The cigarette company knew what would appeal to our children and launched a successful campaign. Our children are a market, and marketers understand our children's fears, aspirations, and fantasies—often better than we do. They use this understanding to shape our children's attitudes and beliefs.

We must pay attention to the values that these industries sell to our children and contrast them with the values that we talk to them about. Most teachers and parents do well to give their children five positive messages a day. In contrast, by the time that day is over, our children will have heard 50 negative messages from their music, television, video games, and radio. It's not that our children don't value our messages. Rather, we are drowned out by the number of negative messages that they hear from other sources.

We have to even out this equation by giving more positive messages of self-worth and by reducing the number of negative messages from others. We must talk with our boys about how they view themselves on the inside and encourage and reward them for focusing on both their internal and external selves.

Mentors

Too many boys lack positive male role models. The number of fathers who are not intimately involved in raising their sons because of separation, divorce, or abandonment has reached staggering proportions. Boys struggle to understand the concept of manhood, and if they don't have positive role models, too many of them look to the streets, to television, or to the movies to understand what it takes to be a man. In these places, they are liable to find manhood defined as a combination of toughness, promiscuity, hard drinking, and a willingness to solve every dispute with violence. Boys emulate those visions of manhood with the youthful exuber-

Boys struggle to understand the concept of manhood, and if they don't have positive role models, too many of them look to the streets, to television, or to the movies to understand what it takes to be a man.

ance with which teens embrace most things.

We must ensure that our boys have male role models who take a personal interest in their moral, intellectual, and emotional development. Where should we look for male mentors? At our institutions of faith, at our college fraternities, at our youth organizations. Boys need not one, but several male mentors in their lives.

What We Can All Do

Can we raise better boys? We can and we must. In one year alone, more than 1.3 million boys under 18 were arrested. One out of every four males in the United States has a record. Fully two-thirds of boys who reach the age of 15 in Harlem can expect to die in young or middle adulthood. If we raise our boys in the same way, we will continue to produce huge numbers of boys who are crippled emotionally and are unprepared to fulfill their roles as fathers, husbands, and productive members of our society. The following are some additional suggestions.

Monitor What They See and Hear

Our children watch too much television, and with the advent of cable, children at very young ages are exposed to violence and sex in a way that was unimaginable 20 years ago. Do you know the lyrics to the latest rap song? Do you watch MTV? Looked at Saturday morning cartoons lately? We should watch what our boys are watching. The mass media shape so much of a boy's sense of himself and his image of manhood. If we spend time watching and listening with them, we will find plenty of opportunities to engage boys in real conversations about real issues before

someone else is allowed to shape their thinking.

Find a Place for Spiritual and Moral Education

Most people from my generation (I'm 47) were introduced to spiritual and moral development through a formal institution of faith. I'm a Christian, and my mother made me go to church every Sunday, even though I didn't want to until I was 12 years old. In church, I heard about good and evil and about the responsibility to give back, to help others, and to do unto others as you would have them do unto you. Too many of our boys receive scant, if any, education in these crucial areas. It doesn't matter what our particular faith is; we must encourage parents to expose their boys to their faith institutions. Too often, we don't think about the moral development of boys until they are in trouble. Everyone who is raising a boy should plan out his moral and spiritual development while he is still young.

Expose Boys to Different Cultures and Points of View

Boys tend to be intolerant of others. They can be racist, sexist, and cruel to other boys who don't conform to their ideas or standards. We give too little thought to broadening the experiences of boys so that early in their lives, they learn about many different cultures, attitudes, and beliefs. We wait until our boys have developed rigid prejudices before we talk with them about differences and tolerance. Our work should begin in elementary school and continue throughout their educational lives.

Know Their Friends

By the time most boys reach puberty, they do what their friends do. If you want to know what any one boy is doing, find out what his friends are doing. Sooner or later, he will do the same thing. This means that when we try to influence a boy, we should not work exclusively with that boy, but also with his friends. Too many times, we try to reach boys as individuals without acknowledging the power of the peer group.

Expose Boys to New Experiences

Take boys on nature walks. Start with frogs and turtles, but include plants and flowers. Teach them about the environment, sailing, singing, sewing, and dancing. By the time boys are 12, they usually say that they don't want to try something new if we haven't made a habit of expanding their experiences when they were young. Very quickly, boys decide that some activities are for boys—riding a bike, playing sports—and some are not—smelling flowers, baking bread. Our job is to not allow hastily developed, arbitrary beliefs to deprive boys of a fuller set of experiences.

Have a Multilayered Support System

I have found (not surprisingly) that boys who have several strong support systems—parents, grandparents, uncles and aunts, cousins their own age, coaches, teachers, and caring adults who run after-school activities—do better than boys who don't. Boys with more support systems get into less trouble, and if they do get into trouble, they get out of it more quickly and are less likely to get back into it. Part of our responsibility in raising better boys is to expand the number of support systems that exist for them. The less influential their family support, the more they need community support.

Reconnecting with All Our Children

Our boys are in trouble, but all is not lost. We have the know-how and the resources in the United States to dramatically change boys' lives for the better. We must find ways to bring new attention and energy to boys—without ever losing our focus on girls. This calls for us to rededicate ourselves to ensuring that we give the best that we have to all our children.

Geoffrey Canada is President of the Rheedlen Centers for Children and Families, 2770 Broadway, New York, NY 10025.

Ethnicity, Identity Formation, and Risk Behavior Among Adolescents of Mexican Descent

Arik V. Marcell

Arik V. Marcell is an MD/Masters in Public Health degree candidate at The University of Illinois College of Medicine, Chicago, and Johns Hopkins University School of Hygiene and Public Health, Baltimore.

Persons of Mexican descent, the largest Hispanic group, make up 50 to 63 percent of the U.S. Hispanic population, which, in turn, comprises about 9 percent of the U.S. population and is one of the fastest growing U.S. ethnic minorities. Mexican Americans are at greater risk of mortality and morbidity than the general U.S. population. However, only a few studies have assessed the health of adolescents of Mexican descent.

High levels of problem behavior, such as alcohol use, unsafe sexual behavior, school dropout, and delinquency, have been cited for youth of Mexican descent. Understanding the factors contributing to risk behavior in adolescents of Mexican descent may help improve health care service delivery and use. Various factors influence the involvement of adolescents of Mexican descent in problem behaviors:

Socioeconomic factors. Hispanic adolescents are more likely to fall below poverty level than white adolescents. A higher proportion of His-panic adolescents are uninsured as compared to white adolescents. Access to care by Mexican American populations is limited due to unfamiliarity with available services, lack of regular health care providers, type of health care facility used, and proximity of facility to residence. Consequently, Mexican Americans are more likely to use public health facilities, hospital outpatient clinics, and emergency rooms than to establish continuity with one primary care physician.

Family factors. Mexican American cultural values traditionally place great importance on family relations and bonds. In the United States, as cultural awareness declines with successive generations, familism may suffer, leading to problems for adolescents in these families. Mexican American adolescents living in single-parent, female-headed households have higher rates of drinking, drug use, overall risk-taking behavior, and earlier sexual activity onset, than adolescents living with both parents. These observations demonstrate that family members engage in risk behavior in the absence of the nuclear family structure in the U.S. It has been argued, however, that quality of the parenting relationship is more significant in predicting social deviance, substance use, and dropping out than the family's com-position. Poor parent-child relationships; insufficient bonding, communication, and guidance; and too authoritative or permissive parents may better predict problem behavior than does family structure.

Community factors. The degree to which an ethnic community is organized with religious institutions, welfare organizations, and ethnic businesses determines its ability to foster ethnic identification and preserve ethnic culture among its members. A community lacking cohesiveness and sense of kinship may decrease self-esteem development among its youth, leading to poor impulse control, less developed sense of right and wrong, and greater risk-taking behavior. Living in high-risk urban settings, where most youth of Mexican descent live, may further expose them to acute problem behavior.

School factors. School environment and quality as well as school teachers' attitudes and classroom practices also may lead to school failure and dropout. Dropout rates are higher among students attending segregated schools, public vocational schools, schools with low teacher-to-pupil ratios, large schools with large classes, and in schools which emphasize tracking and testing. Students of Mexican descent living in urban centers attend schools

From *The Education Digest,* April 1995, pp. 58–62. Condensed from *Journal of School Health,* October 1994, pp. 323–327. Reprinted by permission of Prakken Publications, Inc., Ann Arbor, MI 48107.

characterized by these factors and hence may be at risk for dropping out.

Problem behavior in minority adolescents appears inversely related to identity formation and ethnic identification and directly related to acculturation.

Identity formation. Ethnic identity—a component of a more general process of identity formation which occurs during adolescence—is the commitment made to a social grouping of common ancestry characterized by the sharing of common values, behavioral patterns, or symbols different from the larger society's.

For Mexican American immigrant adolescents, carrying out developmental tasks in the context of a new culture—and also in the presence of language barriers, social constraints as members of a devalued minority group, and social class differences—can greatly influence identity formation. Many decisions immigrant adolescents choose to make regarding their sexuality, independence, and future may be distinct from their parents' choices and at odds with their background values. An achieved ethnic identity, leading to increased self-esteem, results from exploration and resolution of these issues, whereas a foreclosed ethnic identity, leading to low self-esteem, poor mental health outcomes, poor educational performance, and alienation, results from failure to do so.

Cultural retention/acculturation. Retention of ethnic culture among immigrants varies due to length of time in the host society, opportunity to practice the culture, degree of cultural incorporation (taking on elements of the mainstream culture), and degree of structural incorporation (acceptance into host society institutions). In addition, ethnic cultural retention depends on one's degree of ethnic identification (ethnic loyalty), acculturation (acceptance of new cultural traits at the loss of old), and social assimilation (integration of an ethnic minority group into mainstream society).

Rate and degree of Mexican American acculturation depend on generational status. First-generation immigrants encounter more difficulties than second- and third-generation counterparts. Age at immigration also is important: the younger the person, the easier to acquire elements of the mainstream culture. As Hispanics become more acculturated, their health status worsens, tobacco and alcohol use increases, diet worsens, risk-taking behavior increases, and morbidity and mortality for certain diseases increase.

Whereas acculturation, a prerequisite for assimilation, is strongly linked to generational status, it has been argued that ethnic identification with people of Mexican descent is not. One study shows cultural awareness declining significantly in the study population between the first and second generations and continuing to decline through the fourth generation, whereas ethnic loyalty decreases only slightly between the first and second generations and in fact remained virtually constant through the fourth generation. The authors also suggest that social assimilation, a third related process, contributes to ethnic culture change. This study can help in understanding how Mexican Americans adjust to mainstream society and how ethnicity and culture change affect adolescents of Mexican descent as well as their community.

Ethnic Identity. Understanding how Mexican youth identify themselves provides insight into the interaction among ethnic identity, cultural awareness, and risk behavior. A study performed in a California high school examines the interrelatedness of ethnicity and ethnic identity, minority status, and perceptions of adult opportunities in Mexican-descent students.

The students separate themselves into five groups depending on degree of ethnic identification and cultural awareness. Individually perceived ethnic identity has strong implications for success in school,

risk of dropping out, and possible involvement in risk-taking behavior.

Recent Mexican immigrant students have limited English proficiency and claim closer ties with Mexico then any other group. *Mexican-oriented students,* maintaining strong bicultural ties with both Mexico and the United States, are bilingual speakers with varying degrees of English proficiency who perform well in school and have lived in the U.S. more than five years. *Mexican American students,* born in the U.S. and proficient in English (speaking little Spanish), describe themselves as totally assimilated and are the most successful of the Mexican-descent student population. *Chicanos* (U.S. native-born students), representing the majority of the student population, alienate themselves from school activities and favor behavior that promotes failure in school (frequent absence, disruptive activities, noncompliance with classroom assignments). Finally, *Cholos* (low riders or rebellious students) are identified by some of the other groups as "students who had lost their Mexican roots" and as most likely to be gang members or "gang sympathizers."

Membership in the Chicano or Cholo group is identified as derogatory by the other three groups, but not by Chicanos or Cholos themselves. However, identification with Chicanos or Cholos does have negative consequences, since school achievement is defined as antithetical to ethnic solidarity. The fact that most in the Chicano or Cholo groups share the same beliefs predisposes them to dropping out and thereby engaging in risk-taking activities. Recent Mexican immigrant students also could be at risk for dropping out secondary to "negative" influences from Chicano and Cholo youth and due to low English proficiency.

These observations do not imply that successful students do not engage in high-risk behavior. Comprehending ethnic identity formation for adolescents of Mexican descent can only help to identify characteristics which most likely predispose to risky activities. Correspondingly, not all school settings will resemble the California high school referred to here. However, similar subgroupings based on degree of ethnic identification and acculturation may exist in different geographic locations and may apply to other ethnic populations as well.

The following are some recommendations for programs:

1. Promote ethnic identity and appropriate level of prevention.

■ Recognize the heterogeneity among Hispanic and Mexican-origin adolescent populations in health care delivery settings.

■ Identify Mexican American adolescents' degree of ethnic identification and acculturation in health care delivery settings.

■ Develop better ways to identify this population's health needs, how it defines its needs regarding problem behavior, and how it perceives and identifies risk.

■ Learn about the medical conditions for which this population does seek care, and develop better ways and alternative education approaches to increase awareness for services this population does not deem necessary.

■ Develop specifically designed education materials for new immigrant Mexican American adolescents to help them integrate into the school environment and external society.

2. Promote interaction among social workers, schools, families, and communities.

■ Develop education materials to help instruct all persons in the community regarding high-risk behavior and their consequences to increase prevention knowledge.

■ Adolescent clinics, working in concert with social workers and school staff, could become advocates for Mexican American adolescents from deteriorating families.

■ Integrate youth centers into the clinic setting to help encourage youth of Mexican descent to use preventive services.

■ Examine teacher expectations of students, making teachers aware of personal stereotypes and prejudices that may affect student-teacher relations.

3. Adapt program activities.

■ Use same-ethnic and same-gender staff trained to collect information from these youth regarding their backgrounds to help better understand the needs of this population and enhance communication between staff and youth.

■ Use bilingual personnel and appropriately translated literature to help break down language barriers in providing services and help improve the relationship with the community.

■ Include representative youth in program planning to facilitate use of health services and prevention programs.

■ Develop leadership training for adolescents of Mexican descent to help bridge health care providers with their peers.

■ Develop specific risk-factor programs, such as dropout prevention, to target potentially high-risk individuals. Provision of health services, counseling, and self-efficacy/work-study programs may help these individuals remain in school.

■ Establish referral systems with health settings used by this population, such as public health facilities and emergency rooms, to target youth of Mexican descent who are out of school and may not have access to care.

■ Together with the schools, develop communication strategies such as school presentations, one-on-one dialogues, and small-group discussions to encourage these youth to explore their feelings and attitudes regarding ethnicity, family, and community. Identify discrepancies between adolescents of Mexican descent and their parents regarding degree of acculturation and ethnic identification to stimulate changes in health-related behavior and motivate these students to take an active role in their own health education.

■ Develop more qualitative and health status assessment research to address adequately this population's needs and concerns.

☐ WHITE ☐ BLACK ☐ ASIAN ☐ OTHER

"I'm just who I am"

Race is no longer as simple as black or white.
So, what does this mean for America?

By JACK E. WHITE WASHINGTON

HIS NICKNAME NOTWITHSTANDING, professional golfer Frank ("Fuzzy") Zoeller saw Tiger Woods quite clearly. He gazed upon the new king of professional golf, through whose veins runs the blood of four continents, and beheld neither a one-man melting pot nor even a golfing prodigy but a fried-chicken-and-collard-greens-eating Sambo. Zoeller saw Woods, in short, as just another stereotype, condemned by his blackness to the perpetual status of "little boy."

Zoeller soon paid a price for saying openly what many others were thinking secretly. K Mart, the discount chain with a big African-American clientele, unceremoniously dumped him as the sponsor of a line of golf clothing and equipment, and he abjectly withdrew from the Greater Greensboro Open tournament. "People who know me know I'm a jokester. I just didn't deliver the line well," Zoeller tearfully explained. But his real crime was not, as he and his defenders seem to think, merely a distasteful breach of racial etiquette or an inept attempt at humor. The real crime was falling behind the times. The old black-white stereotypes are out of date, and Zoeller is just the latest casualty of America's failure to come to grips with the perplexing and rapidly evolving significance of racial identity in what is fast becoming the most polyglot society in history.

If current demographic trends persist, midway through the 21st century whites will no longer make up a majority of the U.S. population. Blacks will have been overtaken as the largest minority group by Hispanics. Asians and Pacific Islanders will more than double their number of 9.3 million in 1995 to 19.6 million by 2020. An explosion of interracial, interethnic and interreligious marriages will swell the ranks of children whose

MELDING POT

Children of interracial marriages in millions

Interracial marriages in millions

1970 1980 1990

Percentage of African Americans marrying whites

8.9

Women
Men 3.9

1.9
0.7

1970 1993

mere existence makes a mockery of age-old racial categories and attitudes. Since 1970, the number of multi-racial children has quadrupled to more than 2 million, according to the Bureau of the Census. The color line once drawn between blacks and whites—or more precisely between whites and nonwhites—is breaking into a polygon of dueling ethnicities, each fighting for its place in the sun.

For many citizens the "browning of America" means a disorienting plunge into

an uncharted sea of identity. Zoeller is far from alone in being confused about the complex tangle of genotypes and phenotypes and cultures that now undercut centuries-old verities about race and race relations in the U.S. Like many others, he hasn't got a clue about what to call the growing ranks of people like Woods who inconveniently refuse to be pigeonholed into one of the neat, oversimplified racial classifications used by government agencies—and, let's face it, most people. Are they people of color? Mixed race? Biracial? Whatever they like?

And if we don't know what to call them, how are we supposed to cope with them? Are they a new and distinct category of "real" Americans, due the same respectful recognition—and governmental protections—as more familiar groups? Or should they be lumped into the demeaning catchall category of "minorities" or "other"? How we eventually answer these questions will affect everything from the first Census forms of the 21st century, which will be issued a mere three years from now, to university admissions policies to the way civil rights laws are enforced. Even more important, it may ultimately transform the way Americans identify themselves and the tribe or tribes they belong to. In one grandiose vision, shared by conservative analyst Douglas Besharov of the American Enterprise Institute and communitarian sociologist Amitai Etzioni of American University, the ambiguous racial identity of mixed-race children may be "the best hope for the future of American race relations," as Besharov puts it. Letting people define themselves as multiracial, Etzioni argues, "has the potential to soften the racial lines that now divide America by rendering them more like economic differences and less like harsh, almost immutable, caste lines." Those who blend many streams of ethnicity within their own bodies, the argument goes, will render race a meaningless concept, providing a biological solution to the problem of racial justice. This idea reflects a deeply pessimistic view of human nature. It suggests that people can get along with each other only if they are all the same, instead of learning to accept and respect differences.

In any event, the way Americans think and talk about race will have to catch up with the new reality. Just how anachronistic our racial vocabulary has become was made clear by Woods in an appearance last week on *The Oprah Winfrey Show*. When asked if it bothered him, the only child of a black American father and a Thai mother, to be called an African American, he replied, "It does. Growing up, I came up with this name: I'm a 'Cablinasian,' " which he explained is a self-crafted acronym that reflects his one-eighth Caucasian, one-fourth black, one-eighth American Indian, one-fourth Thai and one-fourth Chinese roots with a precision that a racial-classifications expert under South African apartheid would admire. He said that when he was asked to check a box for racial background, he couldn't settle on just one. "I checked off 'African American' and 'Asian.' Those are the two I was raised under, and the only two I know."

KERBOOM! A MINI-RACIAL FIRE STORM erupted. Woods' remarks infuriated many African Americans who hailed his record-setting triumph at the Masters as a symbol of racial progress but see him as a traitor. To them Woods appeared to be running away from being an African American—a condition, they were quick to point out, that he himself had emphasized when he paid tribute to black golf pioneers Teddy Rhoades, Charlie Sifford and Lee Elder in his graceful victory speech. In a mirror image of Zoeller's constricted views, some blacks saw Woods' assertion of a multiracial identity as a sellout that could touch off an epidemic of "passing." Arthur Fletcher, a black member of the U.S. Commission on Civil Rights, testified at a 1993 congressional hearing devoted to whether a new, "multiracial" category should be added to U.S. Census forms that "I can see a whole host of light-skinned black Americans running for the door the minute they have another choice. All of a sudden they have a way of saying, 'In this discriminatory culture of ours, I am something other than black.'"

In their rush to judgment, the fearful apparently never stopped to consider that Woods was not turning his back on any part of his identity but instead was embracing every aspect of it. As he put it, "I'm just who I am, whoever you see in front of you"—and that includes his Asian side. "The influence of Tiger's mother Kultida in his life is very important," declares a family friend. "He goes to the temple with her oc-

"YOU CAN'T BE A FAIRY"

WHEN SHEBA HOWERTON AUDItioned for a sixth-grade performance of *Sleeping Beauty*, two white girls in the play told her to forget it. "You're black," they said. "You can't be a fairy." But when she tried to mix with a group of African Americans in high school, she got another challenge. "Why is your skin so light?" one demanded. Says Howerton, 15, whose father is of African, Cherokee and Irish descent and whose mother comes from a family of German Jews: "I can't pass for white, and I can't pass for black. But I definitely feel there is a lot of pressure to align myself with one group or another."

Instead Howerton has tried to find a middle ground, choosing friends of all races and switching between ethnic cliques at De Anza High School in Richmond, California. "I flow back and forth," she says. To combat further their alienation, Sheba and her 12-year-old sister Shira have joined Generation Pride, a group of a dozen teenagers of interracial background in the San Francisco Bay Area. The group holds social gatherings and discussions about interracial issues, offering a rare space free from racial pigeonholing. The group is an offshoot of an adult group, Interracial/Intercultural Pride, whose members are of mixed races or in mixed couples. Doug Howerton, Sheba's father, is I-Pride's vice president. "Those that are biracial and multiracial have a unique look" at things, he says. "They see from both sides, and they try to be more just."

casionally. She's a devout Buddhist. He wears a family heirloom Buddha around his neck. He's a hybrid of a lot of things, and that's how he sees himself. He honestly sees himself as a somewhat separate person from the norm—not in terms of talent but in terms of his makeup."

Woods grew up in a suburb of Los Angeles with mostly white friends. But over the years he has made four visits to Thailand, where locals like to say he's "Asian from the eyes up," and he has also embraced the role model of his father Earl, who was the first black to play baseball in the Big Eight (for Kansas State). Now Tiger seems to be saying that if acknowledging the totality of his genetic and cultural makeup is difficult for many Americans, they will just have to try harder.

If history is any guide, a lot of them won't try at all. "It's very hard for other folks to embrace our philosophy without thinking we are being racist or trying to create a new race," says Nancy G. Brown, a Jewish woman who is married to a black man and is a past president of the 10-year-old advocacy group Multiracial Americans of Southern California. "It's hard for people to believe we are just looking for equality and that we are able to live with the concept of duality. Constantly calling Tiger Woods black is a good example of what we are talking about."

Groups like Brown's have lobbied for a multiracial category on government forms, but they also point out that recognizing multiracialism is more than just a matter of "psychic comfort." There are important health issues, for example, such as bone-marrow matching and how such race-specific syndromes as Tay-Sachs manifest themselves and get treated in biracial individuals. And most multiracial Americans have had the experience of being arbitrarily assigned an ethnic identity by a school principal, a caseworker or an employer that may differ from other family members'—or from one form to the next.

THE NOXIOUS PRACTICE OF PIGEONholing people in narrow racial classifications is a deeply ingrained American habit that predates independence. It began with a desire to enforce firm distinctions between free citizens and slaves. In 1661, for example, Virginia decreed that the legal status of the mother would determine whether a black child was a slave or free. Three years later, Maryland went a step further, declaring that if either of a child's parents was a slave, the child would also be. The purpose of this law, its authors said, was to deter "divers freeborn English women" from marrying black slaves. But it did nothing to deter white male slave owners from trying to expand their human holdings by impregnating black female slaves.

Eventually, these pioneering efforts at codifying racial distinctions hardened into so-called miscegenation laws, which aimed to preserve the "purity" of the white race by making interracial sex a crime. Though upholding such laws required ever more tortured legal definitions of who was black and who wasn't, 16 states continued to ban interracial marriages until 1967, when the U.S. Supreme Court struck down such laws. In what was perhaps the most ridiculous example of racial pigeonholing, Louisiana ordained that anyone with a "trace" of black ancestry would be classified as black. Then, in an ostensibly "humane" 1970 reform, it enacted the "one thirty-second rule," by which anyone with a single black great-great-great-great-grandparent and 31 white great-great-great-great-grandparents was legally black. That regulation went unchal-

WHO WOULD "SEE THE ASIAN IN ME"?

FAY YARBROUGH, 21, CAN STILL FEEL the tug of ethnic loyalties from her Korean mother. "In high school," recalls the daughter of an African-American serviceman, "after I cut my hair, my mother looked at me with this really sad expression on her face. She said people would not be able to see the Asian in me, and that was hard for her. I didn't feel I was making some kind of statement, but my mother took it as a rejection of that cultural side of me."

When she was a freshman at Rice University in Texas, she recalls, she walked to a meeting of the Korean Student Association and stunned a fellow student by talking to her in Korean. The schoolmate had just said, " 'Oh, no, we couldn't possibly be going to the same place. I am eating with the Korean Student Association.' The other students looked at me the same way, even though I was one of a handful who could speak Korean and who ever had lived in Korea."

Yarbrough now leans toward her black heritage, finding African Americans more receptive. "Blacks come in all shapes and colors," she says. "Koreans are very homogenous. Someone like me is a much bigger issue for them." She is dating a black man. "Asian men don't date women who look like me."

For many decades, people on all sides of the color line chafed at these legal restraints on their ability to love and procreate. Even where black-white marriages were legal, these couples had to seek refuge in more tolerant black neighborhoods and raise their children as African Americans. But in the past 20 years, as the number of mixed-race marriages has increased dramatically, to more than 3 million by some estimates, attitudes among all racial groups have evolved. Tracey Mandell, 26, is an English instructor at Loyola Marymount University. Her partner Michael Bartley is a black man from Jamaica, and their son Noah is coming up on his first birthday. Mandell remembers last March, when she and members of her family were taking a get-acquainted tour of the maternity ward at Santa Monica Hospital. "There were about 50 couples on the tour," she says. "At least half of them were multiracial. My cousin, who lives in Minnesota, pointed it out to me. I hadn't even noticed. I think in L.A. there are so many multiracial people you don't even pay attention. But it's different when you leave Los Angeles."

IT IS PRECISELY BECAUSE THEY FEEL UNder attack and in need of solidarity that many American minorities fear the blurring of racial lines. Congressional black leaders argue that adding a multiracial category to Census forms, which the Office of Management and Budget will be considering through June of this year, would make it much harder to detect and combat racial discrimination. For example, according to a recent article in Emerge, the black news magazine, in 1991 some 35,000 people chose "other" on Home Mortgage Disclosure Act papers meant to track bias in lending. Allowing people to opt out of traditional race categories, says Congressional Black Caucus chairwoman Maxine Waters, a California Democrat, "just blurs everything. [People pushing for a multiracial category] want to be seen for all they are, but I don't think they're making the connection about how it could affect how they're represented, or who's being an advocate for them when they're mistreated." Among the many programs administered on the basis of racial tallies: minority employment on government contracts, court-ordered school desegregation plans and protection of minority voting rights. All would have to be retooled, at great cost, if the categories change.

In the end, however, the impact of multiracialism will be decided not by the content of a Census form but in the hearts of Ameri-

A MOTHER'S CRY: "MY SON IS THREE RACES"

MELISSA MEYER AND THALLIEUS Massey don't simply want to check off a box marked "multiracial" for their eight-year-old son Jordan. With light brown skin, golden, wavy hair and light brown eyes, Jordan Massey is clearly the product of several races. Yet when his mother enrolled him in a second grade at Coconut Grove Elementary in Dade County, Florida, the school registrar gave her a form that asked her to pick just one of the following: black, white, Hispanic, American Indian/Alaskan Native, or Asian/Pacific Islander. Meyer, 31, who is white and whose husband's ancestors included both Africans and Native Americans, refused to select a box. "My son is three races," she said. "Can I choose all three?"

When the school said no, Meyer contacted the American Civil Liberties Union, and after a lot of wrangling, Dade County public schools agreed in 1995 to add a multiracial option on school-registration forms. But Meyer and Massey are not satisfied, because their son still cannot choose all three races. "We're not saying one race is better than the other," she says. "But he is our child, and we want him to understand exactly who he is." Sitting in his Boy Scout uniform, Jordan proclaims, "I'm American Indian, African American, European, American Indian."

lenged until Susie Guillory Phipps, the wife of a wealthy seafood importer who had always considered herself white, got a look at her birth certificate when applying for a passport and discovered that according to the state, she was black. In 1982 she sued the state, which hired a genealogist to delve into Phipps' ancestry. He dug up, among other ancestors, Phipps' great-great-great-great-grandmother—the black mistress of an Alabama plantation owner back in 1760—and concluded that Phipps was precisely three thirty-seconds black. The preposterous law stayed on the books until 1983.

cans. Tiger Woods can proclaim his personal diversity, but if most people, like Zoeller, just see a "boy," it won't make much difference. Multiracial Americans will not get the right to define themselves as they choose without a fight.

—Reported by Tamala M. Edwards/Washington, Elaine Lafferty and Sylvester Monroe/Los Angeles and Victoria Rainert/New York

The EQ Factor

New brain research suggests that emotions, not IQ, may be the true measure of human intelligence

NANCY GIBBS

IT TURNS OUT THAT A SCIENTIST CAN SEE THE future by watching four-year-olds interact with a marshmallow. The researcher invites the children, one by one, into a plain room and begins the gentle torment. You can have this marshmallow right now, he says. But if you wait while I run an errand, you can have two marshmallows when I get back. And then he leaves.

Some children grab for the treat the minute he's out the door. Some last a few minutes before they give in. But others are determined to wait. They cover their eyes; they put their heads down; they sing to themselves; they try to play games or even fall asleep. When the researcher returns he gives the children their hard-earned marshmallows. And then, science waits for them to grow up.

By the time the children reach high school, something remarkable has happened. A survey of the children's parents and teachers found that those who as four-year-olds had the fortitude to hold out for the second marshmallow generally grew up to be better adjusted, more popular, adventurous, confident and dependable teenagers. The children who gave in to temptation early on were more likely to be lonely, easily frustrated and stubborn. They buckled under stress and shied away from challenges. And when some of the students in the two groups took the Scholastic Aptitude Test, the kids who held out longer scored an average of 210 points higher.

When we think of brilliance we see Einstein, deep-eyed, woolly haired, a thinking machine with skin and mismatched socks. High achievers, we imagine, were wired for greatness from birth. But then you have to wonder why, over time, natural talent seems to ignite in some people and dim in others. This is where the marshmallows come in. It seems that the ability to delay gratification is a master skill, a triumph of the reasoning brain over the impulsive one. It is a sign, in short, of emotional intelligence. And it doesn't show up on an IQ test.

For most of this century, scientists have worshiped the hardware of the brain and the software of the mind; the messy powers of the heart were left to the poets. But cognitive theory could simply not explain the questions we wonder about most: why some people just seem to have a gift for living well; why the smartest kid in the class will probably not end up the richest; why we like some people virtually on sight and distrust others; why some people remain buoyant in the face of troubles that would sink a less resilient soul. What qualities of the mind or spirit, in short, determine who succeeds?

The phrase "emotional intelligence" was coined by Yale psychologist Peter Salovey and the University of New Hampshire's John Mayer five years ago to describe qualities like understanding one's own feelings, empathy for the feelings of others and "the regulation of emotion in a way that enhances living." Their notion is about to bound into the national conversation, handily shortened to EQ, thanks to a new book, *Emotional Intelligence* (Bantam; $23.95) by Daniel Goleman. Goleman, a Harvard psychology Ph.D. and a *New York Times* science writer with a gift for making even the chewiest scientific theories digestible to lay readers, has brought together a decade's worth of behavioral research into how the mind processes feelings. His goal, he announces on the cover, is to redefine what it means to be smart. His thesis: when it comes to predicting people's success, brainpower as measured by IQ and standardized achievement tests may actually matter less than the qualities of mind once thought of as "character" before the word began to sound quaint.

At first glance, there would seem to be little that's new here to any close reader of fortune cookies. There may be no less original idea than the notion that our hearts hold dominion over our heads. "I was so angry," we say, "I couldn't think straight." Neither is it surprising that "people skills" are useful, which amounts to saying, it's good to be nice. "It's so true it's trivial," says Dr. Paul McHugh, director of psychiatry at Johns Hopkins University School of Medicine. But if it were that simple, the book would not be quite so interesting or its implications so controversial.

This is no abstract investigation. Goleman is looking for antidotes to restore "civility to our streets and caring to our communal life." He sees practical applications everywhere for how companies should decide whom to hire, how couples can increase the odds that their marriages will last, how parents should raise their children and how schools should teach them. When street gangs substitute for families and schoolyard insults end in stabbings, when more than half of marriages end in divorce, when the majority of the children murdered in this country are killed by parents and stepparents, many of whom say they were trying to discipline the child for behavior like blocking the TV or crying too much, it suggests a demand for remedial emotional education. While children are still young, Goleman argues, there is a "neurological window of opportunity" since the brain's prefrontal circuitry, which regulates how we act on

From *Time*, October 2, 1995, pp. 60–66, 68. © 1995 by Time Inc. Magazine Company. Reprinted by permission.

what we feel, probably does not mature until mid-adolescence.

And it is here the arguments will break out. Goleman's highly popularized conclusions, says McHugh, "will chill any veteran scholar of psychotherapy and any neuroscientist who worries about how his research may come to be applied." While many researchers in this relatively new field are glad to see emotional issues finally taken seriously, they fear that a notion as handy as EQ invites misuse. Goleman admits the danger of suggesting that you can assign a numerical yardstick to a person's character as well as his intellect; Goleman never even uses the phrase EQ in his book. But he (begrudgingly) approved an "unscientific" EQ test in *USA Today* with choices like "I am aware of even subtle feelings as I have them," and "I can sense the pulse of a group or relationship and state unspoken feelings."

"You don't want to take an average of your emotional skill," argues Harvard psychology professor Jerome Kagan, a pioneer in child-development research. "That's what's wrong with the concept of intelligence for mental skills too. Some people handle anger well but can't handle fear. Some people can't take joy. So each emotion has to be viewed differently."

EQ is not the opposite of IQ. Some people are blessed with a lot of both, some with little of either. What researchers have been trying to understand is how they complement each other; how one's ability to handle stress, for instance, affects the ability to concentrate and put intelligence to use. Among the ingredients for success, researchers now generally agree that IQ counts for about 20%; the rest depends on everything from class to luck to the neural pathways that have developed in the brain over millions of years of human evolution.

It is actually the neuroscientists and evolutionists who do the best job of explaining the reasons behind the most unreasonable behavior. In the past decade or so, scientists have learned enough about the brain to make judgments about where emotion comes from and why we need it. Primitive emotional responses held the keys to survival: fear drives the blood into the large muscles, making it easier to run; surprise triggers the eyebrows to rise, allowing the eyes to widen their view and gather more information about an unexpected event. Disgust wrinkles up the face and closes the nostrils to keep out foul smells.

Emotional life grows out of an area of the brain called the limbic system, specifically the amygdala, whence come delight and disgust and fear and anger. Millions of years ago, the neocortex was added on, enabling humans to plan, learn and remember. Lust grows from the limbic system; love, from the neocortex. Animals like reptiles that have no neocortex cannot experience anything like maternal love; this is why baby

snakes have to hide to avoid being eaten by their parents. Humans, with their capacity for love, will protect their offspring, allowing the brains of the young time to develop. The more connections between limbic system and the neocortex, the more emotional responses are possible.

It was scientists like Joseph LeDoux of New York University who uncovered these cerebral pathways. LeDoux's parents owned a meat market. As a boy in Louisiana, he first learned about his future specialty by cutting up cows' brains for sweetbreads. "I found them the most interesting part of the cow's anatomy," he recalls. "They were visually pleasing—lots of folds, convolutions and patterns. The cerebellum was more interesting to look at than steak." The butchers' son became a neuroscientist, and it was he who discovered the short circuit in the brain that lets emotions drive action before the intellect gets a chance to intervene.

A hiker on a mountain path, for example, sees a long, curved shape in the grass out of the corner of his eye. He leaps out of the way before he realizes it is only a stick that looks like a snake. Then he calms down; his cortex gets the message a few milliseconds after his amygdala and "regulates" its primitive response.

Without these emotional reflexes, rarely conscious but often terribly powerful, we would scarcely be able to function. "Most decisions we make have a vast number of possible outcomes, and any attempt to analyze all of them would never end," says University of Iowa neurologist Antonio Damasio, author of *Descartes' Error: Emotion, Reason and the Human Brain*. "I'd ask you to lunch tomorrow, and when the appointed time arrived, you'd still be thinking about whether you should come." What tips the balance, Damasio contends, is our unconscious assigning of emotional values to some of those choices. Whether we experience a somatic response—a gut feeling of dread or a giddy sense of elation—emotions are helping to limit the field in any choice we have to make. If the prospect of lunch with a neurologist is unnerving or distasteful, Damasio suggests, the invitee will conveniently remember a previous engagement.

When Damasio worked with patients in whom the connection between emotional brain and neocortex had been severed because of damage to the brain, he discovered how central that hidden pathway is to how we live our lives. People who had lost that linkage were just as smart and quick to reason, but their lives often fell apart nonetheless. They could not make decisions because they didn't know how they felt about their choices. They couldn't react to warnings or anger in other people. If they made a mistake, like a bad investment, they felt no regret or shame and so were bound to repeat it.

If there is a cornerstone to emotional intelligence on which most other emotional skills depend, it is a sense of self-awareness, of being smart about what we feel. A person whose day starts badly at home may be grouchy all day at work without quite knowing why. Once an emotional response comes into awareness—or, physiologically, is processed through the neocortex—the chances of handling it appropriately improve. Scientists refer to "metamood," the ability to pull back and recognize that "what I'm feeling is anger," or sorrow, or shame.

Metamood is a difficult skill because emotions so often appear in disguise. A person in mourning may know he is sad, but he may not recognize that he is also angry at the person for dying—because this seems somehow inappropriate. A parent who yells at the child who ran into the street is expressing anger at disobedience, but the degree of anger may owe more to the fear the parent feels at what could have happened.

In Goleman's analysis, self-awareness is perhaps the most crucial ability because it allows us to exercise some self-control. The idea is not to repress feeling (the reaction that has made psychoanalysts rich) but rather to do what Aristotle considered the hard work of the will. "Anyone can become angry—that is easy," he wrote in the *Nicomachean Ethics*. "But to be angry with the right person, to the right degree, at the right time, for the right purpose, and in the right way—that is not easy."

Some impulses seem to be easier to control than others. Anger, not surprisingly, is one of the hardest, perhaps because of its evolutionary value in priming people to action. Researchers believe anger usually arises out of a sense of being trespassed against—the belief that one is being robbed of what is rightfully his. The body's first response is a surge of energy, the release of a cascade of neurotransmitters called catecholamines. If a person is already aroused or under stress, the threshold for release is lower, which helps explain why people's tempers shorten during a hard day.

Scientists are not only discovering where anger comes from; they are also exposing myths about how best to handle it. Popular wisdom argues for "letting it all hang out" and having a good cathartic rant. But Goleman cites studies showing that dwelling on anger actually increases its power; the body needs a chance to process the adrenaline through exercise, relaxation techniques, a well-timed intervention or even the old admonition to count to 10.

Anxiety serves a similar useful purpose, so long as it doesn't spin out of control. Worrying is a rehearsal for danger; the act of fretting focuses the mind on a problem so it can search efficiently for solutions. The danger comes when worrying blocks thinking, becoming an end in itself or a path to resignation instead of perseverance. Over-worrying about failing increases the likelihood of failure; a salesman so concerned about his falling sales that he can't bring himself to pick up the phone guarantees that his sales will fall even further.

But why are some people better able to "snap out of it" and get on with the task at hand? Again, given sufficient self-awareness, people develop coping mechanisms. Sadness and discouragement, for instance, are "low arousal" states, and the dispirited salesman who goes out for a run is triggering a high arousal state that is incompatible with staying blue. Relaxation works better for high energy moods like anger or anxiety. Either way, the idea is to shift to a state of arousal that breaks the destructive cycle of the dominant mood.

The idea of being able to predict which salesmen are most likely to prosper was not an abstraction for Metropolitan Life, which in the mid-'80s was hiring 5,000 salespeople a year and training them at a cost of more than $30,000 each. Half quit the first year, and four out of five within four years. The reason: selling life insurance involves having the door slammed in your face over and over again. Was it possible to identify which people would be better at handling frustration and take each refusal as a challenge rather than a setback?

The head of the company approached psychologist Martin Seligman at the University of Pennsylvania and invited him to test some of his theories about the importance of optimism in people's success. When optimists fail, he has found, they attribute the failure to something they can change, not some innate weakness that they are helpless to overcome. And that confidence in their power to effect change is self-reinforcing. Seligman tracked 15,000 new workers who had taken two tests. One was the company's regular screening exam, the other Seligman's test measuring their levels of optimism. Among the new hires was a group who flunked the screening test but scored as "superoptimists" on Seligman's exam. And sure enough, they did the best of all; they outsold the pessimists in the regular group by 21% in the first year and 57% in the second. For years after that, passing Seligman's test was one way to get hired as a MetLife salesperson.

Perhaps the most visible emotional skills, the ones we recognize most readily, are the "people skills" like empathy, graciousness, the ability to read a social situation. Researchers believe that about 90% of emotional communication is nonverbal. Harvard psychologist Robert Rosenthal developed the PONS test (Profile of Nonverbal Sensitivity) to measure people's ability to read emotional

One Way to Test Your EQ

UNLIKE IQ, WHICH IS GAUGED BY THE FAMOUS STANFORD-Binet tests, EQ does not lend itself to any single numerical measure. Nor should it, say experts. Emotional intelligence is by definition a complex, multifaceted quality representing such intangibles as self-awareness, empathy, persistence and social deftness.

Some aspects of emotional intelligence, however, can be quantified. Optimism, for example, is a handy measure of a person's self-worth. According to Martin Seligman, a University of Pennsylvania psychologist, how people respond to setbacks—optimistically or pessimistically—is a fairly accurate indicator of how well they will succeed in school, in sports and in certain kinds of work. To test his theory, Seligman devised a questionnaire to screen insurance salesmen at MetLife.

In Seligman's test, job applicants were asked to imagine a hypothetical event and then choose the response (A or B) that most closely resembled their own. Some samples from his questionnaire:

You forget your spouse's (boyfriend's/girlfriend's) birthday.
A. I'm not good at remembering birthdays.
B. I was preoccupied with other things.

You owe the library $10 for an overdue book.
A. When I am really involved in what I am reading, I often forget when its due.
B. I was so involved in writing the report, I forgot to return the book.

You lose your temper with a friend.
A. He or she is always nagging me.
B. He or she was in a hostile mood.

You are penalized for returning your income-tax forms late.
A. I always put off doing my taxes.
B. I was lazy about getting my taxes done this year.

You've been feeling run-down.
A. I never get a chance to relax.
B. I was exceptionally busy this week.

A friend says something that hurts your feelings.
A. She always blurts things out without thinking of others.
B. My friend was in a bad mood and took it out on me.

You fall down a great deal while skiing.
A. Skiing is difficult.
B. The trails were icy.

You gain weight over the holidays, and you can't lose it.
A. Diets don't work in the long run.
B. The diet I tried didn't work.

Seligman found that those insurance salesman who answered with more B's than A's were better able to overcome bad sales days, recovered more easily from rejection and were less likely to quit. People with an optimistic view of life tend to treat obstacles and setbacks as temporary (and therefore surmountable). Pessimists take them personally; what others see as fleeting, localized impediments, they view as pervasive and permanent.

The most dramatic proof of his theory, says Seligman, came at the 1988 Olympic Games in Seoul, South Korea, after U.S. swimmer Matt Biondi turned in two disappointing performances in this first two races. Before the Games, Biondi had been favored to win seven golds—as Mark Spitz had done 16 years earlier. After those first two races, most commentators thought Biondi would be unable to recover from his setback. Not Seligman. He had given some members of the U.S. swim team a version of his optimism test before the races; it showed that Biondi possessed an extraordinarily upbeat attitude. Rather than losing heart after turning in a bad time, as others might, Biondi tended to respond by swimming even faster. Sure enough, Biondi bounced right back, winning five gold medals in the next five races.
—By Alice Park

cues. He shows subjects a film of a young woman expressing feelings—anger, love, jealousy, gratitude, seduction—edited so that one or another nonverbal cue is blanked out. In some instances the face is visible but not the body, or the woman's eyes are hidden, so that viewers have to judge the feeling by subtle cues. Once again, people with higher PONS scores tend to be more successful in their work and relationships; children who score well are more popular and successful in school, even [though] their IQs are quite average.

Like other emotional skills, empathy is an innate quality that can be shaped by experience. Infants as young as three months old exhibit empathy when they get upset at the sound of another baby crying. Even very young children learn by imitation; by watching how others act when they see someone in distress, these children acquire a repertoire of sensitive responses. If, on the other hand, the feelings they begin to express are not recognized and reinforced by the adults around them, they not only cease to express those feelings but they also become less able to recognize them in themselves or others.

Empathy too can be seen as a survival skill. Bert Cohler, a University of Chicago psychologist, and Fran Stott, dean of the Erikson Institute for Advanced Study in Child Development in Chicago, have found that children from psychically damaged families frequently become hypervigilant, developing an intense attunement to their parents' moods. One child they studied, Nicholas, had a horrible habit of approaching other kids in his nursery-school class as if he were going to kiss them, then would bite them instead. The scientists went back to study videos of Nicholas at 20 months interacting with his psychotic mother and found that she had responded to his every expression of anger or independence with compulsive kisses. The researchers dubbed them "kisses of death," and their true significance was obvious to Nicholas, who arched his back in horror at her approaching lips—and passed his own rage on to his classmates years later.

Empathy also acts as a buffer to cruelty, and it is a quality conspicuously lacking in child molesters and psychopaths. Goleman cites some chilling research into brutality by Robert Hare, a psychologist at the University of British Columbia. Hare found that psychopaths, when hooked up to electrodes and told they are going to receive a shock, show none of the visceral responses that fear of pain typically triggers: rapid heartbeat, sweating and so on. How could the threat of punishment deter such people from committing crimes?

It is easy to draw the obvious lesson from these test results. How much happier would we be, how much more successful as individuals and civil as a society, if we were more alert to the importance of emotional

---

Square Pegs in the Oval Office?

IF A HIGH DEGREE OF EMOTIONAL INTELLIGENCE IS A PREREQUISITE FOR OUTSTAND-ing achievement, there ought to be no better place to find it than in the White House. It turns out, however, that not every man who reached the pinnacle of American leadership was a gleaming example of self-awareness, empathy, impulse control and all the other qualities that mark an elevated EQ.

Oliver Wendell Holmes, who knew intelligence when he saw it, judged Franklin Roosevelt "a second-class intellect, but a first-class temperament." Born and educated as an aristocrat, F.D.R. had polio and needed a wheelchair for most of his adult life. Yet, far from becoming a self-pitying wretch, he developed an unbridled optimism that served him and the country well during the Depression and World War II—this despite, or because of, what Princeton professor Fred Greenstein calls Roosevelt's "tendency toward deviousness and duplicity."

Even a first-class temperament, however, is not a sure predictor of a successful presidency. According to Duke University political scientist James David Barber, the most perfect blend of intellect and warmth of personality in a Chief Executive was the brilliant Thomas Jefferson, who "knew the importance of communication and empathy. He never lost the common touch." Richard Ellis, a professor of politics at Oregon's Willamette University who is skeptical of the whole EQ theory, cites two 19th century Presidents who did not fit the mold. "Martin Van Buren was well adjusted, balanced, empathetic and persuasive, but he was not very successful," says Ellis. "Andrew Jackson was less well adjusted, less balanced, less empathetic and was terrible at controlling his own impulses, but he transformed the presidency."

Lyndon Johnson as Senate majority leader was a brilliant practitioner of the art of political persuasion, yet failed utterly to transfer that gift to the White House. In fact, says Princeton's Greenstein, L.B.J. and Richard Nixon would be labeled "worst cases" on any EQ scale of Presidents. Each was touched with political genius, yet each met with disaster. "To some extent," says Greenstein, "this is a function of the extreme aspects of their psyches; they are the political versions of Van Gogh, who does unbelievable paintings and then cuts off his ear."

History professor William Leuchtenburg of the University of North Carolina at Chapel Hill suggests that the 20th century Presidents with perhaps the highest IQs—Wilson, Hoover and Carter—also had the most trouble connecting with their constituents. Woodrow Wilson, he says, "was very high strung [and] arrogant; he was not willing to strike any middle ground. Herbert Hoover was so locked into certain ideas that you could never convince him otherwise. Jimmy Carter is probably the most puzzling of the three. He didn't have a deficiency of temperament; in fact, he was too temperate. There was an excessive rationalization about Carter's approach."

That was never a problem for John Kennedy and Ronald Reagan. Nobody ever accused them of intellectual genius, yet both radiated qualities of leadership with an infectious confidence and openheartedness that endeared them to the nation. Whether President Clinton will be so endeared remains a puzzle. That he is a Rhodes scholar makes him certifiably brainy, but his emotional intelligence is shaky. He obviously has the knack for establishing rapport with people, but he often appears so eager to please that he looks weak. "As for controlling his impulses," says Willamette's Ellis, "Clinton is terrible." *—By Jesse Birnbaum. Reported by James Carney/Washington and Lisa H. Towle/Raleigh*

---

intelligence and more adept at teaching it? From kindergartens to business schools to corporations across the country, people are taking seriously the idea that a little more time spent on the "touchy-feely" skills so often derided may in fact pay rich dividends.

In the corporate world, according to personnel executives, IQ gets you hired, but EQ gets you promoted. Goleman likes

to tell of a manager at AT&T's Bell Labs, a think tank for brilliant engineers in New Jersey, who was asked to rank his top performers. They weren't the ones with the highest IQs; they were the ones whose E-mail got answered. Those workers who were good collaborators and networkers and popular with colleagues were more likely to get the cooperation they needed to reach their goals than the socially awkward, lone-wolf geniuses.

When David Campbell and others at the Center for Creative Leadership studied "derailed executives," the rising stars who flamed out, the researchers found that these executives failed most often because of "an interpersonal flaw" rather than a technical inability. Interviews with top executives in the U.S. and Europe turned up nine so-called fatal flaws, many of them classic emotional failings, such as "poor working relations," being "authoritarian" or "too ambitious" and having "conflict with upper management."

At the center's executive-leadership seminars across the country, managers come to get emotionally retooled. "This isn't sensitivity training or Sunday-supplement stuff," says Campbell. "One thing they know when they get through is what other people think of them." And the executives have an incentive to listen. Says Karen Boylston, director of the center's team-leadership group: "Customers are telling businesses, 'I don't care if every member of your staff graduated with honors from Harvard, Stanford and Wharton. I will take my business and go where I am understood and treated with respect.'"

Nowhere is the discussion of emotional intelligence more pressing than in schools, where both the stakes and the opportunities seem greatest. Instead of constant crisis intervention, or declarations of war on drug abuse or teen pregnancy or violence, it is time, Goleman argues, for preventive medicine. "Five years ago, teachers didn't want to think about this," says principal Roberta Kirshbaum of P.S. 75 in New York City. "But when kids are getting killed in high school, we have to deal with it." Five years ago, Kirshbaum's school adopted an emotional literacy program, designed to help children learn to manage anger, frustration, loneliness. Since then, fights at lunchtime have decreased from two or three a day to almost none.

Educators can point to all sorts of data to support this new direction. Students who are depressed or angry literally cannot learn. Children who have trouble being accepted by their classmates are 2 to 8 times as likely to drop out. An inability to distinguish distressing feelings or handle frustration has been linked to eating disorders in girls.

Many school administrators are completely rethinking the weight they have been giving to traditional lessons and standardized tests. Peter Relic, president of the National Association of Independent Schools, would like to junk the SAT completely. "Yes, it may cost a heck of a lot more money to assess someone's EQ rather than using a machine-scored test to measure IQ," he says. "But if we don't, then we're saying that a test score is more important to us than who a child is as a human being. That means an immense loss in terms of human potential because we've defined success too narrowly."

This warm embrace by educators has left some scientists in a bind. On one hand, says Yale psychologist Salovey, "I love the idea that we want to teach people a richer understanding of their emotional life, to help them achieve their goals." But, he adds, "what I would oppose is training conformity to social expectations." The danger is that any campaign to hone emotional skills in children will end up teaching that there is a "right" emotional response for any given situation—laugh at parades, cry at funerals, sit still at church. "You can teach self-control," says Dr. Alvin Poussaint, professor of psychiatry at Harvard Medical School. "You can teach that it's better to talk out your anger and not use violence. But is it good emotional intelligence not to challenge authority?"

SOME PSYCHOLOGISTS GO FURTHER AND challenge the very idea that emotional skills can or should be taught in any kind of formal, classroom way. Goleman's premise that children can be trained to analyze their feelings strikes Johns Hopkins' McHugh as an effort to reinvent the encounter group: "I consider that an abominable idea, an idea we have seen with adults. That failed, and now he wants to try it with children? Good grief!" He cites the description in Goleman's book of an experimental program at the Nueva Learning Center in San Francisco. In one scene, two fifth-grade boys start to argue over the rules of an exercise, and the teacher breaks in to ask them to talk about what they're feeling. "I appreciate the way you're being assertive in talking with Tucker," she says to one student. "You're not attacking." This strikes McHugh as pure folly. "The author is presuming that someone has the key to the right emotions to be taught to children. We don't even know the right emotions to be taught to adults. Do you really think a child of eight or nine really understands the difference between aggressiveness and assertiveness?"

The problem may be that there is an ingredient missing. Emotional skills, like intellectual ones, are morally neutral. Just as a genius could use his intellect either to cure cancer or engineer a deadly virus, someone with great empathic insight could use it to inspire colleagues or exploit them. Without a moral compass to guide people in how to employ their gifts, emotional intelligence can be used for good or evil. Columbia University psychologist Walter Mischel, who invented the marshmallow test and others like it, observes that the knack for delaying gratification that makes a child one marshmallow richer can help him become a better citizen or—just as easily—an even more brilliant criminal.

Given the passionate arguments that are raging over the state of moral instruction in this country, it is no wonder Goleman chose to focus more on neutral emotional skills than on the values that should govern their use. That's another book—and another debate.

—Reported by Sharon E. Epperson and Lawrence Mondi/New York, James L. Graff/Chicago and Lisa H. Towle/Raleigh

Unit 5

Key Points to Consider

❖ What kinds of crises may parents face when their children reach adolescence? How may each of these crises affect the manner in which parents interact with their children? How may these crises differ for mothers as compared to fathers? For single parents as compared to intact families?

❖ What kinds of demands may adolescents make of their parents that differ from those of childhood? What kinds of arguments may adolescents start presenting to their parents?

❖ What are the attitudes of Americans to gay families? What are the major problems faced by children in gay families? How has the legal system treated gay families?

❖ How does father absence affect the self-esteem of boys? How does it affect their relationships with their peers?

 **Links** **www.dushkin.com/online/**

16. **CYFERNET: Cooperative Extension System's Children, Youth and Family Information Service**
    http://www.cyfernet.org
17. **Help for Parents of Teenagers**
    http://www.bygpub.com/parents/
18. **Mental Health Net: Facts for Families Index**
    http://mentalhelp.net/factsfam/
19. **Stepfamily Association of America**
    http://www.stepfam.org

These sites are annotated on pages 4 and 5.

When 17-year-old Marie was rejected by the college of her choice, she sought her parents for comfort. But when her parents suggested going to a movie with her, she was stunned: why would she want to go with them when she could go with a friend instead? Clearly the family is important to the adolescent, but the relationship is not the same as it was in childhood. How should parents react? How involved should parents be with their adolescent? In order to understand the influence of the family on its members, the family needs to be viewed as a system. This means that parents do not simply shape their child; rather, each part of the family influences the other parts. For example, just as parents influence their children's behavior, children influence not only their parents' behavior, but their parents' relationship with each other. A child who complies with parental rules may put less stress on the parents than a child who is consistently in trouble. The compliant child's parents may then argue less with each other over issues like discipline. Similarly, the parents' marital relationship influences how each parent interacts with the children. Parents whose marriage is stressed may have less patience with children or may be less available to help their children.

Because the family is a system, factors that affect one part of the system will have implications for the rest of the system. This can be seen in how changes in the adolescent or in the parent affect the rest of the family. Adolescents may be described as changing in three major areas: biologically, cognitively, and socially. As adolescents enter puberty, parents see their children become sexually mature individuals. How parents react to this may be influenced by a variety of factors, including the parents' view of their own aging. Parents who see their attractiveness or health or sexuality as in decline may react to their child's development very differently than do parents who have a more positive view of themselves.

Adolescents' cognitive development may also stress their relationship with their parents. As adolescents become more cognitively sophisticated, they frequently become more questioning of parental behavior and rules. Although the adolescent's demand for reasons underlying parental judgments may reflect newly developed cognitive skills—a positive development from an intellectual perspective—it may increase conflicts with parents. Parents who expect their rules to be obeyed without question may be more upset by their child's arguments than will parents who expect to discuss rules.

Concurrent with these physical and cognitive changes, adolescents also undergo social changes. These include increased demands for autonomy or independence. Parents whose children were docile and compliant prior to adolescence may feel their authority threatened by these changes. Parents may find it more difficult to discipline children than they had before. This may be especially problematic for families who had difficulty controlling their children earlier in childhood.

Although families may be viewed as a system, there is no one form that this system must take. In the 1950s the ideal form of the family system was a breadwinner father, a homemaker mother, and their children. Today families take many different forms. About 50 percent of American adolescents will live in single-parent families for some period. This rate is higher for African Americans. About 75 percent of women with school-age children are employed outside the home. About 21 percent of American children live in blended families. It is clear that there is no "typical" family. Does this mean that the family plays a less significant role in the life of the adolescent? The research indicates no: The family is still among the most important influences on an adolescent. How well adolescents resist peer pressure, how successful they are in developing an identity, how capable they become in making independent decisions, and what they strive for in the future all seem to be predominantly influenced by the family. What characteristics of the family predict success in these areas?

Diana Baumrind, a leading researcher on the effects of differing parenting styles on adolescent development, proposed that some styles of parenting result in more competent, independent children than do other styles. She classified parents as either authoritative, authoritarian, or permissive. Authoritative parents encourage their children to discuss rules, rather than expecting children to obey without question. When the rules are broken, parents address this in a nonpunitive manner. That is, they neither ignore the offense nor do they use punitive discipline. Like authoritative parents, authoritarian parents have clear rules and limits. However, authoritarian parents are more likely to expect their children to obey without question. Permissive parents fall into two categories. Some permissive parents have a warm relationship with their children, but they do not impose many controls on them. Other permissive parents are basically uninvolved in the lives of their children.

Baumrind and others investigated the relationship between parenting styles and social competence in adolescents. Issues such as how well adolescents resisted peer pressure, how well adjusted they were, or how many problems they had with delinquency were investigated. It was found that children from authoritative families, where parents are emotionally warm to their children but have clear rules, limits, and controls, generally scored best. This was found to be the case regardless of family structure.

The articles in this unit demonstrate aspects of the family system. The first two articles emphasize the ways in which crises faced by parents may then affect the way parents interact with their adolescents. In the next article, Richard Lerner and Cheryl Olson provide advice on how parents may effectively respond to adolescents' increased demands and arguments. They suggest that parents maintain rules while treating their children as rational individuals. The article by Lee Beaty examines the influence of father absence on the family. The final article, by Barbara Kantrowitz, describes gay families, societal attitudes to these families, and the prejudice the members of these families may face. The conclusion of the article is that children of these families are at no more psychological risk than are the children of heterosexuals.

Family Relationships

Adolescence
Whose Hell Is It?

The image of teenagers as menacing and rebellious is a big fiction that's boomeranging on kids. We've mythologized adolescence to conceal a startling fact: It is indeed a difficult and turbulent time—for parents. The trouble is, kids look like adults much sooner than ever before. Kids wind up feeling abandoned—and angry at the loss of their safety net. If we haven't got adolescence exactly figured out yet, there's some consolation in the fact that it's a brand-new phenomenon in human history.

Virginia Rutter

I recently spent the weekend with a friend's 13-year-old son. In contrast to the tiny tots most of my friends have, Matthew seemed much more like an adult. The time spent with him wasn't so much like baby-sitting; it was like having company. It was impressive to see how self-sufficient he was. Simple matters struck me: he didn't need someone to go to the bathroom with him at the movies; he could help himself to ice cream; he was actually interested in following the O. J. Simpson story, and we discussed it.

He was polite, thoughtful, and interesting. While the intensive caretaking necessary for smaller children has its own rewards (I suppose), Matthew's contrasting autonomy was pleasant to me. And so I imagined it would be for parents of adolescents. But then, I am not a parent. And most parents report not feeling pleasant about their adolescents.

The weekend reminded me of how easy it is to think of these youngsters as adults. Compared to an eight-year-old, an adolescent is a lot like an adult. Can't reason like an adult, but doesn't think like a child anymore, either. Some parents are tempted to cut 'em loose rather than adjust to the new status of their teenager. Others fail to observe their adolescent's new adultlike status, and continue monitoring them as

> *A couple of teachers are my heroes. My history teacher is great because he listens to what everybody has to say and never judges.*
> —*Chelsea, 14, Bakersfield, California*

closely as a child. But it's obvious that adolescents aren't miniature adults. They are individuals on their way to adulthood; their brains and bodies—to say nothing of their sexuality—stretching uneasily toward maturity.

Yet the sight of kids reaching for some form of adult status commonly evokes contempt rather than curiosity. Negative feelings about teenagers have a strong grip on American culture in general, and on surprising numbers of parents in particular. It's not uncommon for parents to anticipate their child's adolescence with fear and trepidation even before they've gotten out of diapers. They expect a war at home.

"It becomes a self-fulfilling prophesy that adolescence is seen as this bizarre, otherworldly period of development, complete with a battleground set for World War III," says Tina Wagers, Psy.D., a psychologist who treats teens and their families at Kaiser Permanente Medical Center in Denver.

We were all once 13, but it seems we can no longer imagine what kind of parenting a 13-year-old needs. Perhaps it's gotten worse with all the outside opportunities for trouble kids have—gangs, guns, drugs. Families used to extend their turf into their children's schools, friends, and athletic activities. But kids now inhabit unknown territory, and it is scary for parents. "I think

Reprinted with permission from *Psychology Today*, January/February 1995, pp. 54–60, 62, 64, 66, 68. © 1995 by Sussex Publishers, Inc.

this fear and lack of understanding makes some parents more likely to back off and neglect teenagers," reports Wagers. "There is an expectation that you can't influence them anyhow."

This skeptical, sometimes hostile view of teens, however, was countered by my experience with Matthew. I found him hardly a "teenager from hell." Like most teens, Matthew prefers to be with his own friends more than with family or other grown-ups. He's not good with time, and music, basketball, and girls are more central to him than achievement, responsibility, and family. (Despite his tastes, he does very well in school.) At home there is more conflict than there has been in the past, though not less love and commitment to his mom, with whom he lives in eastern Washington.

The story of Matthew falls in line with new research on adolescents, and it's causing psychologists to totally revise conventional wisdom on the subject. According to psychologist Laurence Steinberg, Ph.D., of Temple University, the majority of adolescents are not contentious, unpleasant, heartless creatures. They do not hate their parents—although they do fight with them (but not as much as you might think). "In scrutinizing interviews with adolescents and their families, I reaffirmed that adolescence is a relatively peaceful time in the house." Kids report continued high levels of respect for their parents, whether single, divorced, or together, and regardless of economic background.

When fighting does occur, it's in families with younger teenagers, and it has to do at least in part with their burgeoning cognitive abilities. Newly able to grasp abstract ideas, they can become absorbed in pursuing hypocrisy or questioning authority. In time, they learn to deploy relativistic and critical thinking more selectively.

NOT A DISEASE

If adolescents aren't the incorrigibles we think—then what to make of the endless stream of news reports of teen sexism, harassment, drug abuse, depression, delinquency, gangs, guns, and suicide?

Any way you measure it, teens today are in deep trouble. They face increasing rates of depression (now at 20 percent), suicide (12 percent have considered it, 5 percent attempted), substance abuse (20 percent of high school seniors), delinquency (1.5 million juvenile arrests—about 1 percent of teens—in 1992), early sexual activity (29 percent have had sexual relations by age 15), and even an increased rate of health problems (20 percent have conditions that will hamper their health as adults). And kids' problems appear to be getting worse.

How to reconcile the two parts of the story: adolescents aren't so bad, but a grow-

ing number are jeopardizing their future through destructive behavior? Though we look upon teenagers as time bombs set to self-destruct at puberty, in fact the problems teens face are not encoded in their genes. Their natural development, including a surge of hormonal activity during the first few years of adolescence, may make them a little more depressed or aggressive—but how we treat them has much more to do with teenagers' lives today. From the look of it, we aren't treating them very well.

A CRISIS OF ADULTS

If what goes on in adolescence happens largely in the kids, what goes wrong with adolescence happens primarily in the parents. "It wasn't until I turned to the parents' interviews that I really got a sense that something unusual was going on," reports Steinberg of his ongoing studies of over 200 adolescents and their families. As he details in his recent book, *Crossing Paths: How Your Child's Adolescence Triggers Your Own Crisis* (Simon & Schuster), Steinberg finds that adolescence sets off a crisis for parents.

Teenagers say that parents are not understanding and I don't think it is always that way.
—Gabriel, 16, Alburquerque, New Mexico

Parents do not have positive feelings during the time their kids go through adolescence, and it isn't simply because they expect their kids to be bad (although that's part of it). Scientists have studied the behavior and emotions of parents as well as their adolescent children, and found that when children reach puberty, parents experience tremendous changes in themselves. What's more, they shift their attitudes toward their children. It isn't just the kids who are distressed. Parents are too. Consider the following:

- Marital satisfaction, which typically declines over the course of marriage, reaches its all-time low when the oldest child reaches adolescence. Married parents of adolescents have an average of seven minutes alone with each other

every day. For the marriages that don't pass the point of no return during their kids' teen years, there is actually an increase in satisfaction after the kids complete adolescence.

- Happily married parents have more positive interactions with their kids than unhappy parents. In single-parent families, parental happiness also influences their response to adolescence.

Adults want kids to learn to take care of themselves. Kids need guides and advice. That is how you help people mature—not by leaving them alone.
—Michelle, 16, Clackamas, Oregon

- In a surprising finding, the marital satisfaction of fathers is directly affected by how actively their adolescents are dating. Especially when sons are busy dating, fathers report a marked decline in interest in their wives. Dads aren't lusting for the girls Johnny brings home, they just miss what now seem like their own good old days.

- In family discussions, parents become increasingly negative toward their adolescents—there's more criticism, whining, frustration, anger, and defensiveness expressed verbally or in grimaces. While the kids are always more negative than their parents (it comes with increasing cognitive ability, in part), the parents are actually increasing the amount of negativity toward their children at a higher rate.

- Working mothers don't spend less time at home with their teenagers than non-working moms do, but they do risk higher levels of burnout, because they continue to cover the lioness' share of work at home. On the other hand, a mother's employment makes her less vulnerable to the ups and downs of parenting an adolescent. Maternal employment also benefits kids, especially teen daughters, who report higher levels of self-esteem.

- Despite their fulfillment, mothers' self-esteem is actually lower while they are with their adolescents than when they are not. After all, a mother's authority is constantly being challenged, and she is being shunted to the margins of her child's universe.

- Teenagers turn increasingly to their friends, a distancing maneuver that feels like an emotional divorce to parents. Since mothers are generally more emotionally engaged with their children than are fathers, the separation can feel most painful to them. In fact, mothers typically report looking forward to the departure of their kids after high school. After the kids leave, mothers' emotional state improves.

- Fathers' emotional states follow a different course. Fathers have more difficulty launching their adolescents, mostly because they feel regret about the time they didn't spend with them. Fathers have more difficulty dealing with their kids growing into adolescence and adulthood; they can't get used to the idea that they no longer have a little playmate who is going to do what daddy wants to do.

Add it all up and you get a bona fide midlife crisis in some parents, according to Steinberg. All along we've thought that a midlife crisis happens to some adults around the age of 40. But it turns out that midlife crisis has nothing to do with the age of the adult—and everything to do with the age of the oldest child in a family. It is set off by the entry of a family's firstborn into adolescence.

Once the oldest child hits adolescence, parents are catapulted into a process of life review. "Where have I been, where am I now, where am I going?" These questions gnaw at parents who observe their children at the brink of adulthood.

It hits hardest the parent who is the same sex as the adolescent. Mothers and daughters actually have more difficulty than fathers and sons. In either case, the children tend to serve as a mirror of their younger lost selves, and bear the brunt of parents' regrets as parents distance themselves.

Steinberg tracks the psychological unrest associated with midlife crisis in parents:

- The onset of puberty is unavoidable evidence that their child is growing up.
- Along with puberty comes a child's burgeoning sexuality. For parents, this can raise doubts about their own attractiveness, their current sex life, as well as regrets or nostalgia for their teenage sexual experiences.
- The kids' new independence can make parents feel powerless. For fathers in particular this can remind them of the powerlessness they feel in the office if their careers have hit a plateau.
- Teens also become less concerned with their parents' approval. Their peer group approval becomes more impor-

tant. This hits mothers of daughters quite hard, especially single mothers, whose relationship to their daughters most resembles a friendship.

- Finally, de-idealization—kids' often blunt criticism of their parents—is a strong predictor of decline in parental mental health. Parents who used to be the ultimate expert to their kids are now reduced to debating partner for kids who have developed a new cognitive skill called relativism.

A clear picture begins to emerge: parents of a teenager feel depressed about their own life or their own marriage; feel the loss of their child; feel jealous, rejected, and confused about their child's new sexually mature looks, bad moods, withdrawal into privacy at home, and increasing involvement with friends. The kid is tied up in her (or his) own problems and wonders what planet mom and dad are on.

EMOTIONAL DIVORCE

The sad consequence is that parents who experience a midlife crisis begin avoiding their adolescent. Although a small proportion of parents are holding on to their teens too closely—usually they come from traditional families and have fundamentalist religious beliefs—more parents are backing off. The catch is that these teenagers want their parents' guidance. But more and more they just aren't getting it.

Adults need to understand that it is very difficult to be a teenager nowadays. It takes a lot of understanding with so many problems like guns, drugs, AIDS, and gangs.
—Melissa, 14, Dallas, Texas

Some parents back away not out of their own inner confusion but because they think it's hip to do so. Either way, letting go causes confusion in the kids, not help in making their way into adulthood. Even if they are irritating or irritable, or just more withdrawn than they used to be, teens are seeking guidance.

"I have this image of a kid groping through adolescence, kind of by himself,"

confides therapist Wagers, who sees a lot of parents out of touch with their kids. "The parents swarm around him, but don't actually talk to him, only to other people about him."

The mantra of therapists who work with adolescents and their families is "balance." Parents have to hold on, but not too tightly. They need to stay involved, even when their kids are ignoring them. Roland Montemayor, Ph.D., professor of psychology at Ohio State, finds it is not so different from learning how to deal with a two-year-old. You must stay within earshot, and be available whenever they falter or get themselves into trouble.

With a two-year-old, trouble means experimenting with mud pies or bopping a playmate; with a 14-year-old, it means experimenting with your car keys or sex. The task is the same—keep track of them and let them know what the rules are. Parents unfortunately taken up with their own midlife concerns may not embrace the task. God knows, it isn't easy. But it is vital.

Among parents who have gone through a real divorce, the emotional divorce that occurs between adolescents and their parents can heighten difficulty. It may reawaken feelings of sadness. Parents who don't have many interests outside the family are also vulnerable. Their kids are telling them to "Get a life!"—and that is exactly what they need to do.

DROPOUT PARENTS

As an adolescent reaches age 13, the time she is spending with parents is typically half that before age 10. "Teens come home and go into their bedrooms. They start to feel more comfortable by themselves than with siblings or parents around. They talk on the phone with friends, and their biggest worry usually has to do with a romantic interest," explains Reed Larson, Ph.D., who studies families and adolescents at the University of Illinois, Champaign-Urbana. Larson, coauthor of the recent book, *Divergent Realities: The Emotional Lives of Mothers, Fathers, and Adolescents,* studied 55 families who recorded their feelings and activities for one week, whenever prompted at random intervals by a beeper. He surveyed another 483 adolescents with the beeper method.

The families' reports revealed that a mutual withdrawal occurs. "When kids withdraw, parents get the message. They even feel intimidated. As a result they don't put in the extra effort to maintain contact with their kids," observes Larson. The kids feel abandoned, even though they're the ones retreating to their bedroom. The parents, in effect, cut their kids loose, just when they dip their toes in the waters of autonomy.

Separation is natural among humans as well as in the animal kingdom, Larson notes. Yet humans also need special care during this life transition—and suffer from reduced contact with parents and other adults. They still need to be taught how to do things, how to think about things, but above all they need to know that there is a safety net, a sense that their parents are paying attention and are going to jump in when things go wrong. The kids don't need the direct supervision they received at age two or eight, but they benefit emotionally and intellectually from positive contact with their parents.

I don't think adults understand how complicated kids' minds are today, how much they think; they don't just accept something but wonder why it is.

—Adam, 14, Bethesda, Maryland

Despite the tensions in family life, studies continue to confirm that the family remains one of the most effective vehicles to promote values, school success, even confidence in peer relationships. When it works, family functions as what Larson calls a "comfort zone," a place or a relationship that serves as a home base out of which to operate. Kids feel more secure, calm, and confident than those without a comfort zone. Similarly, Steinberg finds, the one common link among the many successful adolescents in his studies is that they all have positive relationships with their parents. Without positive relationships, the kids are subject to depression and likely to do poorly in school.

Parental withdrawal is a prime characteristic of families where adolescents get into trouble. It often catapults families into therapy. Wagers tells the story of a single parent who wasn't simply withdrawn, her head was in the sand: "I was seeing a mother and her 12-year-old son, who had depression and behavior problems. The mother called me up one time to say she had found all this marijuana paraphernalia in her son's room, in his pocket. She said she wasn't sure what it means. When I said 'it means that he's smoking pot,' she was very reluctant to agree. She didn't want to talk to her son about why he was getting

into trouble or smoking pot. She wanted me to fix him." (Eventually, in therapy, the mother learned how to give her son a curfew and other rules, and to enforce them. He's doing much better.)

Marital problems also enter into the distancing equation. Although the marital decline among teens' parents is part of the normal course of marriage, the adolescent can exacerbate the problem. "Here is a new person challenging you in ways that might make you irritable or insecure," explains Steinberg. "That can spill over into the marriage. The standard scenario involves the adolescent and the mother who have been home squabbling all afternoon. Well, the mom isn't exactly going to be in a terrific mood to greet her husband. It resembles the marital problems that occur when a couple first has a new baby." Trouble is, when the parents' marriage declines, so does the quality of the parenting—at a time when more parental energy is needed.

Teenagers know what is happening around them in school but adults hide things. Parents should shield their kids from some things but not so much that kids are afraid to go out into the world.

—Sarah, 17, Hanover, NH

As if there are not enough psychological forces reducing contact between parents and adolescents today, social trends add to the problem, contends Roland Montemayor. Intensified work schedules, increased divorce and single parenthood, and poverty—often a result of divorce and single parenthood—decrease parent-child contact. A fourth of all teenagers live with one parent, usually their mother. Families have fewer ties to the community, so there are fewer other adults with whom teens have nurturing ties. The negative images of teenagers as violent delinquents may even intimidate parents.

ALONE AND ANGRY

Whatever the source, parental distancing doesn't make for happy kids. "The kids I work with at Ohio State are remarkably in-

dependent, yet they are resentful of it," says Montemayor. "There is a sense of not being connected somehow." Kids are angry about being left to themselves, being given independence without the kind of mentoring from their parents to learn how to use their independence.

Adult contact seems to be on teenagers' minds more than ever before. Sociologist Dale Blythe, Ph.D., is an adolescence researcher who directs Minneapolis' noted Search Institute, which specializes in studies of youth policy issues. He has surveyed teens in 30 communities across the country, and found that when you ask teens, they say that family is not the most important thing in their lives—peers and social activities are. Nevertheless a large proportion of them say that they want more time with adults—they want their attention and leadership. They want more respect from adults and more cues on how to make it in the adult world. What a shift from 25 years ago, when the watchword was "never trust anyone over 30"!

So it's up to parents to seek more contact with their kids—despite the conflict they'll encounter. "The role of parents is to socialize children, to help them become responsible adults, to teach them to do the right thing. Conflict is an inevitable part of it," says Montemayor. He notes that one of the biggest sources of conflict between parents and teens is time management. Teens have trouble committing to plans in advance. They want to keep their options wide open all the time. The only surefire way to reduce conflict is to withdraw from teenagers—an equally surefire way to harm them.

I am insecure about my future. The main view toward people in my generation is that we are all slackers and it's kind of disturbing. We are actually trying to make something of ourselves.

—Jasmine, 16, Brooklyn, New York

"In other countries parents don't shy away from conflict. In the United States we have this idea that things are going to be hunky-dory and that we are going to go

The Invention of Adolescence

Are Romeo and Juliet the Quintessential adolescents? On the yes side, they were rebelling against family traditions, in the throes of first love, prone to melodrama, and engaged in violent and risky behavior. But the truth is that there was no such thing as adolescence in Shakespeare's time (the 16th century). Young people the ages of Romeo and Juliet (around 13) were adults in the eyes of society—even though they were probably prepubescent.

Paradoxically, puberty came later in eras past while departure from parental supervision came earlier than it does today. Romeo and Juliet carried the weight of the world on their shoulders—although it was a far smaller world than today's teens inhabit.

Another way to look at it is that in centuries past, a sexually mature person was never treated as a "growing child." Today sexually mature folk spend perhaps six years—ages 12 to 18—living under the authority of their parents.

Since the mid-1800s, puberty—the advent of sexual maturation and the starting point of adolescence—has inched back one year for every 25 years elapsed. It now occurs on average six years earlier than it did in 1850—age 11 or 12 for girls; age 12 or 13 for boys. Today adolescents make up 17 percent of the U.S. population and about a third of them belong to racial or ethnic minorities.

It's still not clear exactly what triggers puberty, confides Jeanne Brooks-Gunn, Ph.D., of Columbia University Teachers College, an expert on adolescent development. "The onset of puberty has fallen probably due to better nutrition in the prenatal period as well as throughout childhood. Pubertal age—for girls, when their first period occurs—has been lower in the affluent than the nonaffluent classes throughout recorded history. Differences are still found in countries where starvation and malnutrition are common among the poor. In Western countries, no social-class differences are found." Although adolescence is a new phenomenon in the history of our species, thanks to a stable and abundant food supply, we've already hit its limits—it's not likely puberty onset will drop much below the age of 12.

If kids look like adults sooner than ever before, that doesn't mean they are. The brain begins to change when the body does, but it doesn't become a grown-up thinking organ as quickly as other systems of the body mature. The clash between physical maturity and mental immaturity not only throws parents a curve—they forget how to do their job, or even what it is—it catapults teens into some silly situations. They become intensely interested in romance, for example, only their idea of romance is absurdly simple, culminating in notes passed across the classroom: "Do you like me? Check yes or no."

Puberty isn't the only marker of adolescence. There's a slowly increasing capacity for abstract reasoning and relative thinking. Their new capacity for abstraction allows teens to think about big things—Death, Destruction, Nuclear War—subjects that depress them, especially since they lack the capacity to ameliorate them.

The idea that everything is relative suddenly makes every rule subject to debate. As time passes, teens attain the ability to make finer abstract distinctions. Which is to say, they become better at choosing their fights.

Teens also move toward autonomy. They want to be alone, they say, because they have a lot on their minds. Yet much of the autonomy hinges on the growing importance of social relationships. Evaluating the ups and downs of social situations indeed requires time alone. Family ties, however, remain more important than you might expect as teens increase identification with their peers.

Whatever else turns teens into the moody creatures they are, hormones have been given far too much credit, contends Brooks-Gunn. In fact, she points out, the flow of hormones that eventually shapes their bodies actually starts around age seven or eight. "Certain emotional states and problems increase between ages 11 and 14, at the time puberty takes place. These changes are probably due to the increased social and school demands, the multiple new events that youth confront, their own responses to puberty, and to a much lesser extent hormonal changes themselves."

The nutritional abundance that underlies a long adolescence also prompted the extension of education, which has created a problem entirely novel in the animal kingdom—physically mature creatures living with their parents, and for more years than sexually mature offspring ever have in the past. College-bound kids typically depend on their parents until at least age 21, a decade or more after hitting puberty.

Historically, children never lived at home during the teen years, points out Temple University's Laurence Steinberg. Either they were shipped out to apprenticeships or off to other relatives.

Among lower primates, physically mature beasts simply are not welcome in the family den; sexual competition makes cohabiting untenable. But for animals, physical maturity coincides with mental acuity, so their departure is not a rejection.

The formal study of adolescence began in the 1940s, just before James Dean changed our perception of it forever. There is a long-standing tradition of professional observers looking at adolescence as a pathology—and this one really did start with Freud. It continues still.

A 1988 study reported that although the under-18 population actually declined from 1980 to 1984, adolescent admissions to private psychiatric hospitals increased—450 percent! The study suggests a staggering cultural taste for applying mental health care to any problem life presents. It also hints at the negative feelings Americans have toward adolescence—we consider it a disease.

The study of adolescence has come with a context—a culture of, by, and for youth, arising in the postwar boom of the 1950s and epitomized by James Dean. Once the original badass depressive teenager from hell, Dean seems quaintly tame by today's standards. But the fear and loathing he set in motion among adults is a powerful legacy today's teens are still struggling to live down.—V.R.

Many times teenagers are thought of as a problem that no one really wants to deal with. People are sometimes intimidated and become hostile because teenagers are willing to challenge their authority. It is looked at as being disrespectful. Teenagers are, many times, not treated like an asset and as innovative thinkers who will be the leaders of tomorrow. Adults have the power to teach the younger generation about the world and allow them to feel they have a voice in it.—Zula, 16, Brooklyn, NY

A postpubescent child introduces a third sexually mature person into the household, where once sex was a strictly private domain restricted to the older generation. It's difficult for everyone to get used to.

No matter how you slice it, sex can be an awkward topic. For parents, there's not only the feeling of powerlessness, there's discomfort. Most parents of adolescents aren't experiencing much sexual activity—neither the mechanics of sex nor its poetry—in this stage of the marriage (though this eventually improves).

The fact that fathers' marital satisfaction decreases when their kids start to date suggests the power of kids' sexuality, no matter how silenced, to distort parental behavior. Sex and marital therapist David Schnarch, Ph.D., points out that families, and the my-

I think Al Gore is a super environmentalist. With no ozone layer, the world is just going to melt. It's hard not to worry. The environment is really messed up and with no environment there will be no economy, no education, nothing. I hate it when people throw six-pack rings in the lake. We need to think about the environment because we need to get on with the rest of our lives. I don't think adults generally look to kids for opinions.—Sam, 13, New York City

we teach a biological model of sexuality, we imply to the kids 'we know you can't delay. We think these are the best years of your life.' "

Parents can help their children by letting them know that they understand sex and have valuable experience about decisions related to sex; that they know it isn't just a mechanical act; that they recognize that teens are going to figure things out on their own with or without guidance from their parents; and that they are willing to talk about it. But often, the experience or meaning of sex gets lost.

bowling and have fun together. Most people in the world would find that a pretty fanciful idea. There is an inevitable tension between parents and adolescents, and there's nothing wrong with that."

SILENCED SEX

Who can talk about teens without talking about sex? The topic of teenage sexuality, however, heightens parents' sense of powerlessness. Adults hesitate to acknowledge their own sexual experience in addressing the issue. They resolve the matter by pretending sex doesn't exist.

I think there is going to be a lot of destruction and violence. There are all these peace treaties, but I don't think they are going to work out.

—Julia, 12, Albuquerque, NM

Doing the right thing and being good at what you're doing is important to me.

As teenagers we have a lot of things on our back, a lot of people are looking for us to do many great things. We also take in a lot of things and we know a lot of things. I care about the environment because it's a place that we all have to live in, not just us but our families and children. Even though I'm 15, I still have to keep those things in mind because it's serious. As for my own future, I've had a good upbringing and I see all open doors.—Semu, 15, New York City

The future sounds alright. It is probably going to be more modern and really scientific. Things will be run by computers and computers will do more for people. —Emily, 13, New York City

Sexuality was conspicuous by its absence in all the family interviews Steinberg, Montemayor, or Larson observed. Calling sex a hidden issue in adolescence verges on an oxymoron. Sprouting pubic hair and expanding busts aren't particularly subtle phenomena. But adolescent sexuality is only heightened by the silence.

thology of the culture, worship teen sexuality, mistakenly believing adolescence is the peak of human sexuality. Boys have more hard-ons than their dads, while the girls have less cellulite than their moms.

These kids may have the biological equipment, says Schnarch, but they don't yet know how to make love. Sex isn't just about orgasms, it is about intimacy. "All of our sex education is designed to raise kids to be healthy, normal adults. But we are confused about what we believe is sexually normal. Textbooks say that boys reach their sexual peak in late adolescence; girls, five to 10 years later. The adolescent believes it, parents believe it, schools believe it. In the hierarchy dictated by this narrow biological model of sexuality, the person with the best sex is the adolescent. On the one hand we are telling kids, 'we would like you to delay sexual involvement.' But when

I asked a woman whose parents had handed her birth control pills at age 15 how she felt about it now, at age 30. "I wish sex had been a little more taboo than it was. I got into a lot more sexual acting out before I was 20, and that didn't go very well for me. Even though my parents talked about the health consequences of sex, they did not mention other consequences. Like what it does to your self-esteem when you get involved in a series of one-night stands. So I guess I wish they had been more holistic in their approach to sex. Not just to tell me about the pill when I was 15, but to understand the different issues I was struggling with. In every other aspect of my life, they were my best resource. But it turns out sex is a lot more complicated than I thought it was when I was 15. At 30, sex is a lot better than it was when I was a teenager."

The distortions parents create about teen sexuality lead directly to events like the "Spur Posse," the gang of teenage football stars in Southern California who systematically harassed and raped girls, terrorizing the community in the late 80s. The boys' fathers actually appeared on talk shows—to brag about their sons' conquests. "The fathers were reinforcing the boys' behavior. It was as if it were a reflection on their own sexuality," observes Schnarch.

By closing their eyes to teen sexual behavior, parents don't just disengage from

> I don't feel any pressure about sex. It's a frequent topic of conversation, but we talk about other things, too—when I'm going to get my history paper done, movies, music. I listen to classical music a lot. I think about my maturity a lot, because I have recently had losses in my immediate family and it feels like I am maturing so fast. But then sometimes I feel so young compared to everything out there. I think adults have always felt that teens were more reckless.—**Amanda, 16, New York City**

> Teenagers, like adults, are all different. One has a job that is hard, another has more money and more education, and one just gets by. It is unfair to look at all teens the same way. You have maturity in you, but you just don't want to show it because it's no fun. We've got problems, but not really big ones like my uncle who came over from China when he was 16, or going to war when you're 18. If teenagers make it through this era, adults will just bash the next generation of teenagers.—**Mike, 14, Brooklyn, New York**

their kids. They leave them high and dry about understanding anything more than the cold mechanics of sex. Kids raised this

Jackie Joyner-Kersee, the Olympic track star, is my hero because she has accomplished so much and she is one of the main female athletes.
—Kristy, 12, Woodbridge, New Jersey

way report feeling very alone when it gets down to making intimate decisions for the first time. They feel like they haven't been given any help in what turns out to be the bigger part of sex—the relationship part of it.

Returning to the authoritarian, insular family of Ward, June, Wally, and the Beaver

My hero is Queen Latifah. She is herself and doesn't try to be somebody else. My mother is also my hero because she raises me as well as she can and she is a single parent.
—Maria, 15, Bronx, New York

is not the solution for teenagers any more than it is for their parents. But teenagers do need parents and other responsible adults actively involved in their lives, just as younger children do. Only when it comes to teenagers, the grown-ups have to tolerate a lot more ambiguity—about authority, safety, responsibility, and closeness—to sustain the connection. If they can learn to do that, a lot of young people will be able to avoid a whole lot of trouble.

How Teens Strain the Family

What's most likely to set off a parent's midlife crisis?
The presence of a child entering adolescence, says a psychologist
who studied the stresses in 204 families.

Murray Dubin
Inquirer Staff Writer

When Dad makes a mistake around the house, 10-year-old Benjamin Steinberg of Ardmore either laughs hysterically "or he'll rub my face in it," says his father, Laurence Steinberg.

Steinberg, 42, the director of the developmental psychology department at Temple University, understands what's happening psychologically with his pre-adolescent son.

He knows that in the next few years, Benjamin will alter his view of his parents and take them off the pedestal. He knows that it's necessary for his son to separate himself and establish his own identity. Intellectually he understands, but it's still annoying when the kid pokes fun at the old man. And it will likely become more annoying as Benjamin gets older.

The reaction of adults to their adolescents' behavior is the subject of Steinberg's new book, *Crossing Paths—How Your Child's Adolescence Triggers Your Own Crisis* (Simon & Schuster), co-authored with his wife, Wendy, public relations coordinator at the Institute of Contemporary Art.

The book focuses on 204 families with adolescents that Steinberg and his project team studied in Wisconsin. It was there he discovered that the trigger for a parent's midlife crisis is likely to be a child becoming an adolescent.

Adolescence, Steinberg learned, has a far greater impact than previously imagined on the emotional well-being of parents. And it doesn't matter whether the parents are divorced, stepfamilied or in an intact family, living in a city or a suburb, working in a factory or a law firm, skin color of black, white or brown.

What does matter is the age of the children. If it's between 11 to 14 or so, there's a good chance that the kids are making mom or dad a little crazy.

Most of the psychological literature about families with teens looks at the impact that parents have on children. Just twice in the family life cycle has the literary spotlight illuminated children's impact on parents—at birth and when the kids leave home. For the most part, says Steinberg, the in-between time has been ignored by those who study and write about families.

And he did not set out to study it, either.

Steinberg's expertise is adolescent behavior and development. He set out in Wisconsin to find out more about how families "negotiated the change" as children grew into adolescence. A series of detailed questionnaires to family members was the initial research tool. Interviews came later.

"We had a good sense beforehand that this was a time of transformation of relationships in the family and we knew it was more likely to happen in early adolescence—11 to 14—than in late," he says in his Temple office.

"But we didn't know for sure it was affecting people's well-being. There's a difference between parents complaining about their adolescents and really being affected psychologically by what's going on. The surprise was the extent that they were affected.

"We looked at midlife literature and almost none of it talks about kids. They talk about work. They talk about physical changes."

He found that about 40 percent of the parents studied in a three-year period had a decline in their "psychological well-being" during their children's adolescence.

Steinberg is quick to point out that most adolescents get through adolescence fine and most adults get through their midlife just fine, thank you. But the 44-year-old parent with

Reprinted with permission from *The Philadelphia Inquirer,* November 16, 1994, pp. H1, H3.

Laurence Steinberg and his wife, Wendy, of Ardmore know what to expect in the years ahead with their son, Benjamin, 10.

a 13-year-old is more likely to have difficulty than the 44-year-old parent with an 8-year-old.

One reason is de-idealization, a long word to describe the process in which a growing child learns that mom and dad make mistakes, too.

"The kids filled out the questionnaire, too, and the more they de-idealized their parents, the lower the parents' mental health.

"The kids are pointing out things and criticizing, and it all has an element of truth to parents. Some parents are more susceptible than others. Just because something is normative, that doesn't mean it won't bother you.

"Some of the criticism goes on in front of the spouse. It can be, 'You're no good at math. I'll ask Dad.' We don't talk much in this society about the ambivalent feelings that parents have about their children and we don't talk much about criticism of parents by kids."

Besides causing a decline in mental health, adolescence also may cause a decline in marital happiness.

Steinberg points out that most marriages that fail collapse early, but that marital happiness does dip into a trough at about 15 years. Couples that do not have children experience the same dip, but the decline is more precipitous for parents with teens.

"Bickering and squabbling between parents and kids and de-idealization makes a contribution to worsening marriages," he says. "When parents feel worse about themselves, it hurts the marriage."

Steinberg studied three types of families with teens or pre-teens: single parents, stepfamilies, and intact two-parent families.

SINGLE PARENTS

All of the single parents in the study were divorced women.

"Even good parents become less good following a divorce. They become less consistent, less vigilant, less organized."

Other studies show that single mothers and their sons—more so than their daughters—have a difficult time in the two-to-three-year period following a divorce.

"In the face of adversity, boys seem to do worse. We saw a lot of power struggles between single mothers and sons. In all families, the period of adolescence is when moms and sons go at it. In an intact family, the mom may say, 'Wait until your father gets home.' That works. Kids are more afraid of their fathers. In single-parent families, there's no backup defense to bring in."

In fact, a single mother is more likely to simply let her adolescent son go his own way than a mother in an intact family or in a stepfamily. "I was really surprised by this, but single mothers would say, 'He's so big, I can't control him anymore.' Must be something symbolic that he's now bigger and stronger."

While sons may be a problem, single mothers draw closer to their teenage daughters.

"There's an increase in closeness following the divorce and an increase in the quality of the closeness. Many single mothers had better relationships with their daughters than married mothers."

But, Steinberg says, when that daughter begins to separate and seek her own friends and her own space, "the single mom has more to lose if the adolescent becomes more emotionally distant."

Faced with the fact that adolescents are more likely to get into serious trouble than younger children, single parents react in one of two ways:

"One pattern is that the mother throws up her hands and sort of checks out. It is a to-hell-with-them attitude and it underlies the powerlessness and helplessness they feel. The second way is to start a crackdown, but they are unable to do that consistently and it doesn't work."

Steinberg says that it's difficult to be stricter as a child ages because the teenager is seeking fewer strictures.

He adds that single mothers are more permissive than mothers in intact families or in stepfamilies. The only more permissive parent is a single father.

STEPFAMILIES

New stepfamilies with teenagers have a more difficult time than if the children are small.

"The most common situation is mom remarries. Now there's a divided loyalties problem. She's torn between her children and her husband, and that's much more of a problem in adolescence because kids speak up at that age, they challenge."

The relationship between spouses is not on the firmest ground because the relationship is a new one. "Stepfamilies are sometimes like newlyweds, and when you are a newlywed you're more interested in pleasing your spouse."

Another problem is the break in continuity. "In two-parent families, parents may disagree, but not after doing things one way for five years. Stepfamilies have abrupt changes in family routines," Steinberg says.

"Lack of a biological and historical connection between father and child makes the authority of the parent less legitimate in the child's eye."

Unlike sons with divorced mothers, it is daughters who have the most difficulty with stepparents.

"If a remarriage occurs, it pulls the mother away from the daughter. They perceive their mother's remarriage as a loss of their mother. We didn't anticipate that. The reaction is more variable for boys."

He adds that other research shows that the story of the evil stepparent is a myth. "Most often it is really the evil stepchild."

INTACT FAMILIES

The dip in mental and emotional health strikes parents in intact families as well.

One parent may react well to the transformation of a child into an adult while the other may see it as a loss of control or, perhaps, an unwanted change in the parent-child relationship. Dad may be jealous of a son's success or mom may be depressed that a daughter is repeating youthful mistakes that she once made.

"If at the end of the day where you have been bickering and squabbling with your teenager, how ready are you to have fun with your spouse?"

Steinberg acknowledges that there is a flip side. "When the marriage is very happy, then marriage provides a buffer. Happily married men and women are less affected."

Work is also a buffer, no matter what the family configuration is. "We measured work satisfaction, and parents with satisfying careers are less likely to be negatively affected by their children's adolescence."

Many parents with adolescents are coping very well. The ones that seem to do the best have pleasures and pursuits other than parenting.

"A lot of parents out there, in a valiant way, have invested every part of themselves in being a parent," Steinberg says. "They are terrific parents, but . . . if all your eggs are in the parenting basket, that parent is the most vulnerable and will be hit hardest by their children becoming adolescents."

As They Grow • 11 to 13 years

"Don't talk back!"

Does your preteen have to argue about about <u>everything</u>? Yes, but you can keep it all in perspective.

R<small>ICHARD</small> M. L<small>ERNER</small>, P<small>H</small>.D.,
<small>AND</small> C<small>HERYL</small> K. O<small>LSON</small>

Richard M. Lerner, Ph.D., is the director of the Institute for Children, Youth, and Families at Michigan State University, in East Lansing.
Cheryl K. Olson is a specialist in youth and health communications.

Mark Twain once wryly noted, "When I was a boy of 14, my father was so ignorant that I could hardly stand to have the old man around. But when I got to be 21, I was astonished at how much he had learned in seven years."

If you're the parent of a preteen, you know all too well what it's like to be on the receiving end of that attitude. The youngster who once saw you as the source of all wisdom now cuts you off in midconversation with utterances such as "You can't tell me what to do" and "Why do I bother explaining things to you? You can't possibly understand." In addition, he suddenly seems to question every statement that comes out of your mouth. He may even use the occasional obscenity.

It's easy for a parent to lose patience when a child starts mouthing off

this way; none of us enjoys being treated disrespectfully or having to justify everything we say. Back talk is also disturbing because it signifies your loss of control over your child's behavior.

But as inappropriate and disrespectful as a preteen's language might be, it's actually a step toward mature behavior. Learning to assert individual opinions is a developmental milestone every bit as significant, and universal, as cutting teeth or walking. As annoying as this stage in your child's life can be at times, there is no way you can absolutely abolish back talk. There are, however, a number of ways for you to recognize and provide outlets for your child's opinions, emotions, and growing skills at debate.

Begin by understanding why your child needs to talk back. Her "smart mouth" is, in some ways, exactly that—a sign that she's smarter. Her logic is growing more sophisticated, although it's not quite up to adult level yet. She now sees her parents' opinions, once regarded as the absolute truth, as one possible truth—and a version of it that she sometimes finds hard to swallow.

Chalk that up to another aspect of preadolescence: your child's need to establish herself as a person separate from you. Just as it is your job to watch over and protect your child, it is your child's job to stake out her own emotional turf, to discover who she is and what she stands for.

An increase in back talk often coincides with a developmental transition, such as starting middle or junior high school. Hanging out with a new group of kids may lead your child to think that a certain level of repartee is expected of her. You may need to tell your adolescent, "I know you talk this way with your friends, but I find it unpleasant to hear that kind of language at home."

Don't belittle your child. In the heat of the moment, this rule can be tough to follow, but it's crucial. No matter how adult your preteen wants to be, he is still a child, with easily hurt feelings and little experience in the art of persuasion.

For example, if you take your child to task for doing his homework in front of the television, he may answer you dismissively with, "This isn't homework. It's just answering questions." You could easily answer him with something like, "That's ridiculous! Do you think I don't know what homework is?"

Although understandable, this response will only serve to embroil you further in an unproductive argument. What you might do instead is say something such as, "Whatever you call it, I want you to try your best at your schoolwork, and I don't think you can do that if you're working in front of the television."

Similarly, if your child is using unpleasant language toward a sibling and you tell him to stop it, he might say, "I'm not being mean; I'm just defending myself!" Your impulse might well be to say, "That's baloney! I heard the way you talked to her." But it's probably more helpful if you respond by saying something like, "Standing up for yourself is a good thing, but you have to try to do it without using words that hurt others' feelings."

Fight fair, even when your child doesn't. Resist the temptation to fight fire with fire, especially if your preteen gets so angry during an argument that she curses at you, shoves you, or even spits on you. If something like this happens, as calmly as you can, say, "I want you to let me know how you feel about things, but I can't tolerate this behavior. The conversation is over." Follow up with appropriate discipline.

Stick to your values. Debates with your child will be more fruitful for both of you if you know what is negotiable and what is not. If you have a habit of arguing and then giving in, you'll get more of an argument from your child because he knows that it pays off. Put forward your deeply held values, and don't retreat from them—but be prepared to justify your position to your child.

If your child is hanging out with a new group of kids, he may start talking like them.

Set limits on profanity. Preadolescents often use foul language to signal their grown-up status. It's hard to deny that cursing is an activity associated with adults. It is as reasonable to set limits on profanity, however, as it is on other adult behaviors, such as staying up late. What those limits are depends on how much foul language upsets you.

If your child says, "How come you get to say any words you want, and I don't?" tell her that using profanity is a habit of yours that you don't especially like and are trying to control, but that it sometimes happens when you're very angry or upset. You can also say to her, "By using those words, you're going to offend someone or create an impression you'll regret later on."

Make sure you give your child credit for what he does right. Because one of your child's primary motives for talking back is to show that he is capable of holding his own in a grown-up conversation, acknowledge him when he succeeds. You won't lose ground by saying, "That's a good point you've made."

Suppose your 12-year-old son wants to sleep over at a friend's house and you say, "No, I don't want you to spend the night there. Blair's parents are lax about supervision."

Your child might respond with, "How do you know? *You've* never spent the night there."

Instead of treating this response as insolence, you might reply, "That's absolutely true. I've heard from other parents, however, that Blair's mom and dad sometimes go out and leave the kids alone. Maybe that isn't so, but the possibility worries me because I'm concerned about your safety."

After some discussion, your child might suggest a solution: "I'll call and make sure his parents will be there all night." After you agree to this—with the understanding that you can telephone the parents to confirm the arrangement—praise your child for respecting your concerns and solving the problem creatively.

Don't expect conflicts—or back talk—to be solved overnight. Arguments often do not have clear-cut resolutions. If you've both had your say and the conversation has become unproductive, you may have to tell your child, "We've been over this too many times. Let's wrap it up. Maybe if we think about it and talk tomorrow, it'll be easer for us to agree on something."

And remember that arguing with a child you love can be a highly emotional and exasperating experience. Don't expect perfection from yourself. Stay as calm and evenhanded as you can, and keep reminding yourself how smart you're going to be in just a few years.

EFFECTS OF PATERNAL ABSENCE ON MALE ADOLESCENTS' PEER RELATIONS AND SELF-IMAGE

Lee A. Beaty

ABSTRACT

This study explores the extent to which adolescent males experience different peer adjustment and masculine self-image as a function of father deprivation. A sample of 40 middle school boys (20 father-present and 20 father-absent) rated each other on peer adjustment and masculine self-image. Results indicate that father-absent boys evidence a poorer sense of masculinity as well as poorer interpersonal relationships than do father-present boys.

INTRODUCTION

Due to the almost overwhelming complexity of modern society and the consequent socio-cultural factors which impact on the structure of the contemporary American family, it is hardly surprising that the variety of alternative family structures has continued to increase during the past generation. One of the most common characteristics of these alternative family structures is paternal absence. Although maternal absence from the family does exist (and can presumably exert a profound influence on children's development), paternal absence is a much more frequent occurrence.

Reprint requests to Lee A. Beaty, Ph.D., Department of Counselor Education, Northeastern Illinois University, 5500 North St. Louis Ave., Chicago, Illinois 60625-4699.

From *Adolescence,* Winter 1995, pp. 873-880. © 1995 by Libra Publishers, Inc. Reprinted by permission.

The most frequently mentioned causes of paternal absence are divorce and/or separation, death, and career demands (e.g., military service). Of these, divorce and separation occur most often. Steinberg (1989) noted the differences that paternal absence due to divorce or death can have on a child's emotional development. Hetherington's (1972) research found differential effects of paternal absence due to death and divorce on female adolescents. Probably the least traumatic effects due to paternal deprivation result from prolonged but temporary father absence, since these effects are reversible.

There is also a differential effect of age on the severity of impact of father absence on children versus adolescents. This may well be due to the inferior coping mechanisms of children as compared to those of adolescents, who have achieved increased emotional maturity and have access to supportive social networks in the form of peer groups (Steinberg, 1989). The research literature (e.g., Hetherington, 1966; Biller & Bahm, 1971) strongly suggests that children who become father-absent before the age of five suffer more debilitating intrapsychological and interpersonal difficulties than do children who become father-absent after the age of five. In fact, the potentially debilitating effects of father absence which occur in middle childhood and subsequent to middle childhood seem to become equalized when these children are compared with father-present children.

For children who become father-absent prior to the age of five, the overall effects of paternal loss seem to be profound and long-term. This is especially true for male children. Adelson (1980) reviewed research which clearly showed that father absence can seriously affect the sex role development of boys. Consequently, their adjustment to peer groups can be impaired. While Johnson (1979), who investigated the effects of father absence due to divorce on preadolescent peer relations, found significance between the father-child relationship and social interaction for both boys and girls, Armsden (1986), who investigated attachment to parents and peers in late adolescence, obtained different results. She found that the well-being of males was most highly related to father attachment. In their meta-analysis of paternal absence studies, Stevenson and Black (1988) reported that males who became father-absent prior to preschool showed less preference for stereotypical sex-typed toys than did father-present boys. Thus, the conceptions of societally proscribed masculine and feminine roles may have been affected for these boys.

In a discussion of sex role and socialization, Block (1973) stated that individuals who are high in sex-appropriate behaviors and highly socialized seemed to have derived these traits from family contexts " . . . where both parents were available to the child, both

physically and psychologically through adolescence. . . ." (p. 523). If we accept this assertion, then the inverse should be true (i.e., males who are father-deprived should be lower in sex-appropriate behaviors and less well socialized). In other words, their gender role development in general and their peer relationships as well should be affected.

Because of the clear importance of peer relationships in the lives of adolescents, it would seem appropriate to give serious consideration to the impact of father absence on male adolescents. Hughes and Noppe (1991) present a developmentally based hierarchy of peer groups in adolescence. In early adolescence, groups normally consist only of same-sex individuals; in middle adolescence, same-sex groups gradually become heterosexual groups; and in late adolescence, heterosexual groups begin to break down into dyads. This normative developmental sequence can indeed be impinged upon by many variables, including that of father absence.

Lamb (1981) suggested that the masculine role model provided by the peer group can be particularly influential for paternally deprived boys. Such "masculine" attributes as aggressiveness and independence are particularly valued in male unisex peer groups, especially in lower socioeconomic status neighborhoods. In an examination of boys from broken homes, McCord, McCord, and Thurber (1962) found a significant relationship between father-absent boys and female/aggressive behaviors; however, the potential relationship with general delinquency was explained more in terms of the effects of divorce rather than those of father absence.

In their study of Norwegian children, Lynn and Sawrey (1959) postulated that adequate peer adjustment is related to appropriate same-sex identification. Father-absent subjects in their study exhibited poorer peer adjustment, presumably because they were less firmly identified with masculine role models. Hetherington (1966) agreed with this presumption and suggested that early father-absent boys showed greater dependency on peers, showed greater deviation in sex-typed traits, and tended to disfavor activities involving competitive and aggressive play. Biller and Bahm (1971) found that in early father-absent boys, masculinity of self-concept was strengthened when mothers encouraged aggressive behavior. They stated that " . . . ramifications of the quality of the early mother-son relationship (for father-absent boys) may become most apparent during adolescence" (p. 181).

In the present study, the intention was to support the findings of Lynn and Sawrey (1959), Hetherington (1966), and Biller and Bahm (1971) with respect to the effects of father absence on the development of masculine self-concept in male adolescents and the resulting effects on peer relationship

adjustment. The hypothesis was that early father-absent boys (those who experience father absence prior to the age of five) evidence dysfunctional effects due to paternal deprivation both in masculinity of their self-concept and in their poor peer adjustment.

METHOD

Subjects

The sample consisted of 40 7th- and 8th-grade (13- and 14-year-old) boys selected from classes in a major Midwestern suburban area middle school. Subjects were selected from a middle school setting because such schools usually have smaller enrollments than do junior high schools, thus providing students with the opportunity for more frequent and in-depth peer interactions. From an initial sample of 60 subjects, 40 were randomly selected for the research sample. Half of the subjects ($n = 20$) were father-present males and the other half ($n = 20$) were father-absent males who had become father-deprived prior to the age of five years. Father-absent subjects were defined as those who had lived with their mothers or nonpaternal relatives at least two thirds of the time. Mean age for the total sample was 13.4 years; the sample was composed of 59% Caucasian, 30% African-American, and 11% Hispanic subjects. Because the subjects were not of majority age, written parental permission was obtained.

Measures

The primary objective in this attempt to replicate the findings of the studies previously cited was to do so by utilizing a different methodological approach. In this study, sociometric measures were employed to determine the degree of perceived masculinity and the degree of perceived peer group adjustment. Kerr, Nelson, and Lambert (1987) describe two types of sociometric instruments: (a) combination measures, and (b) rating scale measures. With the former, students are asked to nominate a specific number of classmates according to some interpersonal criteria. With the rating scale procedure, a student is asked to rate each of his/her classmates according to a Likert scale. Thus each individual earns a score which is his/her mean rating from peers.

The sociometric instrument employed in this study was of the rating scale type, consisting of two separate subscales: Part A focused on perceived masculinity, and Part B focused on perceived peer adjustment. Each subscale contained 15 words or phrases which described masculinity and/or peer adjustment. Items descriptive of masculinity included such words as "independent," "aggressive," or "self-confident." Peer adjustment descriptors included such phrases as "Gets along well with others," "Is popular" or "Is one of the gang." Responses were made on a five-point Likert scale which ranged from *mostly false* to *partly false* to *no opinion* to *partly true* to *mostly true*. The numeric equivalents for these ratings ranged from 1 (mostly false) to 5 (mostly true).

Procedures

Subjects in the father-present group were given sheets with the names of the father-absent subjects and were asked to rate them; they were told that the scale was attempting to measure masculine self-image and peer adjustment, but were not told that father absence was a criterion. Correspondingly, subjects in the father-absent group were asked to rate father-present subjects and were told the same thing. Data collection schedules were coordinated with division teachers and were completed during a single day. The instrument was given to the students as a group since individual administrations were not time-efficient.

RESULTS

The data were analyzed in a conventional manner. The scoring system for Parts A and B of the sociometric measure was calculated as follows: numeric equivalents to responses ranged from mostly false (equals one) to mostly true (equals five). Each subject in the father-present group rated all 20 subjects in the father-absent group on the 15 criteria for masculine self-image and the 15 criteria for peer adjustment; conversely, the father-absent subjects rated the father-present subjects on the same 30 criteria.

Means of each subscale for both groups were calculated and independent *t*-tests for self-image and for peer adjustment were computed to determine whether differences in group means reached statistical significance. The mean on masculine self-image for father-absent boys was significantly lower than that for father-present boys ($t =2.02[38]$, $p < .05$). Similarly, the mean on peer adjustment for father-absent boys was significantly lower than that for father-present boys ($t =2.70[38]$, $p < .01$). (See Tables 1 and 2 for these data.) In fact, individual means for most of the self-concept and peer adjustment items were lower for father-absent subjects than for father-present subjects. The exceptions were the following items: *Masculine Self-concept—5.* "domineering," 10. "reckless," and 13. "uncaring"; Peer Adjustment—3. "is well liked" and 9. "gets along well with both boys and girls."

DISCUSSION

A review of the relevant research literature (e.g., Lynn & Sawrey, 1959; McCord, McCord, & Thurber, 1962; Hetherington, 1966; Biller & Bahm, 1971) has revealed

TABLE 1: t-TEST FOR MASCULINE SELF-IMAGE SCORES

Group:	Mean:	SD:	t:	Signif:
Father-present	55.1	17.4	----	----
Father-absent	42.3	14.8	----	----
Total	48.7	16.1	2.44	0.05*

*Level of significance for 2-tail test

TABLE 2: t-TEST FOR PEER ADJUSTMENT SCORES

Group:	Mean:	SD:	t	Signif:
Father-present	57.3	19.2	----	----
Father-absent	41.9	11.9	----	----
Total	49.6	15.6	2.97	0.01*

*Level of significance for 2-tail test

some degree of consensus on the negative effects of father absence on the masculine self-concept and peer relationship adjustment of male children and adolescents.

It has been reported that these effects are most traumatic and most long lasting when father deprivation occurs prior to the age of five. In later childhood and subsequently in adolescence, such individuals exhibit tendencies to be more dependent on peers, to be more ambiguous about masculinity, to disfavor competitive games and sports, and to engage in female-aggressive behavior. A commonly cited rationale for the development of such tendencies is the lack of an appropriate male role model during early childhood. It also has been noted that maternal perceptions and behaviors can sometimes have a mediating influence on the severity of these negative effects. However, it has generally been agreed that this mediating effect is less strong when provided by mothers than when provided by fathers.

As Lamb (1981) has suggested, the impact on peer adjustment for paternally deprived boys can hardly be underemphasized since male peers supply a strong role model function for such boys. This function is quite important if we recall that peer groups in adolescence moved through a triarchic developmental sequence from same-sex to heterosexual groups and ultimately to dyads. Thus, the quality of peer interactions for father-absent male adolescents seems to have been affected in some significant way.

In this study, the results support the findings of Hetherington (1966) and Biller and Bahm (1971) with respect to the effects of paternal absence on peer relationship adjustment of adolescent boys. This study departs from earlier methodological approaches by employing a rating scale version of a sociometric measure. These sociometric data do indeed support the hypothesis that statistically significant differences in mean scores of perceived masculine self-image and perceived peer adjustment would be observed between father-present and father-absent adolescent males. Both differences were statistically significant—peer relationships at $p < .01$ and masculine self-concept at $p < .05$. Also, most of the individual item means of the father-present group were higher than those of the father-absent group.

It must be strongly emphasized that these findings are subject to a variety of possible interpretations (i.e., there are certainly many alternative explanations for these observed differences). In a causal/comparative design such as this, it is impossible to know whether alternative independent variables other than paternal presence or absence account for the observed group differences. In particular, it is difficult to generalize the results of this study to other middle school students, since many of the environmental factors associated with a suburban school setting are not similar to those of urban or rural settings. Also, the maturational effects of normal developmental processes do indeed produce a multifactorial explanation of complex psychosocial constructs such as self-concept and peer relations. However, the fact that this study's findings do replicate those of previous studies adds considerable weight to the validity of the paternal absence interpretation.

Such results have implications, not only for additional research, but for counselors, teachers, and other professionals who are attempting to develop appropriate strategies to assist adolescents in identifying and rectifying deficits in peer relationships and self-concept. Deficits which can be linked to early father deprivation might be at least somewhat susceptible to subsequent interventions. The connection between these dysfunctions and problems such as poor academic performance/school attendance, alcohol and drug abuse, and a variety of socially maladaptive behaviors is rather easy to conceptualize. If only a fraction of those youth who experience these types of dysfunctional behaviors as a result of early paternal absence could be helped to improve their self-image and peer interactions, then the time and resources devoted to these interventions would be worthwhile. Simply knowing that this kind of alternative family structure may have a negative effect on a youngster's personal and interpersonal capabilities is in itself an important piece of information for those who are in a position to offer assistance.

REFERENCES

Adelson, J. (1980). *Handbook of adolescent psychology.* New York: Wiley.

Armsden, G.G. (1986). *Attachment to parents and peers in late adolescence: Relationships to affective status, self-esteem and coping with loss, threat and challenge.* Unpublished doctoral dissertation, University of Washington.

Biller, H.B., & Bahm, R.M. (1971). Father absence, perceived maternal behavior, and masculinity of self-concept among junior high school boys. *Developmental Psychology, 4*(2), 178–181.

Block, J.H. (1973). Conceptions of sex role: Some crosscultural and longitudinal perspectives. *American Psychologist, 6,* 512–528.

Hetherington, E.M. (1966). Effects of paternal absence on sex-typed behaviors in Negro and white preadolescent males. *Journal of Personality & Social Psychology, 4*(1), 87–91.

Hetherington, E.M. (1972). Effects of father absence on personality development in adolescent daughters. *Developmental Psychology, 7,* 313–326.

Hughes, F.P., & Noppe, L.D. (1991). *Human development across the life span (2nd ed.).* Columbus, OH: Merrill.

Johnson, L.A. (1979). *Divorce, father absence, and father-child relationship as predictors of pre-adolescent children's peer relationships and perspective-taking performance.* Unpublished doctoral dissertation, Stanford University.

Kerr, M.M., Nelson, C.M., & Lambert, D.L. (1987). *Helping adolescents with learning and behavior problems.* Columbus, OH: Merrill.

Lamb, M. (1981). *The role of the father in child development.* (2nd. ed.). New York: Wiley.

Lynn, D.D., & Sawrey, W.L. (1959). The effects of father absence on Norwegian boys and girls. *Journal of Abnormal & Social Psychology, 59,* 258–262.

McCord, J., McCord, W., & Thurber, E. (1962). Some effects of paternal absence on male children. *Journal of Abnormal & Social Psychology, 64,* 361–369.

Stevenson, M.R., & Black, C.N. (1988). *Paternal absence and sex-role development: A meta-analysis. Child Development, 59,* 793–814.

Steinberg, L. (1989). *Adolescence (2nd ed.).* New York: Knopf.

Gay Families Come Out

SAME-SEX PARENTS are trying to move out of the shadows and into the mainstream. Will they—and their kids—be accepted?

BY BARBARA KANTROWITZ

THERE WERE MOMENTS IN Claire's childhood that seemed to call for a little . . . ingenuity. Like when friends came over. How could she explain the presence of Dorothy, the woman who moved into her Chicago home after Claire's dad left? Sometimes Claire said Dorothy was the housekeeper; other times she was an "aunt." In the living room, Claire would cover up the titles of books like "Lesbian Love Stories." More than a decade later, Claire's mother, Lee, recalls silently watching her daughter at the bookcase. It was, she says, "extremely painful to me." Even today, Lee and Claire—now 24 and recently married—want to be identified only by their middle names because they're worried about what their co-workers might think.

Hundreds of miles away, a 5-year-old girl named Lily lives in a toy-filled house with her mommies—Abby Rubenfeld, 43, a Nashville lawyer, and Debra Alberts, 38, a drug- and alcohol-abuse counselor who quit working to stay home. Rubenfeld and Alberts don't feel they should have to hide their relationship. It is, after all, the '90s, when companies like IBM offer gay partners the same benefits as husbands and wives, and celebrity couples like Melissa Etheridge and Julie Cypher proudly announce their expectant motherhood.

Lily was conceived in a very '90s way; her father, Jim Hough, is a gay lawyer in New York who once worked as Rubenfeld's assistant and had always wanted to have kids. He flew to Nashville and the trio discussed his general health, his HIV status (negative) and logistics. They decided Rubenfeld would bear the child because Alberts is diabetic and pregnancy could be dangerous. They all signed a contract specifying that Hough has no financial or legal obligation. Then Rubenfeld figured out when she would be ovulating, and Hough flew

down to donate his sperm so Alberts could artificially inseminate her at home. Nine months later, Lily was born.

Two daughters, two very different families. One haunted by secrecy, the other determined to be open. In the last few years, families headed by gay parents have stepped out of the shadows and moved toward the mainstream. Researchers believe the number of gay families is steadily increasing, although no one knows exactly how many there are. Estimates range from 6 million to 14 million children with at least one gay parent. Adoption agencies report more and more inquiries from prospective parents—especially men—who identify themselves as gay, and sperm banks say they're in the midst of what some call a "gayby boom" propelled by lesbians.

But being open does not always mean being accepted. Many Americans are still very uncomfortable with the idea of gay parents—either because of religious objections, genuine concern for the welfare of the children or bias against homosexuals in general. In a recent NEWSWEEK survey, almost half of those polled felt gays should not be allowed to adopt, although 57 percent thought gays could be just as good at parenting as straight people. Despite the tolerance of big companies like IBM, most gay partners do not receive spousal health benefits. Congress recently passed—and President Clinton signed—a bill allowing states to ban same-sex marriages. Only 13 states specifically permit single lesbians or gay men to adopt, according to the Lambda Legal Defense and Education Fund, a gay-rights advocacy group. Even then, usually only one partner is the parent of record—leaving the other in

FOR THIS NEWSWEEK POLL, PRINCETON SURVEY RESEARCH ASSOCIATES TELEPHONED 929 ADULTS NATIONWIDE OCT. 17–18. THE MARGIN OF ERROR IS +/– 4 PERCENTAGE POINTS. THE NEWSWEEK POLL © 1996 BY NEWSWEEK, INC.

In the most recent Newsweek Poll, 57% of the adults surveyed said they think gay people can be as good at parenting as straight people; only 31% said they didn't think so

legal limbo. Courts have allowed adoptions by a second parent (either gay or straight) in some of those states, although the law is still in flux. In California, for example, Gov. Pete Wilson has been lobbying hard against his state's fairly open procedure for second-parent adoptions.

Dealing with other people's prejudices continues to be a rite of passage for children in gay families. Merle, 14, lives north of Boston with her mother, Molly, and her mother's partner, Laura. Over the years she has learned to ignore the name-calling—gay, queer, faggot—from kids who know her mother is a lesbian and assume she must be one, too (as far as she knows, she isn't). And there are other painful memories, like the time in fifth grade when a friend suddenly "changed her mind" about sleeping over. Merle later learned that the girl's parents had found out about Molly and Laura and wouldn't let their daughter associate with Merle. One day in sixth-grade health class, the teacher asked for examples of different kinds of families. When Merle raised her hand and said, "lesbian," the teacher responded: "This is such a nice town. There wouldn't be any lesbians living here."

Gays say they hope that being honest with the outside world will ultimately increase tolerance, just as parenthood makes them feel more connected to their communities. "It sort of gets you into the Mom and Dad clubs of America," says Jenifer Firestone, a lesbian mother and gay-family educator in Boston. Having a child can also repair strained family relations; mothers and fathers who may have once turned their backs on gay sons and daughters often find it emotionally impossible to ignore their grandchildren.

Still, the outlook for children in this new generation of gay families is unclear. Only a few have even reached school age, so there are no long-term studies available of what the effects of growing up in such a family might be. Researchers do have some data on kids who grew up about the same time that Claire was living with Lee and Dorothy in Chicago. Most were born to a married mother and father who later split up. If the children were young, they generally wound up living with their mother, as did the majority of children of divorce. Pressures were often intense. The children worried about losing friends, while the mothers worried about losing custody if anyone found out about their

sexual orientation. Yet despite these problems, the families were usually emotionally cohesive. In a comprehensive 1992 summary of studies of gay parenting, psychologist Charlotte Patterson of the University of Virginia concluded that the children are just as well adjusted (i.e., they do not have any more psychological problems and do just as well in school) as the offspring of heterosexual parents. The studies also show that as adults, they are no more likely to be gay than are children of straight parents.

The new generation of gay parents is far more diverse and will be harder to analyze. Often they are already in stable partnerships when they decide to start a family. They include lesbian couples who give birth through artificial insemination (the donors can be friends or anonymous contributors to a sperm bank); gay dads who adopt, hire surrogate mothers or pair up with lesbian friends to co-parent, and the more traditional—in this context, at least—parents who started out in heterosexual unions.

Usually they try to settle in a relatively liberal community within a large urban area like Boston, Chicago or Los Angeles, where their children will be able to mix with all kinds of families. They often join one of the many support groups that have been springing up around the country, like Gay and Lesbian Parents Coalition International or COLAGE, an acronym for

Looking for Comfort Zones

The acceptance of gay men and lesbians as parents varies from state to state. This overview is based on information provided by the Lambda Legal Defense and Education Fund, a gay civil-rights group that looked at adoption law and custody decisions.

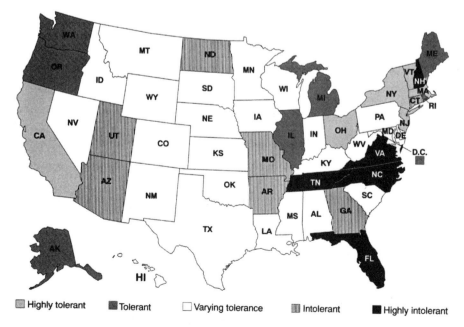

Highly tolerant ■ Tolerant □ Varying tolerance ▥ Intolerant ■ Highly intolerant

36% of those surveyed think gay couples should have the right to adopt, as compared with 29% in 1994; 47% oppose gay adoption rights, down from 65% in 1994

Children of Lesbians and Gays Everywhere. The support groups form a kind of extended family, a shelter against the often hostile outside world.

A decade ago, when gay parents routinely hid their sexual orientation, the issues of differences rarely came up in school. But now gay parents say they try to be straightforward from the first day of class. Marilyn Morales, 34, and her partner, Angela Diaz, 37, live on Chicago's Northwest Side with their son, Christopher, 6, and their 4-month-old daughter, Alejandra, both conceived through artificial insemination. Registering Christopher for school proved to be an education for everyone. Because Morales appeared to be a single mother, a school official asked whether the family was receiving welfare. When Morales explained the situation, the woman was clearly embarrassed. "People don't know how to react," says Diaz. At Christopher's first soccer game, Diaz had to fill out a form that asked for "father's name." She scratched out "father's name" and wrote "Marilyn Morales." Both Morales and Diaz feel Christopher is more accepted now. "At birthday parties people say, 'Here comes Christopher's moms,'" says Morales. Dazelle Steele's son Kyle is a friend of Christopher's, and the two boys often sleep over each other's home. "They're such great parents," Steele says of Diaz and Morales. "Their actions spoke louder to me than rhetoric about their political decisions."

To the parents, each new encounter can feel like coming out all over again. Brian and Bernie are a Boston-area couple who don't want their last names used because they are in the process of finalizing the adoptions of two boys, ages 12 and 6. A few years ago, Brian dreaded meeting the older boy's Cub Scout leader because the man had actively tried to block a sex-education curriculum in the schools. But his son Ryan wanted badly to join the Scouts, and Brian felt he needed to tell the man that the boy's parents were gay. As it turned out, the session went better than Brian had expected. "People challenge themselves, and people grow," Brian says. But, he adds, "as out as I am, I still feel the blood pressure go up, I sweat profusely, I'm red in the face as I tell him I'm gay, that I have a partner and that Ryan has two dads. I always think how it looks to Ryan. I'm always hoping he doesn't see me sweat."

Even in the relatively more tolerant '90s, gay parents "always feel threatened," says April Martin, a New York family therapist who is also a lesbian mother and the author of "The Lesbian and Gay Parenting Handbook." "How can you feel secure when it's still legal for someone to tear apart your family?" The parents are haunted by such well-publicized legal cases as the 1995 Virginia Supreme Court ruling that Sharon Bottoms was an unfit parent because she is a lesbian; she had to surrender custody of her 5-year-old son, Tyler, to her mother. In Florida this summer, the state appeals court ruled that John

Ward, who was convicted of murdering his first wife in 1974, was a more fit parent than his ex-wife Mary, a lesbian.

Catherine Harris, 41, a university administrator in Boston, knows only too well the pain of these legal battles. Ten years ago, she was married and the mother of a toddler daughter, Tayler. Then she fell in love with Paula Vincent, now 38, a nurse-midwife. During the divorce Harris's husband fought for custody of Tayler, and Harris's parents, who disapproved of her new identity as a lesbian, testified against her. Her ex-husband won.

Harris is still on rocky terms with her parents and her ex-husband, but she and Vincent have started a new family of their own that now includes Sora, 7, and her twin siblings, Kaelyn and Marilla, 22 months. In contrast to Tayler, Sora knows her biological father only as "the donor." She has seen the vial his sperm came in and knows that her biological mother, Vincent, and Harris chose him because—according to the questionnaire he filled out at the sperm bank—he was well educated, spiritual and optimistic. "I don't really want a dad," says Sora. "I like having two moms."

But problems can arise even in the most innocent situations. Wayne Steinman and Sal Iacullo didn't truly understand their fragile footing until Labor Day weekend a few years ago, when they drove to Disney World from their home in New York City. As they passed through Virginia, Steinman was at the steering wheel; Iacullo was in the back seat with their adopted daughter, Hope, now 9. They noticed a pickup truck sticking close to them, and when they pulled off the highway to get lunch the truck followed. Just as they were getting ready to pay the bill, two highway patrolmen walked in and started questioning them. The driver of the pickup had called the cops because he suspected the fathers of kidnapping. Fortunately, Steinman and Iacullo were able to convince the patrolmen that they were, in fact, Hope's parents. "From that point on, we carried the adoption papers in our pockets," says Iacullo.

Legalities aside, gay parents—and those who disapprove of gay families—are also concerned about issues of the children's emotional development. Most same-sex parents say they make a special effort to ensure that their kids learn to relate to adults of the opposite sex. Their situation is not that different from that of heterosexual single parents, and the solution is often the same: persuading aunts, uncles or grandparents to be part of their children's lives. Hope Steinman-Iacullo, for example, often visits with her grandmother, her aunts and her teenage cousins. "There are a lot of female role models," says Iacullo.

Psychologists say the best time to tell kids how their families are different is either in childhood or in late adolescence. Young adolescents—from about ages 11 to 15—are particularly vulnerable because they are struggling with their own issues of sexual identity. George Kuhlman and his ex-wife shared joint custody of their daughter, Annie, who was 13 when their marriage fell apart in the early 1980s. But although Annie talked to her father nearly every day of her life, he never told her he was gay. "Several of my friends and even family members had been of the opinion that there might be some real psychological damage and some anger if I didn't make the disclosure," says Kuhlman, now 49 and the ethics counsel for the American Bar Association in Chicago. "That was the bear breathing down my neck." But the timing never seemed right.

Then, one day when Annie was a college freshman, he called to say goodbye as he was about to head off for a Caribbean vacation with a male friend. "She just said, 'Dad, I know. I've known for a long time . . . I just thought you and Tom would have a much nicer time and a happier vacation if you know that I knew and I love you.' I pretty much fell to pieces." Annie, now 24, says she is happy she learned about her father when she was an adult. His sexuality isn't an issue now, she says. "When you have a dedicated parent, it matters less."

And, ultimately, it is the quality of the parenting—not the parents' lifestyle—that matters most to kids. Sexual orientation alone doesn't make a person a good or bad parent. In Maplewood, N.J., Charlie and Marc are raising 17-month-old Olivia, whom they adopted. Last Christmas she had a lead role in their church's holiday pageant. "So you had a little Chinese girl of two gay parents who was the baby Jesus," says Charlie. Adds Marc: "It gives a whole new meaning to the word 'Mary'." As she gets older, Charlie and Marc say, they'll explain to Olivia why her family is unusual. "I think Olivia is so lucky to have the opportunity to be different," says Marc. "And that's what I intend to teach her."

With KAREN SPRINGEN *in Chicago,* CLAUDIA KALB *in Boston,* MARC PEYSER *in New York,* MARK MILLER *in Los Angeles and* DANIEL GLICK *in Denver*

Unit Selections

Key Points to Consider

❖ How has the increased incidence of nontraditional family structures changed the adolescent experience? Do today's adolescents spend less time with adults? Are they growing up too fast? Are they more peer-oriented than other generations?

❖ Does part-time work take too much time away from studies? Do adolescents have too much discretionary income? How does working affect the adolescent? How does working affect the parent-adolescent relationship?

❖ How have adolescent leisure activities changed today? What about the nature of sports activities? What about the role of computers and the Internet?

❖ What drugs are popular with adolescents today? Do most adolescents engage in regular drug and alcohol use because of peer pressure? What smoking and drug prevention techniques are likely to be successful with adolescents?

❖ Do you believe that violence on television, video games, and in music contributes to aggressive behavior in children and adolescents? Why or why not? Will rating TV programs and putting warning labels on music or filtering Internet access make a difference in curbing violence?

 **Links** **www.dushkin.com/online/**

These sites are annotated on pages 4 and 5.

My son won't spend time with the family anymore! All my daughter cares about is what her friends think! Parents bemoan the loss of influence over their children's behavior and the increasing insinuation of peers into their children's lives. The image of the powerless parent versus the persuasive peer is inconsistent with current research and theory about relationships during adolescence. Parents who believe this stereotype run the risk of missing danger signals in their children's behavior and of abdicating too much responsibility when their children still need parental guidance and structure.

Adolescents are without a doubt more peer-oriented than any other age group. But it is simplistic to assume that peer influence is always negative and that it outweighs parental influence. The nature of the parent-child relationship is consistently the best predictor of adolescent psychological health and well-being. Adolescents who have poor relationships with their parents are precisely the adolescents who are most susceptible to negative peer influences. Poor parent-adolescent relationships are not the norm during the pubertal years, but they more likely represent a continuation of poor family relationships from childhood.

Research indicates that most adolescents feel close to and respect their parents. Most adolescents share their parents' values, especially when it comes to moral, religious, political, and educational values. Peers often reinforce parental values as the adolescent's peer group is influenced by parental choices: What school does the adolescent attend? What kind of neighborhood do the parents live in? Do parents attend religious services? What do the parents do for a living? Parental choices such as these have an impact on the network of potential friends for their children.

Several factors have contributed to this misconception that adolescents reject their parents in favor of peers. First, peers do play a greater role in the adolescent's life and influence day-to-day activities, style of dress, and musical tastes. Second, parents often confuse the adolescent's struggle for autonomy with rebellion. G. Stanley Hall's views of adolescence as a biologically necessary time of "storm and stress" contributed to this confusion. Anna Freud, arguing from her father's psychoanalytic tradition and her experience with troubled adolescents, also maintained that the adolescent-parent relationship should be highly conflictual and that adolescents need to turn to peers. Such conflict would ensure a successful resolution of the Oedipus/Electra complex. This model of intense parent-adolescent conflict has not been empirically supported and can be detrimental if parents fail to seek help because they believe that intense conflict is "normal" during adolescence.

Another myth about peer influence during adolescence is that it is primarily negative. As Thomas Berndt discusses in his research, peer influence is mutual and has both positive and negative effects. Peer pressure is rarely coercive, as is popularly envisaged. It is a more subtle process where adolescents influence their friends as well as being influenced by them. Like adults, adolescents choose friends who already have similar interests, attitudes, and beliefs. Until recently, researchers paid little attention to the positive effects of peers on adolescent development. Among other things, friends help adolescents develop role-taking and social skills, conquer the imaginary audience, and act as social supports in stressful situations. Although they decry peer pressure as an influence on their children, no thinking parents would want their son or daughter to be a social outcast with few friends.

Another misconception about peer relations is that teen culture is a unified culture with a single way of thinking and acting. A visit to any secondary school today will reveal the variety of teen cultures that exist. The formation of peer groups and adolescent crowds is partly a function of school structure and school activities. As in past decades, one can find jocks, populars, brains, delinquents, and nerds. One would also encounter members of today's grunge and body-piercing crowds. Media attention is often drawn toward bizarre or antisocial groups, further contributing to the myth that peer influence is primarily negative.

Music is very much a part of youth culture, although there is no universal type of music liked by all adolescents. One way that adolescents have always tried to differentiate themselves from adults has been through music. Adults today are concerned that music lyrics, movies, and television programs have gone too far in the quest for ever more shocking and explicit sexual and violent content. Widespread, easy access to the Internet has also compounded concerns about the types of material today's adolescents are exposed to and can download. Several readings examine positive and negative media influences on today's adolescents.

In addition to school and leisure activities like sports, adolescents today spend considerable time in the part-time work force. Work has usually been seen as a positive influence on adolescent development. Society points to positive outcomes such as developing responsibility and punctuality, knowledge of the working world, and appreciating the value of money. Research does corroborate some positive effects of working, but adolescents have been spending increasing hours in the work force. Recent studies, such as those described in the unit's readings, find that adolescents who work over 20 hours per week are more involved in drug use and delinquent activity, have more psychological and physical complaints, and perform more poorly in school. Although there may be a tendency for adolescents who are predisposed toward such behaviors to be disengaged from school and, therefore, work more in the first place, longitudinal data suggest that working exacerbates these tendencies.

Article 27

They are a generation stuck on fast forward, in a fearsome hurry to grow up. Richer than ever, they're also a retailer's dream, with a seemingly insatiable desire for the latest in everything. What should parents do? BY BARBARA KANTROWITZ AND PAT WINGERT

The Truth About Tweens

LAST YEAR, MAJA KAHN'S LOOK was hip-hop. this year, she's gone glam. Typical outfit: a tight blue tank top, dark blue flare-legged pants, black platforms with silver buckles and nine necklaces of brown or silver beads to match the hoops in her ears. Maja's currently battling with her parents over whether to add a third hole to each earlobe; someday, she hopes to tattoo a spider on her ankle or maybe pierce her navel. Although her mom and dad are as cool as any in Montclair, north of San Francisco, they're resisting her pleas. After all, she's only 12.

Way in the back of Maja's closet, there's a baby doll dressed in pink (a color now banned from her wardrobe). This relic of her past was banished two years ago when Maja shed her polka-dot leggings, pastel shorts and frilly T shirts. No longer a child, not yet a teen, she had officially morphed into a tween, the term marketers have coined for the 27 million children 8 to 14—the largest number in this age group in two decades. "When we're alone," Maja says, "we get weird and crazy and still act like kids. But in public we act cool, like teenagers."

They are a generation stuck on fast forward, children in a fearsome hurry to grow up. Instead of playing with Barbies and Legos, they're pondering the vagaries of love on "Dawson's Creek." The girls wear sexy lingerie and provocative makeup created just for tweens in order to complete what some parents call the Lolita look. The boys affect a tough-guy swagger—while fretting about when their voices will change. In many ways, tweens are blessed. For most of their lives, the economy has been booming. They're likely to have friends from many different ethnic and racial backgrounds. They're computer-savvy, accustomed to a world of information (and a social life based on e-mail) just a mouseclick away. They will also probably be the best-educated generation in history; a substantial majority expect to go on to college.

Tweens are also a retailer's dream: consumers with a seemingly insatiable desire for the latest in everything, from Old Navy cargo pants to Limp Bizkit CDs. But to parents and teachers, they can also be a nightmare, aping the hair, clothes and makeup of celebrities twice their age while still throwing tantrums worthy of a 2-year-old. Psychologists worry that in their rush to act like grown-ups, these kids will never really learn to be grown-up, confusing the appearance of maturity with the real thing. "What we're seeing is a superficial sophistication," says William Damon, director of the Stanford University Center on Adolescence. "There's been no increase in the values that help a kid get through the confusion of life in a steady, productive way."

Of course, every kid's story is unique, and there are certainly lots of youngsters who sail through these years with few problems. But many tweens, even those with sympathetic and supportive parents, say they feel pressured to act older than they feel. Allie Terese Baron-Phillips, 10, of Tarzana, Calif., regularly tells her mother, Brenda Phillips, all the things she's worried about: homelessness, her nightly three hours of homework, the kids in her class who are already pairing off. "My life is really hectic right now," she says. "I'm already doing

what some people in the 1800s weren't doing until they were full-grown adults. I get up at 6:30 every morning, go to school and have to rush through all my classes, come home and work on my homework, go to ice-skating lessons, watch a little TV, talk on the phone, do more homework and practice my violin. If I'm lucky, I get to sleep by 11. And then the entire ordeal starts again."

Allie dreams about building a time machine. "It would be great to just sit around, make quilts and bake pies," she says. "Every day I could meet with my friends and have tea. If I lived on a farm, I could get up and collect the eggs in the morning and spin yarn. It would also be pretty cool to go to a one-room schoolhouse with just 10 or 15 other kids. I wouldn't have to learn as many subjects, and the teacher wouldn't be all stressed out." Her mother sympathizes with Allie's yearning for a simpler time. "When I think of Allie and how advanced she is, how much she's been exposed to, it just amazes me," she says. "I'm not worried, though. I don't look at her and say, 'Oh, it's too bad that she's not a child anymore.' I just say to myself, 'She's a child of the '90s'."

Marketers have seized on these preternaturally frantic kids because it's an oppor-

---

MICHAEL LEWIS, 10

What he likes: "Math is my best subject. And I like roller skating and ice skating and riding my skateboard and playing basketball."
His fears: "I worry about my friends and my family. I worry about them getting hurt, getting hit by a car on their bike, getting beat up by a gang."
On church: "It's fun, but most of the time they just talk and it gets kind of boring. I like the singing."

"Some people want to do chores and some don't. When my mom says, 'Pick up a math book,' I might do that or I might ask if somebody needs something done. I like working around the house."

JENNIFER INGERSOLL, 10

On school: Science is her favorite subject: "We're studying anatomy." Her pack is on wheels "so I don't strain my back carrying my math book."
TV habits: She's "totally obsessed" with "Charmed," "7th Heaven" and "Friends."
Role models: She idolizes Jennifer Love Hewitt "because she's so successful" and also admires Sarah Michelle Gellar and Elizabeth Hurley.

"I love flared pants with flowers on the bottom and anything neon or trendy. My favorite store is Limited Too. I think everything they have there is cool."

tunity to lock in highly impressionable consumers. "They have more market potential than any other demographic group simply because they have all their purchases ahead of them," says James McNeal, professor of marketing at Texas A&M University, who has been studying children's consumer behavior for 30 years. McNeal says tweens have become the "powerhouse" of the kids' market, spending close to $14 billion a year. Increasingly, that money is actually income, he says; younger and younger kids are getting paid for "preparing meals, cleaning the house, mowing the lawn, baby-sitting, working on the computer for their parents." In 1997, McNeal says, a typical 10-year-old had about $13.93 a week to spend, an increase of 75 percent over 1991.

A lot of that money goes for clothes. Kids this age desperately need to belong; they believe that having the right "stuff" is the quickest route to acceptance. They spend millions annually at retailers like Limited Too and the Delia's clothing catalog. They're very brand-conscious, like the students at Franklin elementary school in Chicago who insist on Nikes or Reeboks. Woe to the kid whose mom seeks a bargain. "People tease you, like, 'Ooo, you've got Payless gym shoes'," says 13-year-old Andrea Williams. "I like to stay in Nikes."

Their influence goes beyond their closets. Tweens—Leonardo DiCaprio fans—were a force behind the phenomenal success of "Titanic," as well as groups like the Backstreet Boys; 10- to 14-year-olds now account for about 9 percent of all CD sales. They're a huge part of the audience of the WB network, which has made a specialty of creating programs that appeal to tweens (18.5 percent of its audience), along with their older siblings. They're also the target consumers of magazines like YM and Teen People. McNeal estimates that tweens had direct influence over $128 billion in family spending in 1997, with a say in all kinds of purchases—from soft drinks to cars. "Kids invented the minivan," says McNeal, "and just recently, they've been encouraging their parents to sell them and get an SUV instead."

Why do tweens have so much say? Guilt is one factor. Parents who aren't around much often try to compensate by buying their kids almost anything they ask for. The vast majority of their mothers (more than 75 percent) are in the work force, compared with just over half in the mid-1970s. Then there's the bribery theory of child rearing—often effective in the short run. A new CD can buy cooperation in a hectic week.

But tweens' influence also grows out of a dramatic change in family relationships. The parents, who came of age in the free-spirited late 1960s and '70s, have a more democratic ideal than their mothers and fathers did. "People treat each other more like members of a group, rather than as sons and daughters and moms and dads," says McNeal.

It's Their World: A Guide to Who's Hot

Not yet teens, but not quite kids, the 27 million tweens have huge market potential, and their idols have the shelf life of cotton candy. From "tha bomb" (coolest) to "played" (totally over), here's an up-to-the-minute ranking:

COOLEST BRANDS, 1998
12- TO 15-YEAR-OLDS

Boys	Girls
Nike	Nike
Adidas	Adidas
Tommy Hilfiger	Tommy Hilfiger
Sony	Gap
Pepsi	Cover Girl

FAVORITE TV SHOWS, 1998
12- TO 15-YEAR-OLDS

Boys	Girls
'The Simpsons'	'Dawson's Creek'
'Home Improve.'	'Home Improve.'
'Seinfeld'	'Friends'
'South Park'	'The Simpsons'
'SportsCenter'	'Bev. Hills 90210'

PERSONAL WEEKLY SPENDING
Tweens earn more money from odd jobs and chores, but save relatively less than kids used to.

8- TO 12-YEAR-OLDS

	1989	1994	1997
Income	$6.13	$13.46	$15.64
Spending	3.70	8.90	11.52
Saving	2.43	4.56	4.12

NATIONAL YEARLY SPENDING
Today's superconsuming tweens spend about 300 percent more than they did just a decade ago.

8- TO 12-YEAR-OLDS, IN BILLIONS

	1989	1994	1997
Income	$6.4	$13.9	$16.3
Spending	3.8	9.3	11.9
Saving	2.5	4.6	4.4

INFLUENTIAL SOURCES
The % of 10- to 15-year-olds who learn "a lot" from:

TV, movies	49%
Friends	48
School	41
Mothers	38
Internet	35
Fathers	31
Magazines	26

WHAT THEY WANT TO KNOW
The % of 10- to 12-year olds interested in learning more about:

Violence
Being Safe 80%
Prevention 71

Sex
AIDS 73
STDs 66
Peer Pressure 58
Knowing When 54

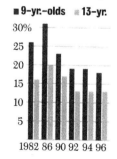

TUBE TIME
The % watching six or more hours a day:

■ 9-yr.-olds ▨ 13-yr.

30%
25
20
15
10
5

1982 86 90 92 94 96

BY THE NUMBERS

According to a 1997 study, kids 9 to 12 play sports for five hours a week—up **50%** from 1981.

In another 1997 study **48%** of boys in grades 5 through 8 reported "high self-confidence." For the girls however, that percentage is lower: **44%**.

(continued on next page)

Editor's note: Refer to *Newsweek*, October 18, 1999, pages 66–67, for additional data.

RESEARCH BY ELIZABETH ANGELL, DEVIN GORDON AND BRET BEGUN. SOURCES; TEENAGE RESEARCH UNLIMITED, JAMES MCNEAL, KAISER FAMILY FOUNDATION, TRENDS IN THE WELL-BEING OF AMERICA'S CHILDREN & YOUTH, THE COMMONWEALTH FUND.

Debra Korn of Bethesda, Md., the mother of 9-year-old Kelly Rakusin, remembers shopping with her own mother decades ago. "She always picked out things for me," Korn says. "She said, 'Boy, that looks good on you,' and I would wear it, but I questioned whether it was the right thing. And I still feel unsure today. I like it that Kelly knows what she likes." Kelly's taste can be fickle. "Today we went through her closet, and anything that wasn't baggy enough or was a little too short or too tight she wanted to get rid of," says Korn. "She says she won't wear them—and she won't. I may as well put them in a bag and give them away." Kelly nods sympathetically: "I don't want to look bad."

Letting kids have their way also means that it's difficult to set limits. "When we ask children, 'What do you think?' it's harder then to turn around and say, 'I was interested in your opinion, but that's not what we're eating for dinner'," says Paula Rauch, a child psychiatrist at Harvard Medical School. Researchers worry that kids may grow up with a false sense of power. They're at the stage where they're beginning to assert their independence; overly compliant parents will give them a distorted view of their place in the world. "They may end up self-centered, self-absorbed, incapable of managing a successful social life, spoiled and unhappy because they're never going to get their own way all the time," says Damon of Stanford.

Although marketers have helped to define tween identity by creating products especially for them, researchers who study adolescents say that the pressure to act like 8 going on 25 really starts at home. Even before they are out of elementary school, many tweens have had to shoulder some pretty serious burdens. "They're being exposed to adult things from birth," says Markus Kruesi, a child and adolescent psychiatrist at the University of Illinois's Institute for Juvenile Research. Nearly half are children of divorce. Too old for child care but not old enough to travel around town on their own, they're often alone in the afternoon with only cartoons or the computer for company, immersed in a culture their parents don't understand.

But that electronic universe is more comforting than the outside world, which can be scary even in the most secure suburbs. As kids returned to school this fall, thoughts of Columbine haunted every middle-school classroom in America. It was only the latest in a lifetime of anxieties. As little kids, tweens worried about being abducted by strangers and having their pictures ending up on milk cartons. Before they'd even been on a date, they'd heard all about AIDS. Parents like Linda Lalande, 45, of Woodland Hills, Calif., mourn for the lost innocence of their own childhoods "when we could play in the woods for hours by ourselves and our parents had no reason to worry." But she believes she has to be on guard with her daughter, Emily, 9, a fourth grader: "You have no choice but to tell them about things like sexual predators and kidnappers."

For some tweens, danger really is just outside the door. Growing up in a single-parent home, 13-year-old Tyler Jimenez of Yucaipa, Calif., learned to look out for himself. Until a year ago, his mother, Dawn Whitson, 37, worked nights as a cocktail waitress. Even when she was home, she was often asleep. "He's had to spend a lot of time alone and learn how to entertain himself," says Whitson, who now has a job with regular hours at the local courthouse. Tyler still gets home first most days. "I do my homework, then clean up around the house," he says. "Sometimes I cook dinner for me and my mom." Whitson worries that Tyler has become something of a loner lately. "He's afraid of being exposed to drugs," she says. "Two older kids on the block . . . got expelled for drugs. Tyler doesn't want to hang out with them anymore. He won't even go out to check the mail. Instead, he just sits with his computer or his videogames. As an excuse, I've heard him say that he's on restriction and he can't go outside."

Under the best circumstances, these can be difficult years. It's a time of tremendous neurological growth, comparable only to the period just after infancy, that psychologists call the "age of obsession." The transformation in their appearance is equally dramatic. "Their bodies undergo more changes than at any time since infancy," says Mary Wright, former principal of Hillview Middle School in East Whittier, Calif., near Los Angeles. "That means the girls are easily brought to tears . . . and the boys try to hide their emotions."

Now those changes begin earlier, thanks largely to improved public health and nutrition. According to a study published this month in the journal Pediatrics, most white girls show signs of puberty before the age of 10 (a year earlier for African-American girls), compared with about 15 at the turn of the 20th century. There are indications that some kids—especially in low-income, inner-city neighborhoods—are also becoming sexually active at an alarmingly early age. According to a 1997 Centers for Disease Control study, 6.5 percent of ninth-

---

HOLLY THOMAS, 12

Mementos of her past: She still has lots of toys in her room. Her childhood favorite, a panda, gets the place of honor on her canopy bed. "I talk to him sometimes."
On put-downs: Her favorite is: "You must think I'm someone who cares."
Her dreams: "If I became an actress or a veterinarian, I'd like to be a famous one. You could make yourself rich, and everyone would know you and want to be with you."

"When I'm with some kids, I act different. I'm quieter. I don't talk much, and I just listen to them talk. With other kids, I'm more hyper. I talk more and I'm bolder. I say whatever I'm thinking."

PATRICK POWER, 13

On TV: He has a set in his room and watches about two hours a day during the week, four hours on weekends.
On games: His PlayStation favorites are Tenchu Stealth Assassin and Metal Gear Solid. "I'd like to go to a paint-ball-fight place, but my parents won't let me."
On money: His weekly allowance is $3.50 "if I do my chores," including cleaning his room and taking out the trash. "I haven't gotten it lately."

"There used to be a lot of groups of kids . . . Now there's mostly one big group—and I'm not in it. Those are the kids who beat up on me. There are some really big kids in my class."

How Parents Can Help

It's a difficult time for the whole family, but there are ways to make these years easier. Your kids still need you.

BY CLAUDIA KALB AND
PAT WINGERT

ONE DAY THEY'RE crawling around in the sandbox; the next day they're prowling the Internet. Tweens like to think of themselves as all grown up—but they still need plenty of support and guidance from parents. Some tips:

BODY CHANGES. Girls may begin to develop breasts as early at 8, and some now get their periods at 10. To prepare for puberty, many boys' and girls' bodies also bulk up during the tween years. Experts warn against putting children on diets or making them feel self-conscious about their weight. Instead, reassure kids that there's a wide definition of "normal" at this age.

SEXUALITY. Few tweens are actually having sex, but they're busy trying to understand it. Some will begin to struggle with sexual orientation. This is a window of opportunity for parental involvement and guidance—once tweens become teens, they're more likely to turn to peers or popular culture for sex ed. They're also sometimes exposed to explicit material on the Internet, and this may confuse and upset them. One good source for parents: the book "Now What Do I Do?" available from the nonprofit group Sexuality Information and Education Council of the United States (www.siecus.org).

SCHOOL. Classes get harder and homework increases as kids move to middle school and junior high. If they're trying hard but still not doing well, parents should talk to teachers about potential learning disabilities that may require special instruction. Overall, parents should coach and support children in homework, but should never be trapped into actually doing it. For general catch-up, afterschool tutors can help.

FRIENDS. For young children, family is the center of the universe. But friends and peer approval become increasingly important during tween years. Cliques emerge and fashion begins to define what's "cool." Still, parents influence on children when it comes to morals and lifelong goals. Get to know your children's friends and their parents. Ask you kids about peer pressure, rather than waiting for them to raise the issue themselves. And act as a role model, exhibiting the kind of behavior around friends and family that you hope to foster in your kids.

INDEPENDENCE. Tweens have one foot in childhood, the others in adolescence. But they're eager to grow up. Experts say the rush is partly due to popular media—especially teen magazines and television shows. Being raised by single parents or in families where both parents work can also accelerate their desire for independence.

Parents should not expect to have absolute control over their tweens, but they should set limits. Regulate the number of hours kids watch TV, and monitor movies; say no to too much violence or graphic sexuality. Make sure you know what they're doing online as well.

MIND AND MOOD. Peer pressure and new academic challenges can overwhelm tweens. Look for symptoms of stress: headaches, stomachaches, sleeping or eating problems. Shifts in hormone levels as tweens advance toward puberty can also cause temporary mood swings. Don't ignore or punish tweens when they become emotional; encourage them to air their feelings. Internalizing sadness or anger is unhealthy. Some tweens can even be clinically depressed. Early signs: feelings of hopelessness, withdrawal and irritability. Parents should intervene and seek professional counseling.

grade girls—compared with only 2.9 percent of 12th graders—said they had had sex before the age of 13. Boys showed a similar increase: 14.7 percent of ninth graders said they'd already been sexually active, while only 6.0 percent of 12th graders said they'd had sex before the age of 13.

There's also some evidence that a few older tweens are experimenting with oral sex—perhaps after hearing so much about it during the Lewinsky scandal last year. "They are copying what they see in adult movies and on the Internet and other places," says Kevin Dwyer, president of the National Association of School Psychologists. "I always tell people that if you have a 12-year-old male in your household, and you have a sex video on the top shelf of your closet that you watch in the privacy of your bedroom, your son has seen it."

Tweens are vulnerable to other problems as well when their physical maturity outpaces their emotional growth. "They're struggling with how they feel about their bodies, what's acceptable and what's not," says Debra Haffner, director of the Sexuality Information and Education Council of the United States, a nonprofit research group. This is a time when girls—attempting to look like the models they see in magazines—often become obsessed with weight; many develop eating disorders. One recent study found that 39 percent of girls in grades five to eight said they were on a diet; 13 percent of those girls said they had already binged and purged, symptoms of bulimia.

Looks have become a measure of self-worth, says Cornell University historian Joan Jacobs Brumberg, author of "The Body Project," a history of American girls. Brumberg says that 50 years ago, when girls talked about self-improvement, they were thinking of doing good works or doing better in school. Now everything comes down to appearance, she says. "In adolescent girls' private diaries and journals, the body is a consistent preoccupation, second only to peer relationships."

Although there are no reliable statistics on substance abuse in this age group (largely because the issue is so new for tweens, few people have studied it), researchers say they think there has been a huge jump in drug use among youngsters in grades six to eight in the past decade. A 1998 University of Maryland study of eighth graders found that 29 percent had tried some illegal drug. More than half—52.5 percent—said they had used alcohol, and 24.7 percent said they had been drunk at least once.

The Age of Obsession

You're worried because they're immersed in a baffling world beyond your reach. Could it really be just a phase?

WHETHER IT'S Pokémon or Harry Potter or Quake III, tweens seem inextricably drawn to mastering complicated worlds with byzantine rules or becoming experts on obscure topics. William Damon, head of the Stanford University Center on Adolescence, talked to NEWSWEEK's Pat Wingert about why the tween years are the age of obsession and how parents should react.

WINGERT: Is obsession a normal part of development?

Damon: It's one of the landmarks that psychologists like Jean Piaget and Erik Erikson have written about. Physiologically, there's a huge increase in the neurological capacity of kids at this stage of development. There are two times when a human goes through tremendous neurological growth—one is just after infancy and the other is around 10, 11 and 12. Kids begin thinking in more complex ways.

So they're looking for a challenge?

Every generation gives it its own twist—and that tells us something about the kids and the culture. In the past, a lot of kids were fascinated in almost an obsessive way with social systems, politics, religious ideology. When I was growing up, everyone collected baseball cards and memorized stats. Some kids use this time to develop skills that can turn out to be incredibly valuable later on—like a fascination with rockets or music. In the '70s a lot of kids, like Steve Jobs and Bill Gates, were fascinated with computers.

If you kid obsesses on the intricacies of Pokémon instead of rocket science, is he wasting an opportunity?

"Wasting" is putting it too strongly. Anything they do to exercise the mental muscle is positive. But it would be more productive to spend time on something that had a deeper meaning, something academic or artistic or civic.

Should parents just say no to the more trivial pursuits as a way to encourage tweens to seek out something more worthwhile?

I would advise against that, because you don't know where they'll turn next with all their energies. They might develop a new type or artificial intelligence, but they might join the Hells Angels. If all you're giving kids is a constraint and censorship, you're setting your kids loose into a risky world and robbing them of your positive guidance. Every parent has to learn to walk the fine line between managing and micromanaging their kids' lives. You should be very careful about what you say no to. I would recommend the other side of the coin: take positive action and help them see a wider range of options.

When should parents get concerned?

Part of this age is discovering private worlds that Mom and Dad are not necessarily promoting, and generally it's harmless. But it can also get weird and scary, and parents need to use their judgment. Parents should get concerned if an obsession gets dangerous, or excessive in ways that could lead to self-destructive habits—like gambling and thrill seeking. Watch for things that can become habit-forming or destructive to themselves or others. Kids are bad about judging risk. These things can get out of control.

Many parents of tweens just don't get what fascinates their child about his or her particular obsession. Is that a bad thing?

To kids, that's the good part.

Researchers say tweens are vulnerable to these high-risk behaviors because they're not getting enough guidance from parents or other responsible adults. "This is a time when they're real curious about the world and they're soaking up other points of view," says Mary Pipher, author of "Reviving Ophelia." "They're not getting enough of that from the people who love them. They're getting it from machines and people who want to sell them stuff." Teachers say that's why an increasing number of kids are becoming behavior problems, unable to deal with everyday conflicts. They see an angry response as the norm. "They spend more time in an unreal environment," says David Eisenstat, a teacher for 20 years, of his fifth graders at Hilltop Elementary School in Inver Grove Heights, outside St. Paul, Minn. "When anything serious crops up in the news, their reaction is based on Bruce Willis movies."

Even in more benign circumstances, they grab on to the fantasies they see on screen. Take 12-year-old Samantha Brooks, a poised seventh grader who lives in Laguna Niguel, Calif. She's got her life all planned out: a career in acting, with a degree from the University of Southern California's film school. She and her pals are particularly fond of the TV program "Friends," especially Courteney Cox's character, Monica, a neat freak who struggles to get her personal life in order. "If you like a show, you take the actors on as a role model," she says. "I think a show like 'Friends' is pretty realistic."

Every generation is an experiment, and there's no way to predict how today's tweens will turn out. According to one recent poll, the "1998 Roper Youth Report: The Mood of Young America," they're optimistic. Eighty percent expected to have a better life than their parents, and most said they liked school. Parents were their most important influences. Too many mothers and fathers step back just when their kids need them most. The best advice: always keep the lines of communication wide open. Get to know their friends. Talk to them about what's going on in school. "They haven't become self-sufficient critters," says W. Andrew Collins, a professor of child development at the University of Minnesota and the president-elect of the Society for Research on Adolescence. "Decision making may be more often left to kids, but it depends on support. It's not a bad thing if parents provide a safety net."

That's exactly what Maja Kahn's parents are trying to do. Roger Kahn, a tennis pro who plays in a rock band, is often home in the afternoons; Marianne, a software tester, usually leaves the office by 5 p.m. Both say they're proud of their daughter's 3.5 GPA and her willingness to do chores. She walks Luna, the family dog, twice a day and empties the dishwasher and vacuums. "She's a good kid," says Marianne. Maja is confident that she has her life under control. "The wild parties, smoking and trying drugs, that takes place in eighth grade at my school," she says, "that's out of my league." At least, for now.

With KAREN SPRINGEN *in Chicago,* ANA FIGUEROA *in Los Angeles and* NICOLE JOSEPH-GOTEINER *in San Francisco*

Teen Jobs:
How Much Is Too Much?

Jon Marshall, Special to The Christian Science Monitor

CHICAGO—It's a classic parent-teen conflict: whether teenagers should get jobs. Derek McDonald, a high school senior in Phoenix, wants to continue working about 30 hours a week as a telemarketing supervisor so he can keep up payments on his 1986 Ford Bronco.

But his parents worry that Derek's long hours are hurting his school work.

"Since he started to work, his grades are getting lower," says his mother, Lupe McDonald. "Sometimes he doesn't have enough time to do homework. But all his friends work, and he wants to also."

Millions of students like Derek spend their afternoons, evenings, and weekends in jobs that include flipping burgers, selling clothes, and baby-sitting. Many of these jobs offer adolescents more than extra spending money—they also teach responsibility, how to budget time and money, and offer a bridge to the worlds of college and career.

But recent research suggests some teens may be working to exhaustion. These studies conclude that working part time can reduce students' academic performance, create undue stress and fatigue, and increase cigarette, alcohol, and marijuana use.

"We see this really clear relationship where 20 or more hours per week is not a good idea," says Michael Resnick, a professor of public health and pediatrics at the University of Minnesota in Minneapolis. "It interferes with the task of being a kid and student." Mr. Resnick co-wrote a recent study in the Journal of the American Medical Association, which found that nearly 1 in every 5 high school students is working at least 20 hours a week.

Too much work can leave students exhausted and irritable, he says. Often their jobs are boring, he says, making them frustrated and cynical about future careers.

In addition, the more time teens spend in the workplace, the more likely they are to imitate the actions of their coworkers, including drinking and smoking, says Jeylan Mortimer, a sociology professor at the University of Minnesota, and author of the 1996 book "Adolescents, Work and Family."

Students often feel caught in a tug of war between their jobs and classwork. Lee Goins of Monroe, Ga., worked bagging groceries during high school but quit. "He came to us and said he didn't have time to study or have a social life," says his mother, Lynne Goins. His parents agreed and decided not to let any of their three children work during the school year, she says.

Teens have always worked, helping out on family farms and filling the factories of the Industrial Revolution. In the first half of the 20th century, however, the percentage of teens in the labor force dropped rapidly. Youths spent more time in school as the demand for cheap, unskilled labor declined and child-labor laws went into effect. By 1940, fewer than 3 percent of US high school students were working while in school, according to Ellen Greenberger and

Laurence Steinberg, authors of the 1986 book "When Teenagers Work."

But after World War II, the number of working teens soared in the US. This American emphasis on working students contrasts with most other industrial countries, where the worlds of work and school are considered separate, the authors say.

'A number of kids who don't do well in school thrive in a job.'—*Terry Stevig, head of the guidance department at Wauconda High School, northern Illinois*

Hours on the Job

About a quarter of high school seniors work between 11 and 20 hours per week.

Males	Percentage of Females	Hours per week
23.8%	22.6%	None
18.8	19.7	1–10
24.0	28.6	11–20
21.8	21.9	21–30
11.6	07.2	31+

Figures are 1995 survey results.

Source: Survey Research Center of the University of Michigan's Institute for Social Research
(TOM BROWN—STAFF)

How Teens Spend Their Earnings

Personal expenses, such as clothing and eating out, top the list of reasons to earn money.

Spending on needs such as clothing, music, and recreation

Percentage of		Proportion
Males	Females	spent
40%	44%	Most
35	33	Some
19	18	A little
5	5	None

Car or car expenses

Percentage of		Proportion
Males	Females	spent
18%	14%	Most
29	23	Some
18	17	A little
36	46	None

Saving for future education

Percentage of		Proportion
Males	Females	spent
10%	9%	Most
19	18	Some
21	22	A litle
51	50	None

Helping to pay family living expenses

Percentage of		Proportion
Males	Females	spent
6%	6%	Most
12	14	Some
24	26	A little
58	54	None

Figures are 1995 survey results

Source: Survey Research Center of the University of Michigan's Institute for Social Research.
(TOM BROWN—STAFF)

'A positive experience'

Government programs over the last two decades have encouraged students to find part-time work. These jobs can help students, many high school counselors say. "Overall, I think it's a positive experience because they learn responsibility, they learn to deal with adults in a more direct, mature way, and they also learn to budget time and money," says Paul Cleary, college and career consultant at William Fremd High School in suburban Chicago.

Jobs often give students a feeling of independence and pride, says Terry Stevig, head of the guidance department at Wauconda High School in northern Illinois. Without the job, they would be spending their time hanging out on the streets, Mr. Stevig says. "A number of kids who don't do well in school thrive in a job," he says.

Andy Theodore agrees. The senior at Evanston Township High School in suburban Chicago works 30 hours a week sweeping sidewalks, trimming hedges, and making repairs for a real estate firm. He says he often feels bored and frustrated in class. At his job, he can see immediate results and feel he is helping people. "It's good money and it's satisfying work," he says. "It makes you feel good about yourself."

But students who work long hours don't have as much time for homework or clubs, sports, and other extracurricular activities. Stevig, who coaches Wauconda's soccer team, has seen players leave practice early so they can get to their jobs on time.

Sometimes parents put the brakes on how many hours their children work. Thomas and Margarita Lang of Phoenix think it's great their sophomore daughter, Jessica, wants to work on weekends and summers to earn extra money. But they are concerned that a weeknight job will hurt her ability to get good grades, do volunteer work, and participate in sports and clubs. "Working over the weekends is not too bad," Mrs. Lang says, "but during the week it's hard. We think it'll interfere with school."

Limiting hours is the key, says Julia Ferguson, a junior at Evanston High School near Chicago. Julia works six hours a week doing clerical work, leaving plenty of time for the pompom squad, friends, and a prep class for college entrance exams. "I like how it's only two hours a day so I can do my schoolwork afterward," she says.

Some students such as Julia use their earnings for college, or to help out their families. But research shows most students are using their income to buy clothes, music, and gadgets. "They want the Nike sneaker for $150," Stevig observes. "They want all the brand clothes and a car."

But what do they gain?

Joel Milgram, an education professor at the University of Cincinnati, wonders how many useful skills students really learn at their jobs. Instead of sweeping floors, they should be spending time in school developing the skills they'll need for the high-tech job market of the future, he says. "It's hard to do well in school when you spend four hours every night as a cashier," he says.

Teens from upper-income families that don't need the extra cash are just as likely to be working as those from poorer families, Mr. Milgram says. Students who need the jobs most in the inner cities and rural areas don't have ready access to the growing job markets in the suburbs, he says.

For some of these students, a part-time job can offer a boost up the career ladder. Despite the potential drawbacks, high school jobs can help teens once they move into the working world, says Professor Mortimer in Minnesota. "Those who work more during high school have a greater ease in joining the full-time labor force and increasing their earnings," she says.

Part-time jobs can teach students useful skills such as working with computers, says Kathryn Borman, an anthropology professor at the University of South Florida who is writing a study on preparing teens for the adult world. But those kinds of good jobs for students are hard to come by, she says.

American businesses have urged schools to teach better job skills, but most companies haven't been creative at giving students good working experiences, Ms. Borman says. Businesses need to do a better job connecting with high schools and community groups to create meaningful job experiences for students, she says. "There needs to be a better way for adolescents to move through that maze to the working world."

INSIDE THE CRAZY CULTURE OF KIDS SPORTS

Competitive athletics can help keep children happy and out of trouble— but it takes over some families' lives

BY ANDREW FERGUSON

KELLY DONNELLY IS BRIGHT AND pretty and lives in Cranford, N.J. She is 13 years old, and she plays soccer. Boy, does she play soccer! Her sister Katie is 15. She plays soccer too. And their dad Pat—well, Pat drives. He drives one girl or the other to soccer practice most every day, and to Virginia for the occasional soccer tournament, and even to Canada once in a while, for more soccer. Last week he drove the girls home from soccer camp in Pennsylvania. Not long ago, Pat logged 300 miles in his green 1994 Dodge Caravan so that Kelly could play in three games on Saturday. Katie had two games that day.

Then they had five on Sunday.

And how was your weekend?

Pretty much the same, probably, if yours is among the growing number of American families that have succumbed to the mania of kids' athletics as they are conceived in the late 1990s: hyperorganized, hypercompetitive, all consuming and often expensive. Never before have America's soccer fields, baseball diamonds, hockey rinks and basketball courts been so as warm with children kicking, swinging, checking and pick-and-rolling.

Some estimates put the number of American youths participating in various organized sports at 40 million. According to the Sporting Goods Manufacturers Association, the number of kids playing basketball now tops 12 million. Not to mention the nearly 7 million playing soccer. Or the 5 million playing

baseball. Hockey, originally played on frozen ponds, is now a year-round sport involving more than half a million kids from Maine down through the Sunbelt. The Turcotte Stickhandling Hockey School, based in Ormond Beach, Fla., of all places, expects 6,400 kids to take part in its clinics this summer, up from 2,600 in 1992.

But it is not just the number of kids playing an organized sport that's unprecedented. It's the way they're playing it—or, to be more precise, the way their parents are arranging for them to play it. Kelly Donnelly's team, the SMC Strikers, offers a good illustration of what is happening to kids' athletics. Not so long ago, games were weekly, teams were local and each sport had its own brief season. And now? "I played varsity soccer in high school and college," says Bob Seiple, a coach for Kelly's team. "During that time, I might have played a total of 50 games. Kelly might play 50 games in a single year."

The Strikers are a travel team—sometimes known as a select or club team—comprising kids who have risen through local soccer squads to be selected for more competitive play. They're drawn from a variety of mostly suburban neighborhoods and towns in a given region, and they will make single-day or weekend-long pilgrimages to meet other similarly skilled teams on distant soccer fields. Their coaches are not volunteer dads but traveling professionals, some of them imported from countries like Britain. Kelly's parents will pay roughly $3,000 a

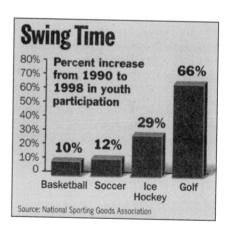

Swing Time

Percent increase from 1990 to 1998 in youth participation

Basketball 10% · Soccer 12% · Ice Hockey 29% · Golf 66%

Source: National Sporting Goods Association

■ TRACK AND FIELD

WHAT IT COSTS
Equipment: $600 to $1,500 a year
Clubs: $100 first year, $50 thereafter
Travel: $100 to $500 a meet
Clinics: $50 to $100 a day; a three-day stay at hurdle camp is $600

HOW MUCH TIME
Schedule: 2 to 9 hours of practice a day, plus a daylong track meet every Saturday

year for her soccer experience, including club dues (which cover the coaches' pay), private clinics, summer camps, travel

■ SOCCER

WHAT IT COSTS
Equipment: $85 to $265 for uniforms and cleats
Clubs: $30 to $400 a year
Travel: $50 to $250 for each tournament
Clinics: $400 to $600 for a week at an overnight camp

HOW MUCH TIME
Schedule: 6 to 16 hours a week of practice and games

and hotels. For the kids, the commitment sometimes seems almost total. Many have abandoned other organized sports—and sometimes even their school's team—to concentrate on the travel squad. "It's tough to play at this level if you don't do it year round," Seiple says.

To be sure, plenty of kids still participate in sports through lower-intensity recreational leagues. But kids' sports, like other American institutions circa 1999, have succumbed to a cycle of rising expectations. More and more parents and kids want better coaching, more of a challenge and the prestige that comes from playing with the best. All of which fuels the growth in travel teams. Says Judy Young, executive director of the National Association for Sport and Physical Education (a professional coaches' association) in Reston, Va.: "Nobody seems to want to play on a little neighborhood team for more than one season." Kids who want to make the big step up from "rec" sports to a travel team often take private instruction, at $70 an hour or more, or attend specialized summer sports camps and clinics, where attendance is booming. The governing body of Little League baseball, for example, has seen attendance more than double, to 2,900 kids, at its five summer-camp locations around the country. Kids' athletics today is not a pursuit for dilettantes—even among 13-year-olds, who used to be dilettantes by nature.

Coaches are recruiting talented children as young as eight, whose after-school hours,

■ BASKETBALL

WHAT IT COSTS
Equipment: $200 to $395 for shoes and uniforms
Clubs: $12.40 to $150 a year
Travel: $60 to $210 a month for a player and parent to attend out-of-town games
Clinics: $100 to $400 a week

HOW MUCH TIME
Schedule: 2 to 6 hours of practice daily, plus games

weekends and summer vacations are occupied by clinics, practices, tournaments and fight-to-the-death competition. The old childhood ideal of goofing off—what the grimmer parenting books term "nonstructured play"—isn't an option. As the kids get older, the more talented rise to ever more selective teams, perhaps representing an entire county, while their less gifted (or less committed) teammates drop away. Family holidays, including Christmas and Thanksgiving, dissolve into long treks to tournaments.

Coaches can get caught in bidding wars—recruited and signed to contracts drawn up by team managers and parents, for annual salaries as high as $60,000. If they don't perform according to expectations, they can be dumped with a dispatch that would make George Steinbrenner smile.

And waiting at the end of the young competitor's rainbow is more than a trophy, more than the thrill of victory, more even than the molding of good character that has been the traditional purpose of children's sports. Now the goal might be a scholarship to defray the stratospheric costs of college, or at least a record of athletic accomplishment that could provide the edge in gaining admission. The dream might be a berth on an Olympic team, or even a career in professional sports.

If all this sounds familiar, it probably should. Throughout the cold war, complacent Americans watched with disdain as promising youngsters behind the Iron Curtain were plucked from home and hearth and sent to spend their childhood in athletic camps where they would be ruthlessly forged into international competitors, exemplars of the totalitarian ideal.

But that was years ago. Watching the crazy culture of kids' sports in America today, a cynic might marvel at how the world has changed. The good news is that the cold war is over. The bad news is that the East Germans won.

That's a harsh view, of course, and it is one not shared by many of the families who crowd the playing fields and gyms. Even in the most intense programs, the kids will tell you this is what they want: the sheer fun of the game, the tribal bond with teammates, the pride of being selected for a team, and the attention from busy parents who might not make as much of a fuss over a triumph in algebra or Spanish.

Any parent knows that few pleasures match the sight of a child who's flushed and beaming after a romp on a stretch of turf. Travel teams in particular can do much to melt away the inhibitions between parents and their teens. "On about the seventh hour of a road trip from western Pennsylvania," says lawyer Robert Luskin of Washington, "you tend to hear things you wouldn't otherwise."

On the practical side, a child busy with sports is less susceptible to the lure of drugs

■ BASEBALL

WHAT IT COSTS
Equipment: $150 to $450 for bats, gloves, uniforms and shoes
Clubs: $25 to $150 a year for league and team fees
Travel: Most youth teams play near home, but kids in élite travel squads spend $10 to $100 a week
Clinics: $200 to $600 for intensive summers and spring breaks

HOW MUCH TIME
Schedule: 3 to 12 hours of practice a week, plus 2 to 4 games

and gangs and the despair we've lately seen in places like Littleton, Colo. "It keeps kids out of trouble and away from the TV," says Leea Kielpinski, 28, a nurse in Oakland, Calif., whose nine-year-old daughter and seven-year-old son play competitive basketball. Most sports programs, despite their excesses, manage to promote the old virtues: self-confidence, personal responsibility, teamwork, persistence, the ability to win and lose with grace. "In an organized sport, Danny's got to learn a little teamwork, some structure and discipline," says Terrence Straub, a Washington steel executive and father of Daniel, 9, and two older sons.

The benefits can even be measured on the child's report card. "We know from a lot of research that kids who participate in sports tend to do better academically," says Mark Goldstein, a child clinical psychologist at Roosevelt University in Chicago. "It forces them to be more organized with their time and to prioritize a lot better."

Of course, the traditional virtues come wrapped in the garb of the less than traditional 1990s, when prosperity is at an all-time high and leisure at an all-time low. In the Glennon household in Lake Forest, Ill., parents John and Kathy and their three younger daughters have re-arranged family

■ TENNIS

WHAT IT COSTS
Equipment: $130 to $750 for rackets, shoes
Clubs: $50 to $700 a year, plus $40 to $100 a week (coaching, court time)
Travel: $100 to $1,500 a month, depending on how many tournaments
Clinics: $600 to $900 a week at tennis camp, $150 for a one-day clinic

HOW MUCH TIME
Schedule: 2 to 6 hours of practice and exercise drills daily, plus weekend tournaments

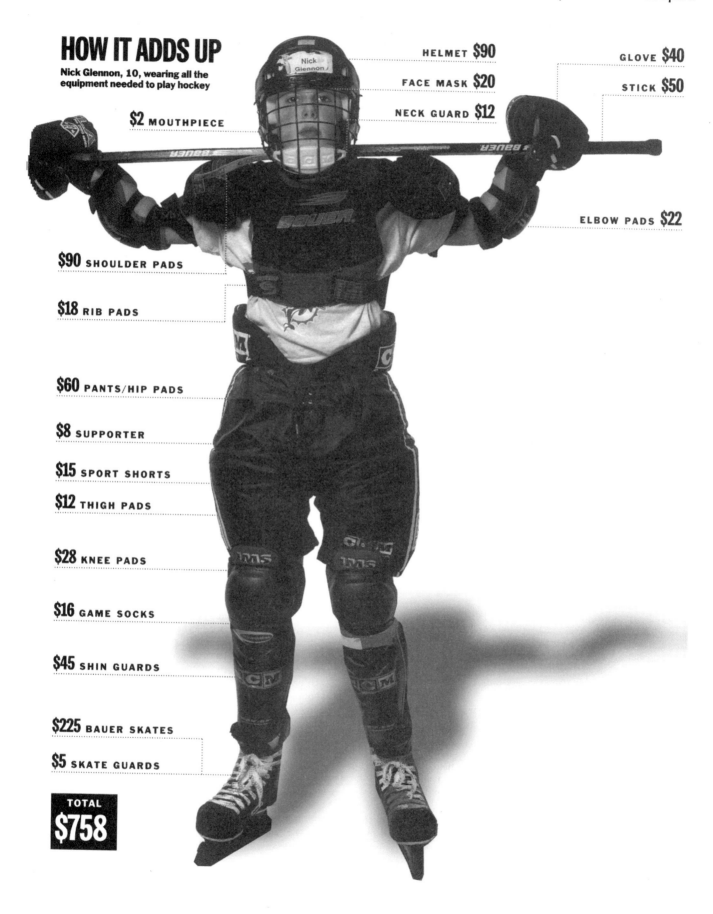

HOW IT ADDS UP

Nick Glennon, 10, wearing all the equipment needed to play hockey

HELMET **$90**

FACE MASK **$20**

NECK GUARD **$12**

GLOVE **$40**

STICK **$50**

$2 MOUTHPIECE

ELBOW PADS **$22**

$90 SHOULDER PADS

$18 RIB PADS

$60 PANTS/HIP PADS

$8 SUPPORTER

$15 SPORT SHORTS

$12 THIGH PADS

$28 KNEE PADS

$16 GAME SOCKS

$45 SHIN GUARDS

$225 BAUER SKATES

$5 SKATE GUARDS

**TOTAL
$758**

■ SWIMMING

WHAT IT COSTS

Equipment: $45 to $100 for suits, goggles and latex caps

Clubs: $25 to $450 a year

Travel: $40 to $150 a month, depending on level of competition and distance traveled

Clinics: About $600 a week: training, room, meals

HOW MUCH TIME

Schedule: 6 to 14 hours of weekly practice, plus strength training

---

life around the hockey schedule of son Nick, 10. One week's lineup: Sunday: practice from 9 a.m. to 10 a.m. Monday: power skating from 7 p.m. to 8 p.m. Tuesday: game night. Friday: a fund-raising dinner dance for the team. Sunday: another game. And several days a week, Nick joins a group of kids who take an hour of private instruction from the former speed coach of the Chicago Blackhawks.

Beyond the expense in time, there is the expense of, well, expense. Hockey is easily the most costly of the team sports. Nick has been playing since he was five, and this year, says John, 46, an investment banker, the family will spend as much as $4,500 on the boy's hockey habit: for equipment, gas and hotel rooms, summer training camps and the membership fee to the local hockey association, which covers coaches' salaries and rink rentals. "It's worth it," says Nick's mom Kathy. "It provides exercise, discipline and camaraderie." Nick has a slightly different take. "I play to win," he says. "I don't play to play. If I find out I have a team that's going to be 0–8, I'll go with a different team."

Some parents hope their kids will win a college scholarship. Single mother Mar Rodriguez of Orlando, for example, is a graduate student at the University of Central Florida. Money is tight. She shuttles her three kids—Virgil, 14; Eva, 13; and Sara, 10—to dozens of youth-basketball events every week, year round. In a recent month, Rodriguez counted only three days without a practice or a game.

Inspired by her idol, Rebecca Lobo of the Women's National Basketball Association, Eva plays on five teams at once. Meals are on the fly, and other social activities are rare. Mar can only pray that the sacrifice will pay off in college aid. "By the time I graduate, it's going to be almost time for the two eldest kids to go to college," she says. "I'll need all the help I can get to pay for their education."

The Saunders family, in Palm Beach Gardens, Fla., nurtures the same hope. Every morning at 4 o'clock, 13-year-old Barry

rises groggily from bed, pulls on his sweat suit and heads out for a 30-min. run at a nearby golf course. Every afternoon he has two hours of track practice. Barry has followed the same routine five days a week since he was seven—all in hopes of winning a college scholarship and eventually a shot at the Olympics. It's not a farfetched dream: already Barry holds the U.S. record for his age in the long jump and for 55-meter hurdles.

Barry's father Stan, an Olympic alternate in track in 1976, coaches his son's club track team, the Roosevelt Express. Last year the club spent $60,000—most of it raised from local companies—to travel to tournaments as far away as Seattle and Antigua. Saunders estimates his out-of-pocket expenses last year at $12,000.

But it's worth it, he says. The kids on the team, many from underprivileged backgrounds, get to go places and meet people they otherwise would not. Also, college coaches are scouting the national competitions for recruits, even among kids as young as Barry. "We just feel very fortunate," Stan says, "that we're able to afford for him to compete at the next level. Because that's where the recruiters are."

For most kids, though, the odds of a scholarship are long. Robert Malina, director of the Institute for the Study of Youth Sports at Michigan State University, says most parents would be better off putting the money they spend on travel teams into a savings account. According to the National Center for Educational Statistics, fewer than 1% of the kids participating in organized sports today will qualify for any sort of college athletic scholarship.

Still, Mar Rodriguez knows parents who have hired private coaches for girls as young as 10. Andrew Roderick, who heads UK-Elite, the company that supplies British coaches for Kelly Donnelly's team, says such parents may be setting up their kids for disappointment. "The big thing is fun," he says. "If you're not having fun with it, you shouldn't be doing it."

Ah, yes, fun. The primary importance of fun—of sport pursued for sheer exhilaration—is a credo repeated, and often honored, by coaches, kids and parents. At the same time, though, the pushy parent, red-faced and screaming from the sidelines or bleachers at a hapless preteen fumbling on the field, has become an American archetype and a symbol of the unmeasured costs of kids' sports.

Violence is rare but not unheard of. Military police were called in to stop a parents' brawl at a "tinymite" football game in Repton, Ala., last October. A T-ball coach in Wagoner, Okla., was sentenced to 12 days in jail for attacking a 15-year-old umpire. California recently passed a law making it a felony to assault a sports official in an amateur contest.

More common is the low-voltage ugliness of parents who just don't know when to let up, or shut up. Hockey parents in suburban Washington are used to such sights as the dad who ran up to his son after an unexpected loss recently to rage at him, "I'm very, very disappointed." The boy sighed, staring at his scuffed toes. "Yeah, Mom's gonna chew me out too."

Jay George, a Washington biochemist whose son Jason, 12, plays on Washington's Little Caps team, had to summon a referee to remove some parents from the opposing team who were overheard telling their kids, "If you're going to get a penalty, really hurt someone." Then there was the time a Squirt-level tournament match ended in a tie and one of the opposing moms celebrated by clawing two of George's son's teammates as they filed off the ice.

And if parents don't spoil the fun, sometimes the coaches will. Bob Bradley, 41, of Chicago tried to suggest quietly to his daughter's soccer instructor that his screaming at the players during a game was inhibiting their play. "Well, you're the parent and I'm the coach," came the reply, "and I'm the one who knows how to play this game." Bradley walked away without mentioning that he had just coached the Chicago Fire to the championship of Major League Soccer.

Critics cite such unpleasantness to account for the 73% of kids who quit their childhood sports by age 13, according to studies. "They drop out because it ceases to be fun, and the pressures put on them by coaches and parents don't make it worthwhile," says Fred Engh of West Palm Beach, Fla. He's a professional coach, father of seven and author of the book Why *Johnny Hates Sports*.

Too often, says Engh, "we take Johnny and Mary and push them into sports without knowing whether they're physically or mentally ready. The travel teams, the all-stars, the championships—they're what the parents want. There's nothing wrong with competition. It makes people successful. But children under the age of 10 don't necessarily want competition. What they want is to have fun, to go out and swing on a swing and go down a sliding board."

Swings? Slides? How hopelessly retro. Nowadays, if a kid waits till she's 10 to decide she wants to compete at an advanced level, the travel team will have already left the station. Her peers will be making deft one-touch passes while she's still learning to dribble. That leaves as her only option the easygoing recreation league, where the coaching is desultory and players often go AWOL. While many parents of kids on "rec" teams equate "keeping it fun" with holding down the level of instruction and competition, the kids often see things differently. Young, of the professional coaches' association, observes, "It's not fun for them when they don't get better."

You can take the testimony of the kids themselves. "It's my life," says Aidan Wolfe, 10, of Portland, Ore., who plays in a recreational league. "I love soccer. If my parents told me I couldn't play anymore, I'd be devastated." During the school year, hockey player Jason George wedges homework into recess and lunch breaks to make the grueling Little Caps schedule, but, he says, "if that's what it takes for me to be good at hockey, I'll do whatever I have to do." His sister Sara, 9, also loves travel hockey because, on the road trips, "I get to spend a lot of time with my mom."

But other youngsters buckle under the load: whether it's that of a single, demanding club sport or a whole basketful of scheduled activities. Stephanie Mazzamaro, 10, of Ridgefield, Conn., complained that in addition to homework, piano lessons, Girl Scouts and religion classes, she had Monday soccer practices and Saturday games. "Mom, I don't want to do all of this anymore," she sobbed. "I don't have time to be a kid."

Her mother Janice, 40, could only agree. "When you live in an area like this, you get caught up in it," Janice says. "If you don't do each step, you feel like you're doing an injustice to your child."

The intensity of today's kids' sports seems to be contributing to an increase in injuries. The Consumer Products Safety Commission reports that roughly 4 million children between the ages of 6 and 16 end up in hospital emergency rooms for sports-related injuries each year. Eight million more are treated for some form of medical problem traceable to athletics: for example, shin splints and stress fractures. Some sports physicians point to specialization—a child playing a single sport year round, which many club teams encourage—as one culprit in sports injuries. Kids who alternate different activities at different seasons are less likely to overuse the same set of muscles and joints.

"It's a very rare thing to see someone playing three sports in high school anymore because of the pressure these clubs put on kids to play in the off season," says Gary Thran, director of athletics at Harvard-Westlake School in Studio City, Calif. Gregg Heinzmann, associate director of the Youth Sports Research Council at Rutgers University in New Brunswick, N.J., observes that these players often have become "specialists who face all the stress of a pro." Why the pressure? According to Thran, college coaches are telling ever younger kids to limit themselves to one sport year round, so they can make the elite traveling clubs.

The Darwinian struggle has gripped girls' sports with a special intensity. Some college recruiters are bypassing high schools and selecting players directly from the club teams. And some high school recruiters are moving even earlier. Charles Morris, 42, of Berkeley, Calif., a technician for Bay Area Rapid Tran-

Poor Kids Need a Sporting Chance

WHILE SURBURBAN AND SMALL-TOWN parents often worry about their kids being overscheduled with sports and not having enough free time, many inner-city families say they would love to have such problems. When kids pour out of school each day in scores of lower-income urban communities, all that awaits them is the street—no soccer, baseball or ice skating. They just hang out, while their parents pray that dead-end afternoons won't lead to sex or drugs or violence. "Most teenage pregnancies happen between 2 and 5 in the afternoon," says Les Franklin, founder of the Shaka Franklin Foundation for Youth, a nonprofit group based in Denver that provides counseling and other services for urban youngsters. "In our neighborhoods, the concept of 'soccer mom' doesn't exist."

Millions of less fortunate families bemoan the scarcity of such basic resources as recreation centers with a staff or basketball hoops with nets on them. In many of their neighborhoods, public money for after-school activities has declined, even in a time of plenty. Instead governments are directing resources toward law enforcement, education and other means of curbing such social ills as teen pregnancy, drug abuse and gang violence.

The result is that many traditional extracurricular activities, from basketball leagues to math clubs and choirs, have all but disappeared from inner-city schools. "If you're a child growing up in a poor community, your chances of being involved in an after-school activity are almost none," says Geoffrey Canada, president of the Rheedlen Centers for Children and Families in New York City.

Consider the contrast between two suburbs of St. Louis. In upscale Clayton, Mo., the after-school menu is crowded with leagues and summer-camp activities ranging from baseball and martial arts to tennis and volleyball. But travel 15 minutes northwest to Clayton's working-class neighbor, the town of Jennings. There the recreation department is understaffed, lacks a gymnasium and relies largely on local public schools and other facilities, creating transportation problems that keep many kids sidelined. "There are some definite barriers," says Cindy Tharp, director of recreation in Jennings. "But if parents want to get their child involved, they'll find a way to do it."

Happily, some of them are getting help. Three years ago, when the U.S. National Park Service was ready to tear down an aging ice-hockey rink in a lower-income section of southeastern Washington, D.C., some parents from more affluent communities banded together and raised enough private and corporate dollars to save it. Today Fort Dupont Ice Arena provides free skating instruction to some 2,500 local kids, with its $500,000 annual budget funded through admission fees, fund raisers and sale of ice time for practicing hockey teams from private schools and local colleges. Says rink general manager Fred Wilson: "The greatest reward we get is seeing the expression on the faces of these kids when they step out on the ice for the first time." It's a step that no child or parent should take for granted.

—By Ron Stodghill II/Chicago

sit, shakes his head as he recalls the coach who, after watching his daughter play basketball, asked what high school she plans to attend. To be sure, the girl, Casey, is a standout player. But she's eight years old.

If kids' sports is undergoing a kind of privatization, with the most talented kids forgoing high school play altogether in favor of the elite travel clubs, the future of high school athletics could be bleak indeed. Dean Crowley, commissioner of athletics at the California Interscholastic Federation, points to the precarious position that sports programs already hold in many cash-strapped schools. "Pretty soon they might say, 'Why do we need to spend all the money we do on sports? These kids are playing all year round anyway.' " And then? "Then you don't have high school athletics." And then too,

the best coaching and the most challenging opportunities would be limited to the kids whose parents can afford private club sports. Which is not what anyone had in mind.

We Americans are a competitive bunch. It was probably inevitable that the striving impulse would sooner or later reshape kids' sports. But the trend has been abetted by other, less predictable changes in American life: the ascendancy of the automobile, the shrinking of open spaces, the ubiquity of the two-earner family and the pervasive fear of crime. Baby-boomer parents may look back wistfully at their own childhood, when playing sports was a matter of heading to the corner sandlot or the neighborhood park after school for a pick-up game. But the sandlot's been filled in by a four-bedroom Cape Cod with a two-story atrium. To pay for the

Cape Cod, Mom and Dad are both working, and with Mom and Dad both working, the kids are signed up for extended-day sessions at school. And by the time extended-day is over, it's dusk. And even if Mom and Dad were home, they'd never let the kids wander alone to the neighborhood park. You never know who they'll find at the neighborhood park.

So what's a parent to do? We do what Americans have always done. This is, after all, a country that systematizes: we create seminars on how to make friends, teach classes in grieving and make pet walking a profession. In that light, Gregg Heinzmann's praise of unstructured play seems almost un-American. Any activity, no matter how innocent or trivial or spontaneous, can become specialized in America. So if our children

are to have sports, we will make leagues and teams, write schedules and rule books, publish box scores and rankings, hire coaches and refs, buy uniforms and equipment to the limit of our means. We will kiss our weekends goodbye—and maybe more than our weekends.

To most parents involved in kids' sports, all the criticisms sound like the dreariest party-poopery. There are joys that can't be organized, pleasures that resist the rigors of systematization. And these remain unextinguished, even in the overwrought world of kids' sports today. In Morristown, N.J., at the Beard School gym, Kelly Donnelly is whiling away the last moments before a soccer clinic. Dad Pat has driven her there, of course. He watches as Kelly spends a minute or so keeping a soccer ball suspended by

bouncing it lightly off her knees, in a kind of airborne dribble—a bit of magic that only the rarest adult could pull off.

"It's quite a commitment from the parents as well as the kids," Pat Donnelly is saying. Suddenly Kelly lets the ball fall to the polished wooden floor and with a deft kick sends it the length of the gym till it narrowly misses a basketball hoop at the far end. The kid's good. Donnelly beams and says, "I think I enjoy it almost as much as she does."

—Reported by William Dowell/New York, Tamala Drummond/Orlando, Julie Grace/Chicago, Maureen Harrington/Denver, Sylvester Monroe/Oakland and Elaine Shannon/Washington

Stop Blaming Kids and TV

MARK S. FISHER

BY MIKE MALES

Children have never been very good at listening to their elders," James Baldwin wrote in *Nobody Knows My Name.* "But they have never failed to imitate them." This basic truth has all but disap-

Mike Males, author of "The Scapegoat Generation: America's War on Adolescents" (Common Courage Press, 1996), is a social-ecology doctoral student at the University of California-Irvine.

peared as the public increasingly treats teenagers as a robot-like population under sway of an exploitative media. White House officials lecture film, music, Internet, fashion, and pop-culture moguls and accuse them of programming kids to smoke, drink, shoot up, have sex, and kill.

So do conservatives, led by William Bennett and Dan Quayle. Professional organizations are also into media-bashing. In its famous report on youth risks, the Carnegie Corporation devoted a full chapter to media influences.

Progressives are no exception. *Mother Jones* claims it has "proof that TV makes kids violent." And the Institute for Alternative Media emphasizes, "the average American child will witness . . . 200,000 acts of [TV] violence" by the time that child graduates from high school.

None of these varied interests note that during the eighteen years between a child's birth and graduation from high school, there will be fifteen million cases of real violence in American homes grave enough to require hospital emergency treatment. These assaults will cause ten million serious injuries and 40,000 deaths to children. In October 1996, the Department of Health and Human Services reported 565,000 serious injuries that abusive parents inflicted on children and youths in 1993. The number is up four-fold since 1986.

The Department of Health report disappeared from the news in one day. It elicited virtually no comment from the White House, Republicans, or law-enforcement officials. Nor from Carnegie scholars, whose 150-page study, "Great Transitions: Preparing Adolescents for a New Century," devotes two sentences to household violence. The left press took no particular interest in the story, either.

All sides seem to agree that fictional violence, sex on the screen, Joe Camel, beer-drinking frogs, or naked bodies on the Internet pose a bigger threat to children than do actual beatings, rape, or parental addictions. This, in turn, upholds the Clinton doctrine that youth behavior is the problem, and curbing young people's rights the answer.

Claims that TV causes violence bear little relation to real behavior. Japanese and European kids behold media as graphically brutal as that which appears on American screens, but seventeen-year-olds in those countries commit murder at rates lower than those of American seventy-year-olds.

Likewise, youths in different parts of the United States are exposed to the same media but display drastically different violence levels. TV violence does not account for the fact that the murder rate among black teens in Washington, D.C., is twenty-five times higher than that of white teens living a few Metro stops away. It doesn't explain why, nationally, murder doubled among nonwhite and Latino youth over the last decade, but declined among white Anglo teens. Furthermore, contrary to the TV brainwashing theory, Anglo sixteen-year-olds have lower violent-crime rates than black sixty-year-olds, Latino forty-year-olds, and Anglo thirty-year-olds. Men, women, whites, Latinos, blacks, Asians, teens, young adults, middle-agers, and senior citizens in Fresno County—California's poorest urban area—display murder and violent-crime rates double those of their counterparts in Ventura County, the state's richest.

Confounding every theory, America's biggest explosion in felony violent crime is not street crime among minorities or teens of any color, but domestic violence among aging, mostly white baby boomers. Should we arm Junior with a V-chip to protect him from Mom and Dad?

In practical terms, media-violence theories are not about kids, but about race and class: If TV accounts for any meaningful fraction of murder levels among poorer, nonwhite youth, why doesn't it have the same effect on white kids? Are minorities inherently programmable?

The newest target is Channel One, legitimately criticized by the Unplug Campaign—a watchdog sponsored by the Center for Commercial-Free Public Education—as a corporate marketing ploy packaged as educational TV. But then the Unplug Campaign gives credence to claims that "commercials control kids" by "harvesting minds," as Roy Fox of the University of Missouri says. These claims imply that teens are uniquely open to media brainwashing.

Other misleading claims come from Johns Hopkins University media analyst Mark Crispin Miller. In his critique of Channel One in the May edition of *Extra!*, Miller invoked such hackneyed phrases as the "inevitable rebelliousness of adolescent boys," the "hormones raging," and the "defiant boorish behavior" of "young men." Despite the popularity of these stereotypes, there is no basis in fact for such anti-youth bias.

A 1988 study in the *Journal of Youth and Adolescence* by psychology professors Grayson Holmbeck and John Hill concluded: "Adolescents are *not* in turmoil, *not* deeply disturbed, *not* at the mercy of their impulses, *not* resistant to parental values, and *not* rebellious."

In the November 1992 *Journal of the American Academy of Child and Adolescent Psychiatry,* Northwestern University psychiatry professor Daniel Offer reviewed 150 studies and concluded, in his article "Debunking the Myths of Adolescence," that "the effects of pubertal hormones are neither potent nor pervasive."

If anything, Channel One and other mainstream media reinforce young people's conformity to—not defiance of—adult values. Miller's unsubstantiated claims that student consumerism, bad behaviors, and mental or biological imbalances are compelled by media ads and images could be made with equal force about the behaviors of his own age group. Binge drinking, drug abuse, and violence against children by adults over the age of thirty are rising rapidly.

The barrage of sexually seductive liquor ads, fashion images, and anti-youth rhetoric, by conventional logic, must be influencing those hormonally unstable middle-agers.

I worked for a dozen years in youth programs in Montana and California. When problems arose, they usually crossed generations. I saw violent kids with dads or uncles in jail for assault. I saw middle-schoolers molested in childhood by mom's boyfriend. I saw budding teen alcoholics hoisting forty-ouncers alongside forty-year-old sots. I also saw again and again how kids start to smoke. In countless trailers and small apartments dense with blue haze, children roamed the rugs as grownups puffed. Mom and seventh-grade daughter swapped Dorals while bemoaning the evils of men. A junior-high basketball center slept outside before a big game because a dozen elders—from her non-inhaling sixteen-year-old brother to her grandma—were all chain smokers. Two years later, she'd given up and joined the party.

As a rule, teen smoking mimicked adult smoking by gender, race, locale, era, and household. I could discern no pop-culture puppetry. My survey of 400 Los Angeles middle schoolers for a 1994 *Journal of School Health* article found children of smoking parents three times more likely to smoke by age fifteen than children of nonsmokers. Parents were the most influential but not the only adults kids emulated. Nor did youngsters copy elders slavishly. Youths often picked slightly different habits (like chewing tobacco, or their own brands).

In 1989, the Centers for Disease Control lamented, "75 percent of all teenage smokers come from homes where parents smoke." You don't hear such candor from today's put-politics-first health agencies. Centers for Disease Control tobacco chieftain Michael Eriksen informed me that his agency doesn't make an issue of parental smoking. Nor do anti-smoking groups. Asked Kathy Mulvey, research director of INFACT: "Why make enemies of fifty million adult smokers" when advertising creates the real "appeal of tobacco to youth?"

Do ads hook kids on cigarettes? Studies of the effects of the Joe Camel logo show only that a larger fraction of teen smokers than veteran adult smokers choose the Camel brand. When asked, some researchers admit they cannot demonstrate that advertising causes kids to smoke who would not otherwise. And that's the real issue. In fact, surveys found smoking declining among teens (especially the youngest) during Joe's advent from 1985 to 1990.

The University of California's Stanton Glantz, whose exposure of 10,000 tobacco documents enraged the industry, found corporate perfidy far shrewder than camels and cowboys.

"As the tobacco industry knows well," Glantz reported, "kids want to be like adults." An industry marketing document advises: "To reach young smokers, present the cigarette as one of the initiations into adult life . . . the basic symbols of growing up."

The biggest predictor of whether a teen will become a smoker, a drunk, or a druggie is whether or not the child grows up amid adult addicts. Three-fourths of murdered kids are killed by adults. Suicide and murder rates among white teenagers resemble those of white adults, and suicide and murder rates among black teens track those of black adults. And as far as teen pregnancy goes, for minor mothers, four-fifths of the fathers are adults over eighteen, and half are adults over twenty.

The inescapable conclusion is this: If you want to change juvenile behavior, change adult behavior. But instead of focusing on adults, almost everyone points a finger at kids—and at the TV culture that supposedly addicts them.

Groups like Mothers Against Drunk Driving charge, for instance, that Budweiser's frogs entice teens to drink. Yet the 1995 National Household Survey found teen alcohol use declining. "Youths aren't buying the cute and flashy beer images," an in-depth *USA Today* survey found. Most teens found the ads amusing, but they did not consume Bud as a result.

By squabbling over frogs, political interests can sidestep the impolitic tragedy that adults over the age of twenty-one cause 90 percent of America's 16,000 alcohol-related traffic deaths every year. Clinton and drug-policy chief Barry McCaffrey ignore federal reports that show a skyrocketing toll of booze and drug-related casualties among adults in their thirties and forties—the age group that is parenting most American teens. But both officials get favorable press attention by blaming alcohol ads and heroin chic for corrupting our kids.

Progressive reformers who insist kids are so malleable that beer frogs and Joe Camel and Ace Ventura push them to evil are not so different from those on the Christian right who claim that *Our Bodies, Ourselves* promotes teen sex and that the group Rage Against the Machine persuades pubescents to roll down Rodeo Drive with a shotgun.

America's increasingly marginalized young deserve better than grownup escapism. Millions of children and teenagers face real destitution, drug abuse, and violence in their homes. Yet these profound menaces continue to lurk in the background, even as the frogs, V-chips, and Mighty Morphins take center stage.

Sex, drugs and rock have worried parents for decades. But now the Net, videogames and no-holds-barred-music are creating new worlds that many adults can't enter. BY JOHN LELAND

The Secret Life of Teens

HI, KIDS, DO YOU LIKE VIOLENCE? WANNA SEE ME STICK NINE-inch nails through each one of my eyelids? Wanna copy me and do exactly like I did?" The bleached-blond pixie could be a refugee from the set of "Friends," all smirk and glimmer. He is Marshall Mathers, better known as Eminem, whose debut rap album has been near the top of the charts for the last two months. In the secret lives of American teenagers, Eminem is large. "By the way," he raps, "when you see my dad, tell him I slit his throat in this dream I had."

Since they first emerged as a demographic entity earlier this century, adolescents of every era have carved out their own secret worlds, inventing private codes of style and behavior designed to communicate only within the in group and to exclude or offend adults. It is a central rite of American passage. But lately this developmental process has come under great strain. "In the past, the toughest decision [teens] had was whether to have sex, or whether to use drugs," says Sheri Parks, who studies families and the media at the University of Maryland. "Those are still

Voices of a Generation

Teens say their lives are stressful, filled with social pressures—especially about looks and dress—worries about safety and fears of being stereotyped. And, of course, some parents just don't understand.

ON CLIQUES

Julia Papastavridis, 15 Freshman, the Paideia School, Atlanta. Student rep on the disciplinary committee, chorus member.

"I see people who don't allow themselves to grow in certain areas, even though they have talent or skill, because they feel that would be out of character or that people wouldn't like them if they changed. Say you're really good at math, but your friends say, "I hate math. It's such a nerdy stupid subject." You can't be good at it because then you're a nerdy brainiac person. And then you feel like you don't fit in."

ON MEDIA VIOLENCE

Chris Haley, 17 Junior, Lewisville High School, Lewisville, Texas. Founder of philosophy group, loves classical music.

"Our generation is far more densensitized to violence than any other generation. TVs raise children now more than parents do, and television caters to children's violent fantasies. Parents are working more and spending less time with their kids."

ON FASHION

Marisol Salguero, 16 Junior, Alexander Hamilton High School, Los Angeles. AP and honors classes, academic tutor.

"The biggest thing here is wearing name-brand clothes. If you even think of wearing a non-name brand, you have guts. Looks are real important, too. If you're not pretty, people won't want to hang out with you. Even the girls with dark hair usually dye their hair blonde. Everything is just one big competition."

ON APPEARANCE

Lauren Barry, 17 Senior, Glenbrook South High School, Glenview, Ill. National Honor Society, alternative theater group.

"I went to a National Honor Society induction. The parents were just staring at me. I think they couldn't believe someone with pink hair could be smart. I want to be a high-school teacher, but I'm afraid that, based on my appearance, they won't hire me. Don't be afraid of us. Don't stereotype us."

ON FEAR

Thomas James, 17 Senior, Northside High School, Ft. Smith, Ark. Plays trombone in the band; does volunteer work.

"I used to not worry about safety at my school. But after the Jonesboro shootings, I started to think about it more. Jonesboro is just across the state from here. I just started to think, if it can happen there, it can happen here. This year we had two bomb threats. It was a hoax this time, but it makes me think that next time it may not be."

ON SCHOOL AND PARENTS

Diane Leary, 17 Senior, Memorial High School, West New York, N.J. Student council, tennis team.

"The school is divided into different groups of kids: the breakdancers, the people who listen to heavy metal, the pretty girls, the ravers and the hip-hop people. But there's no pressure to be in one group or another. If a person is a break-dancer, they can still chill with the ravers. I'm a hip-hopper. We wear baggy jeans and sweatshirts. But if I'm really good friends with a person in the heavy-metal group; I can go chill with them and it's just like, whatever. I don't really worry about violence. And I don't really worry about peer pressure. Like if you're at a party and you don't drink, that's cool.

"Most kids' parents don't know what they are doing. I talk to my mom about everything. She shows up for every parents' night; sometimes she's the only one there. It makes me feel good that I have a mom who cares about what is going on with me."

The Good, the Bad and the Ugly

Parents once just had to contend with Elvis's pelvis thrusting on the family TV. Now teens are off in their own garden of electronic delights. Here's what they're doing:

Shake: *Teen style has long strived to offend adults. Yesterday's bobby-soxer is today's pierced Goth.*

Rattle: *Violent entertainments like the videogame Half-Life and the rapper DMX both reflect and create a harsher cultural climate for adolescents.*

Roll: *Teen luv still conquers all. Amid the sour stuff, candy like 'Dawson's Creek' and Britney Spears tally sweet ratings and sales figures.*

there, but on top are piled all these other issues, which are very difficult for parents or children to decipher." New technologies and the entertainment industry, combined with changes in family structure, have more deeply isolated grown-ups from teenagers. The results are what Hill Walker, codirector of the Institute on Violence and Destructive Behavior in Oregon, calls "almost a virtual reality without adults."

With as many as 11 million teenagers now online, more and more of adolescent life is taking place in a landscape that is inaccessible to many parents. "That is apparent in the geography of households, " says Marlene Mayhew, a clinical psychologist who runs an online mental-health newsletter. With the computer often in the teen's bedroom, Mayhew says, the power structure in the family is turned upside down. "Kids are unsupervised, looking at whatever they please." A parent who might eventually notice a stockpile of Guns & Ammo or pornographic magazines has fewer clues to a child's online activities. "We're missing the opportunity for an adult reality check, adult perspective on the stimulation [teens] are getting exposed to. Kids have less access to parents, more access to potentially damaging information."

The pop-culture industry, marketing tribal styles through MTV and the Internet, makes it harder than ever for adults to read their kids, even parents raised on rock and roll. Parents in the '50s could " read" the ripe sexuality of Elvis—they just might not have approved. But what to make of the much more densely encrypted messages and camp nihilism of Eminem or Marilyn Manson, who dare outsiders to take offense? How to distinguish a kid drawn to gangsta rapper DMX for the rhymes from one drawn to the crimes? Making the process harder, teens have long been adept at lying, dissembling and otherwise conniving to hide their secret lives. Robyn Sykes, a senior at Jordan High School in Long Beach, Calif., reports that the skills are still sharp. "Some girls," she says, "leave the house wearing one thing,

and then change into tight, short skirts when they're here."

Mike L., 13, from suburban New York, is one of the unsupervised millions online. A couple years ago his father spied on him through a window, catching him in a chat room where people swapped pirated software. But now Mike has his own laptop and can do what he wants. Like many kids, he mostly sends e-mail and hangs around chat rooms, where he encounters both adults and other teens. "You go in, and someone offers what they've got stored in their computer," he says. "And maybe one of the things is 'The Anarchist Cookbook'," a notorious handbook that includes instructions for building bombs. Though he doesn't have it, he says, "one of my friends gets called down to the guidance counselor every day because somebody told a teacher that he knows how to make bombs. He's not the kind of guy who would do it. But he found out how on the Internet." Andrew Tyler, 13, from Haddonfield, N.J., used his Internet freedom another way: two weeks ago, while his mother tended the family garden, Tyler placed bids on $3.2 million worth of merchandise via the online auction house eBay, including the winning bid on a $400,000 bedroom set. "I thought [eBay] was just a site," he told NEWSWEEK. "It turned out to be a lot more than that."

The vast majority of adolescents' online activity ranges from edifying to harmless. Though hard numbers on Internet use are notoriously suspect, Malcolm Parks, an Internet researcher at the University of Washington in Seattle, says that most teens use the computer to send e-mail or instant messages, visit chat rooms or fan Web sites, do homework or download songs. For the most part, he says, "I worry more about poor quality of information online, and students' lack of skills for evaluating information, than I worry about frequently discussed evils like pornography."

At Neutral Ground in Manhattan on a recent afternoon, other skills are in play. The

drafty, fourth-floor gaming room, undetectable from the street, is a teen oasis, dotted with interconnected computers. By a quarter to four, it is packed with adolescent boys. Robert, one of eight boys glued to the screens, suddenly curses and bangs on the table. "Die, you stupid whore," he shouts. Then, "I'm gonna go kill Sebastian now." Sebastian, three terminals down, calls back: "You take this game way too seriously."

They are playing Half-Life, known in videogame parlance as a multiplayer "first-person shooter" game, or FPS. As Robert pushes a key, a red shell fires from an on-screen shotgun; arms fly off, blood spatters on the walls. "If my parents came down here now," says Mike, pausing from the carnage, "they'd probably drag me out." The best-known FPS is Doom, the game reportedly favored by the Littleton shooters, but to the kids at Neutral Ground, Doom is already passe. A new game, Kingpin, promises even hairier carnal gratifications. "Includes multiplayer gang bang death match for up to 16 thugs!" coos the ad copy. "Target specific body parts and actually see the damage done including exit wounds."

The videogame business last year topped $6.3 billion, much of it dedicated for play on the home computer. The more violent games are marked for sales to mature buyers only, but like R-rated movies, they are easily accessible to kids. "The people usually tell you you're not old enough," says Eddie, 14, a regular at Neutral Ground, "but they don't stop you from buying it." Eddie says most FPS games "make me dizzy," but he enjoys one called Diablo, which is not just another shoot-'em-up orgy. "It's more like slice 'em up." His parents don't like the games but rarely engage him on it. His mother, he says, "thinks it's too violent, so she doesn't watch."

Most teenagers seem to process the mayhem as mindless pyrotechnics. But not all kids react the same way, warns Dan Anderson, a University of Massachusetts psychologist who has studied the effects of TV on

---

47% of Americans say very few parents really know what their teens are up to; **60%** say the government should restrict access to some Internet material.

children. "It's always been the case that the kids who have been vulnerable to violent messages on television have been a small minority. But a small minority can cause serious havoc. If you're predisposed to violence and aggression, you can find like-minded people who will validate your experience. You can become part of an isolated group that family and friends don't know about, and that group can exchange information on getting or making weapons." Brad Bushman, an Iowa State University psychologist, argues that violent computer games are more harmful than movies, "because the person becomes the aggressor. They're the one that does the killing."

In Santa Monica last week Collin Williams and his friends, a multiracial group of eighth graders, describe a numbing effect. Sure, they shrugged, a tragedy like the one in Littleton could happen in their school.

Though they don't spend much time on computers, says Williams, 14, "we see so much violence on TV and in the movies that it just seems like it's everywhere. We don't go to school thinking we're going to be killed. But maybe it's because we're so used to it."

The challenges for parents may be new, but they are not insurmountable. Many psychologists recommend changing the way the computer is used. Put it in a family room, where adults and teens have more opportunities to discuss what's coming into the house. Every Web browser records what sites users visit; parents can monitor their kids' activities with just elementary computer savvy. Filters, such as Net Nanny, restrict which sites users can visit, but smart kids can get around them often by using a friend's computer. Idit Harel, founder of the kid-friendly site MaMaMedia, highly recommends playing videogames along with your

kids. Even in violent games, she says, "there is learning, visualization; there is analysis of hints." Likewise, parents can either set limits on their kids' pop-cultural diets or just talk to the teens about what they're consuming. Say: "I don't understand this kid Eminem. What's he about?"

Even with such interaction, the secret lives of teenagers are likely to remain secret. They are as unbounded as the Internet and as plebeian as the Backstreet Boys, a daunting world for any parent to enter. But this remains the job of parenting. Today's teens command an electronic landscape more stimulating, vibrant and mysterious than any before. They are the masters of the new domain. But they still need adult guidance on their travels.

With Devin Gordon, Anne Underwood, Tara Weingarten and Ana Figueroa.

Teen tobacco wars

An Antismoking ad blitz vs. new cigarette marketing ploys

By Marianne Lavelle

The girls in the living room lean toward the speakerphone with eyes raised, watching one another's reactions–looking like any prank phone callers at a weekend party. "What is the lucky part about Lucky Strike cigarettes?" asks one teen, maintaining her composure while the others giggle. "Is it that I *might* live?" she continues, prompting the executive at Brown & Williamson Tobacco Corp. to hang up. Laughter drowns out the dead-line buzz.

This TV commercial was part of a Florida campaign that drove teen smoking rates in the state down nearly 20 percent from 1998 to 1999, the greatest annual drop ever recorded by a state. Now health advocates and antismoking activists are trying to repeat that success nationwide. Scheduled to begin as early as next week is the first nationwide anti smoking media campaign since the 1960s. The new ads will be sponsored by the American Legacy Foundation, an independent organization created with $1.5 billion of the $246 billion that's being paid over 25 years by Big Tobacco to settle health claims by the states.

What works? But the Legacy campaign also is touching off a new debate over teens and smoking, about what kind of prevention programs work, and whether the tobacco industry—and even many states—are really serious about stopping young smokers before they start. Last week, Legacy and the Centers for Disease Control and Prevention released figures showing 13 percent of 11-to-13-year-olds have used some form of tobacco, the first time that age group has been thoroughly surveyed. More than a third of older teens use tobacco.

Yet despite the gargantuan size of the tobacco settlement, states have committed only a tiny fraction to efforts to curb

Shocking ads ring true

- **California's "Voicebox" ad "shocked and mesmerized" teen focus groups.**
- **Debi recalls tobacco industry claims that cigarettes aren't addictive. After taking a drag from her laryngectomy hole, she remarks, "How can they say that?"**
- **Teens believed Debi, who said she began smoking when she was young.**
- *"We should not be denying the nation's youth something that's been working in every state where it has been applied."*

youth smoking. The cigarette makers have launched their own campaigns against youth smoking—pouring millions of dollars into school and community programs and TV ads. Antitobacco activists argue that teens' decisions are far more likely to be swayed by the new wave of cigarette advertising: promotional events at bars, rock and blues concert sponsorships, and sleek magazine ads bombarding the 18-to-25-year-old market.

Emblematic of bold marketing to young but legal smokers: RJ Reynolds Tobacco Co. late last year debuted vanilla, citrus, and spice Camel cigarettes, flavors the industry long has believed would appeal to early smokers. RJ Reynolds insists its target is adults, but Matthew Myers, director of the Campaign for Tobacco-Free Kids, says the idea "appeals uniquely to children." It is just one indication, he says, that "the only thing that's changed is the rhetoric.

The tobacco companies haven't changed their marketing behavior at all."

Early users. Myers and other tobacco foes maintain that the youth market always will be critical to Big Tobacco, because 80 percent of the nation's 47 million adult smokers began lighting up before the age of 18. Stop the 3,000 teens who become regular smokers each day, they say, and the pool of tobacco users evaporates. Everyone says curbing youth smoking is essential, but nobody seems to agree on how to do it. Case in point: The big television networks last week held up the initial versions of the Legacy Foundation ads. Network sources told *Ad Week* that they found the ads offensive in their graphic depiction of smoking's ill effects. "All we can say right now is that they are under review," CBS Vice President Dana McClintock told *U.S. News.* It was a frustrating development for Legacy, since its research shows that media-saturated teens need vivid illustrations of tobacco's consequences. "We believe they are very effective ads that reach teens in a new and innovative way," says Legacy's Carlea Bauman.

But whatever the final form of the campaign, at $150 million to $255 million a year, it's tiny compared with the $8.8 billion first installment of settlement dollars flowing to the states. So far politicians have committed less than 2 percent of that cash to antismoking efforts. The CDC has recommended that states spend one third of the money on tobacco control programs.

"A lot of [those programs] impress me as being naive and ineffective," says West Virginia's Attorney General Darrell McGraw. Says Texas state Sen. Bill Ratliff, "We don't know for sure that kids can be convinced." But CDC's Terry Pechacek says that the success of

 From *U.S. News & World Report*, February 7, 2000, pp. 14-16. © 2000 by U.S. News & World Report. Reprinted by permission.

pilot youth prevention programs in states like Florida, Massachusetts, and California cannot be ignored. Largely because of a drop-off in these states, the national smoking rate for high school seniors has fallen slightly in the past two years after rising 30 percent in the mid-1990s, according to a University of Michigan study (chart)."We should not be denying the nation's youth something that's working in every state where it has been applied," Pechacek says.

The CDC says states must do more than hire glitzy advertising agencies. Pechacek says TV spots are merely "air cover," helpful in building public support for what happens on the ground. Since 1992, when Massachusetts voters passed the 25-cent-a-pack tax that funds its tobacco control program, the number of cities and towns with antismoking ordinances quadrupled to 144, with 3.8 million residents. "Reducing public smoking is a golden nugget in its impact on youth," says Lori Fersina, advocate for the American Cancer Society of Massachusetts. "You are changing the world you raise kids in, not just telling them it's bad for them." In November, Massachusetts announced a 15 percent decline in youth smoking in the past two years. That same month, neighboring Rhode Island reported a 60 percent *increase* since 1993. "Massachusetts has taken a far more aggressive approach and is going to have a healthier population," laments Rhode Island's Lt. Gov. Charles Fogarty. Fogarty wants to fund a substantial antismoking drive, but so far, except for a $1 million grant, the legislature has backed Gov. Lincoln Almond's competing plan to pour the first $57 million into the state's general budget. In contrast, Massachusetts is using $20 million of its first settlement installment to expand its antitobacco program to a $54 million effort.

Tobacco companies, to the surprise of some, have advocated use of the settlement money for prevention. But there's a caveat: The industry wants campaigns directed at children, not adults. Health advocates complain that simply telling kids they're too young to smoke, without explaining why adults shouldn't

Tobacco ads stress choice

- Tobacco industry youth prevention ads urge teens to choose not to smoke.
- Lorillard's "Stereo Kid" ad illustrates how cigarettes burn away teens' money.
- Kids say they don't smoke to be cool in Philip Morris's "Think. Don't Smoke" ads.
- Critics say tobacco's ads don't offer teens compelling reasons not to smoke.
- *We might be able to get to the real issues, like self-esteem, risk-taking, and parental involvement."*

USN&WR

Teens keep puffing

In 1999, nearly 35 percent of 12th graders—1 million total—had smoked a cigarette in the past 30 days.

Source: University of Michigan—Monitoring the Future study

smoke either, merely enhances tobacco's appeal. Critics have assailed Philip Morris's partnership with 4-H clubs and Brown & Williamson's program with the Jaycees. Tobacco industry officials say their approach is a legitimate effort to address societal concerns about under-age smoking while continuing to do business with adults who understand the risks. "If [our adversaries] were really concentrating on youth smoking, and not trying to put tobacco companies out of business, we might be able to get at

the real issues, like self-esteem, risk-taking, and parental involvement," says Corky Newton, Brown & Williamson's vice president for youth responsibility programs.

A moving target? Industry officials insist they can afford to be sincere about youth prevention, even if it means fewer adult smokers. "We know how to compete in a declining market," says Carolyn Levy, Philip Morris Co.'s senior vice president for youth smoking prevention. Unfortunately, in the view of tobacco critics, that means an increased focus on the legal market of 18-to-25-year-olds. "The tobacco companies have been repositioning themselves since the settlement, and all for the worse," says Greg Connolly, Massachusetts's tobacco control program director. "The advertising that works best for the 15-year-old is targeting a 25-year-old." The companies have been hosting Kool Nites, Camel Club events, and Marlboro Party Nights in bars across the country, and ads in magazines such as *Rolling Stone* and *Mademoiselle* reinforce the image of cigarettes as an essential element of night life.

But RJ Reynolds spokeswoman Jan Smith notes that the settlement forced tobacco companies to yank down billboards, give up cartoon spokesmen, and withdraw from "youth-oriented" sports sponsorships. "It strikes me as a huge irony" that advocacy groups have criticized the bar nights, she says. "One of the very reasons that we view bars as a good place to be is it's an age-restricted environment." In fact, RJ Reynolds began selling its high-priced flavored cigarettes—Crema, Twist, and Samsun—strictly in bars and by direct mail to smokers over 21. Smith says the new "styles" are directed at adults. But Myers of Tobacco-Free Kids says the new CDC study on youth smoking shows that flavored cigarettes imported from India, "bidis," have become as popular among high school students as chewing tobacco (used by 5 percent to 6 percent of teens). Says Myers: "The only way to interpret [RJ Reynolds's move] is as yet another tobacco industry appeal to the young."

Unit Selections

Key Points to Consider

❖ What kinds of factors should parents consider when deciding whether their children should be allowed to date?

❖ How may acknowledgement of one's sexuality differ for homosexual as compared to heterosexual adolescents? What kinds of problems may homosexual adolescents face that may not even occur to heterosexuals?

❖ How may adults prepare adolescents for the emotional aspects of intimate relationships? What combination of social and educational factors seems to encourage sexual abstinence in adolescents? What are possible emotional consequences of premature sexual involvement?

❖ How common is sexual harassment in middle school? How do children respond to harassment?

❖ How has the sexual behavior of American female adolescents changed since the 1980s?

❖ In what ways has the research on sexual behavior and sex education programs improved in the last two decades? What factors predict high-risk sexual activity? What factors are related to the effectiveness of sex education and intervention strategies?

❖ How can schools and society effectively increase the safer sex behaviors of adolescents?

 **Links** www.dushkin.com/online/

These sites are annotated on pages 4 and 5.

Based on the music they listen to, the television shows they watch, or the movies they attend, it is clear that sex is frequently on the minds of adolescents. In fact, one statistic indicates that teenage boys think of sex on the average of once every 5 minutes! Unfortunately for adolescents today, the sexual issues that concern them run the gamut from "When should I start dating?" to "Will I get AIDS?" How has society, whether in the form of the government, the schools, or the family, dealt with these concerns? The answer seems to be, not very consistently and, frequently, not very well.

The articles in this unit have been organized into two subsections. The first, Sexual Attitudes and Behavior, addresses the concerns adolescents have about a variety of areas related to sexuality, and how adolescents behave in these areas. Although prepubescent children are interested in sex and may engage in some sexual exploration of their own or other people's bodies, interest in dating and in interacting in a sexual manner with others seems to increase rapidly with the onset of puberty. The vast majority of adolescents indicate that they have a boyfriend or girlfriend. By age 13 about 20 percent of boys indicate that they have touched a girl's breasts; a similar proportion of girls concur. By the end of the teen years, the majority of adolescents have engaged in coitus. Ten percent of teenagers in the United States become pregnant each year—twice the rate of other industrialized nations. Twenty-five percent of new cases of HIV are in adolescents under age 18.

Adolescents are clearly engaging in sexual behaviors. This is not only normal, but it is an important part of development. Understanding oneself as a sexual being is a significant component of identity formation. It seems, therefore, that society would want to understand how adolescents view their sexuality. The reality is that research on what adolescents want more information about, and how much adolescents already know, is surprisingly limited. Part of the reason for this lack of information is the taboos our society has concerning talking about sex. For example, when was the last time a study asking adolescents how often they masturbated was described in a magazine? Probably not recently. This is a sensitive topic, and parents are reluctant to allow their adolescents to talk about it even though the majority of people have masturbated. How much less is known, then, about the concerns of adolescents who are homosexual—a far more controversial area? How much is really known regarding how girls feel about sexual harassment and what they are willing to do about it?

Research on sexuality is limited not only by taboos but also by society's clinging to myths involving romantic relationships. Ours is a society that worries about adolescent sexuality, yet it does not train adolescents in social skills for dating or flirting. Adolescents are presented with the myth that they should find love with no problems, yet in reality romance and relationships must be worked on. Adolescents are expected to date, but they are not taught how to act on a date, how to communicate with a partner, or how to avoid or remove themselves from uncomfortable situations while on a date. When adults discuss sex with adolescents they generally focus on the dangers surrounding sexual behavior. They do little to prepare adolescents for the emotional aspects of dating relationships. Knowledge about many significant areas of adolescent sexuality is severely limited. The articles selected for this first section demonstrate the wide variety of issues faced by adolescents, including dating, homosexuality, emotional involvement, sexual harassment, and some of the ways in which adolescents respond to these.

The second subsection, Sex Education, includes articles discussing how parents, teachers, and society inform adolescents about sex and how their approaches to sex education and pregnancy prevention may be improved. Research on where adolescents learn about sex has been performed for about 60 years. The results of this research are quite consistent—adolescents' primary sources of information on sex are other adolescents. Schools and mothers also seem to contribute some information. Adolescents are most likely to learn about sexually transmitted diseases, including HIV, from teachers. Many, though by no means all, girls learn about menstruation and conception from their mothers. Fathers are less frequently cited by adolescents as a source of information on sex.

Why aren't parents and schools assuming more responsibility for educating children about sex? Researchers have speculated that parents do not know what to discuss with their children or how to present information effectively. Parents may also be inhibited by their own embarrassment with the topic. This does not mean parents wish their children to be completely ignorant about sex. Some surveys indicate that 85 percent of American families want schools to include sex education. Part of the reason for this is because parents wish their children to be knowledgeable about transmission of HIV. However, when sex education is left up to the schools, other problems are incurred. For example, what topics should be covered in school? In how much detail should various topics be covered? It may be acceptable to teach adolescents about conception or pregnancy, but if the adolescents have a child, should the school teach child care? How much information on transmission of HIV and prevention of transmission should be included? The first article in this subsection discusses the improvement in research on teenagers' sexual behavior, including the effectiveness of sex education and pregnancy prevention programs. In the second article the effect that school-based programs can have on teen parenting is presented. The final article focuses on AIDS.

Teenage Sexuality

Too Young To Date?

Definitely—and you can help your preteen resist peer pressure.

Debra Morgenstern Katz

Ben began dating last year, when he was 11. According to his mother, Annie, it started when he and his friends suddenly announced that they were "going out" with girls. Ben's first relationship, Annie recalls, lasted all of one day. The second one was a couple of months long, and the third hung on until the end of the school year. These relationships consisted primarily of phone conversations; dating, Annie says, was strictly in name only.

However, now that he's 12, Ben goes on group outings with his current girlfriend and other couples. Although Annie says she doesn't allow the two of them to spend time together alone, she adds, "I constantly think this is happening too soon, but I'm not sure how to put the brakes on."

Putting the brakes on preteen dating is something virtually every expert endorses. "For kids this age, dating is developmentally inappropriate," says Karen Zager, Ph.D., a psychologist in private practice in New York City who specializes in adolescents. "Ten-, 11-, and 12-year-olds are, by and large, not ready. It's like trying to drive an 18-wheel truck before you even know how to drive a car. There's too much information—and too many complicated feelings—for kids that age to integrate."

Furthermore, the same-sex friendships that dominate preteens' lives allow them to develop skills such as sharing emotions and learning give-and-take—skills that come into play in later romantic relationships—without social or sexual pressure. According to David Elkind, Ph.D., professor of child study at Tufts University, in Medford,

Massachusetts, and the author of The Hurried Child (Addison-Wesley), "If children this age spend too much time in opposite-sex relationships, they don't get to hone these skills."

There's no denying that preteens feel pushed to begin their romantic lives at an ever earlier age. It used to be that 13-year-olds were the ones who were forced to straddle the boundary between childhood and adolescence. Zager says, "Now it's an issue with clients I'm seeing who are 10, 11, and 12."

Why? "Kids this age are exposed to much more 'mature' material on TV and in the movies than kids were a generation ago," explains Zager. Another reason is the classic one, peer influence. However, preteens often find that there's another subtle source of pressure: parents themselves. In many neighborhoods all over the country, parents organize dances for elementary-school-age children—even when the children view these events with nervousness and discomfort. In my own neighborhood, several mothers have described their preteens' dating rituals as "cute."

Most parents, thankfully, don't look at preteen romance that way. They are genuinely perplexed about how they should handle this early rush into the dating game. As Annie says, "What do you say when all your son's friends are going out with girls? 'No, you can't go'?" If you're concerned, try these suggestions.

Listen to your child—and yourself. Children this age are still more inclined to listen to their parents' advice than to their friends'. When your child comes to you with questions about her

personal life, it means that she wants and values your honest answer. You'll help a lot if you place a higher priority on hearing your child out than on judging her.

If your daughter came home from sleep-away camp and told you that she didn't know what to do when a boy she met there gave her a French kiss, some parents' instinct would be to say, "French kissing? There's no way you're going to see that boy again!" However, that response is practically guaranteed to close the lines of communication, notes Leah Blumberg Lapidus, Ph.D., professor of psychology at Columbia University and clinical psychologist in private practice. "It shuts down trust. In effect, the parent is saying that the child can't be in charge of her own social life," she explains.

A better response, Lapidus says, is something like, "It sounds like this made you kind of nervous." If your child indicates that it did, you might suggest that the next time she's in a romantic situation that makes her uncomfortable, she might say, "I don't want to do this. Let's go get something to eat." By talking to your daughter in this way, you let her know that she can trust her own feelings, that she doesn't have to go along with peers if their activities make her uncomfortable—and that you are an ally in whom she can confide freely.

Define "dating" clearly. If your preteen tells you he wants to date, your response should depend on whether or not you feel comfortable with what that means in his social group. For some, it is a serious commitment—spending Friday nights, weekend afternoons, and some days after school together. Also part of the definition is the way in which "dating" children spend their time. Do they go to movies, indoor arcades, or ice cream parlors with other couples? Are they alone at each other's houses?

Sometimes their outings resemble traditional dates, with boys paying for girls, and a goodnight kiss when they part. However, in other instances, dating is far more innocent and informal. Kids who call each other boyfriend and girlfriend may not spend much time together, even on the phone.

If you child wants to take dating further than you'd like, don't be afraid to set limits in a firm but loving way. According to Elkind, if your son says he wants to be alone with his girlfriend, "You can say, 'You're not ready for this yet. Some day you will be, but not yet. You're not supposed to drive. You're not supposed to drink alcohol. There are a lot of things you can't do until you're older.' "

If he makes the request with his girlfriend present, calmly say you'd like to speak with him alone for a minute; preteens can easily feel humiliated by parents when peers are around.

Don't hesitate to offer compromises and alternatives. If you have no problem with your child occasionally having phone conversations with a boyfriend, but object to their going to a movie together, suggest another activity that's acceptable. Preteens often enjoy supervised outings such as trips to sports events or amusement parks, where they can be active. Just make sure the activity is suited to their age; even something as supposedly corny as taking a group of preteens bowling is more appropriate than getting them into an R-rated movie—and more fun for the kids, who generally feel less pressure to act grownup when they're among adults than they do in a group of their peers.

If your child is among a mixed-gender group going to a movie, it's not a bad idea to have a parent or two in the theater during the movie; they can sit away from the kids, who will feel independent, but still have the reassuring presence of a grown-up nearly.

Debra Morgenstern Katz is a freelance writer based in North Woodmere, New York

A CLACK OF TINY SPARKS

Remembrances of a gay boyhood

Bernard Cooper

Bernard Cooper is the author of Maps to Anywhere, *a collection of essays published by the University of Georgia Press. His essay "Nick's Barber Shop" appeared in the June 1990 issue of* Harper's Magazine. *He lives in Los Angeles.*

Theresa Sanchez sat behind me in ninth-grade algebra. When Mr. Hubbley faced the blackboard, I'd turn around to see what she was reading; each week a new book was wedged inside her copy of *Today's Equations*. The deception worked; from Mr. Hubbley's point of view, Theresa was engrossed in the value of *X*, but I knew otherwise. One week she perused *The Wisdom of the Orient*, and I could tell from Theresa's contemplative expression that the book contained exotic thoughts, guidelines handed down from high. Another week it was a paperback novel whose title, *Let Me Live My Life,* appeared in bold print atop every page, and whose cover, a gauzy photograph of a woman biting a strand of pearls, head thrown back in an attitude of ecstasy, confirmed my suspicion that Theresa Sanchez was mature beyond her years. She was the tallest girl in school. Her bouffant hairdo, streaked with blond, was higher than the flaccid bouffants of other

girls. Her smooth skin, plucked eyebrows, and painted fingernails suggested hours of pampering, a worldly and sensual vanity that placed her within the domain of adults. Smiling dimly, steeped in day-dreams, Theresa moved through the crowded halls with a languid, self-satisfied indifference to those around her. "You are merely children," her posture seemed to say. "I can't be bothered." The week Theresa hid *101 Ways to Cook Hamburger* behind her algebra book, I could stand it no longer and, after the bell rang, ventured a question.

"Because I'm having a dinner party," said Theresa. "Just a couple of intimate friends."

No fourteen-year-old I knew had ever given a dinner party, let alone used the word "intimate" in conversation. "Don't you have a mother?" I asked.

Theresa sighed a weary sigh, suffered my strange inquiry. "Don't be so naive," she said. "Everyone has a mother." She waved her hand to indicate the brick school building outside the window. "A higher education should have taught you that." Theresa draped an angora sweater over her shoulders, scooped her books from the graffiti-covered desk, and just as she was about to walk away, she turned and asked me, "Are you a fag?"

There wasn't the slightest hint of rancor or condescension in her voice. The tone was direct, casual. Still I was stunned, giving a sidelong glance to make sure no one had heard. "No," I said. Blurted really, with too much defensiveness, too much transparent fear in my response. Octaves lower than usual, I tried a "Why?"

Theresa shrugged. "Oh, I don't know. I have lots of friends who are fags. You remind me of them." Seeing me bristle, Theresa added, "It was just a guess." I watched her erect, angora back as she sauntered out the classroom door.

She had made an incisive and timely guess. Only days before, I'd invited Grady Rogers to my house after school to go swimming. The instant Grady shot from the pool, shaking water from his orange hair, freckled shoulders shining, my attraction to members of my own sex became a matter I could no longer suppress or rationalize. Sturdy and boisterous and gap-toothed, Grady was an inveterate backslapper, a formidable arm wrestler, a wizard at basketball. Grady was a boy at home in his body.

My body was a marvel I hadn't gotten used to; my arms and legs would sometimes act of their own accord, knocking over a glass at dinner or flinching at an oncoming pitch. I was never singled out as a sissy, but I could have been just as easily as Bobby Keagan, a gentle, intelligent, and introverted boy reviled by my classmates. And although I had always been aware of a tacit rapport with Bobby, a suspicion that I might find with him a rich friendship, I stayed away. Instead, I emulated Grady in the belief that being seen with him, being like him, would somehow vanquish my self-doubt, would make me normal by association.

Apart from his athletic prowess, Grady had been gifted with all the trappings of what I imagined to be a charmed life: a fastidious, aproned mother who radiated calm, maternal concern; a ruddy, stoic father with a knack for home repairs. Even the Rogerses' small suburban house in Hollywood, with its spindly Colonial furniture and chintz curtains, was a testament to normalcy.

Grady and his family bore little resemblance to my clan of Eastern European Jews, a dark and vociferous people who ate with abandon—matzo and halvah and gefilte fish; foods the goyim couldn't pronounce; who cajoled one another during endless games of canasta, making the simplest remark about the weather into a lengthy philosophical discourse on the sun and the seasons and the passage of time. My mother was a chain-smoker, a dervish in a frowsy housedress. She showed her love in the most peculiar and obsessive ways, like spending hours extracting every seed from a watermelon before she served it in perfectly bite-sized, geometric pieces. Preoccupied and perpetually frantic, my mother succumbed to bouts of absent-mindedness so profound she'd forget what she was saying mid-sentence, smile and blush and walk away. A divorce attorney, my father wore roomy, iridescent suits, and the intricacies, the deceits inherent in his profession, had the effect of making him forever tense and vigilant. He was "all wound up," as my mother put it. But when he relaxed, his laughter was explosive, his disposition prankish: "Walk this way," a waitress would say, leading us to our table, and my father would mimic the way she walked, arms akimbo, hips liquid, while my mother and I were wracked with laughter. Buoyant or brooding, my parents' moods were unpredictable, and in a household fraught with extravagant emotion it was odd and awful to keep my longing secret.

One day I made the mistake of asking my mother what a "fag" was. I knew exactly what Theresa had meant but hoped against hope it was not what I thought; maybe "fag" was some French word, a harmless term like "naive." My mother turned from the stove, flew at me, and grabbed me by the shoulders. "Did someone call you that?" she cried.

"Not me," I said. "Bobby Keagan."

"Oh," she said, loosening her grip. She was visibly relieved. And didn't answer. The answer was unthinkable.

For weeks after, I shook with the reverberations from that afternoon in the kitchen with my mother, pained by the memory of her shocked expression and, most of all, her silence. My longing was wrong in the eyes of my mother, whose hazel eyes were the eyes of the world, and if that longing continued unchecked, the unwieldy shape of my fate would be cast, and I'd be subjected to a lifetime of scorn.

During the remainder of the semester, I became the scientist of my own desire, plotting ways to change my yearning for boys into a yearning for girls. I had enough evidence to believe that any habit, regardless of how compulsive, how deeply ingrained, could be broken once and for all: The plastic cigarette my mother purchased at the Thrifty pharmacy—one end was red to approximate an ember, the other tan like a filtered tip—was designed to wean her from the real thing. To change a behavior required self-analysis, cold resolve, and the substitution of one thing for another: plastic, say, for tobacco. Could I also find a substitute for Grady? What I needed to do, I figured, was kiss a girl and learn to like it.

This conclusion was affirmed one Sunday morning when my father, seeing me wrinkle my nose at the pink slabs of lox he layered on a bagel, tried to convince me of its salty appeal. "You should try some," he said. "You don't know what you're missing."

"It's loaded with protein," added my mother, slapping a platter of sliced onions onto the dinette table. She hovered above us, cinching her housedress, eyes wet from onion fumes, the mock cigarette dangling from her lips.

My father sat there chomping with gusto, emitting a couple of hearty grunts to dramatize his satisfaction. And still I was not convinced. After a loud and labored swallow, he told me I may not be fond of lox today, but sooner or later I'd learn to like it. One's tastes, he assured me, are destined to change.

"Live," shouted my mother over the rumble of the Mixmaster. "Expand your horizons. Try new things." And the room grew fragrant with the batter of a spice cake.

The opportunity to put their advice into practice, and try out my plan to adapt to girls, came the following week when Debbie Coburn, a member of Mr. Hubbley's algebra class, invited me to a party. She cornered me in the hall, furtive as a spy, telling me her parents would be gone for the evening and slipping into my palm a wrinkled sheet of notebook paper. On it were her address and telephone number, the lavender ink in a tidy cursive. "Wear cologne," she advised, wary eyes darting back and forth. "It's a make-out party. Anything can happen."

The Santa Ana wind blew relentlessly the night of Debbie's party, careening down the slopes of the Hollywood hills, shaking the road signs and stoplights in its path. As I walked down Beachwood Avenue, trees thrashed, surrendered their leaves, and carob pods bombarded the pavement. The sky was a deep but luminous blue, the air hot, abrasive, electric. I had to squint in order to check the number of the Coburns' apartment, a three-story building with glitter embedded in its stucco walls. Above the honeycombed balconies was a sign that read BEACHWOOD TERRACE in lavender script resembling Debbie's.

From down the hall, I could hear the plaintive strains of Little Anthony's "I Think I'm Going Out of My Head." Debbie answered the door bedecked in an Empire dress, the bodice blue and orange polka dots, the rest a sheath of black and white stripes. "Op art," proclaimed Debbie. She turned in a circle, then proudly announced that she'd rolled her hair in orange juice cans. She patted the huge unmoving curls and dragged me inside. Reflections from the swimming pool in the courtyard, its surface ruffled by wind, shuddered over the ceiling and walls. A dozen of my classmates were seated on the sofa or huddled together in corners, their whispers full of excited imminence, their bodies barely discernible in the dim light. Drapes flanking the sliding glass doors bowed out with every gust of wind, and it seemed that the room might lurch from its foundations and sail with its cargo of silhouettes into the hot October night.

Grady was the last to arrive. He tossed a six-pack of beer into Debbie's arms, barreled toward me, and slapped my back. His hair was slicked back with Vitalis, lacquered furrows left by the comb. The wind hadn't shifted a single hair. "Ya ready?" he asked, flashing the gap between his front teeth and leering into the darkened room. "You bet," I lied.

Once the beers had been passed around, Debbie provoked everyone's attention by flicking on the overhead light. "Okay," she called. "Find a partner." This was the blunt command of a hostess determined to have her guests aroused in an orderly fashion. Everyone blinked, shuffled about, and grabbed a member of the opposite sex. Sheila Garabedian landed beside me—entirely at random, though I wanted to believe she was driven by passion—her timid smile giving way to plain fear as the light went out. Nothing for a moment but the heave of the wind and the distant banter of dogs. I caught a whiff of Sheila's perfume, tangy and sweet as Hawaiian Punch.

I probed her face with my own, grazing the small scallop of an ear, a velvety temple, and though Sheila's trembling made me want to stop, I persisted with my mission until I found her lips, tightly sealed as a private letter. I held my mouth over hers and gathered her shoulders closer, resigned to the possibility that, no matter how long we stood there, Sheila would be too scared to kiss me back. Still, she exhaled through her nose, and I listened to the squeak of every breath as though it were a sigh of inordinate pleasure. Diving within myself, I monitored my heartbeat and respiration, trying to will stimulation into being, and all the while an image intruded, an image of Grady erupting from our pool, rivulets of water sliding down his chest. "Change," shouted Debbie, switching on the light. Sheila thanked me, pulled away, and continued her routine of gracious terror with every boy throughout the evening. It didn't matter whom I held—Margaret Sims, Betty Vernon, Elizabeth Lee—my experiment was a failure; I continued to picture Grady's wet chest, and Debbie would bellow "change" with such fervor, it could have been my own voice, my own incessant reprimand.

Our hostess commandeered the light switch for nearly half an hour. Whenever the light came on, I watched Grady pivot his head toward the newest prospect, his eyebrows arched in expectation, his neck blooming with hickeys, his hair, at last, in disarray. All that shuffling across the carpet charged everyone's arms and lips with static, and eventually, between low moans and soft osculations, I could hear the clack of tiny sparks and see them flare here and there in the dark like meager, short-lived stars.

I saw Theresa, sultry and aloof as ever, read three more books—*North American Reptiles, Bonjour Tristesse,* and *MGM: A Pictorial History*—before she vanished early in December. Rumors of her fate abounded. Debbie Coburn swore that Theresa had been "knocked up" by an older man, a traffic cop, she thought, or a grocer. Nearly quivering with relish, Debbie told me and Grady about the home for unwed mothers in the San Fernando Valley, a compound teeming with pregnant girls who had nothing to do but touch their stomachs and contemplate their mistake. Even Bobby Keagan, who took Theresa's place behind me in algebra, had a theory regarding her disappearance colored by his own wish for escape; he imaged that Theresa, disillusioned with society, booked passage to a tropical island, there to live out the rest of her days without restrictions or ridicule. "No wonder she flunked out of school," I overheard Mr. Hubbley tell a fellow teacher

one afternoon. "Her head was always in a book."

Along with Theresa went my secret, or at least the dread that she might divulge it, and I felt, for a while, exempt from suspicion. I was, however, to run across Theresa one last time. It happened during a period of torrential rain that, according to reports on the six o'clock news, washed houses from the hillsides and flooded the downtown streets. The halls of Joseph Le Conte Junior High were festooned with Christmas decorations: crepe-paper garlands, wreaths studded with plastic berries, and one requisite Star of David twirling above the attendance desk. In Arts and Crafts, our teacher, Gerald (he was the only teacher who allowed us—*required* us—to call him by his first name), handed out blocks of balsa wood and instructed us to carve them into bugs. We would paint eyes and antennae with tempera and hang them on a Christmas tree he'd made the previous night. "Voilà," he crooned, unveiling his creation from a burlap sack. Before us sat a tortured scrub, a wardrobe-worth of wire hangers that were bent like branches and soldered together. Gerald credited his inspiration to a Charles Addams cartoon he'd seen in which Morticia, grimly preparing for the holidays, hangs vampire bats on a withered pine. "All that red and green," said Gerald. "So predictable. So *boring.*"

As I chiseled a beetle and listened to rain pummel the earth, Gerald handed me an envelope and asked me to take it to Mr. Kendrick, the drama teacher. I would have thought nothing of his request if I hadn't seen Theresa on my way down the hall. She was cleaning out her locker, blithely dropping the sum of its contents—pens and textbooks and mimeographs—into a trash can. "Have a nice life," she sang as I passed. I mustered the courage to ask her what had happened. We stood alone in the silent hall, the reflections of wreaths and garlands submerged in brown linoleum.

"I transferred to another school. They don't have grades or bells, and you get to study whatever you want." Theresa was quick to sense my incredulity. "Honest," she said. "The school is progressive." She gazed into a glass cabinet that held the trophies of track meets and intramural spelling bees. "God," she sighed, "this place is so . . . barbaric." I was still trying to decide whether or not to believe her story when she asked me where I was headed. "Dear," she said, her exclamation pooling in the silence, "that's no ordinary note, if you catch my drift." The envelope was blank and white; I looked up at Theresa, baffled. "Don't be so naive," she muttered, tossing an empty bottle of nail polish into the trash can. It struck bottom with a resolute thud. "Well," she said, closing her locker and breathing deeply, "bon

voyage." Theresa swept through the double doors and in seconds her figure was obscured by rain.

As I walked toward Mr. Kendrick's room, I could feel Theresa's insinuation burrow in. I stood for a moment and watched Mr. Kendrick through the pane in the door. He paced intently in front of the class, handsome in his shirt and tie, reading from a thick book. Chalked on the blackboard behind him was THE ODYSSEY BY HOMER. I have no recollection of how Mr. Kendrick reacted to the note, whether he accepted it with pleasure or embarrassment, slipped it into his desk drawer or the pocket of his shirt. I have scavenged that day in retrospect, trying to see Mr. Kendrick's expression, wondering if he acknowledged me in any way as his liaison. All I recall is the sight of his mime through a pane of glass, a lone man mouthing an epic, his gestures ardent in empty air.

Had I delivered a declaration of love? I was haunted by the need to know. In fantasy, a kettle shot steam, the glue released its grip, and I read the letter with impunity. But how would such a letter begin? Did the common endearments apply? This was a message between two men, a message for which I had no precedent, and when I tried to envision the contents, apart from a hasty, impassioned scrawl, my imagination faltered.

Once or twice I witnessed Gerald and Mr. Kendrick walk together into the faculty lounge or say hello at the water fountain, but there was nothing especially clandestine or flirtatious in their manner. Besides, no matter how acute my scrutiny, I wasn't sure, short of a kiss, exactly what to look for—what semaphore of gesture, what encoded word. I suspected there were signs, covert signs that would give them away, just as I'd unwittingly given myself away to Theresa.

In the school library, a *Webster's* unabridged dictionary lay on a wooden podium, and I padded toward it with apprehension; along with clues to the bond between my teachers, I risked discovering information that might incriminate me as well. I had decided to consult the dictionary during lunch period, when most of the students would be on the playground. I clutched my notebook, moving in such a way as to appear both studious and nonchalant, actually believing that, unless I took precautions, someone would see me and guess what I was up to. The closer I came to the podium, the more obvious, I thought, was my endeavor; I felt like the model of The Visible Man in our science class, my heart's undulations, my overwrought nerves legible through transparent skin. A couple of kids riffled through the card catalogue. The librarian, a skinny woman whose perpetual whisper and rubber-soled shoes caused her to drift through the room like a phantom, didn't seem to register my presence. Though I'd looked up dozens of words before, the pages felt strange beneath my fingers. *Homer* was the first word I saw. *Hominid. Homogenize.* I feigned interest and skirted other words before I found the word I was after. Under the heading HO · MO · SEX · U · AL was the terse definition: *adj. Pertaining to, characteristic of, or exhibiting homosexuality. —n. A homosexual person.* I read the definition again and again, hoping the words would yield more than they could. I shut the dictionary, swallowed hard, and, none the wiser hurried away.

As for Gerald and Mr. Kendrick, I never discovered evidence to prove or dispute Theresa's claim. By the following summer, however, I had overheard from my peers a confounding amount about homosexuals: They wore green on Thursday, couldn't whistle, hypnotized boys with a piercing glance. To this lore, Grady added a surefire test to ferret them out.

"A test?" I said.

"You ask a guy to look at his fingernails, and if he looks at them like this"—Grady closed his fingers into a fist and examined his nails with manly detachment—"then he's okay. But if he does this"—he held out his hands at arm's length, splayed his fingers, and coyly cocked his head—"you'd better watch out." Once he'd completed his demonstration, Grady peeled off his shirt and plunged into our pool. I dove in after. It was early June, the sky immense, glassy, placid. My father was cooking spareribs on the barbecue, an artist with a basting brush. His apron bore the caricature of a frazzled French chef. Mother curled on a chaise lounge, plumes of smoke wafting from her nostrils. In a stupor of contentment she took another drag, closed her eyes, and arched her face toward the sun.

Grady dog-paddled through the deep end, spouting a foundation of chlorinated water. Despite shame and confusion, my longing for him hadn't diminished; it continued to thrive without air and light, like a luminous fish in the dregs of the sea. In the name of play, I swam up behind him, encircled his shoulders, astonished by his taut flesh. The two of us flailed, pretended to drown. Beneath the heavy press of water, Grady's orange hair wavered, a flame that couldn't be doused.

I've lived with a man for seven years. Some nights, when I'm half-asleep and the room is suffused with blue light, I reach out to touch the expanse of his back, and it seems as if my fingers sink into his skin, and I feel the pleasure a diver feels the instance he enters a body of water.

I have few regrets. But one is that I hadn't said to Theresa, "Of course I'm a fag." Maybe I'd have met her friends. Or become friends with her. Imagine the meals we might have concocted: hamburger Stroganoff, Swedish meatballs in a sweet translucent sauce, steaming slabs of Salisbury steak.

THE NEGLECTED HEART

The Emotional Dangers of Premature Sexual Involvement

THOMAS LICKONA

You didn't get pregnant. You didn't get AIDS.
So why do you feel so bad?
—Leslee Unruh, abstinence educator

There is no condom for the heart.
—Sign at a sex education conference

IN DISCUSSIONS of teen sex, much is said about the dangers of pregnancy and disease—but far less about the emotional hazards. And that's a problem, because the destructive psychological consequences of temporary sexual relationships are very real. Being aware of them can help a young person make and stick to the decision to avoid premature sexual involvement.

That's not to say we should downplay the physical dangers of uncommitted sex. Pregnancy is a life-changing event. Sexually transmitted disease (STD)—and there are now more than 20 STDs—can rob you of your health and even your life. Condoms don't remove these dangers. Condoms have an annual failure rate of 10 percent to 30 percent in preventing pregnancy because of human error in using them and because they sometimes leak, break, or slip off. Condoms reduce but by no means

eliminate the risk of AIDS. In a 1993 analysis of 11 different medical studies, condoms were found to have a 31 percent average failure rate in preventing the sexual transmission of the AIDS virus.[1] Finally, condoms do little or nothing to protect against the two STDs infecting at least one-third of sexually active teenage girls: human papilloma virus (the leading cause of cervical cancer) and chlamydia (the leading cause of infertility), both of which can be transmitted by skin-to-skin contact in the entire genital area, only a small part of which is covered by the condom.[2]

Why is it so much harder to discuss sex and emotional hurt—to name and talk about the damaging psychological effects that can come from premature sexual involvement? For one thing, most of us have never heard this aspect of sex discussed. Our parents didn't talk to us about it. The media don't talk about it. And the heated debate about condoms in schools typically doesn't say much about the fact that condoms do nothing to make sex *emotionally* safe. When it comes to trying to explain to their children or students how early sexuality can do harm to one's personality and character as well as to one's health, many adults are simply at a loss for words, or reduced to vague generalities such as "you're too young" or "you're not ready" or "you're not mature enough."

This relative silence about the emotional side of sex is ironic, because the emotional dimension of sex is what makes it distinctively human.

What in fact are the emotional or psychological consequences of premature, uncommitted sex? These conse-

---

Thomas Lickona is a developmental psychologist and professor of education at the State University of New York at Cortland. He is the father of two sons, ages 20 and 26, and author of the Christopher Award–winning book Educating for Character *(Bantam Books, 1992).*

From *American Educator,* Summer 1994, pp. 34–39. Adapted from *Sex, Love, and You: Making the Right Decision* by Thomas Lickona, Judith Lickona, and William J. Boudreau. © 1994 by Ave Maria Press, Notre Dame, IN 46556. Reprinted by permission.

quences vary among individuals. Some emotional consequences are short-term but still serious. Some of them last a long time, sometimes even into marriage and parenting. Many of these psychological consequences are hard to imagine until they've been experienced. In all cases, the emotional consequences of sexual experiences are not to be taken lightly. A moment's reflection reminds us that emotional problems can have damaging, even crippling, effects on a person's ability to lead a happy and productive life.

Let's look at 10 negative psychological consequences of premature sexual involvement.

1. Worry About Pregnancy and AIDS

For many sexually active young people, the fear of becoming pregnant or getting AIDS is a major emotional stress.

Russell Henke, health education coordinator in the Montgomery County (Maryland) Public Schools, says, "I see kids going to the nurses in schools, crying a day after their first sexual experience, and waiting to be tested for AIDS. They have done it, and now they are terrified. For some of them, that's enough. They say, 'I don't want to have to go through that experience anymore.' "[3]

A high school girl told a nurse, "I see some of my friends buying home pregnancy tests, and they are so worried and so distracted every month, afraid that they might be pregnant. It's a relief to me to be a virgin."

2. Regret and Self-Recrimination

Girls, especially, need to know in advance the sharp regret that so many young women feel after becoming sexually involved.

Says one high school girl: "I get upset when I see my friends losing their virginity to some guy they've just met. Later, after the guy's dumped them, they come to me and say, 'I wish I hadn't done it.' "[4] A ninth-grade girl who slept with eight boys in junior high says, "I'm young, but I feel old."

Girls are more vulnerable than boys because girls are more likely to think of sex as a way to "show you care." They're more likely to see sex as a sign of commitment in the relationship.

If a girl expects a sexual interlude to be loving, she may very well feel cheated and used when the boy doesn't show a greater romantic interest after the event. As one 15-year-old girl describes her experience: "I didn't expect the guy to marry me, but I never expected him to avoid me in school."

Bob Bartlett, who teaches a freshman sexuality class in a Richfield, Minn., high school, shares the following story of regret on the part of one of his students (we'll call her Sandy):

Sandy, a bright and pretty girl, asked to see Mr. Bartlett during her lunch period. She explained that she had never had a boyfriend, so she was excited when a senior asked her out.

After they dated for several weeks, the boy asked her to have sex with him. She was reluctant; he was persistent. She was afraid of appearing immature and losing him, so she consented.

"Did it work?" Mr. Bartlett asked gently. "Did you keep him?"

Sandy replied: "For another week. We had sex again, and then he dropped me. He said I wasn't good enough. There was no spark.

"I know what you're going to say. I take your class. I know now that he didn't really love me. I feel so stupid, so cheap."[5]

Sandy hoped, naively, that sex would keep the guy. Here is another high school girl, writing to an advice column about a different kind of regret. She wishes she could lose the guy she's involved with, but she feels trapped by their sexual relationship.

I am 16, a junior in high school, and like nearly all the other girls here, I have already lost my virginity. Although most people consider this subject very personal, I feel the need to share this part of my life with girls who are trying to decide whether to have sex for the first time.

Sex does not live up to the glowing reports and hype you see in the movies. It's no big deal. In fact, it's pretty disappointing.

I truly regret that my first time was with a guy that I didn't care that much about. I am still going out with him, which is getting to be a problem. I'd like to end this relationship and date others, but after being so intimate, it's awfully tough.

Since that first night, he expects sex on every date, like we are married or something. When I don't feel like it, we end up in an argument. It's like I owe it to him. I don't think this guy is in love with me, at least he's never said so. I know deep down that I am not in love with him either, and this makes me feel sort of cheap.

I realize now that this is a very big step in a girl's life. After you've done it, things are never the same. It changes everything.

My advice is, don't be in such a rush. It's a headache and a worry. (Could I be pregnant?) Sex is not for entertainment. It should be a commitment. Be smart and save yourself for someone you wouldn't mind spending the rest of your life with.

—Sorry I Didn't And Wish I Could Take It Back.[6]

Regret over uncommitted sexual relationships can last for years. I recently received a letter from a 33-year-old woman, now a psychiatrist, who is very much concerned about the sexual pressures and temptations facing young people today. She wanted to share the lessons she had learned about sex the hard way. After high school, she says, she spent a year abroad as an exchange student:

I was a virgin when I left, but I felt I was protected. I had gotten an IUD so I could make my own decisions if and when I wanted. I had steeled myself against commitment. I was never going to marry or have children; I

> *Sometimes guilt about their sexual past ends up crippling people when they become parents by keeping them from advising their own children not to become sexually involved.*

was going to have a career. During that year abroad, from 17½ to 18½, I was very promiscuous.

But the fact is, it cost me to be separated from myself. The longest-standing and deepest wound I gave myself was heartfelt. That sick, used feeling of having given a precious part of myself—my soul—to so many and for nothing, still aches. I never imagined I'd pay so dearly and for so long.

This woman is happily married now, she says, and has a good sexual relationship with her husband. But she still carries the emotional scar of those early sexual experiences. She wants young people to know that "sex without commitment is very risky for the heart."

3. Guilt

Guilt is a special form of regret—a strong sense of having done something morally wrong. Guilt is a normal and healthy moral response, a sign that one's conscience is working.

In his book for teenagers, *Love, Dating, and Sex,* George Eager tells the story of a well-known speaker who was addressing a high school assembly. The speaker was asked, "What do you most regret about your high school days?"

He answered, "The thing I most regret about high school is the time I singlehandedly destroyed a girl."

Eager offers this advice to young men: "When the breakup comes, it's usually a lot tougher on the girls than it is on the guys. It's not something you want on your conscience—that you caused a girl to have deep emotional problems."[7]

One 16-year-old boy says he stopped having sex with girls when he saw and felt guilty about the pain he was causing: "You see them crying and confused. They say they love you, but you don't love them."

Even in an age of sexual liberation, a lot of people who are having sex nevertheless have a guilty conscience about it. The guilt may come, as in the case of the young man just quoted, from seeing the hurt you've caused other people.

The guilt may come from knowing that your parents would be upset if they knew you were having sex. Or it may stem from your religious convictions. Christianity, Judaism, and Islam, for example, all teach that sex is a gift from God reserved for marriage and that sexual relations outside marriage are morally wrong.

Sometimes guilt about their sexual past ends up crippling people when they become parents by keeping them from advising their own children not to become sexually involved. According to counselor Dr. Carson Daly: "Because these parents can't bear to be considered hypocrites, or to consider themselves hypocrites, they don't give their children the sexual guidance they very much need."[8]

4. Loss of Self-Respect and Self-Esteem

Many people suffer a loss of self-esteem when they find out they have a sexually transmitted disease. For example, according to the Austin, Texas-based Medical Institute for Sexual Health, more than 80 percent of people with herpes say they feel "less confident" and "less desirable sexually."[9]

But even if a person is fortunate enough to escape sexually transmitted disease, temporary sexual relationships can lower the self-respect of both the user and the used.

Sometimes casual sex lowers self-esteem, leading a person into further casual sex, which leads to further loss of self-esteem in an oppressive cycle from which it may be hard to break free. This pattern is described by a college senior, a young woman who works as a residence hall director:

There are girls in our dorm who have had multiple pregnancies and multiple abortions. They tend to be filled with self-loathing. But because they have so little self-esteem, they will settle for any kind of attention from guys. So they keep going back to the same kind of destructive situations and relationships that got them into trouble in the first place.

On both sides of dehumanized sex, there is a loss of dignity and self-worth. One 20-year-old college male confides: "You feel pretty crummy when you get drunk at a party and have sex with some girl, and then the next morning you can't even remember who she was."

Another college student describes the loss of self-respect that followed his first sexual "conquest":

I finally got a girl into bed—actually it was in a car—when I was 17. I thought it was the hottest thing there was, but then she started saying she loved me and getting clingy.

I figured out that there had probably been a dozen guys before me who thought they had "conquered" her, but who were really just objects of her need for security. That realization took all the wind out of my sails. I couldn't respect someone who gave in as easily as she did.

I was amazed to find that after four weeks of having sex as often as I wanted, I was tired of her. I didn't see any point in continuing the relationship. I finally dumped her, which made me feel even worse, because I could see that she was hurting. I felt pretty low.[10]

People aren't things. When we treat them as if they were, we not only hurt them; we lose respect for ourselves.

5. The Corruption of Character and the Debasement of Sex

When people treat others as sexual objects and exploit them for their own pleasure, they not only lose self-respect; they corrupt their characters and debase their sexuality in the process.

Good character consists of virtues such as respect, responsibility, honesty, fairness, caring, and self-control. With regard to sex, the character trait of self-control is particularly crucial. The breakdown of sexual self-control is a big factor in many of the sex-related problems that plague our society: rape, promiscuity, pornography, addiction to sex, sexual harassment, the sexual abuse of children, sexual infidelity in marriage, and the serious damage to families many of these problems cause. It was Freud who said—and it is now obvious how right he was—that sexual self-control is essential for civilization.

Sex frequently corrupts character by leading people to tell lies in order to get sex. The Medical Institute for Sexual Health reports: "Almost all studies show that many sexually active people will lie if they think it will help them have sex."[11] Common lies: "I love you" and "I've never had a sexually transmitted disease."

Because sex is powerful, once sexual restraint is set aside, it easily takes over individuals and relationships. Consider the highly sexualized atmosphere that now characterizes many high schools. A high school teacher in Indiana says, "The air is thick with sex talk. Kids in the halls will say—boy to girl, girl to boy—'I want to f— you.'"

In a 1993 study by the American Association of University Women, four of five high school students—85 percent of girls and 75 percent of boys—said they have experienced "unwelcome sexual behavior that interferes with my life" in school.[12] An example: A boy backs a 14-year-old girl up against her locker, day after day. Says Nan Stein, a Wellesley College researcher: "There's a Tailhook happening in every school. Egregious behavior is going on."

Another recently reported example of this corruption of character is the Spur Posse club at Lakewood High School in suburban Los Angeles. Members of this club competed to see how many girls they could sleep with; one claimed he had slept with 63. Sadly, elementary school-age children are beginning to mimick such behavior. In a suburb of Pittsburgh, an assistant superintendent reports that sixth-grade boys were found playing a sexual contact game; the object of the game was to earn points by touching girls in private parts, the most points being awarded for "going all the way."

In this sex-out-of-control environment, even rape is judged permissible by many young people. In a 1988 survey of students in grades six through nine, the Rhode Island Rape Crisis Center found that two of three boys and 49 percent of the girls said it was "acceptable for a man to force sex on a woman if they have been dating for six months or more."[13] In view of attitudes like these, it's easy to understand why date rape has become such a widespread problem.

In short, sex that isn't tied to love and commitment undermines character by subverting self-control, respect, and responsibility. Unchecked, sexual desires and impulses easily run amok and lead to habits of hedonism and using others for one's personal pleasure. In the process, sexual intercourse loses its meaning, beauty, and specialness; instead of being a loving, uniquely intimate expression of two people's commitment to each others, sex is trivialized and degraded.

6. Shaken Trust and Fear of Commitment

Young people who feel used or betrayed after the break-up of a sexual relationship may experience difficulty in future relationships.

Some sexually exploited people, as we've seen, develop such low self-esteem that they seek any kind of attention, even if it's another short-lived and demeaning sexual relationship. But other people, once burned, withdraw. They have trouble trusting; they don't want to get burned again.

Usually, this happens to the girl. She begins to see guys as interested in just one thing: Sex. Says one young woman: "Besides feeling cheap [after several sexual relationships], I began to wonder if there would ever be anyone who would love and accept me without demanding that I do something with my body to earn that love."[14]

However, boys can also experience loss of trust and fear of commitment as a result of a broken relationship that involved sex. Brian, a college senior, tells how this happened to him:

I first had intercourse with my girlfriend when we were 15. I'd been going with her for almost a year, and I loved her very much. She was friendly, outgoing, charismatic. We'd done everything but have intercourse, and then one night she asked if we could go all the way.

A few days later, we broke up. It was the most painful time of my life. I had opened myself up to her more than I had to anybody, even my parents.

I was depressed, moody, nervous. My friends dropped me because I was so bummed out. I felt like a failure. I dropped out of sports. My grades weren't terrific.

I didn't go out again until I got to college. I've had mostly one-night stands in the last couple of years.

I'm afraid of falling in love.[15]

7. Rage Over Betrayal

Sometimes the emotional reaction to being "dumped" isn't just a lack of trust or fear of commitment. It's rage.

Every so often, the media carry a story about a person who had this rage reaction and then committed an act of violence against the former boyfriend or girlfriend. Read these accounts, and you'll find that sex was almost always a part of the broken relationship.

Of course, people often feel angry when somebody breaks up with them, even if sex has not been involved. But the sense of betrayal is usually much greater if sex has been part of the relationship. Sex can be emotional dynamite. It can lead a person to think that the relationship is really serious, that both people really love each other. It can create a very strong emotional bond that hurts terribly when it's ruptured—especially if it seems that the other person never had the same commitment. And the resulting sense of betrayal can give rise to rage, even violence.

> *Teenagers who are absorbed in an intense sexual relationship are turning inward on one thing at the very time in their lives when they should be reaching out.*

8. Depression and Suicide

In *Sex and the Teenager*, Kieran Sawyer writes: "The more the relationship seems like real love, the more the young person is likely to invest, and the deeper the pain and hurt if the relationship breaks up."[16] Sometimes the emotional turmoil caused by the rupture of a sexual relationship leads to deep depression. The depression, in turn, may lead some people to take their own lives.

In the past 25 years, teen suicide has tripled. In a 1988 survey by the U.S. Department of Health and Human Services, one in five adolescent girls said they have tried to kill themselves (the figure for boys was one in 10).

This is the same period during which the rate of teenage sexual activity has sharply increased, especially for girls. No doubt, the rise in youth suicide has multiple causes, but given what we know about the emotional aftermath of broken sexual relationships, it is reasonable to suspect that the pain from such break-ups is a factor in the suicide deaths of some young people.

9. Ruined Relationships

Sex can have another kind of emotional consequence: It can turn a good relationship bad. Other dimensions of the relationship stop developing. Pretty soon, negative emotions enter the picture. Eventually, they poison the relationship, and what had been a caring relationship comes to a bitter end.

One young woman shares her story, which illustrates the process:

> With each date, my boyfriend's requests for sex became more convincing. After all, we did love each other. Within two months, I gave in, because I had justified the whole thing. Over the next six months, sex became the center of our relationship. . . .
>
> At the same time, some new things entered our relationship—things like anger, impatience, jealousy, and selfishness. We just couldn't talk anymore. We grew very bored with each other. I desperately wanted a change.[17]

A young man who identified himself as a 22-year-old virgin echoes this warning about the damage premature sex can do to a relationship:

> I've seen too many of my friends break up after their relationships turned physical. The emotional wreckage is horrendous because they have already shared something so powerful. When you use sex too early, it will block other means of communicating love and can stunt the balanced growth of a relationship.[18]

10. Stunting Personal Development

Premature sexual involvement not only can stunt the development of a relationship; it also can stunt one's development as a person.

Just as some young people handle anxieties by turning to drugs and alcohol, others handle them by turning to sex. Sex becomes an escape. They aren't learning how to cope with life's pressures.

Teenagers who are absorbed in an intense sexual relationship are turning inward on one thing at the very time in their lives when they should be reaching out—forming new friendships, joining clubs and teams, developing their interests and skills, taking on bigger social responsibilities.

All of these are important nutrients for a teenager's development as a person. And this period of life is special because young people have both the time and the opportunities to develop their talents and interests. The growing they do during these years will affect them all their lives. If young people don't put these years to good use, they may never develop their full potential.

The risk appears to be greater for girls who get sexually involved and in so doing close the door on other interests and relationships. Says New York psychiatrist Samuel Kaufman:

> A girl who enters into a serious relationship with a boy very early in life may find out later that her individuality was thwarted. She became part of him and failed to develop her own interests, her sense of independent identity.[19]

REFLECTING ON her long experience in counseling college students and others about sexual matters, Dr. Carson Daly comments:

> I don't think I ever met a student who was sorry he or she had postponed sexual activity, but I certainly met many who deeply regretted their sexual involvements. Time and time again, I have seen the long-term emotional and spiritual desolation that results from casual sex and promiscuity.
>
> No one tells students that it sometimes takes years to recover from the effects of these sexual involvements—if one every fully recovers.

Sex certainly can be a source of great pleasure and joy. But as should be amply clear—and youngsters need our help and guidance in understanding this—sex also can be the source of deep wounds and suffering. What makes the difference is the relationship within which it occurs. Sex is most joyful and fulfilling—most emotionally safe as well as physically safe—when it occurs within a loving, total, and binding commitment. Historically, we have called that marriage. Sexual union is then part of something bigger—the union of two persons' lives.

REFERENCES

1. Susan Weller, "A Meta-Analysis of Condom Effectiveness in Reducing Sexually Transmitted HIV," *Social Science and Medicine*, June 1993, p. 12.

2. See, for example, Kenneth Noller, *OB/GYN Clinical Alert-t*, September 1992; for a thorough discussion of the dangers of human papilloma virus, see "Condoms Ineffective Against Human Papilloma Virus," *Sexual Health Update* (April 1994), a publication of the Medical Institute for Sexual Health, P.O. Box 4949, Austin, Texas 78765.

3. "Some Teens Taking Vows of Virginity," *Washington Post* (November 21, 1993).

4. William Bennett, "Sex and the Education of Our Children," *America* (February 14, 1987), p. 124.

5. Bob Bartlett, "Going All the Way," *Momentum* (April/May, 1993), p. 36.

6. Abridged from Ann Landers, "A Not-So-Sweet Sexteen Story," *Daily News* (September 23, 1991), p. 20.

7. Eager's book is available from Mailbox Club Books, 404 Eager Rd., Valdosta, Ga. 31602.

8. Carson Daly, personal communication.

9. *Safe Sex: A Slide Program.* Medical Institute for Sexual Health, Austin, Texas: 1992.

10. Josh McDowell and Dick Day, *Why Wait: What You Need to Know About the Teen Sexuality Crisis* (Here's Life Publishers, San Bernardino, Calif.: 1987).

11. Medical Institute for Sexual Health, P.O. Box 4919, Austin, Texas 78765.

12. *American Association of University Women Report on Sexual Harassment,* June 1993.

13. J. Kikuchi, "Rhode Island Develops Successful Intervention Program for Adolescents," *National Coalition Against Sexual Assault Newsletter* (Fall 1988).

14. McDowell and Day, op. cit.

15. Abridged from *Choosing the Best: A Values-Based Sex Education Curriculum,* 1993. (5500 Interstate North Parkway, Suite 515, Atlanta, Ga. 30328).

16. Kieran Sawyer, *Sex and the Teenager* (Ave Maria Press, Notre Dame, Ind.: 1990).

17. McDowell and Day, op. cit.

18. Ann Landers, "Despite Urgin', He's a Virgin." *Daily News* (January 15, 1994).

19. Quoted in Howard and Martha Lewis, *The Parent's Guide to Teenage Sex and Pregnancy* (St. Martin's Press, New York: 1980).

Charol Shakeshaft, Laurie Mandel, Yolanda M. Johnson,
Janice Sawyer, Mary Ann Hergenrother, and Ellen Barber

Boys Call Me Cow

**A three-year study of students' experiences and stories
sheds some light on what administrators should know to curb
the pervasive problem of peer harassment.**

If you wear something the other kids will laugh
at or if you sit in something or get caught, you
know, having your period, then the whole class
will see and make fun of you. It's nerve-wracking.
Someone is always saying something. Someone is
always watching. You have to be careful.

—A middle school girl

We hear a lot today about student-to-student harassment in newspapers, on TV, and even from our own children. In an effort to understand how students treat one another—even in ordinary adolescent banter—we (a professor and five doctoral students in educational administration) developed a research team to study peer harassment and understand how it occurs and how we can learn to stop it.

> ## "Unless they're close friends, people talk about each other with no respect," said one boy. "If they don't like you, they pick on you a lot."

During the 1992-95 academic years, we interviewed more than 1,000 Long Island, New York, students in eight middle, junior, and high schools. They represented a suburban mix of middle-class, wealthy, and low-income families. We also observed students in classes and hallways and in social settings, before and after school. Finally, we interviewed and observed school personnel at each site to understand the response of educators to peer harassment.

Patterns of Harassment

Most of the peer harassment we observed and heard about focused on verbal assaults. The pervasive nature of peer harassment—particularly sexual harassment—surprised us the most. Because peer sexual abuse was so widespread, no one appeared safe.

Everywhere we went, kids made fun of other kids—this was more usual than unusual. Although bullies and sexually aggressive students instigated some harassment, most of the persecution—especially in middle school—was random and illogical. Harassment occurred at school events, was unplanned, and, initially, was not thought out. The students we interviewed saw harassment as a way of life for themselves. "People make fun of you," said one student." They make fun of your hair and the way you dress. They're just cruel."

A boy described what most boys told us is normal male behavior when he said, "We're always making fun of each other the whole time we are together." Another student added:

> Unless they're close friends, people talk about each other with no respect. If they don't like you, they pick on you. You can just be sittin' at the table and they start dissin' on you and stuff or talkin' about you.

We saw and heard about more harassment by boys than by girls, but both sexes harassed their peers. Girls believed that boys only picked on girls, whereas boys described their male peers as harassers.

In general, boys targeted both boys and girls in a direct style that one student described as "in your face." Girls made fun of other girls indirectly or behind their backs. When a girl harassed a boy, it was almost always a response to his attack on her.

Name-calling was the most common form of harassment. In fact, practically everyone had a story to tell about their classmates' names and labels. "This one boy calls me Miss Piggy." "Boys call me cow." "Boys say things like joker to a girl with big lips and they call this other girl greasy." "Boys call one girl popcorn because she has zits." "Boys say you're stacked."

While all students were vulnerable to general harassment, some students were targeted more than others. In general, most girls were harassed by peers at some time during their school experience—more likely by boys than by girls. Not only did females experience more kinds of abuse more often, but it upset them more than it did males.

The Main Targets

Girls were teased because of how they looked and boys for how they acted.

Unattractive or unstylish girls. Males harassed females in this category more frequently, although sometimes females made fun of other females. Girls perceived as physically unattractive were often called fat or cows. When they entered a classroom, the boys made loud mooing sounds. One student described a repeated attack on her friend by a group of boys: "The girl isn't fat, but they call her cow, and they moo at her." Comments about a girl's weight were common, although a larger than average boy was seldom harassed.

Physically mature girls. Girls who developed breasts earlier than their classmates were at higher risk for name-calling. Other students accused them of sexual activity and circulated rumors about their so-called exploits. In addition, boys quizzed more physically developed girls with questions such as, "What did you do last night?" and "How much did he pay you?" In one incident, boys teased an 8th grade girl because of her physical appearance. "They call her slut," remarked a student. "They say how far they've gotten. A lot of boys will talk about her. They'll say she's easy. Everybody talks."

Boys often confronted these girls directly, making sexual demands and comments. It was not uncommon for a boy to target a girl for sexual confrontation before, after, or during a class, as a middle school girl explained:

In English class, right in front of the teacher, Joey will say, "I think I'm getting hard" when his girlfriend walks in or when he wants to embarrass some girl. The teacher only says, "Joey, calm

Surprisingly, the double standard for girls remained strong. Fears of damage to their reputations by rumors were pervasive.

down." Joey will say to girls, "I want you now." He does this to the unpopular girls to embarrass them and make them feel uncomfortable. Everybody laughs at the girl. She blushes or walks away.

Surprisingly, the double standard for girls remained strong. Fears of damage to their reputations by rumors were pervasive. Despite increased sexual activity by *all* adolescents, girls still suffered the most if they were considered sexually active. One girl described what we heard from many:

Girls get called whores. If it gets around, even if you are not, it ruins your reputation. I had a friend who the boys called a whore. She wasn't, but she got the name. It ruined her reputation.

Boys who don't fit the stereotypic male mold. Harassment of boys often took the form of homophobic insult, in which boys were called queer, old lady, girl, sissy, or any name that linked them to a female or feminine behavior. Fear of being labeled a homosexual was much more common than fear of actually being one. Boys didn't want others to believe they were homosexual and worked hard to make sure that their behavior fit an imagined norm. Such insults were hurled at boys for any perceived weakness. Many boys told us that the most common verbal assault among their male peers was to equate the boy with femininity. "You'd call a person a pussy if they were afraid to do something," said one middle school boy. "Like if we were drinking and they were afraid to drink."

This description of treatment by 7th and 8th grade boys was typical of the homophobic club wielded against boys who didn't conform to a macho image:

If they were quiet, if they acted different in the way they walked or acted in the hall—like hyper or something—or if they were into karate, or acted in any way different from the rest, they'd get laughed about. Kids make up nicknames like gay and faggot.

A 7th grade boy told us that if a boy didn't talk about having sex with girls, then his peers assumed he was a homosexual.

If he's not interested in girls, they might call him gay. When we're talking about girls there is this one kid who is silent, and we wonder why he is not talking about having sex with girls. We say, "What's wrong with him?"

Boys who didn't excel in athletics became targets. A 9th grader told us,

If someone isn't good at sports, they'll call him a faggot. One time a kid missed the ball or he did something stupid, and they called him a f_____ fag.

Our study showed that fear of being labeled a homosexual was central to male adolescent life and was a strong influence on male behavior.

How Do Students Respond?

Female and male responses to name-calling were the same: They felt bad about themselves. One girl told us that she felt "sad and worthless." A middle school boy said, "They make fun of me—it's depressing. I would change schools if I could." Another girl reported, "It makes you feel powerless. The guys think it is a joke." One girl described the constant verbal abuse as wearing.

It's tiresome. It worries me. I know that I'm affected by it, but I have a tendency to pretend I'm not. We get used to it.

Five responses by the students to verbal harassment included ignoring it, rationalizing it, fighting it, changing behavior, or becoming part of a group to shield themselves from it. They often used more than one of these strategies to stop attacks. No matter which defense they took, however, students reported that verbal abuse hurt.

How Do Adults Respond?

Typical adult responses to allegations of harassment in schools almost always discouraged students from further reports, seldom curbed harassment, and left kids feeling as though they had no place to turn for help. Very often, when students reported harassment, they felt uncomfortable and responsible for the harassment. In many cases, staff and other students penalized them for going public by reporting a crime. In these cases, students were violated twice—first by the harassment and then by the treatment of adults and other students.

The majority of students didn't report harassment in schools. Only about 6 percent of students told an adult in authority when they were harassed. The rest either didn't tell anyone or only told a friend. Because adults seldom heard harassment complaints, they mistakenly believed that the climate was not troublesome to adolescents. When students did report peer harassment, they were often told: "You're overreacting," "That's the way life is," or "What do you expect when you wear clothes like that?" Thus, students didn't feel particularly supported by staff when they reported abuses, and most students in our study believed that teachers and administrators didn't care or that it wasn't their job to stop them.

Students said that teachers and administrators rarely intervened when harassment occurred. Some students believed that teachers saw the harassment, but didn't want to get involved. This incident is typical:

In science class, the boys snap our bras. The [male] teacher doesn't really care. He doesn't say anything. The teacher has to keep teaching. The boys just laugh.

Other students believed that teachers didn't stop peer harassment because they didn't care about students. A few thought the teachers had too much to do, and that stopping abuse was not part of their job description. "Teachers don't really have time—they have 200 people to think about. I don't expect them to care."

Either way, students didn't view talking to school personnel as a possible recourse. One girl spoke for most when she said, "No way I'd report harassment to the principal or anyone else. I'd be the laughing stock of the school."

In cases of peer abuse, teachers—particularly male teachers—often sided with student athletes accused of harassment, especially sexual. They defended the athletes, often describing a female target as setting a trap or encouraging the athletes. These same teachers often isolated the student accuser or failed to act on allegations of sexual abuse by male athletes. These teachers gave male students this message: "Watch out or you will be falsely accused." Rarely did we find evidence that teachers talked with males, particularly athletes, about sexual harassment. Instead, most male students got the message to be careful *not* to get caught.

In cases of verbal harassment, most students and teachers alike reported that teachers only intervened minimally. One girl said:

For name-calling, they'll [teachers] just say, "I don't want to hear that," and then that's it. They really don't do anything else.... I wish teachers would stop it right away; even if they hear only one thing.

Another student described ineffectual teacher response this way:

They [teachers] don't take as much control as they should. They say, "Don't do it next time." And when they [the harassers] do it the next time, they [the teachers] keep on saying the same thing. They don't take control.

Supporters of victims tended to be quiet, often not even telling the other student they believed the story. Many students thought that anyone who was harassed brought it on themselves. For example, one student said, "If girls are flirting or flaunting, then both guys and girls would call them names, like 'ho'." Another student reported that any student who "wears short shorts is a slut." Although this student and her friends wore short shorts, she stressed that "we're definitely not sluts. There are a lot of other girls in our grade who are."

Putting an End to It

Stopping peer harassment requires changing the adolescent culture of the school. Because students don't report harassment and because the peer culture requires that they act as though it doesn't affect them, adults must take the lead in behavioral change.

Help the school community become conscious of harassing behavior. This takes some time and involves students, teachers, other staff, and parents. Students initially downplay the effects of harassment. Therefore, we need to use reflective activities to raise consciousness and raise students' awareness of their own feelings. Teachers can plan these activities through academic projects and assignments in all areas. In literature classes, focus on the issues of acceptable community behavior when discussing fiction. In science and math classes, ask students to conduct surveys about teasing and harassment and analyze the results. In art courses, encourage students to portray in paintings and other representations how they feel about verbal attacks.

Westbury Friends School in Westbury puts a priority on conflict resolution.[1] This school is an institution that honors its Quaker roots by its peaceful settlement of everyday conflict. Teachers try to spot potential conflicts between students and defuse them by talking to students before conflicts get out of hand.

Define appropriate behavior. Once aware of the extent of harassment and the harm it does, students and faculty can move toward defining the behavior they would like to see replace harassment. These definitions must include detailed explanations of what students and teachers believe is acceptable behavior. In small-group activities, community participants can share their definitions of respectful and caring behavior. For example, students can explain how and when they feel it is appropriate to be touched by others. Teachers might share list of words they prefer that students do not use. During this phase, allow students and faculty to freely speak about the kind of language that makes them feel uncomfortable. Remember that teachers and other staff members are part of the community. Expecting students to conform to the comfort level of the adults is not only a reasonable expectation but it is also a responsible one. The purpose is to end up with guidelines for behavior in a caring, inclusive environment.

Monitor and change the behavior. If teachers give these problems at least a year of close attention, three things can happen: students and faculty will learn about expectations; teachers will monitor student behavior; and students will realize the harmful consequences of unchanged behavior.

The main point is to stay attentive to behavior. Teachers can use staff meetings, student meetings, assemblies, staff in services, special projects, plays, school newspaper articles, PTA meetings, and other community activities to discuss harassment issues. Teachers must also monitor their own behavior because sarcasm and ridicule by teachers is no more acceptable than peer harassment.

Changing adolescent culture isn't easy. It is necessary, however, if we are to ensure a safe environment for learning and growing.

[1] J. Hildebrand (March 11, 1996), "Taking the Fight Out of Students in School" (*Newsday,* p. A23).

Charol Shakeshaft is Professor and Chairperson of Administration, Policy Studies, and Literacy at Hofstra University, 124 Hofstra University, Hempstead, NY 11550 (e-mail: CharolSS@aol.com). **Laurie Mandel** and **Janice Sawyer** are Adjunct Assistant Professors at the university. **Yolanda M. Johnson** is a doctoral student working on her dissertation. **Mary Ann Hergenrother** is Program Administrator at Cooperative Educational Services in Trumbull, Connecticut. **Ellen Barber** is an Assistant Professor at North Adams State College in North Adams, Massachusetts.

TRENDS IN SEXUAL ACTIVITY AMONG
Adolescent American Women: 1982–1995

By Susheela Singh and Jacqueline E. Darroch

Context: The formulation of policies and development of programs regarding adolescent sexual and reproductive health requires up-to-date information on levels of and trends in teenage sexual activity.

Methods: Analysis of three NSFG surveys, carried out in 1982, 1988 and 1995, allows examination of the sexual behavior of teenage women over a 13-year time period, using comparable data for the entire time period.

Results: The proportion of adolescent women who ever had sexual intercourse increased somewhat during the 1980s, but this upward trend stabilized between the late 1980s and the mid-1990s. Throughout the period, there has been little change in the proportion currently sexually active: In each of the surveys, about 40% of all 15–19-year-olds had had sexual intercourse in the last three months. The average number of months in the past year in which sexually experienced teenagers had had intercourse declined during the 1980s, with no change in the continuity of sexual intercourse taking place between 1988 and 1995, when the mean remained at 8.6 months. Differences in teenage sexual behavior across poverty and racial and ethnic subgroups were large in the early 1980s, but narrowed over the 13-year period.

Conclusions: Only continued monitoring will tell whether the patterns observed during 1988–1995 signify a temporary leveling off in the trend toward increasing adolescent sexual activity, stability in behavior or the beginnings of a decline. Nevertheless, the sustained level of initiation of sexual activity during adolescence is by now a recognized pattern of behavior, and is an important characteristic of the transition to adulthood in the United States.

Family Planning Perspectives, 1999, 31 (5):212-219

Susheela Singh is director of research and Jacqueline E. Darroch is senior vice president and vice president for research at The Alan Guttmacher Institute, New York. The authors thank Suzette Audam, Selene Oslak and Manasi Tirodkar for assistance with data processing and analysis. The authors also are grateful to Akinrinola Bankole, Stanley Henshaw, Beth Fredrick and Jeannie Rosoff for comments on earlier drafts of this article. The research on which this article is based was funded by a grant from the Marion Cohen Memorial Foundation.

A series of national surveys conducted by researchers at the Johns Hopkins University charted a steady rise during the 1970s in the proportion of U.S. women aged 15–19 who had ever had sexual intercourse before marriage.[1] In 1982, the federal government fully incorporated young women aged 15–19 into its National Survey of Family Growth (NSFG). The 1982 NSFG confirmed that levels of premarital sexual intercourse had risen steadily, from 32% in 1971 to 38% in 1976, 43% in 1979 and 45% in 1982. However, the 1982 NSFG analysis suggested that by the early 1980s, the earlier rise in the level of premarital sexual experience had leveled off among white adolescents, and that a decrease had occurred among black teenagers.[2]

The 1988 NSFG, however, revealed another large increase in the proportion of all American adolescent women who had had premarital sexual intercourse, from 45% in 1982 to 52% in 1988.[3] The newly available national trend data also showed that the proportion of all 15–19-year-old women who had ever had sexual intercourse had increased during the 1980s, from 47% in 1982 to 53% in 1988.[4]

For several reasons, this general increase in sexual experience among adolescents has attracted societal attention.[5] It has given rise to fears of declines in morals and values; worries about rising rates of sexually transmitted diseases (STDs); and concern about other negative consequences, such as unwanted pregnancy and the potential public and private costs of childbearing by unmarried adolescents.

At the same time, this broad trend is known to characterize most developed countries.[6] Thus, it is increasingly acknowledged that sexually active unmarried youth need comprehensive sexuality education and that such education should begin at younger ages than is now the case, so that adolescents have the knowledge and skills they need to make and carry out decisions concerning their sexual behavior. Moreover, it is also recognized that sexually active adolescents need ready access to services for the prevention of STDs and unwanted pregnancy.[7]

This has led to the formulation of policies and programs, both public and private and in a variety of settings, to try to meet these needs. Recent examples are the increased provision of HIV and AIDS education, an increased emphasis on teaching abstinence within sexuality education programs, and implementation by most states of abstinence-only education programs (as part of states' response to the 1996 welfare reform law).[8]

Given the heightened importance of trends and levels of adolescent sexual behavior for public policies and programs, up-to-date information on trends is greatly needed. With the most recent NSFG (carried out in 1995), it is now possible to follow these trends into the mid-1990s. By comparing the new 1995 data with information from 1982 and 1988, we can examine changes in the sexual experiences of American teenage women over a 13-year time period, using data collected in similar ways over the entire time period.

As with earlier studies, this article examines trends and differentials in sexual intercourse across various racial and ethnic groups and among younger and older adolescents. We also look at differences by the economic level of the young woman's family. Indeed, economic status has been shown to be a strong predictor of adolescent pregnancy and childbearing, and of negative consequences for young women in terms of health, education and employment.[9] While it is difficult to measure, it is probably more relevant than race or ethnicity to young women's opportunities and risk behaviors.

This article presents findings on the proportion of teenagers who have ever had and who are currently having sexual intercourse, and on the mean number of months in the past year during which adolescents had intercourse. Each of these measures describes a different aspect of adolescent sexual behavior; using all three yields a more comprehensive (although not complete) picture of the sexual behavior of adolescent women.

The proportion who have ever had intercourse is a broad measure of the extent of sexual initiation during the adolescent years, and provides an indicator of exposure to pregnancy and STDs, as well as of the need for related health services. However, more current or point-in-time measures are needed because, in the early adolescent years, sexual relationships are unlikely to be long-lasting. In fact, studies show that more than half of adolescents who have ever had sexual intercourse have been in at least two sexual relationships, often with some time between them.[10]

For these reasons, the proportion currently in a sexual relationship (measured as the percentage who had intercourse in the three-month period before interview) is a useful additional measure, providing a minimum indicator of the extent of risk for pregnancy and STDs and of the need for health services. The number of months of sexual activity in the past year describes another dimension—the extent of continuity in sexual intercourse, once a teenager has become sexually active.

Data and Methods

The data for most of the analysis come from the 1982, 1988 and 1995 cycles of the NSFG. All three surveys interviewed large, nationally representative samples of women aged 15–44 who were living in households, including all females aged 15–19, both those in school and those not in school.*

The basic measures that we use in this article are comparable across surveys. All three surveys used similar questions to obtain information on when first intercourse took place and the respondent's age at that time. However, in the 1995 round of the NSFG only, questions on intercourse more clearly defined intercourse as heterosexual by including the phrase "with a man." (In 1995, the question used was: "Think back to the very first time in your life that you ever had sexual intercourse with a man. In what month and year was that?") Also, in the 1995 survey, the interviewer was directed not to count oral sex, anal sex, sex with a female partner, heavy petting or other forms of sexual activity that did not involve vaginal penetration.

The definition of teenage sexual behavior used in this article has some limitations, particularly in measuring risk for STDs. With a focus on understanding exposure to pregnancy, the 1982 and 1988 NSFGs imply that "intercourse" should be interpreted to mean heterosexual vaginal intercourse, and the 1995 NSFG clearly defines it as such (i.e., that "intercourse" excludes oral and anal sex). Although

---

*Although a telephone survey was conducted in 1990 to reinterview women who had been interviewed in the 1988 NSFG (as well as an added subsample of 15–17-year-olds), the 1990 survey data are not analyzed here. This is because of the especially low response rate in the 1990 sample for younger teenagers (53%), compared with that among women aged 17–44 (68%). (Source: Peterson LS, Contraceptive use in the United States: 1982–90, Advance Data, 1995, No. 260, Feb. 14, 1995, technical notes, p. 12.) In addition, the interviews were short and conducted by telephone, which may affect response on the sensitive topic of sexual behavior, particularly among adolescents.

the prevalence of homosexual relationships may be relatively low, the level of genital sexual activities among adolescent females who have never had vaginal intercourse has been found to be about 10%.[11] The results presented here therefore provide only a minimum estimate of sexual behavior that puts adolescents at risk for STDs.

A second variation across surveys is that in measuring the timing of first intercourse, both the 1982 and the 1988 surveys excluded intercourse before menarche, while the 1995 survey did not. (The question asked in 1982 and 1988 was: "Thinking back, after your first menstrual period, when did you have sexual intercourse for the first time—what month and year was that?") In addition, the 1995 survey obtained new information on whether first intercourse was voluntary; the earlier surveys did not collect this information. To maintain comparability across all three surveys, we defined first intercourse to exclude intercourse prior to menarche, and to include any experience of intercourse after menarche, regardless of whether it was voluntary. Because in 1995 those who only ever had involuntary sex were not asked about sexual activity in the three months before the 1995 survey, we assumed that the 0.4% of all teenagers who only ever had involuntary intercourse did not have sex in the last three months.[†]

To maintain comparability across surveys, our analyses use the respondent's age at the time of the actual interview, not at the estimated midpoint of the data collection period—the point in time that was used in the two most recent surveys to select women into the sample. We consider age at the time of the interview the more appropriate of the two measures. In light of the steep increase in the likelihood of sexual debut as adolescents age, even small differences between surveys in how age is measured could affect the proportion reported to be sexually active at given ages, and could result in an inaccurate depiction of trends over time. The results presented here differ slightly from previously published estimates for both 1988 and 1995 largely

because of the difference in measurement of age.[12] However, differences in the definition of sexual intercourse (inclusion or exclusion of those adolescents who had only had involuntary intercourse or who had only had intercourse before menarche) can also affect estimates.[‡]

To examine the effect of changes in the age composition of teenagers over the period 1982–1995, we standardized the data for selected basic measures (such as the proportion of 15–19-year-olds who had ever had intercourse), using the 1990 census distribution of 15–19-year-olds by single year of age as the standard. However, changes in age composition accounted for little of the time trend. As a result, the actual unstandardized results are presented in this article.

Never-married adolescents exclude both those who had ever been formally married and those who had ever been in a cohabiting union.[*] However, data limitations lead the results to be inconsistent across surveys: The NSFG data for 1988 and 1995 fully identified past marital and cohabiting unions, whereas the 1982 NSFG obtained current cohabiting status but did not ob-

tain information on cohabiting unions that had ended. The number of never-married adolescents who were formerly in a cohabiting union is likely to be smaller in 1982 than it was by the mid-1990s, given the overall upward trend in cohabitation as a type of union during the 1980s.[13] We expect that the net effect should not introduce any substantial element of noncomparability into the analyses of trends in sexual activity levels among the never-married or of trends in the proportion who had ever had premarital intercourse. In fact, the proportion of all adolescent women who have ever been in a marital or cohabiting union has changed very little between 1982 and 1995, and remains quite low, as can be seen below:

Status	1982	1988	1995
Married	6.4	3.1	4.0
Cohabiting	1.5	3.7	4.2
Formerly married	0.8	0.1	0.6
Never-married	91.3	93.1	91.2
Formerly cohabited	na	3.7	3.2
Never cohabited	na	89.4	88.0
Total	100.0	100.0	100.0

Because of the importance of economic status, we present differentials by income group. However, classifying adolescents according to what they say their families earn is somewhat unreliable: Many teenagers may report family income incorrectly because they simply are unlikely to have this information, and thus give approximate answers. To minimize potential error, we used a dichotomy, dividing adolescents into those with a family income below 200% of the federally designated poverty level and those with an income at or above 200% of the poverty level. In addition, we present differences according to racial and ethnic subgroups—Hispanic, non-Hispanic white and non-Hispanic black.

All percentages reported in this article are weighted national estimates. Unweighted sample sizes are shown in Table 1 to give an indication of the potential reliability of the estimates. Non-Hispanic adolescents of races other than white and black are excluded from subgroup analyses because of the small size of this group, although they are included in the totals.

As can be seen in Table 1, despite the large total samples used in the NSFG, the numbers of respondents in some subgroups are small (fewer than

---

[†]This is in agreement with the recoded variable provided by NCHS on the 1995 NSFG data file. It is also largely supported by analysis of month-by-month reporting over the past year: Eighty percent of this small group of women were not sexually active throughout most or all of the year (60% did not have intercourse in any of the last 12 months, and 20% did not do so in nine of the last 12 months).

[‡]In the 1988 NSFG, the proportion of participants aged 15–19 who had ever had intercourse after menarche varied depending on how age was defined. This proportion was estimated to be 52.9% when age was based on the women's age at the date used to determine the sample (March 15, 1988—approximately the midpoint of the period in which the survey was fielded). In comparison, this proportion was 52.6% when based on respondents' age at the actual date of interview. In the 1995 NSFG, the proportion of 15–19-year-olds who had ever had intercourse after menarche (including those who had had only involuntary intercourse postmenarche) was 50.6% when age was based on the sample date (April 1, 1995), but was 51.5% when age was based on women's actual age at interview (source: special tabulations). In 1988, inclusion of those who only had had intercourse prior to menarche increased the proportion by 0.3% (source: reference 4), while in 1995, such an approach adds 0.2% (source: special tabulations). For 1995, using the postmenarche definition and excluding those who had had involuntary intercourse only would reduce the proportion who had ever had intercourse among those aged 15–19 at interview by 0.4% (source: reference 12).

---

[*]Premarital sexual activity is defined to include married and cohabiting women who first had intercourse at least one month prior to the month in which they married or started to cohabit, as well as all never-married women who had initiated sexual activity.

Table 1. Unweighted number of adolescent respondents interviewed in the National Survey of Family Growth (NSFG), by age at interview and selected characteristics, according to year

Age at interview and characteristic	1982	1988	1995
Total			
15–19	1,888	1,231	1,396
15–17	939	713	815
18–19	949	518	581
Never married/never cohabited			
15–19	1,711	1,097	1,231
15–17	909	687	776
18–19	802	410	455
Income <200% of poverty			
15–19	1,001	634	574
15–17	471	383	330
18–19	530	251	244
Income ≥200% of poverty			
15–19	887	597	822
15–17	468	330	485
18–19	419	267	337
Non-Hispanic white			
15–19	1,120	711	842
15–17	511	397	474
18–19	609	314	368
Non-Hispanic black			
15–19	562	368	289
15–17	320	224	177
18–19	242	144	112
Non-Hispanic other†			
15–19	37	34	55
15–17	16	24	41
18–19	21	10	14
Hispanic			
15–19	169	118	210
15–17	92	68	123
18–19	77	50	87

†Analyses are not presented for this subgroup because of its small sample size.

100 among some Hispanic subgroups, for example). Thus, we may be unable to identify some differences as being statistically significant, even when absolute differences appear large.

Some changes at the national level may also prove not to be statistically significant, even when the change appears substantial. For example, the proportion of 18–19-year-olds who ever had sexual intercourse increased between 1982 and 1988; this change was not statistically significant at the standard level of p<.05, although it was weakly significant (at p<.10). The ability to have a 90% power to detect change at a 5% level of significance between 1982 and 1988 would have required a slightly larger number of respondents. Any smaller change that might have occurred would have required a much larger sample of respondents to detect with confidence whether it was statistically significant.

As a result, in this article we present information on levels of significance in four categories: at the 5–10% level (p<.10); at the 1–5% level (p<.05); at the 0.1–1% level (p<.01); and lower than 0.1% (p<.001). We discuss some findings even if they are significant at relatively weak levels (5–10%), because with small sample sizes, these findings may indicate differences that might prove to be statistically significant if the sample were larger. However, we place greater confidence in findings that are statistically significant at p=.05 or less.

We assessed statistical significance between percentages using two-tailed t-tests. For all three surveys, we estimated standard errors using approaches that take the surveys' complex sample designs into account, following procedures recommended by the National Center for Health Statistics, the government agency in charge of the NSFG.[14]

While these and other surveys have used similar definitions and questions for three decades, it is nevertheless possible that any of the three surveys may actually underestimate levels of sexual intercourse, given the fact that women are sometimes reluctant to report their sexual activity. (Males, on the other hand, are believed to overreport their sexual behavior.[15]) There is, however, little research examining adolescents' tendencies to underreport or overreport whether they have had sexual intercourse while still single. Neither is there any documentation of whether younger teenagers are likely to report less accurately than older adolescents are, or whether the likelihood of accurate reporting has changed over time in response to changing sexual attitudes and mores.

A related question is whether the trends reported in the NSFG measure actual changes in behavior or reflect differences in young women's comfort in reporting their behavior. Adolescents' willingness to report sexual activity could have increased during the 1980s, as society became more accepting of nonmarital sex; in addition, although there is no hard information on this issue, such willingness to report may have lessened through the 1990s, with the increased emphasis on the teaching of abstinence in sexuality education.[16]

As a check on the 1982–1988 trends, we constructed retrospective cohort estimates of the proportion of women sexually active by age 20 in 1982 and 1988 from all three NSFG surveys. The results of the cohort analysis indicate a trend similar to that derived from the cross-sectional measures over the period of the 1980s (not shown). Although there are small inconsistencies, the retrospective cohort estimates are very close to, and serve to confirm, the point-in-time estimates derived from the 1982 and 1988 NSFGs. This comparison, therefore, basically supports the validity of reported age of onset of sexual intercourse. However, these results do not mean that period differences in the reporting of current sexual activity did not occur, at least among the unmarried.

Results

Proportion Who Ever Had Sex

Between 1982 and 1988, the proportion of all adolescent women aged 15–19 who had ever had sexual intercourse increased from 47% to 53% (Table 2). In absolute terms, the increase between 1982 and 1988 was twice as large among women aged 18–19 (from 64% to 74%) as it was among those aged 15–17 (from 32% to 38%). During this same period, there were substantial increases in this measure among adolescents at every single year of age, although these changes were not statistically significant (not shown).

There was little change between 1988 and 1995 in the proportion of all adolescents who had ever had sexual intercourse (Table 2), and while trends were somewhat different for younger and older adolescents, none were statistically significant at p<.05. Among women aged 15–17, the proportion sexually experienced increased slightly, while among those aged 18–19 it decreased somewhat.

If the age composition of 15–19-year-olds had been the same in 1988 as it was in 1982, the increase in the proportion of young women who had ever had sexual intercourse over the period 1982–1988 would actually have been slightly greater. However, age-composition did not contribute to the observed pattern of stability between 1988 and 1995 (not shown).

Trends in the proportions of women 15–19 who have ever had premarital sexual intercourse—that is, who first had intercourse before marriage or cohabitation—essentially paralleled those in the proportion who ever had intercourse. The proportion who were sexually active premaritally increased significantly between 1982 and 1988, both among all adolescents and especially among 18–19-year-olds (Table 2). This is not surprising, since almost all women who begin intercourse in their adolescence do so before marriage or cohabitation—93.6% in 1982, 99.8% in 1988 and 98.3% in 1995 (not shown).

Current Sexual Activity

The proportion of all American women aged 15–19 who were currently sexually active—that is, who had had intercourse at some time during the three months preceding the survey—showed no significant change between 1982 and 1988 (Table 2). Although the increase among those aged 18–19 was large in absolute terms (from 55% to 63%), it was not statistically significant (p=.12). Likewise, none of the other changes in the proportion currently sexually active, whether among adolescents aged 15–17 or among all 15–19-year-olds, were statistically significant.

Over the period 1988–1995, the same pattern of stability observed in the proportion who had ever had sexual intercourse can also be seen in the proportion currently sexually active. Among all young women aged 15–19, the proportion currently sexually active in 1995 was 40%, slightly but not significantly less than in 1988 (43%). Similarly, change was minimal among adolescents aged 15–17, while a small, nonsignificant decline occurred among those aged 18–19.

Continuity of Sexual Intercourse

Among all those who had ever had sex, the proportion currently in a sexual relationship declined over the 13-year period, from 85% in 1982 to 81% in 1988 and 79% in 1995 (not shown). The decline between 1982 and 1995 was marginally statistically significant (at p=.06), while the declines in the periods 1982–1988 and 1988–1995 were not. This trend suggests that although adolescent women are now more likely to begin having intercourse during their teenage years than was the case in the early 1980s, those who do so are somewhat less likely to be continu-

ously sexually active than their counterparts in the early 1980s.

In 1982, the average sexually experienced adolescent had had sex during 9.1 months in the year before the interview; this average had declined significantly (to 8.6 months) by 1988, but remained unchanged between 1988 and 1995 (Table 2).* This trend suggests decreasing continuity of sexual activity since 1982, which is consistent with the drop in the proportion of sexually experienced teenagers currently in a sexual relationship. It reflects the fact that teenage sexual relationships tend to be short-term and sporadic. Indeed, one-quarter of sexually active adolescents have intercourse in fewer than six months out of a year.[17]

Sex Among Adolescents
Never in a Union

The level of sexual activity among adolescent women who have never married and never cohabited (referred to as "never-married" subsequently) is of special interest to policy makers and service providers because of this group's heightened risk of STDs,[18] childbearing outside of a union and abortion.[19] Policies and programs to motivate and support youth to be abstinent until marriage have chiefly focused on this group.[20] Overall, the proportions ever sexually active and currently sexually active would be expected to be slightly lower among never-married teenagers than among all teenagers. Otherwise, because the vast majority of adolescent women have never been married, most measures for this group would be expected to closely parallel those for all adolescent women.

As expected, the proportion of never-married adolescent women who have ever had intercourse and the proportion currently in a sexual relationship are slightly lower among never-married teenagers than among all adolescents (Table 2). For example, in 1995, 45% of never-married teenage

---

*In 1982, the recoded variable on the number of months sexually active in the year before interview did not provide this information for currently pregnant women. Pregnant teenagers constituted 4.8% of all adolescents in 1982. Data from 1988 and 1995 show that the mean number of months sexually active in the past year is somewhat higher among pregnant teenagers than among other sexually experienced teenagers, suggesting that the 1982 estimate of mean number of months sexually active in the past year was slightly understated.

Table 2. Selected measures of current and lifetime sexual activity among women aged 15–19, by age at interview, according to year

Measure	1982	1988	1995
ALL ADOLESCENTS			
% who ever had intercourse			
15–19	46.9[a]	52.6	51.5
15–17	32.2	37.6	38.5
18–19	64.1[a]	74.3	70.8[c]
% who ever had premarital intercourse[g]			
15–19	43.9[b]	52.2	50.6[f]
15–17	31.1[a]	37.5	38.3[e]
18–19	58.6[b]	73.7	69.0[f]
% who had intercourse in past 3 months			
15–19	40.0	42.6	40.3
15–17	26.8	28.5	28.0
18–19	55.2	63.0	58.7
Mean no. of months in past year in which sexually experienced women had sex			
15–19	9.1[a]	8.6	8.6[d]
15–17	8.7	8.2	8.0[c]
18–19	9.2	8.9	9.1
NEVER-MARRIED ADOLESCENTS[h]			
% who ever had intercourse			
15–19	41.8[a]	47.0	44.9
15–17	30.0	35.3	35.6[c]
18–19	57.6[a]	67.7	62.2
% who had intercourse in past 3 months			
15–19	34.3	36.6	32.9
15–17	24.4	26.3	24.6
18–19	47.4	54.9	48.3

[a]Significantly different from 1988 at p<.10.
[b]Significantly different from 1988 at p<.001.
[c]Significantly different from 1982 at p<.10.
[d]Significantly different from 1982 at p<.05.
[e]Significantly different from 1982 at p<.01.
[f]Significantly different from 1982 at p<.001.
[g]Those who first had sex one month or more prior to the month they first married or cohabited.
[h]Excludes those who have been married and those who have ever cohabited.
Note: No differences between 1988 and 1995 were statistically significant at p<.10.

women had ever had intercourse, compared with 52% of all 15–19-year-olds.

Trends in the proportion of never-married 15–19-year-olds who had ever

Table 3. Percentage of women aged 15–19 who ever had sexual intercourse, percentage who had intercourse in the past three months and mean number of months in the past year in which sexually experienced adolescents had sex, by poverty status and age at interview, according to year

Measure and age	1982	1988	1995
% WHO EVER HAD INTERCOURSE			
<200% of poverty			
15–19	55.4	55.5	57.0
15–17	45.4	40.4	45.6
18–19	65.0[a]	80.1	72.7
≥200% of poverty			
15–19	39.4[c]	49.7	48.0[f]
15–17	22.5[c]	34.8	34.3[f]
18–19	63.0	69.5	69.5
% WHO HAD INTERCOURSE IN PAST 3 MONTHS			
<200% of poverty			
15–19	49.2	44.5	45.3
15–17	38.5	30.4	34.7
18–19	59.5	67.3	60.1
≥200% of poverty			
15–19	31.8[b]	40.7	37.1[e]
15–17	18.3[b]	26.6	23.9[e]
18–19	50.7	59.4	57.8
MEAN NO. OF MONTHS IN PAST YEAR IN WHICH SEXUALLY EXPERIENCED WOMEN HAD SEX			
<200% of poverty			
15–19	9.4[d]	8.5	8.9e
15–17	9.1[a]	8.2	8.3
18–19	9.6[a]	8.8	9.4
≥200% of poverty			
15–19	8.7	8.7	8.4
15–17	8.3	8.2	7.7
18–19	8.9	9.0	8.9

[a]Significantly different from 1988 at p<.10.
[b]Significantly different from 1988 at p<.05.
[c]Significantly different from 1988 at p<.01.
[d]Significantly different from 1988 at p<.001.
[e]Significantly different from 1982 at p<.10.
[f]Significantly different from 1982 at p<.001.
Note: No differences between 1988 and 1995 were statistically significant at p<.10.

17-year-olds and 48% of 18–19-year-olds. Over the entire period 1982–1995, there was little change in the proportion of never-married adolescents currently sexually active. Only among 15–17-year-old never-married adolescents was an increase over this period in the proportion who had ever had intercourse even marginally significant (p=.06). Marginally significant increases between 1982 and 1988 in the proportion of never-married 18–19-year-olds who had ever had intercourse were paralleled by nonsignificant increases in the proportion currently sexually active at these ages.

The decline between 1982 and 1995 in the proportion of all sexually experienced adolescent women who were currently in a sexual relationship was also seen among never-married women, with this proportion decreasing from 82% of never-married 15–19-year-olds in 1982 to 73% in 1995 (p<.01, not shown).

Trends by Income
Overall, there were no statistically significant changes during the period 1982–1995 in the proportion of lower income adolescents who had ever had sex or were currently sexually active. However, somewhat erratic and opposing trends occurred among younger and older lower income adolescents (Table 3). Although none of these changes were significant, the proportion of lower-income 15–17-year-olds who had ever had sex decreased between 1982 and 1988 and increased from 1988 to 1995. In contrast, among 18–19-year-olds, levels of sexual activity rose and then fell.

Among adolescents from higher income families, however, the proportions who had ever had intercourse and who were currently sexually active increased significantly between 1982 and 1988: Among all 15–19-year-olds, the proportion who were sexually experienced increased from 39% to 50%, and the proportion currently sexually active increased from 32% to 41%.

Between 1988 and 1995, as was true in the general population, there was no change among higher income teenagers in the proportion who ever had sex, and there was a small, nonsignificant decrease in the proportion currently sexually active. Changes among the two age-groups were generally similar and not statistically significant.

The net result was that between 1982 and 1995, the proportions who had ever had sex or who were currently sexually active increased sharply among all higher income teen-

agers and among young higher income adolescents.

Because levels of sexual activity stayed fairly stable among lower income teenagers but rose during the period 1982–1988 among those with a higher income, differentials between these subgroups narrowed over time. For example, among 15–19-year-old females, the difference between the two income groups in the proportion who had ever had sexual intercourse was 16 percentage points in 1982 and nine percentage points in 1995.

Nevertheless, both among young adolescents and among all 15–19-year-olds, lower income adolescents still were significantly more likely to have ever had or to be currently having sexual intercourse than were higher income adolescents. By late adolescence, however, lower income and higher income teenagers were about equally likely to have ever had intercourse or to be currently sexually active.

Among higher income adolescents who had had intercourse, there was relatively little change in the mean number of months in the past year in which they had been sexually active. On the other hand, among lower income teenagers, the number of months spent sexually active declined significantly from 1982 to 1988, but rose only slightly and nonsignificantly between 1988 and 1995.

Racial and Ethnic Trends
Trends in levels of sexual activity among white adolescents were very similar to the national pattern and to that seen among higher income adolescents. This is not unexpected, given that white teenagers represent the largest population subgroup and that most are above poverty level.* Over the period 1982–1988, the proportions of non-Hispanic white adolescents aged 15–19 and aged 18–19 who had ever had intercourse increased significantly (Table 4). Similarly, the proportion of 18–19-year-old white adolescents who were currently sexually active increased significantly. However, trends among white adolescents in the period 1988–1995 were similar to those found among all adolescent women: Essentially, little change occurred, except for nonsignificant small declines among older teenagers.

In contrast to the experience of non-Hispanic white adolescents, the pro-

had sex were similar to trends among all adolescent women: Small, weakly significant increases occurred between 1982 and 1988. Trends between 1988 and 1995 in the proportions of never-married women who had ever had intercourse were also similar to those among all adolescent women, and not statistically significant.

In 1995, the proportion of never-married adolescents who were currently sexually active remained moderately high, at 33% of 15–19-year-olds, 25% of 15–

*"White" includes only non-Hispanic whites. Non-Hispanic women of other backgrounds are excluded from Table 4 and from this discussion, but they are included in the totals.

portion of black teenagers aged 15–19 who had ever had intercourse changed little throughout the whole period 1982–1995. Although this proportion increased somewhat among young black adolescents from 1982 to 1988 (from 44% to 50%), the change was not statistically significant.

From 1982 to 1995, the proportion of black adolescents who were currently sexually active declined somewhat; for example, among all black 15–19-year-olds, this proportion fell from 54% to 47%. However, none of these changes were statistically significant. Among all black adolescents 15–19 who had ever had intercourse, the proportion currently sexually active declined from 91% in 1982 to 77% in 1995 (not shown), a change that was significant (p<.01).

The proportions of Hispanic teenagers who had ever had sexual intercourse remained virtually unchanged between 1982 and 1988. Hispanic adolescents became slightly less likely to be currently sexually active between 1982 and 1988, but this change was not statistically significant. Among Hispanic teenagers who had ever had intercourse, the proportion currently sexually active dropped from 85% in 1982 to 66% in 1988, yet this decline, although large, was not statistically significant.

During the period 1988–1995, trends among Hispanic adolescents differed from the overall pattern: There was a large, statistically significant increase among younger Hispanics in the proportion currently sexually active (from 20% to 39%), and a marginally significant increase among all Hispanic 15–19-year-olds (from 31% to 45%, p=.06). Similarly, there was a marginally significant rise in the proportion of younger Hispanics who had ever had sexual intercourse (from 34% to 49%, p=.09). And during this period, the proportion currently sexually active among Hispanic 15–19-year-olds who had ever had intercourse rose from 67% to 80%, although this increase was not statistically significant. The wide variations observed over time in measures of sexual activity among Hispanic teenagers clearly are mainly a result of the small samples on which these results are based (Table 1). The lack of statistical significance for trends in all groups except 15–17-year-olds suggests that only these younger Hispanic adolescents experienced substantial change—a trend toward increased levels of sexual activity between 1988 and 1995.

The net result of these changes is that by 1995, racial and ethnic differences had narrowed: Across subgroups of 15–19-year-olds by race and ethnicity, the difference seen in 1982 in the proportion who had ever had sexual intercourse (15 percentage points) had narrowed substantially (to about 10 percentage points) by 1995. This resulted primarily from the substantial rise in the proportion of white teenagers who had had sex, combined with little change among black teenagers. While Hispanic adolescents were more similar to white non-Hispanic teenagers in 1982, by 1995 their levels of sexual activity were closer to those of black non-Hispanic adolescents.

There was relatively little change among sexually experienced non-Hispanic white teenagers in the mean number of months in the past year that were spent sexually active. Among young Hispanic adolescents, the mean rose substantially, from 5.8 months in 1982 to 7.8 months in 1995, but this increase was only weakly significant. However, non-Hispanic black teenagers reported significant declines from 1982 to 1988 in the mean number of months sexually active in the past year.

Discussion

Our analysis of three NSFG surveys spanning the period 1982–1995 confirms that the proportion of adolescent women who had ever had sexual intercourse increased during the 1980s, a continuation of the trend observed during the 1970s. This upward trend appears to have stabilized between the late 1980s and the mid-1990s. While a small decline between 1988 and 1995 has been heralded, it is not statistically significant, even at a very weak level (p<.20). These broad patterns of increase followed by stabilization characterize the experience of both never-married adolescent females and all teenage women.

The trends identified in the NSFG are supported by findings from the Youth Risk Behavior Survey (YRBS).* The YRBS shows that the proportion of female high school students who had ever had intercourse increased somewhat between 1990 and 1995 (from 48% to 52%), but this change was not statistically significant.[21] Thus, both surveys essentially show no

*Based on a national sample of schools, the YRBS surveys high school students (those in grades 9–12, who are approximately 14–18 years of age). Interviews are self-administered, and only adolescents attending school are represented.

Table 4. Percentage of women aged 15–19 who have ever had sexual intercourse, percentage who had intercourse in the past three months and mean number of months in the past year in which sexually experienced adolescents had sex, by race or ethnicity and age at interview, according to year

Measure and age	1982	1988	1995
% WHO EVER HAD INTERCOURSE			
Non-Hispanic white[h]			
15–19	44.4[b]	52.2	50.7[d]
15–17	29.7	35.6	36.2[c]
18–19	60.5[b]	74.5	70.7[e]
Non-Hispanic black			
15–19	58.9	60.8	60.4
15–17	44.1	50.2	48.9
18–19	79.1	78.1	78.8
Hispanic			
15–19	49.9	26.7	56.0
15–17	34.4	33.6[f]	49.4
18–19	70.1	70.9	65.6
% WHO HAD INTERCOURSE IN PAST 3 MONTHS			
Non-Hispanic white[h]			
15–19	37.1	43.2	39.9
15–17	25.2	27.6	26.2
18–19	50.3[b]	63.6	58.8[d]
Non-Hispanic black			
15–19	53.6	50.6	46.8
15–17	38.8	39.1	34.9
18–19	73.9	69.3	65.6
Hispanic			
15–19	42.2	31.2[f]	44.9
15–17	22.0	19.9[g]	38.5[d]
18–19	68.3	52.1	54.3
MEAN NO. OF MONTHS IN PAST YEAR IN WHICH SEXUALLY EXPERIENCED WOMEN HAD SEX			
Non-Hispanic white[h]			
15–19	8.9	8.7	8.5
15–17	8.8	8.5	7.9[c]
18–19	9.0	8.8	8.9
Non-Hispanic black			
15–19	9.8[b]	9.0	9.3
15–17	9.5[a]	8.5	8.6[c]
18–19	10.1	9.6	10.0
Hispanic			
15–19	8.5	7.7	8.5
15–17	5.8	6.6	7.8[c]
18–19	9.9	8.7	9.2

[a]Significantly different from 1988 at p.10.
[b]Significantly different from 1988 at P.05.
[c]Significantly different from 1982 at p.10.
[d]Significantly different from 1982 at p.05.
[e]Significantly different from 1982 at p.01.
[f]Significantly different from 1995 at p.10.
[g]Significantly different from 1995 at p.01.
[h]The small subgroup consisting of non-Hispanic respondents of other races is excluded.

significant change during the early 1990s in the proportion of adolescent women who had ever had intercourse.

In contrast, over the entire period 1982–1995, the NSFG data show little change in the proportions of female adolescents who were currently sexually active, with about 40% of all 15–19-year-olds reporting that they had had intercourse in the most recent three months. The YRBS yields a similar result for female high school students: Although there appeared to be a small increase between 1990 and 1995 in the proportion currently sexually active (from 36% to 40%), it was not statistically significant.

The fact that both the YRBS and the NSFG show approximately the same proportion currently sexually active in 1995 (40%) may be interpreted as evidence of inconsistency between the two surveys: The YRBS represents a younger age-group (students in grades 9–12, who were approximately ages 14–18) than the NSFG (all 15–19-year-olds). Given this, we would expect the YRBS to show a lower proportion of adolescents sexually active than the NSFG.

Possible explanations for the higher than expected level of sexual activity in the YRBS include differences in how the questions on sexual behavior were asked. The question used in the YRBS is: "Have you ever had sexual intercourse?" There is no further elaboration. In all questions concerning sexual behavior in the 1995 NSFG, homosexual relationships, oral and anal sex, heavy petting or any other form of sexual activity that did not involve vaginal penetration were specifically excluded. In addition, the YRBS measured current sexual activity based on the question: "During the past three months, with how many people did you have sexual intercourse?" In contrast, the 1995 NSFG used a more specific and detailed approach, and asked a series of questions on the dates of periods in which intercourse did not take place.

Increases between 1982 and 1988 in the percentage of teenagers who had ever had sex, but stability in the percentage who had had sex in the past three months, reflect a reduction in the continuity of sexual relationships among those who had ever had intercourse. Thus, while the proportion of teenagers who had initiated intercourse increased from 1982 to 1988, the mean number of months in the past year during which sexually experienced adolescents had sex decreased. However, there was no change in the mean number of months sexually active between 1988 and 1995.

Patterns of change were generally similar across ages—that is, we saw similar trends among younger and older adolescents. However, in some cases, trends by income and race or ethnicity differed from the overall trend. In the subgroups that in the early 1980s were most likely ever to have had intercourse (lower income teenagers and black teenagers), the proportion who had done so remained more or less stable between 1982 and 1988. Conversely, levels of sexual experience rose during the 1980s among those who had lower rates at the beginning of the 1980s (such as higher income teenagers and non-Hispanic whites).

The net result of these trends is that formerly large differences among population subgroups appear to have narrowed. In the case of the proportion of teenagers who were currently sexually active (which hardly changed among all teenagers throughout the period), there were significant increases during the 1980s among teenagers with an income above 200% of poverty and among non-Hispanic white adolescents aged 18–19. During the period 1988–1995, younger Hispanic teenagers also seem to have experienced significant increases in both the proportion currently sexually active and the proportion who had ever had intercourse. The proportion of all Hispanic adolescents 15–19 who were currently sexually active also increased.

However, the number of respondents to the NSFG surveys limits the extent to which changes over time and differences between subgroups can be analyzed, especially for population subgroups. Even though these national surveys are very large, ranging from 8,000 to 10,800 respondents per survey, the limited number of teenagers in the sample provides little statistical power to identify even relatively sizable changes as being statistically significant. Plans for the next NSFG cycle (expected to be conducted in the year 2001) include oversampling adolescents to increase the number of female respondents aged 15–19 from 1,400 (in the 1995 survey) to 2,500. While this will not solve the limitations of small sample size for all population subgroups, it will greatly enhance efforts to identify differences between major subgroups and across time periods.

In most subgroups and for both measures, the level of sexual activity among adolescent women in 1995 is higher than it was in 1982, and in some cases it is significantly higher. By 1995, about half of all 15–19-year-old adolescent women had already had sexual intercourse, and 40% were currently sexually active. Overall, relatively few very young adolescents are sexually active: In 1995, about 14% of 20–24-year-olds reported that they had intercourse before age 15. Nevertheless, 81% had done so before their 20th birthday.[22]

A central aspect of long-term trends in sexual activity is that the increase occurred almost wholly among unmarried adolescents. In contrast, the proportion of adolescents who were either married or cohabiting showed little change in this same period, although cohabitation increased and marriage declined over the 13-year period. The proportion whose first experience of intercourse occurred within marriage or cohabitation actually declined slightly.[23] Throughout the period studied here, the large majority of adolescent women who were in a current sexual relationship were unmarried.

The tendency over recent decades for adolescent women to begin their sexual lives at ever earlier ages and before marriage or cohabitation—a trend observed in most developed countries—reflects greater tolerance of sexual activity among the unmarried and the delinking of sex and marriage. The proportion of all never-married adult U.S. women who had ever had intercourse also increased over the period 1982–1995. For example, among 20–24-year-olds who had never legally married, the proportion who were currently sexually active increased from 54% in 1982 to 58% in 1988 and to 62% in 1995.[24]

However, social and political responses to this general societal trend show wide variation within the United States and reflect a range of values concerning sexual activity among adolescents, especially the timing of initiation of sexual intercourse. Some are concerned about the urgent need to minimize the potential for negative consequences, such as by providing comprehensive sexuality education and contraceptive and STD education and services. But while educating adolescents to make informed and responsible decisions about sex has long been a common goal of sexuality education, more attention has recently been focused on abstinence-only education and on programs aimed at convincing young people not to have sex, providing social support to those who abstain and taking some direct policy actions, such as tightening enforcement of statutory rape laws.[25]

It is not clear what effects such efforts will have. For example, will an increase or a decline follow the stabilization of sexual activity levels among adolescent women between 1990–1995? One factor suggesting that young women may experience a decline is the fact that a significant decline has occurred in the proportion of adolescent men who have ever had intercourse.[26] On the other hand, a sharp decrease seen in the YRBS between 1995 and 1997 in the proportion of female high school students who had ever had intercourse (from 52% to 48%) was not statistically significant. The large size of this decrease over such a short time period suggests that measurement or sample fluctuations may account for at least some of the change. Only further analyses of data that will be collected over the next few years will indicate whether this change was a short-term fluctuation or the beginning of a downward trend.

Should a decrease occur, and if it is combined with vigorous efforts to expand information, education and health services, for both pregnancy prevention and protection against STDs, some negative consequences will be ameliorated and the drop in teenage pregnancy that has been recently observed is likely to continue, and may proceed at a more rapid pace.[27] However, the limitations of available data on adolescent sexual behavior must be borne in mind, and efforts are needed to achieve more comprehensive and more accurate measurement of sexual behavior.

Our findings suggest that trends in levels of sexual activity among American adolescents must be viewed from a longer term perspective. Focusing on short–run fluctuations may lead to incorrect conclusions. Only continued monitoring of change over the next years will tell us whether the patterns observed during 1988–1995 signify a new stability, a temporary leveling off in a generally upward trend in levels of adolescent sexual activity or the precursor of a decline. Nevertheless, the sustained level of initiation of sexual activity during adolescence over the past decade and one-half is by now a recognized pattern of behavior, and is an important characteristic of the transition to adulthood in the United States.

References

1. Zelnik M and Kantner JF, Sexual activity, contraceptive use and pregnancy among metropolitan-area teenagers: 1971–1979, *Family Planning Perspectives*, 1980, 12(5):230–237.

2. Hofferth SL, Kahn JR and Baldwin W, Premarital sexual activity among U.S. teenage women over the past three decades, *Family Planning Perspectives*, 1987, 19(2):46–53.

3. Ibid.

4. Forrest JD and Singh S, The sexual and reproductive behavior of American women, 1982–1988, *Family Planning Perspectives*, 1990, 22(5):206–214.

5. Driscoll AK, Moore KA and Lindberg LD, *A Statistical Portrait of Adolescent Sex, Contraception and Childbearing*, report prepared for the National Campaign to Prevent Teen Pregnancy, Washington, DC, Feb. 1998; Ehrhardt AA, Editorial: our view of adolescent sexuality—a focus on risk behavior without the developmental context, *American Journal of Public Health*, 1996, 86(11):1523–1524; The Alan Guttmacher Institute (AGI), *Sex and America's Teenagers*, New York: AGI, 1994; Centers for Disease Control and Prevention (CDC), Premarital sexual experience among adolescent women, United States, 1970–1988, *Morbidity and Mortality Weekly Report*, 1991, 39(51 & 52):929–932; and AGI, *Teenage Pregnancy: The Problem That Hasn't Gone Away*, New York: AGI, 1981.

6. Jones EF et al., *Teenage Pregnancy in Industrialized Countries*, New Haven, CT: Yale University Press, 1986.

7. Kirby D, *No Easy Answers: Research Findings on Programs to Reduce Teen Pregnancy*, Washington, DC: National Campaign to Prevent Teen Pregnancy, 1997; and Frost JJ and Forrest JD, Understanding the impact of effective teenage pregnancy prevention programs, *Family Planning Perspectives*, 1995, 27(5):188–195.

8. Donovan P, School-based sexuality education: the issues and challenges, *Family Planning Perspectives*, 1998, 30(4):188–193; and Donovan P, The 'illegitimacy bonus' and state efforts to reduce out-of-wedlock births, *Family Planning Perspectives*, 1999, 31(2):94–97.

9. AGI, 1994, op. cit. (see reference 5).

10. Kost K and Forrest JD, American women's sexual behavior and exposure to risk of sexually transmitted diseases, *Family Planning Perspectives*, 1992, 24(6):244–254.

11. Michael RT et al., Private sexual behavior, public opinion and public health policy related to sexually transmitted diseases: a U.S.-British comparison, *American Journal of Public Health*, 1998, 88(5):749–754; and Schuster MA, Bell RM and Kanouse DE, The sexual practices of adolescent virgins: genital sexual activities of high school students who have never had vaginal intercourse, *American Journal of Public Health*, 1996, 86(11):1570–1576.

12. Abma JA et al., Fertility, family planning, and women's health: new data from the 1995 National Survey of Family Growth, *Vital and Health Statistics*, Series 23, No. 19, 1997, Table 19, p. 30, and Table 24, p. 35.

13. Bumpass LL, Sweet JA and Cherlin A, The role of cohabitation in declining rates of marriage, *Journal of Marriage and the Family*, 1991, 53(4):913–927.

14. National Center for Health Statistics (NCHS), National Survey of Family Growth, Cycle III: tape contents manual, mimeo report, Hyattsville, MD: NCHS, undated; NCHS, *Public Use Data Tape Documentation: National Survey of Family Growth, Cycle IV*, 1988, Hyattsville, MD: NCHS, 1990; and Potter FJ et al. Sample design, sampling weights, imputation and variance estimation in the 1995 NSFG, *Vital and Health Statistics*, Series 2, No. 124, 1998.

15. Smith TW, A methodological review of sexual behavior questions on the 1988 and 1989 GSS, *GSS Methodological Report*, Chicago: National Opinion Research Center, 1988, No. 65.

16. Donovan P, 1998, op. cit. (see reference 8); and Mayer R, Trends in opposition to comprehensive sexuality education in public schools in the United States, *SIECUS Report*, 1996–1997, 25(6):20.

17. AGI, 1994, op. cit. (see reference 5), p. 24; and special tabulations of the 1982 and 1995 NSFG surveys.

18. Kost K and Forrest JD, American women's sexual behavior and exposure to the risk of sexually transmitted diseases, *Family Planning Perspectives*, 1992, 24(6):244–254; and American Social Health Association (ASHA), Sexually transmitted diseases in America: how many cases and at what cost? report prepared for the Henry J. Kaiser Family Foundation, Research Triangle Park, NC: ASHA, Dec. 1998.

19. Henshaw SK and Kost K, Abortion patients in 1994–1995: characteristics and contraceptive use, *Family Planning Perspectives*, 1996, 28(4):140–147 & 158; and Department of Health and Human Services, *Report to Congress on Out-of-Wedlock Childbearing*, Washington, D.C.: U.S. Government Printing Office, 1995.

20. Saul R, Teen pregnancy: progress meets politics, *The Guttmacher Report on Public Policy*, 1999, 2(3):6–9.

21. Warren CW et al., Sexual behavior among U.S. high school students, 1990–1995, *Family Planning Perspectives*, 1998, 30(4):171–172 & 200; and CDC, Trends in sexual risk behaviors among high school students, United States, 1991–1997, *Morbidity and Mortality Weekly Report*, 1998, 47(36):749–752.

22. AGI, *Into a New World: Young Women's Sexual and Reproductive Lives*, New York: AGI, 1998, Appendix Table 3; and tabulations of 1995 NSFG data file.

23. Abma JA et al., 1997, op. cit. (see reference 12), Table 25, p. 36.

24. Forrest JD and Singh S, The sexual and reproductive behavior of American women, 1982–1988, *Family Planning Perspectives*, 1990, 22(5):206–214, Table 3; and tabulations of 1995 NSFG data file.

25. Donovan P, 1998, op. cit. (see reference 8).

26. Sonenstein FL et al., Changes in sexual behavior and condom use among teenaged men: 1988 to 1995, *American Journal of Public Health*, 1998, 88(6):956–959; and Ku L et al., Understanding changes in sexual activity among young metropolitan men: 1979–1995, *Family Planning Perspectives*, 1998, 30(6):256–262.

27. Henshaw SK, Unintended pregnancy in the United States, *Family Planning Perspectives*, 1998, 30(1):24–29 & 46.

Reflections on Two Decades of Research on Teen Sexual Behavior and Pregnancy

ABSTRACT: *During the past 20 years, both researchers and program developers made great progress in their efforts to reduce adolescent unprotected sex and prevent teen pregnancy. Research studies are now more likely to employ experimental designs with random assignment, to have large sample sizes with adequate statistical power, to measure actual sexual and contraceptive behaviors, to measure longer-term effects, to employ proper statistical methods, and to report results in an unbiased manner. As a result of this body of research, large advances have occurred in our understanding of: 1) the incidence of teen pregnancy and its consequences; 2) the effects of improving adolescent knowledge, increasing access to contraception, and improving parent/child communication; and 3) the characteristics of effective programs. The on-going evaluation of sex and HIV education programs coupled with creativity and perseverance on the part of program developers led to two groups of effective programs—sex and HIV education programs that reduce sexual risk-taking behavior, and youth development programs that reduce teen-age pregnancy and childbearing.* (J Sch Health, 1999;69(3):89–94)

Douglas Kirby

Exactly 20 years ago, I began doing research on sex education programs designed to reduce unprotected sex and teen pregnancy. At that time there was increased national concern about teen-age pregnancy; a

Douglas Kirby, PhD, ETR Associates, P.O. 1830, Santa Cruz, CA 95061-1830. Douglas Kirby received the 1998 Distinguished Scientist Award from the Research Council of the American School Health Association. This paper summarizes the presentation that followed his acceptance of that award.

belief that sex education programs could provide American youth with needed information about sexual behavior, contraception, and pregnancy; and a desire to find effective sex education programs and demonstrate their effectiveness through research. At that time HIV/AIDS was not known, and not part of our concerns, but there was concern about STD more generally. During these past 20 years, our field has come a long way, both in the development and use of research methods and in its understanding of adolescent sexual behavior, teen pregnancy, and programs that

From the *Journal of School Health*, March 1999, pp. 89-94. © 1999 by the American School Health Association. Reprinted by permission.

affect them. This paper highlights some of those advances.

ADVANCES IN RESEARCH METHODS

Our field has made tremendous advances in research methods—both in its understanding of how to conduct rigorous research and in its actual use of more rigorous research methods. There are at least five different areas in which major improvements have taken place.

Measurement of Sexual Behavior

Twenty years ago, only a few studies measured the impact of sex education programs, and of those studies which measured impact, still fewer measured impact upon the very behavior that the programs were designed to change, namely the sexual and contraceptive behaviors of youth. It was even less common to ask questions about sexual behavior in school settings, and still less common to do so with federal funds. When the Center for Health Promotion and Education (the forerunner of the Division of Adolescent and School Health) at the Centers for Disease Control (CDC) funded a group of us to measure the impact of sex education programs on student sexual attitudes and behavior, many people clearly stated that it simply could not be done.

And indeed, it almost could not. People opposed to using taxpayer dollars in this manner obtained copies of our proposed questionnaires, selected questions about attitudes and behavior that they felt were particularly egregious, and sent them with a highly critical cover letter to every Congress person in Washington. Shortly thereafter, I received a concerned call that the Center had received a Congressional inquiry—this seemed unprecedented for that Center, and clearly of grave concern. And then there was a second inquiry, and then more, and then many, many more. Fortunately, the Center, and CDC more generally, remained committed to the study and resisted the pressure to terminate the study or to abstain from measuring sexual behavior.

Today, questions about adolescent sexual behavior are routinely asked in surveys, even in school settings. Questions are commonly asked about whether the students have ever had sex, their frequency of sexual activity, their number of sexual partners, their use of condoms, their use of other forms of contraception, whether they have ever been pregnant and whether they have ever had an STD.[1] Some more recent studies have even refined these questions to assess the behaviors that are most highly related to pregnancy, HIV, and STD (ie, frequency of sex without any kind of contraception, frequency of sex without condoms, and number of sexual partners without condoms). Indeed, some of these questions about sexual and contraceptive behavior are asked not only of high school students, but of middle school students. Studies asking these questions now provide reasonably accurate estimates of student sexual and contraceptive behavior in many individual schools, communities, states, and even the entire United States. Studies employing these questions have also given us a better understanding of the behavioral impact of different programs.

This very positive picture should, however, be balanced by the recognition of efforts to thwart and limit survey research. For example, there are efforts to make it more difficult to ask students any personal questions and it is difficult, if not impossible, in most schools to ask questions about sexual orientation, even though such questions could help us better understand how to meet the needs of some youth at higher risk of HIV.

Sample Sizes and Calculations of Statistical Power

Twenty years ago studies typically had small sample sizes. For example, the seminal work of Schinke certainly shaped subsequent sex education programs, but his first three studies included samples of only 30, 36 and 53 students.[2,3] Sample sizes of a few hundred were considered quite large.

And 20 years ago, few researchers in our field calculated statistical power (ie, the sample size needed to have a reasonable chance of finding a certain difference in our results to be statistically significant). Sometime during the past 20 years, most researchers in our field discovered formulas to calculate statistical power. Frankly, when I first encountered them, I was less than enthusiastic; I didn't fully understand or trust them, and they represented additional work to be completed during proposal writing time. Also, I never liked what they told me!

Fortunately, most researchers realized that what they were telling us was very important.

Given reasonable assumptions about the initiation of sex in many communities or the use of condoms or contraceptives, completed sample sizes of 500 to 2,000 youth are often needed. And given the sample losses due to obtaining parental consent, student absenteeism, inability to follow up all students, and other factors, studies often need to start with 1,000 to 4,000 students. Even larger samples are needed if schools, rather than individual youth, are assigned to treatment and control groups.

Though people have often claimed that it is either impossible or infeasible to conduct such large studies, during the past 5 to 10 years, several studies with completed sample sizes greater than 2,000 have been completed (eg, the studies of Healthy and Alive, the McMaster Teen Program, Project Action, Safer Choices, the Self Center, Skills for Healthy Relationships, and the Summer Training and Education Program).[4-9] The study of Postponing Sexual Involvement in California even had a completed sample size of more than 7,500.[10]

Unfortunately, these same power calculations have informed us that many studies have been underpowered. That is, many studies did not have a sufficiently large sample size to find program effects to be statistically significant when in fact they were programmatically important. Thus, there are undoubtedly some programs which had important effects upon the behavior of youth, but these programs were incorrectly found to be ineffective when the studies employed sample sizes that were too small to find these effects to be significant.

Use of Experimental Designs with Random Assignment

Twenty years ago, few studies, especially those in schools, used experimental designs with random assignment.[11] People often believed that it was both ethically improper and administratively infeasible to randomly assign individual youth, classrooms of youth, or entire schools to treatment and control groups.

Subsequently, our field learned two things that moderated this view. First, it realized that many "standard" programs did not have a marked impact upon behavior. Thus, researchers became more comfortable comparing a new intervention with the standard intervention instead of comparing a new intervention with nothing at all. This made random assignment less ethically challenging and more administratively feasible.

Second, our field became more conscious of how subtle and insidious self-selection effects can be. For example, one study of school-based clinics examined the pregnancy rates of students who were sexually active and had used the clinic to obtain contraception with students who were sexually active and had never used the clinic to obtain contraception. Those students who had used the clinic for contraception were more likely to report having been pregnant. Fortunately, the study survey had asked several questions about the timing of the pregnancy, and analyses revealed that students had become pregnant before using the clinic, and then after their pregnancy, they came to the clinic for contraception to prevent subsequent pregnancies. Thus, there existed a powerful self-selection effect that was not recognized prior to the study.[12] Other self-selection effects or biases often exist whenever random assignment is not employed.

Now, 20 years later, there is still controversy and opposition to random assignment, but this opposition has diminished, and it has been well demonstrated that schools are willing to participate in studies in which individual students, classrooms of students, or entire schools are randomly assigned to receive either their existing intervention or a new, hopefully more effective, intervention. Accordingly, there are an increasing number of studies that have employed random assignment (eg, studies of Becoming a Responsible Teen, Be Proud–Be Responsible, ENABL, Healthy and Alive, McMaster Teen Program, Safer Choices, SNAPP, Summer Training and Education Program, the Teen Incentives Program, Teen Talk and the Youth AIDS Prevention Project).[4,5,7,8,13-19]

Measurement of Long-Term Effects

Twenty years ago most studies measured only the short-term effects of programs. Some studies used a simple pretest/posttest design with the posttest data collected immediately after the end of the program. A few studies measured three-month or six-month data. Only rarely did studies track youth from one school year to the next.

Subsequently, three changes increased our field's motivation and ability to track youth for longer periods of time. First, researchers more fully recognized the greater importance of long-term effects versus short-term effects. If a program has an impact on adolescent behavior for only a few weeks, then that program will not have much of an impact on the many adolescent years prior to marriage. Second, researchers more fully realized that some effects cannot be measured in the short term. For example, if a program is designed to delay the initiation of sex, then youth must be tracked for many months (eg, 12 to 24 months) to determine whether fewer youth in the intervention group initiate sex than in the comparison group. After only a few months, few youth in the control group will have initiated sex and it is impossible for the intervention group to do significantly better. Third, researchers developed a variety of techniques that enabled them to track large percentages of youth for longer periods of time.

Now, studies measure much longer effects. For example, at least four studies have tracked youth for one year,[2,13,14,19] three studies have tracked youth for about 18 months,[15,16,20] three studies for about two years,[8,21,22] and another three studies for about three to four years.[4,7,23]

Use of Proper Statistical Techniques

Twenty years ago researchers in our field used simpler and more basic statistical tests. Sometimes this was justified and proper. However, often data violated important assumptions required by these statistical tests, and the tests were not fully valid.

Today, our strategies for analyzing data are far more sophisticated and better match the characteristics of the data. Although there have been many improvements, one seems particularly important to me—the proper adjustment for the clustering of study participants.

Imagine two situations. In the first, 2,000 students are individually randomly assigned to treatment and control groups. We can be confident that the two groups will be quite similar. In the second, an entire mainstream school with 1,000 students and an entire alternative school with 1,000 higher risk students are randomly assigned to treatment and control groups—that is, the schools, not the individuals within the schools are randomly assigned. In this second situation, we can be confident that the two groups of students will not be quite similar, because "clusters" of 1,000 students, not individual students, were randomly assigned, and one cluster had more higher risk students.

"Multilevel" statistics properly adjust for this clustering. My own experience with these statistics indicates that sometimes adjusting for the clustering makes a small difference, and other times it makes a very large difference. However, it almost always make a difference. Past studies that assigned clusters of students rather than individual students should have used multi-level statistics, but typically did not. Thus, their analyses (both their tests of significance and their estimates of other parameters) are biased by unknown amounts, and some of their conclusions are undoubtedly incorrect.

Recently, studies have begun to use multi-level statistics or to adjust for clustering in other ways.[4,24]

Proper Reporting of Results

Twenty years ago, researchers more often measured the impact of a program on numerous outcomes, and then somewhat selectively reported those findings that were positive. Such reporting helped build the case that a program was effective. But, of course, such reporting was also biased. Sometimes this was more blatant; sometimes it was more subtle. For example, if there were multiple ways of recoding variables or analyzing the data, researchers would present the results that were most positive, believing that these results properly captured the "true" impact of the program.

Today, this still happens, but less commonly. More commonly, before conducting the analyses, researchers identify both the primary hypotheses to be tested and the precise procedures to test these hypotheses, and then they report those findings regardless of whether they are positive. This, of course, is the proper way to evaluate programs and it builds our knowledge about the effectiveness of programs.

ADVANCES IN UNDERSTANDING TEEN PREGNANCY AND SOLUTIONS

In addition to advances in research methods, our field has also made large advances in our understanding of the problem of teen pregnancy and programs to reduce it. Twenty years ago, there were five commonly mentioned pillars to our teen pregnancy prevention movement. These were reflected in assumptions and even explicit statements commonly made in our field.

1. Teen pregnancy rates in the United States are terribly high; there is an epidemic of teen pregnancy in the United States. Indeed, data on teen pregnancy in the United States indicate that teen pregnancy is a serious and common phenomenon: about 10% of 15-19-year-old females become pregnant each year;[25] more than 40% become pregnant before they turn 20[26]; and almost 890,000 teens become pregnant each year.[25] As a result of this high pregnancy rate, the teen birth rate is about 5.3% and is much higher than in other Western industrialized countries—for instance, 0.6% in the Netherlands, 0.9% in Denmark, 1.3% in Sweden, 2.3% in Austria, and 3.2% in Great Britain.[27,28] All of this was and remains true.

However, our view is now balanced by some other statistics. In particular, when the US pregnancy rates or birth rates are adjusted for poverty and ethnicity, they are somewhat higher, but not so dramatically higher than the statistics for other English speaking countries. For example, the birth rate for white 15-19-year-old females in the U.S. is 3.6%, while the birth rate for 15-19-year-old teens in England is 2.9%,[28] 2.5% in Canada, and 3.4% in New Zealand?[29]

Furthermore, as several people have recognized, there never was an "epidemic" of teen pregnancy. The word, epidemic, suggests something that is rapidly increasing. In fact, the teen pregnancy rate was much lower in the 1970s, 1980s and 1990s, than it was in the 1950s. It did increase somewhat during the 1980s, but it has now decreased for the last six years.

What did increase rapidly were the pregnancy and birth rates for unmarried teens. And this was the cause of legitimate concern.

2. Adolescent childbearing produces a huge cost to the teen-ager and to our society more generally. Twenty years ago, some studies of the impact of teen pregnancy compared teens who gave birth with those who did not. Not surprisingly, they found large differences. A second wave of studies measured and statistically controlled background characteristics that preceded the pregnancy and were not caused by the pregnancy (eg, poverty, ethnicity, and other family characteristics). These studies found that the differences between teens who gave birth and those who did not were considerably smaller than previously es-

timated, but that substantial differences still remained, suggesting that these differences were caused by early childbearing.

A third wave of studies used innovative methods to further control for preexisting differences that could not be measured and statistically controlled. For example, these studies examined sisters (who shared many family characteristics), teens who had a miscarriage with teens who gave birth, and teens who had twins with teens who had only one child. Some of these studies suggested that teen childbearing had remarkably little long-term impact on either the teen mothers or fathers.[30]

The most recent reviews of these innovative studies indicate that their methodological limitations would tend to obscure the impact of childbearing upon teens.[31] Currently, the general consensus is that there are some long-term costs of teen childbearing to the mother, especially to the infant, and also to society, but that these costs are not nearly as great as we believed they were 20 years ago.

3. Increasing knowledge about sex, contraception, and sexuality more generally will reduce teen sexual risk-taking behavior and reduce teen pregnancy rates. Twenty years ago, many people in our field recognized that youth believed in various myths (eg, you won't get pregnant the first time you have sex, you won't get pregnant if you have sex standing up; it won't happen to me). Program developers believed that if they corrected these myths and provided accurate information about the probability of pregnancy and STD and methods of protecting against pregnancy and STD, then youth would use that information, act more rationally, and refrain from having as much unprotected sex. In short, some people believed that increasing knowledge would have an impact on behavior although few program developers perceived increasing knowledge as the panacea for teen pregnancy.

Twenty years of research has informed the field that knowledge level is only weakly related to behavior,[32] and that programs that focus on knowledge acquisition do increase student knowledge, but they do not significantly change sexual or contraceptive behavior.[10]

This does not mean that ignorance is the answer—ignorance is not the answer, and knowledge does help build the foundation for behavioral change. However, increasing knowledge, alone, is typically insufficient to change behavior markedly.

4. Increasing access to contraception will increase teen use of contraception and reduce teen pregnancy rates. Twenty years ago, many people believed that if access to contraception was improved, then more sexually active teens would use contraception. Thus, for example, many people supported school-based clinics which provided more convenient access to contraceptives.

Most studies that have been conducted during the past 20 years have indicated that improving access to contraception did not significantly increase contraceptive use or decrease teen pregnancy.[10] For example, even when schools opened clinics that provided contraceptives, employed clinic staff who could relate to youth and were trained in adolescent medicine, made contraceptives available free of charge, and offered a variety of health services so that contraceptive visits would be confidential, students did obtain a wide range of health services, significant numbers of sexually active youth did obtain contraceptives from the clinics, and a few students who would not have obtained contraceptives anyway probably did so through the clinic, but school-wide rates of contraceptive use typically did not increase and pregnancy or childbearing rates did not decrease.[33,34] When community clinics improved their programs to make them more adolescent friendly, the percentage of sexually active youth in communities near those clinics who used contraceptives did not increase?[35]

On the other hand, more comprehensive multi-component interventions that included the provision of contraception did appear to increase contraceptive use. For example, after the Self Center in Baltimore provided educational, counseling, and reproductive health services in the clinic and educational and counseling services in two schools, contraceptive use appeared to increase.[9] Similarly, a media campaign in Portland, Ore., in combination with improved access to condom and instructional components led to an increase in condom use with casual partners.[6] Thus, simply improving access to contraception has not appeared to markedly increase contraceptive use, but improving access to contraception and doing other things to motivate teens to use contraception may lead to greater contraceptive use.

5. Increasing parent-child communication about sexuality will reduce teen sexual risk-taking behavior. Twenty years ago people believed that if parents would communicate more with their own children about sexuality—if they would convey accurate information, answer their children's questions, and express their own beliefs and values—then adolescents would act in a manner more consistent with that knowledge and those values, and would either initiate sex later in life or use contraception more consistently if they had sex.

Reviews of numerous studies of the impact of parent-child communication about sexuality upon adolescent sexual behavior conclude that there is no simple relationship between such communication and adolescent sexual behavior. Some studies suggest there is no relationship; some studies suggest that greater communication is associated with more sexual risk-taking behavior (possibly because the parents anticipate that sexual behavior), and other studies indicate that greater communication is associated with less sexual risk-taking behavior.[36] It may be the case that greater communication has positive effects under some conditions, but not others, but even this is now being questioned. Although many adults—and also adolescents—believe that greater parent-child communication about sexuality is a good thing, in and of itself, simply increasing parent/child communication about sexuality probably does not have the marked behavioral impact that we once believed it had. Instead, other qualities of family interaction (eg, overall connectedness) may be far more important.[37]

NEW RESEARCH-BASED PILLARS FOR PREGNANCY PREVENTION

The past 20 years of research have not only clarified the five pillars our field held 20 years ago, that body of research has also created two new pillars which can be well substantiated by multiple research studies—sex and HIV education programs with specific characteristics can reduce sexual risk-taking behavior and some youth development programs can reduce teen pregnancy and childbearing.

Numerous studies reveal that there are two broad groups of antecedents of adolescent sexual risk-taking behavior that have the potential for being changed. The first group are the sexual antecedents (eg, sexual beliefs, attitudes, norms, skills, self-efficacy, and intentions). These can be addressed by sex and HIV education programs and other reproductive health programs. The second group are the nonsexual antecedents. At the individual level they include school performance, belief in the future, and general risk-taking behavior. At the family and community level, they include many manifestations of poverty, social disorganization, and connectedness. Although many people once believed that these antecedents were impervious to change with politically acceptable methods, we now know that they can be changed.

Sex and HIV Education Programs

Several studies have now demonstrated that sex and HIV education programs with specified characteristics can delay the initiation of sex, reduce the frequency of sex, or increase the use of condoms or other forms of contraception.[4,14,19,20,38] Thus, they have the potential for reducing unintended pregnancy and STD, including HIV. These programs may be especially effective with high-risk youth.

These effective curricula: 1) focused on reducing one or more sexual behaviors that lead to unintended pregnancy or HIV/STD infection; 2) were based upon theoretical approaches that have been demonstrated to be effective in influencing other health-related risky behaviors and specified the risk and protective factors to be modified by curriculum activities; 3) gave a clear message by continually reinforcing a clear stance on these behaviors; 4) provided basic, accurate information about the risks of unprotected intercourse and methods of avoiding unprotected intercourse; 5) included activities that address social pressures on sexual behaviors; 6) provided modeling and practice of communication, negotiation, and refusal skills; 7) employed a variety of teaching methods designed to involve the participants and have them personalize the information; 8) incorporated behavioral goals, teaching methods, and materials that were appropriate to the age, sexual experience, and culture of the students; 9) lasted a sufficient length of time to complete important activities adequately; and 10) selected teachers or peers who believed in the program they were implementing and then provided training for those individuals.

Effective Youth Development Programs

Some youth development programs that address nonsexual risk factors apparently can reduce actual rates of pregnancy and child-bearing. Independent studies of five different programs all indicate that their respective programs decreased pregnancy and childbearing: the Youth Incentive Entitlement Employment Program (YIEEP),[39] the Teen Outreach Program (TOP),[40] the American Youth and Conservation Corps,[41] the Seattle Social Development Program,[42] and the Quantum Opportunities Program.[43] While each of these studies has its own limitations, and while the relative strengths of these studies vary considerably, in combination they provide rather strong evidence that some youth development programs do reduce pregnancy and childbearing.

Because these programs are so different, and also because the ways in which they have an impact are not yet known, there is much to learn about these and other youth development programs. This represents one of many challenges for the next 20 years of research.

CONCLUSION

Conducting research during these past 20 years has not always been easy for researchers in this field. On the one hand, there have been all the challenges to overcome in conducting good research. Perhaps even more important, for many of us, at times, it has been depressing, frustrating, and even painful to believe in programs, to conduct impact evaluations of those programs, and then to report to friends and colleagues that these programs did not have the impact we originally believed they had.

However, all of us—both researchers and program developers—persevered. When we learned that our early approaches were not effective, we struggled and tried to develop more effective programs. When we learned that some of those programs were not effective, we struggled and again tried to design more effective programs. Most important, we ultimately succeeded. We now have at least two groups of programs that have reasonably good evidence that they reduce sexual risk-taking behavior, pregnancy, or childbearing. All of us should be incredibly proud of our efforts and our success.

Our efforts and our success will have an impact upon adolescents in this country. As more and more effective programs are implemented, youth will benefit. During each of the past six years, rates of teen childbearing have declined in this country. There is no question but these declines reflect, in part, broad forces in this country over which we have little control. However, it is also true that those declines may reflect, in part, the broader dissemination and implementation of more effective programs. If so, then this is a great accomplishment and is historic.

Furthermore, the impact of all of our programmatic and research efforts extend well beyond this country. Most of the good research on programs to reduce adolescent sexual risk-taking behavior is conducted in this country. Numerous people from around the world are reviewing what we have learned and are applying it in their own countries. There are more than 1 billion 10-19-year-old youth in the world. That number is growing every year, and the proportion of them that is engaging in unprotected sex is also growing. Thus, in the coming years, the research base that we create here will probably have an impact upon an increasing number of them. That is an awesome thought!

As I look back over the last 20 years, I reach at least three conclusions:

- Rarely is anything as simple as we initially perceive it to be, especially when it comes to adolescent sexual behavior.
- Research really can play a critical role in defining the problem and helping identify effective programs and approaches.
- Some programs actually do reduce adolescent sexual risk-taking behavior, pregnancy, and childbearing.

As we look ahead to the next 20 years, all of us—both researchers and program developers—should fully realize that we are building a foundation of knowledge that will affect future generations of youth, both in this country and throughout the world. We have come a long way in the past 20 years, and we still have an exciting path to follow.

References

1. Centers for Disease Control. Trends in sexual risk behaviors among high school students—United States, 1991–1997. *MMWR.* 1998;47(36):749–752.
2. Schinke S, Blythe B and Gilchrist L. Cognitive-behavioral prevention of adolescent pregnancy. *J Couns Psychol.* 1981;28:451–454.
3. Schinke SP, Blythe BJ, Gilchrist LD and Burt GA. Primary prevention of adolescent pregnancy. *Soc Work Groups.* 1981;4(1-2):121–135.
4. Coyle KK, Basen-Enquist KM, Kirby DB, et al. Short-term impact of a multi-component school-based HIV, other STD and pregnancy prevention program, in press.
5. Grossman JB, Sipe CL. *Summer Training and Education Program: Report on Long-Term Impacts.* Philadelphia, Pa: Public/Private Ventures; 1992.
6. Polen MR, Freeborn DK. *Outcome Evaluation of Project ACTION.* Portland, Ore: Kaiser Permanente Center for Health Research; 1995.
7. Thomas B, Mitchell A, Devlin M, Goldsmith C, Singer J, Watters D. Small group sex education at school: the McMaster teen program. In: Miller B, Card J, Paikoff R, Peterson J, eds. *Preventing Adolescent Pregnancy.* Newbury Park, Calif: Sage Publications; 1992.
8. Warren WK, King AJC. *Development and Evaluation of an AIDS/STD/Sexuality Program for Grade 9 Students.* Kingston, Ontario: Social Program Evaluation Group; 1994.
9. Zabin LS, Hirsh MB, Smith EA, Streett R, Hardy JB. Evaluation of a pregnancy prevention program for urban teenagers. *Fam Plann Perspect.* 1986;18(3):119–126.
10. Kirby D. *No Easy Answers: Research Findings on Programs to Reduce Teen Pregnancy.* Washington, DC: National Campaign to Prevent Teen Pregnancy; 1997.
11. Kirby D. *Sexuality Education: An Evaluation of Programs and Their Effects.* Santa Cruz, Calif: Network Publications; 1984.
12. Kirby D, Waszak C, Ziegler J. *An Assessment of Six School-based Clinics: Services, Impact and Potential.* Washington, DC: Center for Population Options; 1989.
13. Eisen M, Zellman GL. A health beliefs field experiment: Teen talk. In Miller BC, Card JJ, Paikoff RL and Peterson JL, eds. *Preventing Adolescent Pregnancy.* Newbury Park, Calif: Sage Publications; 1992.
14. Jemmott JB, Jemmott LS, Fong GT. Abstinence and safer sex: a randomized trial of HIV sexual risk-reduction interventions for young African-American adolescents. *JAMA.* 1998;279(19):1529–1536.
15. Kirby D, Korpi M, Adivi C, Weissman J. An impact evaluation of SNAPP, a pregnancy- and AIDS-prevention middle school curriculum. *AIDS Prev Educ.* 1997;9;suppl A:44–67.
16. Kirby D, Korpi M, Barth RP, Cagampang HH. The impact of the "Postponing Sexual Involvement: curriculum among youths in California. *Fam Plann Perspect.* 1997;29(3):100–108.
17. Levy SR, Perhats C, Weeks K, Handler A, Zhu C, Flay BR. Impact of a school-based AIDS prevention program on risk and protective behavior for newly sexually active students. *J Sch Health.* 1995;65(4):145–151, 1995.
18. Smith MAB. Teen incentives program: evaluation of a health promotion model for adolescent pregnancy prevention. *J Health Educ.* 1994;25(1):24–29.
19. St. Lawrence JS, Jefferson KW, Alleyne E, Brasfield TL. Comparison of education versus behavioral skills training interventions in lowering sexual HIV risk behavior of substance dependent adolescents. *J Consult Clin Psychol.* 1995;63(2):221–237.
20. Kirby D, Barth R, Leland N, Fetro J. Reducing the Risk: A new curriculum to prevent sexual risk-taking. *Fam Plann Perspect.* 1991;23(6):253–263.
21. Nicholson HJ, Postrado LT. *Girls Incorporated Preventing Adolescent Pregnancy: A Program Development and Research Project.* New York, NY: Girls Inc; 1991.
22. St. Pierre TL, Mark MM, Kaltreider DL, Aikin KJ. A 27-month evaluation of a sexual activity prevention program in Boys and Girls Clubs across the nation. *Family Rel.* 1995;44:69–77.
23. Howard M. Delaying the start of intercourse among adolescents. *Adolescent Medicine: State of the Art Reviews.* Philadelphia, Pa: Hanley & Belfus; 1992.
24. Kirby D, Brener ND, Brown NL, Peterfreund N, Hillard P, Harrist R. The Seattle school condom availability program: subsequent changes in sexual behavior and condom use. *Am J Public Health.* in press.
25. Henshaw SK. *US Teenage Pregnancy Statistics.* New York, NY: Alan Guttmacher Institute; 1998.

26. *Whatever Happened to Childhood? The Problem of Teen Pregnancy in the United States.* Washington, DC: National Campaign to Prevent Teen Pregnancy; 1997.

27. Moore KA, Sugland BW, Blumenthal C, Glei D, Snyder N. *Adolescent Pregnancy Prevention Programs: Interventions and Evaluations.* Washington, DC: Child Trends, Inc; 1995.

28. Ventura SF, Anderson RN, Martin JA, Smith BL. *Births and Deaths: Preliminary Data for 1997.* National Vital Statistics Reports, DHHS; October 1998.

29. New Zealand. *Demographic Trends 97.* 1998.

30. Maynard RA. *Kids Having Kids: A Robin Hood Foundation Special Report on the Costs of Adolescent Childbearing.* New York, NY: The Robin Hood Foundation; 1996.

31. Hoffman S. Teenage childbearing is not so bad after all . . . or is it: a review of the new literature. *Fam Plann Perspect.* 1998;30(5):236–239, 243.

32. Whitley BE, Schofield JW. A meta-analysis of research on adolescent contraceptive use. *Popular Environment.* 1986;173–203.

33. Kirby D, Waszak C, Ziegler J. Six school-based clinics: their reproductive health services and impact on sexual behavior. *Fam Plann Perspect.* 1991;23:6–16.

34. Kisker EE, Brown RS, Hill J. *Health Caring: Outcomes of the Robert Wood Johnson Foundation's School-based Adolescent Health Care Program.* Princeton, NJ: Robert Wood Johnson Foundation; 1994.

35. Hughes ME, Furstenberg FF Jr, Teitler JO. The impact of an increase in family planning services on the teenage population of Philadelphia. *Fam Plann Perspect.* 1995;27(2):60–65, 78.

36. Miller BC. *Families Matter: A Research Synthesis of Family Influences on Adolescent Pregnancy.* Washington, DC: National Campaign to Prevent Teen Pregnancy; 1998.

37. Resnick MD, Bearman PS, Blum RW, et al. Protecting adolescents from harm: findings from the National Longitudinal Study on Adolescent Health. *JAMA.* 1997;278(10):823–832.

38. Main DS, Iverson DC, McGloin J, et al. Preventing HIV infection among adolescents: evaluation of a school-based education program. *Prev Med.* 1994;23:409–417.

39. Olsen RJ, Farkas G. The effects of economic opportunity and family background on adolescent cohabitation and childbearing among low-income blacks. *J Labor Econ.* 1990;8:341–362.

40. Allen JP, Philliber S, Herrling S, Kuperminc GP. Preventing teen pregnancy and academic failure: experimental evaluation of a developmentally-based approach. *Child Dev.* 1997;64(4):729–742.

41. Jastrzab J, Masker J, Blomquist J, Orr L. *Evaluation of National and Community Service Programs: Impacts of Service: Final Report on the Evaluation of American Conservation and Youth Service Corps.* Cambridge, Mass: Abt Associates Inc; 1996.

42. Catalano RF, Hawkins JD, Kosterman R, Abbott RD, Hill KG. Long-term effects of the Seattle social development project: Implications for theory and practice, meeting of the Society for Research on Adolescence, San Diego Calif: February 27, 1998.

43. Hahn A, Leavitt T, Aaron P. *Evaluation of the Quantum Opportunities Program (QOP): DM the Program Work?* Waltham, Mass: Center for Human Resources, Brandeis University; 1994.

KEY SKILL FOR TEEN PARENTS:
Having Realistic Expectations

Today's parenting programs teach teen-age mothers how to care for their children and themselves.

Bridget Murray
Monitor staff

Becky Piatt is convinced she's become a better mother to her son, Christopher, ever since she took a parenting class at Kishwaukee College in rural Illinois near DeKalb.

Kishwaukee's parenting, or "family enrichment," program is geared for teen-age mothers like Piatt, who gave birth to Christopher when she was 17. She entered the program at age 19 when Christopher's bad behavior started to frustrate her.

"It taught me to turn something negative into something positive," said Piatt of the program. Instead of scolding Christopher and telling him to stop riding his bike on the street, she now uses a problem-solving approach and suggests that he ride it on the sidewalk.

Psychologist Karen Stoiber, PhD, a professor at the University of Wisconsin–Milwaukee who worked with teens at Kishwaukee, says such parenting programs strive to establish positive relations between mothers and children and to promote financial independence for mothers.

In accordance with goal two of the National Education Goals 2000 legislation, which calls for more emphasis on high school completion, teen-parenting programs enable young mothers to finish school. The programs first caught on in the 1980s when pregnancy rates began to escalate, and psychologists have been heavily involved with them from the outset.

Teen-pregnancy rates rose 23 percent between 1972 and 1990, and as rates continue to climb and Congress threatens to reduce welfare support for single mothers, programs that move teen moms toward independence are becoming a necessity, experts say.

Counseling and school psychologists often coordinate and run the programs, while others act as consultants. Stoiber sees consulting with teen programs as a new frontier for school psychologists, in particular.

"There's room for school psychologists to become more aware of the issues pregnant and parenting teens face—to help keep them in school and respond to their mental health needs," Stoiber said.

Improving Lives

A range of studies show that teen-parenting programs work. Psychologist Alice Honig, PhD, of Syracuse University found that a parenting program for inner-city teens in Syracuse lowers rates of child abuse and neglect from 40 percent to between 15 percent and 20 percent.

The program, funded by New York State and run by Syracuse's Consortium for Children's Services, sends child development specialists to the homes of first-time teen mothers on a weekly basis for 18 to 24 months. Home visitors often become surrogate mothers to the teens, who tend to live

Photo by Lloyd Wolf

mutual trust and appreciation, it starts off wrong and stays that way.

"We teach moms that they can have a happy relationship with their child and a good life for their child by understanding kids' needs and what to expect," said Sheridan.

In parenting groups Stoiber runs, she teaches that certain kinds of play, like shaking a rattle, and certain kinds of teaching, such as toilet training, are appropriate at specific developmental levels. At Kishwaukee, Stoiber tapped into young mothers' nurturing feelings by having them and their children wrap baby dolls in blankets and stick band-aids on them. To prevent parents from yelling and striking their children, she showed videos that demonstrate the difference between harsh and firm parenting.

Gearing Teens for Work

Teens need career strategies too. Hence, many programs are multifaceted, like the Lady Pitts school-age parenting program, a school for pregnant and parenting teens that Stoiber now works with in Milwaukee. Lady Pitts is geared towards predominantly African-American inner-city 12- to 18-year-olds who are either pregnant or have children and are at risk of dropping out of school.

The program aims to keep teen mothers in school by providing them with high school courses and job counseling. Like Kishwaukee, it provides daycare for babies.

The programs teach teen mothers to put their job expectations in perspective, said Stoiber. Some mothers have spotty school attendance records and low grade point averages, but still think they can become physicians. Programs move them toward goals they can realistically achieve.

When financial independence became the primary goal for a young mother Stoiber worked with at Kishwaukee, she decided to pursue a two-year associate's degree and later a bachelor's degree in nursing.

"If I quit school now, I couldn't support my son and myself," the mother told Stoiber. "I just figure if I

alone, draw welfare and relate poorly to their own families, said Honig.

Honig has also been studying outcomes of a teen-parenting program at Syracuse University that she and psychologist J. Ronald Lally, PhD, directed in the 1970s. Called the Family Development Research Program, the project served teen mothers who dropped out of school. Mothers received parenting and nutrition training from home visitors while other staff cared for their children. As the kids grew older, kindergarten teachers prepared them for kindergarten.

Honig's follow-up studies show that children of mothers who participated in the program had lower rates of delinquency than control children on such counts as burglary, robbery and assault. Girls had lower rates of school failure and, in early adolescence, girls performed better in school. Mothers reported higher rates of family unity and greater pride in their children.

At a time in their lives when teen mothers probably would rather have been flirting or dating than be tied down with baby, the program taught them how to empathize with their infants and see them as people, said Honig.

"Teens need to understand that language and love are the two most powerful gifts a parent can give a child," said Honig. "Language develops only as we give it."

Stopping Child Abuse

Teen-parenting programs aim in part to prevent child abuse, says parenting expert Susan Sheridan, PhD, an associate professor in educational psychology at the University of Utah. To do that, they teach mothers to have more realistic expectations about parenting.

Teens learn that parenting is challenging work and a full-time commitment, Sheridan said. If the mother-child relationship is not based on

plug away at it long enough, I'll get somewhere some day."

Including Fathers

The Really Awesome Parent groups in Minneapolis have made a point of including fathers and other partners of teen mothers in their teen-parenting program. University of Minnesota psychologist Patricia McCarthy, PhD, who ran the program last year and is awaiting funding to run it again, says dads are usually overlooked, but can make a positive difference in their children's lives.

The RAP program draws a large percentage of its participants from area alternative high schools and learning centers, which give students credit if they complete the program. The clientele are predominantly 15- to 20-year-old inner-city or suburban teen moms living below the poverty level.

Program leaders encourage participants to support and socialize with each other. In 15 sessions, the groups cover topics such as managing stress, disciplining children and building self-esteem.

Mothers tested after the program show a significant increase in parenting knowledge. The real challenge, says McCarthy, is getting them to attend sessions.

"They can't attend class because they get sick, their car breaks down, they get in fights with their boyfriends, or they're just being a teenager," McCarthy said. "If we could provide transportation for them as well, we'd have a lot more of them attend."

Research on the program also shows that parent education improves families' lives and benefits the communities they live in.

"Teen-parenting programs cut costs everywhere by lowering delinquency, abuse, neglect and joblessness," she said.

Young adults and AIDS: 'It can't happen to me.'

Many young heterosexuals still shun condoms and have a false sense of security about their own risk for contracting HIV.

By Nathan Seppa
Monitor staff

Young Americans know all about safe sex. They've seen the statistics on AIDS risks, the MTV warnings and those "Russian roulette" public service announcements. And, as one might expect, young adults are practicing sex more safely than any previous generation.

But they still take chances. Studies of college students, for example, show a disturbing trend: New sweethearts often use condoms during their first month or two of sex, then discard the condoms in favor of another form of birth control, such as contraceptive pills, said Christopher Agnew, PhD, assistant professor of psychology science at Purdue University.

Ironically, it is trust in each other that places them at risk. They equate monogamy with security, regardless of their sexual histories. And many never get tested for the human immunodeficiency virus (HIV) that causes AIDS, said Paul Poppen, PhD, associate professor of psychology at George Washington University. Many young heterosexuals, whether in college or not, consider AIDS something that happens to "other people," he said. Studies show that at most, they use condoms only about half the time they have sex.

John Michael Yanson

In the United States, young gay men and intravenous drug users face the greatest risk of contracting HIV. Historically they have been the main targets of education campaigns and other interventions.

But even as gains are made in the gay community and among drug users, the strides of *non-IV-drug-using* heterosexuals toward safer sex have stalled.

"The heterosexual population is where the greatest risk is to society,

From *APA Monitor,* January 1997, pp. 38-39. © 1997 by the American Psychological Association. Reprinted by permission.

Condom sales are dropping

Condom sales in the United States fell between 1991 and 1994, based on scanner data from retail outlets.

Other research supports the notion that much unsafe sex is still being practiced in the young heterosexual community:

Of sexually active college students, only 35 percent of females and 45 percent of males reported using a condom during their most recent sexual intercourse, the Centers for Disease Control and Prevention (CDC) reported in July.

In 1995, 53 percent of high school students ages 14 to 18 had had sex at some point and 38 percent were still active sexually, numbers largely unchanged from five years earlier. But condom use during their most recent intercourse rose only slightly, from 46 percent in 1990 to 53 percent in 1995, the CDC found.

A study of 109 black and adolescent girls in an East Coast city found that of the nearly three-fourths who had had intercourse in the past three months, only 29 percent had used a condom every time. Another 19 percent said they never used a condom in those three months.

—Nathan Seppa

because of their huge numbers," said Stevan Hobfoll, PhD, professor and director of the Applied Psychology Center at Kent State University. The data show that risk is rising: AIDS cases caused by heterosexual transmission in 1983 constituted 1 percent of the U.S. total; by 1993, the number rose to 9 percent. While a large portion of that rise stems from IV-drug users or their partners, the fact remains that getting other young heterosexuals to change their sexual practices has been a difficult task for psychologists and public health officials.

But sometimes events do it for them. For example, after pro basketball star Earvin "Magic" Johnson announced in 1991 that he had contracted HIV through unprotected heterosexual sex, condom use among blacks who had more than one sex partner in the past year rose significantly, research shows. Johnson stood as a real-life reminder that HIV can be spread by heterosexual sex—and that condoms, for the most part, prevent it.

Meanwhile, IV-drug use and unsafe sex form a dangerous combination. Most of the roughly 41,000 annual new HIV infections in the United States occur among IV drug users, their sexual partners or their off-

spring, said John Anderson, Phd, director of APA Office on AIDS.

For U.S. women, the second-highest cause of HIV infection—after IV drug use—is having sex with an HIV-positive man, according to a study in *Health Psychology,* 1992, Vol. 11. As a result, inner-city women are at risk because their partners have higher-than-average incidences of IV drug use, the study found.

The Centers for Disease Control and Prevention (CDC) reported in 1991 that nearly two-thirds of women who contracted HIV through heterosexual sex got it from an IV drug user.

And in 1994, African-American and Hispanic women showed the highest rates of new HIV/STD (sexually transmitted disease) infections, said psychologist Joseph Catania, PhD, associate professor in the department of medicine/Center for AIDS Prevention at the University of California–San Francisco.

But overall, these risks and incidents haven't ignited mass behavioral changes in the large population of young heterosexuals, most of whom have never met an IV-drug user or had sex with anyone in such a high-risk network. Thus, the move toward greater condom use in this broader group may be stalling in part because they simply don't know anyone who

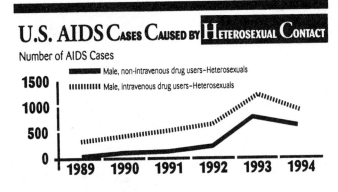

U.S. AIDS Cases Caused by Heterosexual Contact

Number of AIDS Cases
- Male, non-intravenous drug users–Heterosexuals
- Male, intravenous drug users–Heterosexuals

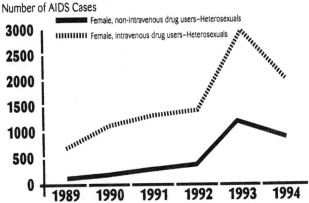

Number of AIDS Cases
- Female, non-intravenous drug users–Heterosexuals
- Female, intravenous drug users–Heterosexuals

Sources: U.S. Department of Health and Human Services, Public Health Service, Centers for Disease Control and Prevention, National Center for Infectious Diseases.

is HIV-positive and still see AIDS only in the abstract, psychologists say.

In any case, their risks could rise in the future as other strains of HIV arrive from abroad (see "New HIV strain likely to come West").

The question is why

Why aren't young people using condoms? Hobfoll and his colleagues found that some fear that broaching the topic will wreck the mood during sexual encounters, cause embarrassment or ultimately limit sexual enjoyment. Adolescents often find sex to be awkward anyway, he said, and the embarrassment can run deep.

On study found that 12 percent of adolescent boys stole their first condom rather than ask a friend for one or face a check-out clerk. Other research found that adolescent girls asking for help in buying condoms in Washington, D.C., drug stores encountered resistance or condemnation from store clerks 40 percent of the time.

Moreover, young people find HIV transmission perplexing because it can be spread heterosexually after only a single sexual contact or not at all after 100, research shows.

And because HIV infection can take months to show up on a basic antibody test, getting tested with a new partner may not yield a valid picture of a person who has had multiple partners in recent months.

Gender role differences complicate heterosexual sex and can hinder condom use as well. Despite social changes of the past 30 years, men are still expected to ask women out on a date, propose marriage and initiate sex, psychologists note. But other research shows that men are several times more likely to give a woman HIV than to get it from a woman.

Communication is key. For example, while condom use has risen in colleges in the past 15 years, discussions about contraception *prior to sex* occurred no more often—about half the time—in 1989 as was the case in 1979, Poppen found.

Many young people also suffer from misconceptions about HIV. In a study of 289 single, pregnant inner-city

New HIV strain likely to come West

While most HIV infections in Europe and North America are spread through intravenous drug use or by anal sex among gay men, HIV in Asia and Africa is largely a heterosexual disease. In Africa, for example, a much higher percentage of AIDS victims are women than in North America.

In the March 1996 issue of *Science,* a group of researchers from the Harvard AIDS Institute unveiled laboratory findings, which suggest that certain HIV subtypes (strains) seen in Asia and Africa are better able to infect an individual via the kinds of cells that appear along vaginal walls—through heterosexual sex.

Some scientists believe it's only a matter of time before heterosexuals in the West face these other strains of HIV.

If these strains are shown to behave in the population the same way they act in the laboratory, it could result in an incursion of HIV in the heterosexual community, said Joseph Catania, PhD, of the University of California–San Francisco. Unsafe sex, little knowledge of personal histories and multiple partners—combined with the arrival of new HIV strains—could spell trouble, he said.

"If you reach this set of conditions, where heterosexuals have all thrown their condoms away and said, '[HIV] isn't going to affect us,' you risk what happened to the gay community in '79 through '81," when many were unknowingly exposed to HIV, Catania said.

—Nathan Seppa

women (average age 21), researchers in Ohio found that many didn't feel at risk for HIV because they had only one sex partner in the past year.

They failed to perceive the inherent risk they faced as a result of their partner's current or past behavior, Hobfoll and four colleagues wrote in *Health Psychology* (Vol. 12, 1993, pp. 481–488). White and black women were equally represented in the study.

Also, many college students feel safe from HIV because they are geographically isolated from big cities, where AIDS is more prevalent. They are, in some ways, correct, Poppen said. Only about one in 500 college students is HIV-positive, a 1990 study showed.

What to do?

Some encouraging data has surfaced. Between 1979 and 1989, college students' condom use rose from 35 percent to 49 percent for first-time-ever sex and 17 percent to 51 percent for first-time sex with the respondent's current sexual partner, Poppen said.

But young adults still account for nearly 70 percent of all STDs in the United States, according to data from the 1993 National AIDS Behavioral

Survey. The U.S. Public Health Service has found that 25 percent of sexually active women contract an STD by age 21. Hobfoll believes young adults need to learn better negotiation skills to satisfy their partner without reverting to unsafe sex.

Also, people need to become more forthcoming, to facilitate frank communication about sex between partners, he said.

Poppen promotes a multifaceted approach to changing sexual behavior among young people, including more condom use and better education. But most importantly, the norms of sexual behavior must change to include safe sex until a partner's sexual history is established, he said.

On the other hand, young people often "fall in love with the person they are having sex with," Poppen said; the idealized vision of their lover can fool them into thinking they can't catch the disease.

Young people need to remember that the AIDS epidemic is not like the flu, something that passes by, Catania said. Many young heterosexuals ignore the stealth nature of HIV and its ability to lie dormant in a person, he said.

Unit Selections

Key Points to Consider

❖ How can parents, schools, and communities work together to prevent adolescents from engaging in high-risk activities?

❖ What are the roles adolescents play in teen courts? What kinds of sentences are given by these courts? How do teens benefit from participating in these courts?

❖ What are the benefits and limitations of using computer profilers to identify teens at risk for the commission of violent crimes?

❖ What are problems associated with men's search for the perfect body?

❖ What are the symptoms of depression in teens? What factors may contribute to depression? What drugs may be used to treat depression? What are the pros and cons of drug therapies for depression?

❖ What are the characteristics of adolescents who are attracted to cults? What can adults do to protect adolescents from the influence of cults?

 **Links**   **www.dushkin.com/online/**

These sites are annotated on pages 4 and 5.

School shootings, teenage pregnancy, drug abuse—are these what come to mind when people think of adolescents? Are adolescents somehow more vulnerable than either children or adults? And, most importantly, how can the problems associated with adolescence be prevented? That many adolescents engage in high-risk behavior is not subject to much debate. The statistics on causes of adolescent fatalities demonstrate their risk taking. The leading causes of death in adolescence are violent: accidents, suicide, and homicide. Alcohol use is frequently involved in these deaths, particularly in motor vehicle fatalities. About half of the fatal motor vehicle accidents involving an adolescent also include a drunk driver.

Why adolescents engage in high-risk behaviors is debated. Some researchers believe the cause of adolescent risk taking is related to their cognitive development. They propose that adolescents have a sense of invulnerability. Adolescents believe that they are special and unique; things that could happen to others could not possibly happen to them. Other researchers believe this may apply at best to only young adolescents. By their mid-teens, most older adolescents are too sophisticated in their thinking to consider themselves invulnerable. Despite this, however, adolescents still take more risks than do adults.

If adolescents do not perceive themselves as invulnerable, then why do they take risks? There are several possible explanations. One proposal is that adolescents may not perceive the risk. For example, adults may have a better sense of how fast they can safely drive given differing road conditions. Adolescents, simply because they are less experienced, may not recognize when road conditions are dangerous and so may not adjust their speed. Adolescents may engage in more high-risk behaviors than adults do simply because they have the time and energy to do so. Many adolescents have free time, money, and a car. Access to these may allow adolescents to put themselves in dangerous situations. Adults, in contrast, may work, do household chores, and take care of their children. These adults may not have the time to drink, or take drugs, or joy ride. Adolescents may also be less adept than are adults in extricating themselves from high-risk situations. For example, adults who attend a party where drugs are consumed may be more comfortable in declining offered drugs than are adolescents, or they may be able to leave the party without relying on transportation from others. Some researchers indicate that society must be somewhat to blame for adolescents' risk taking. If adolescents living in poverty have no chance of getting a meaningful job, have limited access to recreational activities, and have little encouragement in school, then participation in drug-related or violent activities may be the only options open to them. It is up to society to provide these adolescents with an increased number of safe choices.

Adolescents' risk taking activities may take many forms. The U.S. Public Health Service identifies several categories of behavior related to health risks for adolescents. Included are behaviors that may cause injuries, such as suicide and violence; use of tobacco; use of drugs (including alcohol); and, risky behaviors related to eating. All these can clearly threaten adolescents. Alcohol use seems to exacerbate many of the other risks, as indicated by the statistics on alcohol use and violent death. Drug use can be related to accidents, health problems, and violence. Violent behaviors are an increasing concern to society. Murder is the second leading cause of death in adolescence; it is the leading cause of death for African American male teenagers. Suicide rates in young people have tripled since the 1950s. Eating disorders are another threat to adolescents. Millions of adolescents suffer from eating disorders in the United States. Teenagers' attraction to cults has also become a serious problem.

The first unit article discusses programs that involve parents, schools, communities, and adolescents in an attempt to prevent drug abuse. The following two articles focus on criminal behavior in adolescence. The first describes teen courts, where the layers, judges, and defendants all are adolescents. The second addresses the problems with using computer programs for the criminal profiling of adolescents. The next article addresses adolescents' concerns with their bodies. In "Never Too Buff" the problems faced by an increasing number of American men who strive to have the perfect body are discussed. The article that follows is concerned with depression in adolescents. In the final article of the unit, Eagan Hunter describes the factors that characterize adolescents who are attracted to cults and what may be done to protect them from cult influences.

Programs Go Beyond 'Just Saying No'

Innovative programs teach children the skills they need to resist substance abuse.

Bridget Murray
Monitor staff

Psychologists' new school-based approaches to drug-abuse prevention go a step beyond telling teen-agers to 'just say no.' They're teaching teens *how* to say no.

Instead of bombarding students with antidrug dogma that they often ignore, the programs build kids' drug-resistance skills and encourage them to get involved in their schools and communities, social scientists say.

"The programs show alienated kids that society offers better options than taking drugs and strengthen kids' ability to take advantage of those options," said Ronda C. Talley, PhD, APA's assistant executive director for education and head of the APA Center for Psychology in Schools and Education.

These new drug-abuse prevention programs are better than traditional drug-education programs at targeting risk factors for drug abuse, such as boredom, lack of parental support, feelings of failure and social pressures to drink or smoke, said Talley.

Moreover, using such programs to prevent drug abuse is ultimately less expensive and probably more effective

(Photo by Lloyd Wolf)

than treating it, some psychologists contend.

But there is a hitch. The programs fail to reach adolescents who have already started smoking and drinking, said substance-abuse expert John Swisher, PhD, a psychology professor at Pennsylvania State University. Those adolescents do need more intensive treatment programs, he said.

The need for effective drug-abuse prevention programs has reached new heights, according to national survey data. An ongoing, annual study of 50,000 eighth-, 10th- and 12-graders led by social psychologist Lloyd Johnston, PhD, of the University of Michigan's Institute for Social Research, finds that adolescents are reporting greater use of illegal drugs, especially marijuana, than they did in the late 1980s.

School psychologists are working to curb these rates by developing students' social skills and fostering student support systems within and beyond the school, says Swisher.

A Social Fabric That Connects

One program that aims to substitute drug use with community responsibility is the Child Development Project, or CDP, run in elementary schools and based out of the Developmental Studies Center in Oakland, Calif. By building a social fabric that connects kids, parents and teachers with each other and the school, CDP seeks to build children's commitment to such community values as helpfulness and responsibility. Funded in part by the Center for Substance Abuse Prevention at the U.S. Department of Human Services, CDP helps kids become more responsible and academically motivated *before* they're exposed to drugs.

"We try to help schools provide children with a stronger sense of autonomy, belonging and competence—a new sense of the ABCs," said the program's founder, social psychologist Eric Schaps, PhD, director of the Development Studies Center.

CDP revamps school climate, discipline practice and parental involvement. For example, hall monitors report on peers' behavior, and in "buddies" programs, teachers assign each older student to a younger "buddy" to support during the school year. Families become more involved in school life through participation in events such as Family Read Aloud Nights, and in homework activities that relate family experience to what kids are learning in school.

The program also boosts the curriculum: Teachers receive intensive training in teaching methods and discipline practice over three years, and CDP staff provide them with on-site consultation and curriculum materials such as reading supplements. Longitudinal research shows that CDP significantly reduces alcohol and marijuana

"THE PROGRAMS SHOW ALIENATED KIDS THAT SOCIETY OFFERS BETTER OPTIONS THAN TAKING DRUGS AND STRENGTHEN KIDS' ABILITY TO TAKE ADVANTAGE OF THOSE OPTIONS."

RONDA C. TALLEY, PHD
APA'S CENTER FOR PSYCHOLOGY
IN SCHOOLS AND EDUCATION

use relative to other schools. Students also work more collaboratively on classroom tasks, interact more with each other, and behave less violently. Since 1992, schools have gradually phased in CDP in White Plains, N.Y.; Dade County, Fla.; Louisville, Ky.; and Salinas, Cupertino and San Francisco, Calif.

A Community Approach

Project Star is another community-oriented program developed to steer kids away from alcohol and cigarettes. This program aims to stop youngsters from taking these "gateway drugs" and to prevent them from being tempted by "harder" illegal drugs.

The five-year program, partially funded by the National Institute on Drug Abuse and designed by school psychologist Mary Anne Pentz, PhD, has been adopted in the Indianapolis schools. Project Star is school-based but reaches out to parents and the community with prevention education.

The program, which usually starts in junior high school, involves five stages:

- **First year**—Students are taught drug awareness and resistance skills.

- **Second year**—Parents, children, teachers and principals communicate about drug abuse, and parents create stronger rules about drug use.
- **Third year**—Experts train community leaders about prevention strategies and schools sponsor community-wide prevention activities like smoke-outs and alcohol-free sporting events.
- **Fourth year**—Program participants work on policy change such as creating a tax on beer and creating drug-free school zones.
- **Fifth year**—Participants target the mass media to deliver anti-drug messages in advertisements and talk shows.

When community norms are addressed along with schools' prevention efforts, drug-abstinence levels are higher than when school-based programs are implemented alone, says Pentz.

In-school prevention programs typically report a 15 percent to 44 percent drop in drug-use, whereas Project Star reports a 20 percent to 60 percent decline. The program has been shown to lower occasional use of gateway drugs throughout high school and to quell heavier use, such as daily drunkenness and chain-smoking, Pentz said.

Resistance Training

Still another preventive approach is Life Skills Training, which seeks to build adolescents' ability to deal with life stress rather than escaping it through drug use. LST is one of the first school-based projects to demonstrate durable prevention effects over time.

The project was developed by developmental and clinical psychologist Gilbert Botvin, PhD, director of the Institute for Prevention Research at Cornell University Medical College in New York City. LST is funded by NIDA and is being tested in New York State.

Botvin documented the program's success in 56 rural and suburban public schools in upper New York State and Long Island. In this study, nearly 6,000 seventh-graders were coached in LST in 1985. Botvin surveyed 3,600 of them six years later in 1991, and found that those exposed to LST were less likely to use alcohol, drugs and cigarettes than those not exposed to the program.

To implement the program, Botvin and his colleagues train teachers to conduct 15 LST classes, lasting from 45 to 50 minutes, to seventh-graders, each focused on a specific life skill objective. Instruction includes showing students such techniques as muscle-relaxation exercises to ease the anxiety and tension that can lead them to drugs and alcohol.

LST explains how to weigh options and think about long-term consequences of behavior. The program teaches students assertiveness skills, such as building up the nerve to return defective merchandise, and, most importantly, to resist offers and advertising pressure to drink, take drugs and smoke cigarettes.

LST also strives to polish students' conversation skills and improve their rapport with others. Kids learn how to introduce people, to sustain and gracefully end a conversation and to compliment people, said Botvin. The intention is to build supportive social networks that steer children toward academics and away from the isolation that sometimes leads them to drugs.

These classes are supported by out-of-class behavioral "homework," such as encouraging students to introduce themselves to five new people. These skills are reinforced and expanded though a series of 15 "booster" classes in the eighth and ninth grade.

Although programs designed by research psychologists typically rely on classroom teachers and health educators to deliver lessons, school psychologists can take an active role in setting up programs and training teachers, said Botvin. He hopes to see school health professionals, including psychologists, running LST in teams as they work to bring it into more schools and communities.

Courtroom Justice

for Teens—by Teens

In many states, teens in trouble can choose Teen Court—a jury and trial by peers.

by Kathiann M. Kowalski

Seventeen-year-old Zach knew it was illegal, but he drank at the party anyway. On the way home, he was arrested. Charged with illegal alcohol consumption and curfew violation, Zach suddenly became a criminal defendant.

Zach's name has been changed to protect his privacy, but his story is real. Teens who break the law find themselves facing criminal charges. For Zach and other youths, however, a teen court is providing a second chance.

Teens in Charge

Teens run teen courts, deciding real cases for teen defendants. Teen volunteers are trained as bailiffs, clerks, prosecutors, and defense attorneys. Volunteers and former teen offenders who had been defendants in the court make up the jury.

Teen courts provide an alternative: They divert offenders from regular juvenile court. Last year, more than 500 teen courts operated in 45 states plus the District of Columbia. Generally, only first-time offenders can appear in teen court. Moreover, offenses must be misdemeanors. Felonies—serious crimes that if committed by an adult would be punishable by more than a year in prison—generally are not diverted to a teen court.

In most teen courts, defendants must plead guilty and waive their right to a licensed adult attorney. Then teen prosecuting and defense attorneys present their arguments for sentencing to the jury. When defendants complete all parts of their sentence, charges are dismissed. All proceedings remain confidential, there is no criminal record.

"It's not going to follow you the rest of your life," explains Phillip Wolford, a teen defense attorney and juror in Abingdon, Illinois. "Twenty years down the road, nobody's ever going to know or be able to find out you went through teen court."

It's No Slap on the Wrist

Teen court defendants don't get off easily, however. Juries consider the seriousness of the offense, the circumstances surrounding the case, and the defendant's attitude. Then they tailor sentences to the facts of each case.

For example, the jury felt Zach's case was serious. He was 17 already—old enough to drive and to know better. Plus, he knew beforehand there would be drinking at the party.

Zach was sentenced to perform 60 hours of community service. He also had to complete various educational activities. These included making a collage showing nonalcoholic drink choices, listing 25 things he could have done instead of attending a party with alcohol, and describing 25 things that *could have* happened if he hadn't been arrested that night.

Often teens must also attend educational programs or substance abuse assessments. Does this sound like more work than standing before a real judge, paying a fine, and serving probation? It can be. But teens often feel more comfortable with their peers. By accepting responsibility in front of other teens, defendants deal with their own problems.

As part of their sentences, many defendants attend programs emphasizing communication, decision making, anger management, or shoplifting prevention. They use these skills to avoid bad choices in the future. "More than one [teen] has told me it was good that [he or she] got caught and that Teen Court was here," says Bruce Steinmetz, program supervisor for the Bethel Teen Court in Eugene, Oregon. Otherwise, defendants say, they would have continued breaking the law until something worse happened.

In fact, most teen court defendants avoid becoming repeat offenders. This is in contrast to some regular juvenile courts that report success rates of less than 50 percent.

From *Current Health 2*, April/May 1999, pp. 29-31. © 1999 by Weekly Reader Corporation. All rights reserved. Reprinted by permission.

Getting Involved

Teen court sentences almost always involve adult-supervised community service. As they work at food depositories for the homeless, help at hospitals, clean parks, or do other services, defendants give something back to the community they offended when they committed a crime. They accept responsibility for performing tasks properly. They see firsthand the plight of other people who are often in desperate straits.

Most defendants must also return to teen court—to serve as jurors. Then, as part of the system, they must work with a group to decide sentences for other offenders. "I think it makes them see how the other side can be," says teen court volunteer Rachael Junk.

"I believe this is the biggest responsibility some of them have ever been entrusted with," Steinmetz adds. "I think all teen court coordinators have stories about defendants who stay on voluntarily to become regular teen court members, attorneys, etcetera."

Volunteers Benefit, Too

By getting involved, teen court volunteers directly address the problem of juvenile crime. "They gain a sense of personal and community power," Steinmetz says.

Volunteers learn respect for the legal system, too. At Knox County Teen Court in Galesburg, Illinois, only one of 350 volunteers was later arrested. That was for a traffic violation, says program coordinator Lolita Junk. "This proves to me that teens helping other teens make good decisions themselves," she says.

Besides learning about the judicial system, volunteers gain important skills. "Probably the number-one skill would be communication," says Phillip Wolford.

"The bailiff definitely needs leadership skills," says Rachael Junk. "You have to know how to get people to listen to you." Bailiffs maintain order in the courtroom.

Jury duty gives teens from different backgrounds problem-solving experience. They must listen to each other and function as a group—a skill they'll need for almost every real-world job.

Reflecting on her experience as a volunteer attorney, high school junior Annie Hawkinson says, "It made me understand more why people do things." That's empathy—the ability to see things from another person's perspective. Empathy helps everyone get along better.

For more information

Knox Country Teen Court Home Page
http://hyperion.advanced.org/2640
(provides info about teen courts nationwide and pointers for starting teen courts)

LOOKING FOR TROUBLE

More and more schools are trying to spot the potential killers in their midst. But what about the innocents?

By JODIE MORSE LOS ANGELES

THE GRADE-SCHOOL DRAWING looked typically innocent, at least in its style. The subjects were two stick figures, one of them wearing a loopy smile. But the teacher in San Bernardino, Calif., who found it stowed in a student's desk was alarmed by the story line. One grinning stick figure wielded a gun. The other, frowning, had just been shot.

The sketch, from the hand of an eight-year-old with a penchant for nasty temper tantrums, was drawn only days after a six-year-old in Michigan fatally shot a class-mate, so school officials decided to be on the safe side. They brought the drawing to the attention of Gary Underwood, chief of police for the city's public schools, who ran the child's case through the department's new computer "threat-assessment" program, called Mosaic-2000. With a battery of 42 questions—Is the student harassed by peers? Has the student recently experienced rejection?—Mosaic purports to calculate rough odds on whether a child will turn violent.

Long used by law-enforcement and government agencies to examine threats made against their personnel, Mosaic software is now being field-tested in about 20 public school districts from Jonesboro, Ark., to Los Angeles to Salem, Ore. In its assessment of the stick-figure artist, the program suggested that the boy shared several traits with past violent offenders and guided the school to put him in counseling and under close watch. "When those kids walked into Columbine with bombs, no one was expecting it," says Underwood. "We're now on alert if this child comes into school with a bulge in his pocket."

This is the level of vigilance in the American public school a year after Columbine. On average, it may be a safer place than ever—the number of school-associated violent deaths dropped 40% from 1997 through 1999—but it feels scarier with each new well-publicized shooting and threat. In the year since the Columbine massacre, understandably nervous school officials have cycled through a series of responses, from lock-down drills to see-through knapsacks, with the impulsiveness of seventh-graders buying the boy-band CD of the moment.

Now, though, administrators are quietly shifting their sights from metal detectors to "mental detectors." Commonly known as profilers, these programs aim to detect violence-prone kids before they act by comparing them to those who have already snapped. Investigators from Columbine and Jonesboro have tutored administrators across the U.S. on the telltale signs that in their cases went tragically undetected or unheeded. The FBI, which last fall circulated a 20-point "offender profile" culled from common characteristics of school shooters, will release a report on the topic next month. And the Secret Service, at work on its own study, is interviewing school shooters to see what makes them tick—and then explode.

Along with its findings, the Secret Service plans to give schools an instructional video and a set of probative questions. In addition, numerous questionnaires and checklists are being sold by private firms or

SOME OF THE TRAITS

... the FBI says may help identify a kid at risk of committing violence

☑ **RED FLAG** Experiences an event, like rejection by girlfriend, that leads to depression, thoughts of suicide and killing **WHO FITS** Barry Loukaitis, Moses Lake, Wash.; **Luke Woodham**, Pearl, Miss.; **Michael Carneal**, West Paducah, Ken.; **Andrew Golden** and **Mitchell Johnson**, Jonesboro, Ark.; **Kipland Kinkel**, Springfield, Ore.; **Eric Harris, Dylan Klebold**, Littleton, Colo.; **Thomas Solomon**, Conyers, Ga.

☑ **RED FLAG** Has a history of mental health treatment **WHO FITS** Loukaitis, Carneal, Kinkel, Harris, Solomon

☑ **RED FLAG** Tends to dislike popular students or those who bully others **WHO FITS** Loukaitis, Harris, Klebold, Solomon

☑ **RED FLAG** Openly expresses a desire to kill others **WHO FITS** Loukaitis, Carneal, Golden, Johnson, Kinkel, Harris, Klebold, Solomon

☑ **RED FLAG** Is cruel to animals, sets fires, wets bed beyond normal age **WHO FITS** Woodham, Johnson, Kinkel

☑ **RED FLAG** Is fascinated by firearms and has access, usually through a family member **WHO FITS** Loukaitis, Woodham, Carneal, Golden, Johnson, Kinkel, Harris, Klebold, Solomon

drawn up by school officials themselves. One screening test for students is titled simply "Questions for Killers."

Support for the trouble-spotting approach is growing. Proponents contend it has systematically helped nail would-be assassins and mass killers in other settings. In a new poll by TIME and the Discovery Channel, 53% of parents surveyed said they approve of such measures. But their kids are leery: 60% said they disapprove, fearing such programs could be used unfairly against students not prone to violence. A growing number of critics agree, contending that there is simply no reliable way to weed out the world's Dylans and Erics from their merely cranky classmates without trampling on privacy and constitutional rights in the process. "These programs treat children as suspects, not students," says Barry Steinhardt, associate director of the American Civil Liberties Union.

Front and center in the debate is the controversial Mosaic-2000 program. Its creator, Gavin de Becker, 45, a Hollywood security consultant and author of the best-selling self-help book *The Gift of Fear,* works out of a windowless Los Angeles office festooned with gushing thanks from the likes of Goldie Hawn, Robert Redford—and the CIA. This last client speaks to de Becker's lesser-known line of work. For the past decade he has dispensed "artificial-intuition" software to police departments, Governors and even the U.S. Supreme Court. The programs rank numerically the danger posed by celebrity

MOMS FOR GUN CONTROL

If there were a recipe for creating a late-blooming activist—take a devoted parent, add a worst nightmare, mix with official intransigence—Carole Price, 37, would be the final product. The Maryland mother of three says she "hadn't organized anything more complicated than a car pool" until gun violence ripped into her family. On Aug. 20, 1998, Price's son John, 13, was accidentally killed by a 9-year-old wielding a 9-mm Luger pistol that he had found in his home. Since that day, Price and her husband John have put themselves on the front lines of the war over gun safety.

After her son was killed, Carole Price was stunned to learn that in Maryland it was only a misdemeanor to leave a loaded gun accessible to a child. She started attending gun-control rallies and was host at meetings in her home. After she showed up with a TV news crew at a local Republican fund raiser that was raffling off a 9-mm handgun, Price gained the attention of other local media and legislators.

Her testimony before the Maryland legislature helped push through a new law that requires trigger locks and a firearms-safety course for all new handgun owners. When

the measure was signed into law last week, President Clinton traveled to Annapolis to praise the Prices' efforts.

Since November, Carol Price has been an organizer of the Million Mom Match on behalf of "commonsense" gun control, scheduled for Mother's Day on the Mall in Washington. Donna Dees Thomases, the New Jersey publicist and mother of two who launched plans for the march, says that Prices's public anguish speaks for thousands of families branded by gun violence—and furious at legislative inaction.

—**By Amy Dickinson/ Washington**

stalkers, angry employees or potential assassins by comparing their actions to those of known offenders.

A similar logic drives the new schoolhouse version of Mosaic. First, a child acts in a manner considered threatening—he draws a worrisome sketch or strikes another

SURVEY: YOUTH VIOLENCE

THE PERCEPTION GAP

A YEAR AFTER COLUMBINE, parents and teenagers hold strikingly different views on the problem of youth violence, according to a new poll by TIME and the Discovery Channel in conjunction with the National Campaign Against Youth Violence. Fewer teens feel very safe from violence in schools today (33%) than shortly after the Columbine killings a year ago (42% in a similar poll). But more parents believe that teens feel safe in school today (45%) than felt that way last year (27%). Nearly a third of teens say they have witnessed a violent situation

at school, while only 8% of parents think that's the case. About half of teens in the poll. say they have been insulted or threatened in the past year, but only 22% of parents believe their kids have experienced that type of situation.

While 8 in 10 parents say they have talked with their kids about ways to protect themselves from violence, only 6 in 10 kids remember having such conversations. And while about half of parents wish they could talk more with their kids about this subject, only 18% of teens want more such talks. One reason may be

that most parents encourage kids to stand up for themselves, while most kids are worried about the possible violent consequences. Two-thirds of parents believe it is nearly impossible for teens to walk away from an angry confrontation without being teased, but only 37% of teens agree. Both parents and teens believe that youth violence has increased in recent years, even though school-related violent deaths have been in decline. Extensive news coverage of school shootings may account for this misperception.

student. Then, out of the child's presence and without his or her knowledge, school psychologists, principals or police answer a list of multiple-choice questions drafted by de Becker and a committee including law-enforcement and education officials. (Sample queries: What is the student's demeanor toward authority figures? Has there recently been media attention to school shootings or other acts of violence? What is the student's home-life situation?) If the responses seem particularly troubling, a "trigger text" immediately pops up, prompting officials to contact law-enforcement or mental-health professionals. At the end of the exercise, the program computes whether the student has "few," "several" or "some" factors in common with violent perpetrators and a detailed report is printed out.

"Schools are doing all this same stuff anyway, but they're doing it willy-nilly," says de Becker. "Mosaic will give them the participation of experts in those high-stakes decisions." Those experts, however, remain a fiercely divided bunch. While some maintain that school shootings are simply too rare for sound comparisons to be drawn, others who have studied the case histories have found that the shooters share many key traits. "There's no one set of characteristics that can be ascribed to these shooters," cautions Bryan Vossekuil, who is leading the Secret Service's ongoing study. Perhaps the agency's most interesting finding so far is that the shooters rarely made public threats. Instead, they tended to confide their intentions to a few select peers.

There are more specific challenges to Mosaic's pedigree. The U.S. Marshals Ser-

Poll

■ Overall, do you think that in the past few years youth violence has increased, decreased or stayed about the same?

	TEENS	PARENTS
Increased	70%	59%
Decreased	7%	1%
Stayed about the same	23%	40%

■ Do you feel safe from violence at school?

	TEENS
Very safe	33%
Somewhat safe	53%
Not too safe	9%
Not safe at all	5%

■ Biggest problem in school:

ACCORDING TO TEENS

Drugs	32%
Violence	14%
Other	8%
Discipline problems	4%
Peer pressure	4%

ACCORDING TO PARENTS

Drugs	25%
Lack of good teachers	15%
Other	12%
Lack of good education/ college prep	9%
Violence	7%

■ What are the most important solutions to reducing youth violence, both in and out of schools?

ACCORDING TO TEENS

More counseling services in school	15%
Teaching people not to hate	14%
Mentoring programs	11%
More police in schools	10%
More afterschool programs	10%

ACCORDING TO PARENTS

More counseling services in school	26%
Better identification of emotional problems in kids	20%
Teaching people not to hate	14%
Getting drugs out of schools	12%
More recreational opportunities for kids	10%

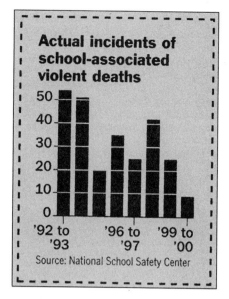

Actual incidents of school-associated violent deaths

Source: National School Safety Center

through a proper scholarly review. Mike Furlong, a psychologist at the University of California at Santa Barbara, recently test-drove the Mosaic-2000 program and concluded, "This is just a private firm asking America's schools to create an open experiment." De Becker says his method is scheduled to undergo two academic evaluations.

Many civil libertarians have a more pressing concern. They fear the program will single out or profile students who are simply maladjusted but not menacing. And because schools use Mosaic to study kids without their knowledge, they may never know they are under suspicion. De Becker says Mosaic is not used for what he calls "the p word"—profiling—but rather for "threat assessment." Students, he says, are not examined unless they single themselves out by making a threat. But in today's anxious classrooms, threats are often defined broadly. Phyllis Hodges, an assistant principal at Chicago's Von Steuben High School, used the program to examine a student who was constantly picked on by peers for being effeminate. He had made disturbing comments in the past—for example, he vowed he would hurt classmates—yet his offense this time was less clear-cut. He refused to hand in a test after his teacher called time. A run of his particulars through the Mosaic program indicated there was no immediate cause for concern.

Better that result, de Becker contends, than the more haphazard approach of a school district like Granite City, Ill., which has hand-crafted its own profiling policy. Students who exhibit certain risky behaviors—cursing, mood swings, writing about "the dark side of life"—can face expulsion or worse. In December, teachers in Granite City found a note by a student promising to "settle some scores." He was read his Miranda warning, arrested by the city police and suspended for 10 days. In the meantime, teachers investigating the matter found that

■ Do you agree or disagree that by the time students with emotional and behavioral problems are 16 or 17, it is too late to change their behavior?

	TEENS	PARENTS
Agree	29%	61%
Disagree	69%	38%

■ Which one of the following groups do you think would have the greatest impact on kids in the effort to reduce violence in schools?

	TEENS
Parents/guardians	37%
Celebrities	19%
Media	13%
Support groups	13%
Teachers and school officials	6%

	PARENTS
Parents/guardians	68%
Support groups	7%
Teachers and school officials	6%
Police	5%
Media	2%
Religious organizations	2%

■ If you or your teenager had an idea but were not completely sure, that another student might do something violent, whom would you tell?

	Teens	Parents
A teacher	26%	3%
A parent	18%	61%
A guidance counselor	16%	1%
No one	15%	18%

■ Do you agree or disagree that it is almost impossible to walk away from an angry scene without fighting and not be teased for it?

	Teens	Parents
Strongly Agree	13%	53%
Somewhat Agree	24%	12%
Somewhat disagree	24%	15%
Strongly disagree	35%	19%

■ Do you think the way the media portray violence is a major factor in causing youth violence?

	TEENS	PARENTS		TEENS	PARENTS
Yes	38%	59%	No	60%	41%

From a Discovery Channel/TIME poll of 400 American teenagers 14 to 17, 400 parents of teenagers and 200 adults without teenage children taken in April by Penn, Schoen & Berland

vice and the L.A. police department may swear by the earlier versions of Mosaic, but many psychologists insist it has not been

the note was only the concoction, as superintendent Steve Balen puts it, "of a goofy freshman having fun."

Tales like that have begun to sway some policymakers. Last week the office of California Governor Gray Davis issued a report urging schools to proceed with caution on Mosaic, and other such programs. The U.S. Education Department is backing away from the checklist of warning signs it sent to every school in the nation in 1998. In a mass mailing this week, the department declares that relying on such lists can "harm children and waste resources." Instead, it counsels teachers and parents to use the much lower-tech and more labor-intensive approach of keeping their eyes and ears alert at all times, not only for overt threats but also for troubled students who need help.

That method seemed to do the trick last week in Lake Station, Ind., where a parent's call helped school officials head off an alleged plot by three first-grade girls to kill a classmate. "The answer is not going to come from just throwing something up on the computer," says Bill Modzeleski, head of the government's school-safety programs. "It's got to come from the teachers in classrooms who really know the problem kids."

Or there's the all-of-the-above approach embraced by schools in a district like Carroll County, Md. In the past year, they have adopted 25 safety initiatives, including a "red flags" profile of their own design. "The threats are way down, and the kids are learning," reports the director of pupil services, Cynthia Little. "They've even stopped saying 'I'm going to kill you.'" But have they stopped thinking it?

—With reporting by Elaine Shannon/ Washington

POLICE PREPARATIONS

READY AND WAITING

POLICE DETECTIVE BRIAN Braswell of Petersburg, Va., thinks he's "three-quarters" prepared for the next Columbine. Last month, the local high school was the stage for a hostage drill complete with blaring fire alarms, 60 kids from Junior ROTC playing the wounded and scared, and an officer portraying a revenge-seeking killer, firing blanks from a shotgun. Braswell's team of officers had to push through waves of fleeing, panicked students and step over wounded children tugging at their pant legs crying "Help me!" Says Braswell: "From Columbine, we've learned that you have no choice but to go in and stop the carnage."

A year after a tragedy that left 15 dead—and scores of questions about why the police moved so slowly—crisis training that was once reserved for big-city SWAT teams has entered the curriculum for street cops. The Los Angeles police hope to have 5,000 patrol officers trained in rapid-deployment techniques by June. The National Tactical Officers Association, a SWAT training organization, has put more than 1,000 officers through "R.U. Ready High School" in Moyock, N.C., a $45,000 facility specifically built to simulate Columbine-style carnage. A school-hostage drill in Pinellas County, Fla., last month featured 600 middle schoolers hiding inside locked-down classrooms. It was enough to make baby-boomer parents long for the good old days of duck-and-cover.

The old rules on how to respond to school and office shootings—set up a perimeter and wait for SWAT—are gone. Now cops are trained that when they hear shootings, they should go in immediately, guns drawn, and stop the violence. "We had to make a change," says SWAT trainer Randy Watt. "Fifteen years ago, you didn't see people going in just for the sake of creating mayhem and planning their own demise."

During the Petersburg drill, several cops blinked back tears when they had to step over injured kids. "All your instincts tell you to help them," says Detective Braswell, a father of two. "But I understand what needs to be done." Some agencies have armed their patrol officers with rifles and equipped patrol cars with computers that can quickly call up school blueprints.

Would any of this have helped at Columbine, where patrolmen waited outside the school for late-arriving SWAT teams rather than barging inside to confront the gunmen? Colorado Governor Bill Owens told TIME that he thinks those slow and deliberate tactics were probably inappropriate and will be assessed by his Columbine Review Commission. But most departments aren't waiting for more studies—rapid deployment is the order of the day.

—By Andrew Goldstein

NEVER TOO BUFF

A new book reveals a troubling obsession: How male self-worth is increasingly tied to body image

By **JOHN CLOUD** Boston

POP QUIZ. WHO ARE MORE LIKELY TO BE dissatisfied with the appearance of their chests, men or women? Who is more likely to be concerned about acne, your teenage son or his sister? And who is more likely to binge eat, your nephew or your niece?

If you chose the women and girls in your life, you are right only for the last question—and even then, not by the margin you might expect. About 40% of Americans who go on compulsive-eating sprees are men. Thirty-eight percent of men want bigger pecs, while only 34% of women want bigger breasts. And more boys have fretted about zits than girls, going all the way back to a 1972 study.

A groundbreaking new book declares that these numbers, along with hundreds of other statistics and interviews the authors have compiled, mean something awful has happened to American men over the past few decades. They have become obsessed with their bodies. Authors Harrison Pope and Katharine Phillips, professors of psychiatry at Harvard and Brown, respectively, and Roberto Olivardia, a clinical psychologist at McLean Hospital in Belmont, Mass., have a catchy name to describe this obsession—a term that will soon be doing many reps on chat shows: the Adonis Complex.

The name, which refers to the gorgeous half man, half god of mythology, may be a little too ready for *Oprah*, but the theory behind it will start a wonderful debate. Based on original research involving more than 1,000 men over the past 15 years, the book argues that many men desperately want to look like Adonis because they constantly see the "ideal," steroid-boosted bodies of actors and models and because their muscles are all they have over women today. In an age when women fly combat missions, the authors ask, "What can a modern boy or man do to distinguish himself as being 'masculine'?"

For years, of course, some men—ice skaters, body builders, George Hamilton—have fretted over aspects of their appearance. But the numbers suggest that body-image concerns have gone mainstream: nearly half of men don't like their overall appearance, in contrast to just 1 in 6 in 1972. True, men typically are fatter now, but another study found that 46% of men of normal weight think about their appearance "all the time" or "frequently." And some men—probably hundreds of thousands, if you extrapolate from small surveys—say they have passed up job and even romantic opportunities because they refuse to disrupt workouts or dine on restaurant food. In other words, an increasing number of men would rather look brawny for their girlfriends than have sex with them.

Consider what they're spending. Last year American men forked over $2 billion for gym memberships—and another $2 billion for home exercise equipment. *Men's Health* ("Rock-hard abs in six weeks!" it screams every other issue) had 250,000 subscribers in 1990; now it has 1.6 million. In 1996 alone, men underwent some 700,000 cosmetic procedures.

At least those profits are legal. Anabolic steroids—the common name for synthetic testosterone—have led to the most dramatic changes in the male form in modern history, and more and more average men want those changes for themselves. Since steroids became widely available on the black market in the 1960s, perhaps 3 million American men have swallowed or injected them—mostly in the past 15 years. A 1993 survey found that 1 Georgia high school boy in every 15 admitted having used steroids without a prescription. And the Drug Enforcement Administration reports that the percentage of all high school students who have used steroids has increased 50% in the past four years, from 1.8% to 2.8%. The abuse of steroids has so alarmed the National Institute on Drug Abuse that on Friday it launched a campaign in gyms, malls, bookstores, clubs and on the Internet to warn teenagers about the dangers. Meanwhile, teenagers in even larger numbers are buying legal but lightly regulated food supplements, some with dangerous side effects, that purport to make you bigger or leaner or stronger.

As they infiltrated the body-building world in the '70s and Hollywood a decade later, steroids created bodies for mass consumption that the world had literally never seen before. Pope likes to chart the changes by looking at Mr. America winners, which he called up on the Internet in his office last week. "Look at this guy," Pope exclaims when he clicks on the 1943 winner, Jules Bacon. "He couldn't even win a county body-building contest today." Indeed, there are 16-year-olds working out at your gym who are as big as Bacon. Does that neces-

BODY BOOSTERS Here are some of the substances some men use to bulk up:

PROTEINS

Protein is the building block of muscle growth. It repairs muscle tissue broken down while training. It's sold in powders and bars under names like MET-Rx and Myoplex. These are acceptable sources of protein, but there is little evidence that they are superior to ordinary foods like skim milk or lean meat. Long-term use of very high doses of protein may cause kidney and liver damage.

FAT BURNERS

Include the drug ephedrine, which comes from the plant Ephedra. Ephedrine is a powerful stimulant used in diet pills, herbal ecstasy and energy-booster products. It promotes fat loss, but weight is quickly retained when use stops. It has caused seizures and strokes, especially among those with high blood pressure and diabetes. The FDA says it has been associated with at least 58 deaths since 1994.

CREATINE

A nutrient found in red meat, it produces energy and helps restore muscle tissue after strenuous exercise. Several studies show it increases lean body mass, though some of this gain is probably water. Long-term use of high doses of creatine hasn't been studied, though there are no known short-term dangers. It comes in many forms: powder, liquid, gum.

ADRENAL HORMONES

Naturally produced in humans and animals, these hormones are partly metabolized into testosterone in the body, and thus are claimed to promote muscle growth. Mark McGwire said he had used them to get a more efficient workout and a faster recovery from weight lifting. (He says he no longer uses them.) It may increase levels of cholesterol and help develop female breast tissue. Long-term dangers are unknown.

DUBIOUS DRUGS

Anabolic steriods classified as controlled substances, are synthetic testosterone that is injected into muscle tissue or taken orally to promote muscle growth and enhance athletic performance. Serious side effects include liver damage, cancer and heart disease. Other prescription products are growth hormones like GHB, which is thought to stimulate natural hormone secretion but is also used as an alternative to ecstasy.

sarily mean that today's body builders—including those 16-year-olds—are 'roided? Pope is careful. "The possibility exists that rare or exceptional people, those with an unusual genetic makeup or a hormonal imbalance," could achieve the muscularity and leanness of today's big body builders, he says.

But it's not likely. And Pope isn't lobbing dumbbells from an ivory tower: the professor lifts weights six days a week, from 11 a.m. to 1 p.m. (He can even mark historical occasions by his workouts: "I remember when the *Challenger* went down; I was doing a set of squats.") "We are being assaulted by images virtually impossible to attain without the use of drugs," says Pope. "So what happens when you change a million-year-old equilibrium of nature?"

A historical loop forms: steroids beget pro wrestlers—Hulk Hogan, for one, has admitted taking steroids—who inspire boys to be just like them. Steroids have changed even boys' toys. Feminists have long derided Barbie for her tiny waist and big bosom. The authors of *The Adonis Complex* see a similar problem for boys in the growth of G.I. Joe. The grunt of 1982 looks scrawny compared

with G.I. Joe Extreme, introduced in the mid-'90s. The latter would have a 55-in. chest and 22-in. biceps if he were real, which simply can't be replicated in nature. Pope also points out a stunning little feature of the three-year-old video game Duke Nukem: Total Meltdown, developed by GT Interactive Software. When Duke gets tired, he can find a bottle of steroids to get him going. "Steroids give Duke a super adrenaline rush," the game manual notes.

To bolster their argument, the *Adonis* authors developed a computerized test that allows subjects to "add" muscle to a typical male body. They estimate their own size and then pick the size they would like to be and the size they think women want. Pope and his colleagues gave the test to college students and found that on average, the men wanted 28 lbs. more muscle—and thought women wanted them to have 30 lbs. more. In fact, the women who took the test picked an ideal man only slightly more muscular than average. Which goes a long way toward explaining why Leonardo DiCaprio can be a megastar in a nation that also idealizes "Stone Cold" Steve Austin.

But when younger boys took Pope's test, they revealed an even deeper sense of inadequacy about their bodies. More than half of boys ages 11 to 17 chose as their physical ideal an image possible to attain only by using steroids. So they do. Boys are a big part of the clientele at Muscle Mania (not its real name), a weight-lifting store that TIME visited last week at a strip mall in a Boston suburb. A couple of teenagers came in to ask about tribulus, one of the many over-the-counter drugs and body-building supplements the store sells, all legally.

A FRIEND OF MINE," ONE BOY BEGINS, fooling no one, "just came off a cycle of juice, and he heard that tribulus can help you produce testosterone naturally." Patrick, 28, who runs the store and who stopped using steroids four years ago because of chest pain, tells the kid, "The s___ shuts off your nuts," meaning steroids can reduce sperm production, shrink the testicles and cause impotence. Tribulus, Patrick says, can help restart natural testosterone production. The teen hands over $12 for 100 Tribulus Fuel pills. (Every day, Muscle Mania does $4,000 in sales of such products, with protein supplements and so-called fat burners leading the pack.)

Patrick says many of his teen customers, because they're short on cash, won't pay for a gym membership "until they've saved up for a cycle [of steroids]. They don't see the point without them." The saddest customers, he says, are the little boys, 12 and 13, brought in by young fathers. "The dad will say, 'How do we put some weight on this kid?' with the boy just staring at the floor. Dad is going to turn him into Hulk Hogan, even if it's against his will."

What would motivate someone to take steroids? Pope, Phillips and Olivardia say the Adonis Complex works in different ways for different men. "Michael," 32, one of their research subjects, told TIME he had always been a short kid who got picked on. He started working out at about 14, and he bought muscle magazines for advice. The pictures taunted him: he sweated, but he wasn't getting as big as the men in the pictures. Other men in his gym also

made him feel bad. When he found out they were on steroids, he did two cycles himself, even though he knew they could be dangerous.

But not all men with body-image problems take steroids. Jim Davis, 29, a human-services manager, told TIME he never took them, even when training for body-building competitions. But Davis says he developed a form of obsessive-compulsive disorder around his workouts. He lifted weights six days a week for at least six years. He worked out even when injured. He adhered to a rigid regimen for every session, and if he changed it, he felt anxious all day. He began to be worried about clothes, and eventually could wear only three shirts, ones that made him look big. He still felt small. "I would sit in class at college with a coat on," he says. You may have heard this condition called bigorexia—thinking your muscles are puny when they aren't. Pope and his colleagues call it muscle dysmorphia and estimate that hundreds of thousands of men suffer from it.

Even though most boys and men never approach the compulsion of Davis or Michael (both eventually conquered it), they undoubtedly face more pressure now than in the past to conform to an impossible ideal. Ripped male bodies are used today to advertise everything that shapely female bodies advertise: not just fitness products but also dessert liqueurs, microwave ovens and luxury hotels. The authors of *The Adonis Complex* want guys to rebel against those images, or at least see them for what they are: a goal unattainable without drug use.

Feminists raised these issues for women years ago, and more recent books such as *The Beauty Myth* were part of a backlash against the hourglass ideal. Now, says Phillips, "I actually think it may be harder for men than women to talk about these problems because it's not considered masculine to worry about such things." But maybe there is a masculine alternative: Next time WWF comes on, guys, throw the TV out the window. And order a large pizza.

VIEWPOINT ■ Joel Stein

I BLED FOR THIS COLUMN

I CANNOT WAIT TO LATHER UP MY NAKED, HAIRY BODY IN AN INflatable pool full of testosterone gel. I have felt testosterone deficient since I was five, when, surrounded by female friends, I spent my days compiling my sticker collection, listening to the *Annie* sound track, baking in my Easy-Bake Oven and arranging my glass-animal collection. Peggy Fleming had a more masculine childhood than I did.

But I needed to know precisely how unmanly I am, so I went to my doctor to get my T count checked. Unfortunately, my doctor could not administer the test via saliva; he would need a blood sample. That made me consider canceling my appointment, which in and of itself delivered the result I needed. But I made the appointment anyway. In 48 hours I would know how much man was in me.

For a long time, I've overcompensated for my lack of manliness through sportswriting, porn watching and stock buying, but deep down I know I'm a little shy on T. I cannot yell at other drivers, raise my voice, pick up women in a bar or grow a full beard. All whiskey, no matter how expensive, just tastes like burning. Yet deep inside I long to sleep around, to kick some ass, to release my first rap album. As I saw it, I had little choice but to score some of that testosterone gel when it comes out this summer. I could keep it in my jacket pocket for emergency situations, next to my lip balm and antibacterial hand gel. I'm thinking about marketing this as a first-aid kit for wusses.

Waiting for my results, feeling especially insecure, I called my masculinity mentor, Adam Carolla, the host of Comedy Central's *The Man Show*. "I'm guessing you're a little light," Carolla said. He suggested that I sign up for the AndroGel now. "A little extra

aggression, a couple of extra inches on the biceps, a little body hair could help you," he said. When I mentioned my concern about taking unprescribed medication, Carolla suggested that I just eat a lot of beef jerky. "I believe there is a lot of testosterone in jerky. That would be the most logical food to put it in, anyway," I suggested I might enjoy it more as a pasta with a light tomato-basil sauce, which I could market as "testosteroni." Carolla said he had to go.

Still anxious about my results, I called a former girlfriend, figuring she'd make me feel better. "I bet it's freakishly low," she said. "You're afraid of dogs; you once owned an Easy-Bake Oven; and you've never been much for fighting." Now I remembered there were good reasons our relationship didn't work out (one of them being that I told her about the Easy-Bake Oven).

After two neurosis-filled days, my doctor called and told me my testosterone level was totally normal. When I pressed him for a number, he said it was within the normal range of 260 to 1,000. When I really pressed him for a number, he told me it was 302. When I started to freak out about being in the bottom 10%, he again reassured me that it was completely normal. Yeah, normal in that I don't have breasts.

One of my female friends tried to comfort me, saying that women may have hot, wild flings with high-testosterone men, but they settle down with hormonally balanced guys. This did not make me feel better. You'd have to have a T count of 20 for this to make you feel any better. All I could think about was that now I have one less excuse for having an affair. Unless, of course, I'm all hopped up on man gel.

ESCAPING FROM THE DARKNESS

Drugs like Prozac, Paxil and Luvox can work wonders for clinically depressed kids. But what about the long-term consequences?

By HOWARD CHUA-EOAN

MEGAN KELLAR IS BUBBLY AND bouncing and lip-synching to the Backstreet Boys. *Get down, get down and move it all around!* The sixth-grader is dancing to the synthesized bubble-gum beat at a talent show at the John Muir Elementary School in Parma, Ohio. *Get down, get down and move it all around!* There is nothing down about Megan, even as she gets down in front of the audience. Her mother remembers a similar effervescence half a dozen years ago. "She'd be singing to herself and making up songs all the time," says Linda Kellar. And sure enough, that part of her is still there. "Megan's such a happy child," the mother of a girl on Megan's baseball team remarked to Linda. Yes, Linda agreed, but there's something you ought to know. Megan is clinically depressed and on the antidepressant Paxil. Says Linda: "She couldn't believe it."

Six years ago, Linda wouldn't have believed that her daughter was clinically depressed either. But shortly after her parents separated, Megan stopped singing. When other kids came over to play, she would lie down in the yard and just watch. At Christmas she wouldn't decorate the tree. Linda thought her daughter was simply melancholy over her parents' split and took her to see a counselor. That seemed to help for a while. Then for about eight months, when Megan was 10, she cried constantly and wouldn't go to school. She lost her appetite and got so weak that at one point she couldn't get out of bed. When a doctor recommended Paxil in conjunction with therapy, Linda recoiled. "I did not want to put my baby on an antidepressant," she says. Then she relented because, she says, "Megan wasn't liv-

ing her childhood." Linda noticed changes in just two weeks. Soon Megan was singing again. "She's not drugged or doped," says Linda. "She still cries when she sees *Old Yeller* and still has moody days." But, as Megan says, "I'm back to normal, like I used to be."

Megan Kellar shares her kind of normality with hundreds of thousands of other American kids. Each year an estimated 500,000 to 1 million prescriptions for antidepressants are written for children and teens. On the one hand, the benefits are apparent and important. Experts estimate that as many as 1 in 20 American preteens and adolescents suffer from clinical depression. It is something they cannot outgrow. Depression cycles over and over again throughout a lifetime, peaking during episodes of emotional distress, subsiding only to well up again at the next crisis. And as research increasingly shows, depression is often a marker for other disorders, including the syndrome that used to be called manic depression and is now known as bipolar disorder. If undetected and untreated in preteens, depressive episodes can lead to severe anxiety or manic outbursts not only in adulthood but as early as adolescence.

On the other hand, come the questions. How do we tell which kids are at risk? Has science fully apprised us of the effects on kids of medication designed for an adult brain? Have we set out on a path that will produce a generation that escapes the pain only to lose the character-building properties of angst?

TO MEDICATE OR NOT TO MEDICATE? THE DIlemma can be traced back to 1987, when the FDA approved Prozac as the first of a new class of antidepressants known as selective

serotonin reuptake inhibitors (SSRIs). Prozac had none of the more serious side effects and risks of the earlier antidepressants and worked faster to control depressive symptoms. Prozac and the other SSRIs (they now include Zoloft, Paxil, Luvox and Celexa) had one other advantage over the older, tricyclic antidepressants: children responded to them. One of the few recent studies on the subject showed that among depressed children ages 8 to 18, 56% improved while on Prozac, in contrast to 33% on a placebo. Says Dr. David Fassler, chair of the American Psychiatric Association's Council on Adolescents and Their Families: "Physicians have a lot of experience using the medications with adult patients with good results, and recent research increases their general level of comfort in using them with children and adolescents."

But which kids?

Not so long ago, many psychiatrists argued that children and young teens could not get depressed because they were not mature enough to internalize their anger. Today, says Fassler, "we realize that depression does occur in childhood and adolescence and that it occurs more often in children than we previously realized."

Still, depression is slightly harder to diagnose in adolescents than in adults, and not because teens are expected to be moodier and more withdrawn. They are less likely to realize that they are depressed and thus less likely to seek help. "Younger kids also have more difficulty expressing their feelings in words," says Dr. Boris Birmaher, a child psychiatrist at the University of Pittsburgh. "When kids become depressed, they become irritable, act out, have temper tantrums and other behavioral problems. It's hard to ascertain that these are the symptoms of depression unless you ask them questions in a language they can understand."

Furthermore, the very definition of being a child—what makes him survive and grow—is being able to move up and down

> ## "I would have sold my house ... to get Nick taken care of."
> —SUSAN DUBUQUE,
> author and mother

emotionally, having a basic elasticity. Says Dr. Peter Jensen, child and adolescent psychiatrist at the National Institute of Mental Health: "A child is more fluid and plastic than an adult. A child may look depressed one day because his dog died but seem O.K. three days later."

But if parents live in a world of family mood swings, that doesn't mean they are prepared to put their own child on mind-altering drugs. That prospect can lead to major soul searching: Will they be thought less of as parents? And if they do agree to antidepressants, will the child still be the one they know?

Donna Mitchell was told her daughter, eight-year-old Sawateos, had attention-deficit hyperactivity disorder, but she also showed signs of serious depression and anxiety, which are often found in combination. Mitchell's first reaction was, "I can pray this away. I thought, Listen, nobody in my family is going on drugs. That's an insult. I figured all we needed was family talks." But two years after the diagnosis, Mitchell has agreed to put her child on the ADHD drug Ritalin. She still resists the idea of antidepressants. It's her preteen daughter who's making the case for doing it. "Mama, it's in our genes," Sawateos tells her.

All this may help explain why it is so hard for the people closest to children to detect that anything is really wrong. Studies show that parents consistently miss the signs of depression. In one survey by researchers at Ball State and Columbia universities, 57% of teens who had attempted suicide were found to be suffering from major depression. But only 13% of the parents of suicides believed their child was depressed.

Diagnosis is critical because depressed children tend to develop increasingly severe mental disorders and in some cases psychosis as teens and adults. Three studies on children who were depressed before puberty show that as adults they had a higher rate of antisocial behavior, anxiety and major depression than those who experienced their first depressive episode as teens. "Prepubertal depression does occur, and those who get it are more susceptible to [the] mania [of bipolar disorder] later," says Dr. John March, director of the program on pediatric psychopharmacology at Duke University. "The earlier you get it, the more likely you will develop chronic depressive and anxiety symptoms."

So how do psychiatrists pick out kids who are depressed from those who are simply moody? In his book *"Help Me, I'm Sad,"* Fassler lists a number of physical symptoms in three age groups—preschoolers, young school-age children and adolescents. Among preschoolers, the signs include frequent, unexplained stomachaches, headaches and fatigue. Depressed school-age children frequently weigh 10 lbs. less than their peers, may have dramatic changes in sleep patterns and may start speaking in an affect-less monotone. Adolescents go through eating disorders, dramatic weight gains or losses, promiscuity, drug abuse, excessive picking at acne, and fingernail biting to the point of bleeding.

Fassler cautions that none of these symptoms may ever be present and a whole constellation of more subjective manifestations must be considered. Adults and adolescents share many of the same warning signs—low self-esteem, tearfulness, withdrawal and a morbid obsession with death and dying. Among adolescents, however, depression is often accompanied by episodes of irritability that, unlike mood swings, stretch for weeks rather than days.

Dr. Elizabeth Weller, professor of psychiatry and pediatrics at the University of Pennsylvania, has developed techniques for detecting depression in kids. First she establishes a rapport with a child. Then she asks, for example, whether he still has fun playing softball or whether it is taking him longer to finish his homework—both of which are ways to figure out whether the child has lost motivation and concentration. Crying is another marker for depression, but Weller says boys rarely admit to it. So she asks them how often they *feel* like crying.

She then quizzes parents and teachers for other signs. Parents can tell her if a child no

> ## "Depression occurs in children more often than we realized."
> —DAVID FASSLER,
> psychiatrist

longer cares about his appearance and has lost interest in bathing or getting new clothes. Teachers can tell her whether a child who used to be alert and active has turned to daydreaming or has lost a certain verve. As Weller puts it, "Has the bubble gone out of the face?"

There are several other complicating factors. Some psychiatrists believe depression

WHAT KIDS ARE TAKING

The most commonly prescribed antidepressants for children are not approved in the U.S. for those under 18, but anecdotal reports show that they appear to be safe and work well for this group. Some manufacturers of these drugs are currently conducting studies of their effect on depressed children.

	Prozac	Zoloft	Paxil	Luvox	Celexa
Approved for adults with	■ Depression ■ Bulimia ■ Obsessive-Compulsive Disorder	■ Depression ■ Obsessive-Compulsive Disorder ■ Panic Disorder	■ Depression ■ Obsessive-Compulsive Disorder ■ Panic Disorder ■ Social Phobia (approval pending)	■ Obsessive-Compulsive Disorder	■ Depression
Characteristics	Remains in body for at least two weeks. Makes some patients agitated, anxious	Remains in body for one week	Has sedating effect on many patients	Also approved for use in children with OCD	Produces fewer adverse reactions with other drugs

in younger children often appears in conjunction with other disorders. "Many depressed kids," notes Fassler, "are initially diagnosed with ADHD or learning disabilities. We need to separate out the conditions and treat both problems." But there's a chicken-and-egg problem here: antisocial behavior or a learning disability can lead a child to become isolated and alienated from peers and thus can trigger depression. And depression can further interfere with learning or bring on antisocial behavior.

But does a diagnosis of depression in a child require medication? Consider Nancy Allee's 10-month journey with SSRIs and other drugs. At 12, she was as bubbly as Megan Kellar is now. She soon developed "a five-month-long headache" and started having nightmares. After about a year in counseling, things seemed to be going better and, her mother Judith says, "we terminated it so as not to make it a way of life." A few months later, Nancy became hostile and rebellious but nothing that Judith considered "out of the bounds for a normal teenager." Then, "without any warning, she [took an] overdose" of her migraine medication, was hospitalized and depression was diagnosed. While Judith thought the overdose was out of the blue, Nancy says, "I'd had depression for a long time. If I'd had bad thoughts, I'd always had them and kind of grew up with them. I was always very bubbly, even when I was depressed. A lot of people didn't notice it. To me, suicide had always been an option."

Nancy was put on Zoloft. When that didn't work, the doctor added Paxil and then several other drugs. But there was a panoply of side effects: her hands would shake, she would bang her head against the wall. A voracious reader, she became too withdrawn and listless to pick up a book. There were times she couldn't sleep, but on one occasion she slept 72 hours straight.

"I was seeing five different doctors, and it was overkill," says Nancy. "At one point, I was taking 15 pills in the morning and 15 in the evening. I wound up burying my medication in the backyard. I didn't want to take it anymore." Then Nancy was tested for allergies, a process that required her to be medication free. "It was like the sky was blue again," says Nancy, who at 18 is still off drugs but sees a counselor occasionally. "The colors came back. It was a total change from the medication stupor. Everything wasn't peachy, but I was able to appreciate doing things again."

Most psychiatrists, despite their enthusiasm for the new antidepressants, write prescriptions for only six months to a year and taper the dosage toward the end. Even Fassler admits, "We try to use medication for the minimum amount of time possible. And with a younger child, we're more cautious about using medication because we have less research concerning both the effectiveness and the long-term consequences and

side effects." Says Michael Faenza, president of the National Mental Health Association: "I feel very strongly that no child should be receiving medication without counseling. Medication is just one spoke in the wheel."

HOW TO SPOT A DEPRESSED CHILD

The key thing to watch for is drastic changes in teen behavior. Other red flags to consider:

■ **DIFFICULTY MAINTAINING RELATIONSHIPS** May become antisocial, reject friends or refuse to take part in school and family events

■ **REDUCED PHYSICAL ACTIVITY** May suffer from lethargy or appear to drag self around

■ **MORBID OR SUICIDAL THOUGHTS** May seek out games, music, art or books with death-related themes

■ **LOW SELF-ESTEEM** May feel that they are worthless and that their peers, teachers and family disapprove of them

■ **SELF-DESTRUCTIVE BEHAVIOR** May harm their body by, for example, biting fingernails to the point of bleeding

■ **PROBLEMS AT SCHOOL** Grades may drop or classroom troublemaking rise

■ **CHANGES IN SLEEP PATTERNS** May either have restless nights or sleep away the day

Preschoolers

■ Frequent unexplained stomachaches, headaches, or fatigue

■ Overactivity or excessive restlessness

■ A sad appearance

■ Low tolerance for frustration

■ Irritability

■ Loss of pleasure in activities

■ Tendency to portray the world as bleak

The lack of science about the effects of these drugs on childhood development is the reason the FDA has required all manufacturers of SSRIs that treat depression to conduct studies on the subject. Says Dr. Peter Kramer, professor of psychiatry at Brown University and author of *Listening to Prozac:*

"Anyone who thinks about this problem is worried about what it means to substantially change neurotransmission in a developing brain. We don't know if these kids would compensate on their own over time and if by giving them these medicines we are interfering with that compensatory mechanism."

Until we know more, some argue, the risks of such medication are just too great, if only because of the message it sends to children. Says Dr. Sidney Wolfe, director of Public Citizen's Health Research Group: "We are moving into an era where any quirk of a personality is fair game for a drug. On one hand, we are telling kids to just say no to drugs, but on the other hand, their pediatricians are saying, 'Take this. You'll feel good.'"

Teen rebellion can put a twist on even that, however. One New York couple, becalmed by antidepressants themselves and openly concerned about the depression of their 18-year-old, were castigated by their son for their "weakness" and dependence on Prozac. His argument: your drugs change who you really are. In place of their drugs, the young man argued for his "natural" remedy: marijuana.

Indeed, pot and alcohol are common forms of self-medication among depressed teens. Weller estimates that about 30% of her teen patients have used pot or alcohol after a depressive episode, most of them at the urging of friends who said smoking and drinking would make them feel better. A high school social worker in Minnesota decided to look into the case of a troubled girl who was still a freshman at 17. The girl admitted she smoked pot as a constant habit but did not understand why she craved it so much. A psychological evaluation found the girl was suffering from clinical depression as well as ADHD. She was prescribed an antidepressant, which had striking results. It not only elevated her mood and helped her focus but also reduced her desire for pot and tobacco.

"IT USED TO BE SAID THAT ADOLESCENCE IS the most common form of psychosis," says Kramer, the man who helped make Prozac famous. Then he turns serious. "But if a child has a prolonged period of depressive moods, he needs to be evaluated for depression." Even if little is known about the long-term effects of SSRIs on young bodies, most doctors in the field argue that the drugs are a blessing to kids in pain. Says Duke's March, who is doing a comparative study of the benefits of Prozac and cognitive-behavior therapy: "My clinical experience is that it's worse to risk a major mental illness as a child than to be on medication. If you weigh the risks against the benefits, the benefits are probably going to win."

Susan Dubuque of Richmond, Va., is convinced of the benefits. Her son Nick went through "seven years of testing hell." At seven, ADHD was diagnosed and he was put

The Danger of Suppressing Sadness

What if Holden Caulfield had been taking Prozac?

CONSIDERING HIS WEALTH OF SYMPTOMS—lethargy, forgetfulness, loss of interest in friends and studies—can there be any doubt that Holden Caulfield, the dropout hero of J.D. Salinger's 1950s masterpiece *The Catcher in the Rye,* would be on Luvox, Prozac or a similar drug if he were a teenager today? No doubt whatsoever. A textbook teen depressive by current standards, Caulfield would be a natural candidate for pharmaceutical intervention, joining a rising number of adolescents whose moodiness, anxiety, and rebelliousness are being interpreted as warning signs of chemical imbalances. Indeed, if Caulfield had been a '90s teen, his incessant griping about "phonies" and general hostility toward mainstream society might have been nipped in the neurological bud. The cultural consequences? Incalculable.

With the stroke of countless pens on thousands of prescription pads, the American coming-of-age experience—the stuff of endless novels, movies and pop songs—could gradually be rendered unrecognizable. Goodbye Salinger, Elvis and Bob Dylan; hello psychopharmacology. "The kids in my school traded Zoloft and Prozac pills the way kids used to trade baseball cards," says Stephen Morris, an Episcopal priest and former chaplain at a Texas parochial school. Of course, this school experience doesn't prove that schoolyards everywhere have turned into bustling prescription-drug bazaars. But Morris, who headed a schoolwide committee called Addressing Behaviors of Concern, recalls that "the problems we focused on were not dramatically different from my own youthful experiences." At least three-quarters of the time, says Morris, the kids in question were placed on medication in what he saw as the beginning of a vicious cycle that frequently worsened the original problem. "Challenges that teachers used to handle are being handed over to psychiatrists. Instead of dealing with kids inside the classroom, they yank them out, put them on drugs and stick them back in with glazed eyes a few days later. No wonder the kids end up as outcasts."

Such outcasts may someday form their own majority, if this trend continues. The pain and confusion of growing up, once considered the proper subject of gloomy poetry read under the blankets and angry rock songs rehearsed in the garage, can now mean a quick ticket to the doctor's office. And it doesn't take a lot of acting up for a restless teenager to attract professional attention. On a website sponsored by Channel One, a television network for school-age youth, a recent posting written with the help of the National Association for Mental Illness classified the following behaviors as possible symptoms of manic depression in teens: "increased talking—the adolescent talks too much," "distractibility," unrealistic highs in self-esteem—for example, a teenager who feels specially connected to God."

That last one is a doozy. And heartbreaking. Could it be that Cassie Bernal, who bravely professed her religious faith while staring down the barrel of a gun at the height of the Columbine massacre, was not so much a hero and a martyr as an untreated candidate for lithium? For the education establishment to go on red alert at the first sign of spirituality in their students would be a devastating development.

What is happening here? For better or worse, an institutional drug culture has sprung up in the hallways of All-American High, mimicking the one already established among depressed adults. As was pointed out in the May issue of *Harper's* magazine, the line between illicit, feel-good drugs such as marijuana and amphetamines and legal mood-altering substances such as Luvox, Wellbutrin, and Effexor is a blurry one. Many of the same optimistic claims—enhanced concentration, decreased anxiety, a renewed capacity for feeling pleasure—are made for both types of magic bullet, whether they are bought on the street or in a pharmacy. A profoundly mixed message is being sent to teens when certain substances are demonized for promoting the same subjective states touted on the labels of other compounds. Adolescents, who are famously alert to hypocrisy among their elders, will surely be the first to catch this irony.

At least one hopes so. Teenage skepticism—Holden Caulfield's bitter gift for discerning inconsistencies in the solemn pronouncements of adults—may be one of the troubling traits on the medicators' target list. A pill that tones down youthful b.s. detectors would certainly be a boon to parents and teachers, but how would it enrich the lives of teenagers? Even if such a pill improved their moods—helping them to stick to their studies, say, and compete in a world with close to zero tolerance for unproductive monkeying around—would it not rob them (and the rest of us) of a potent source of social criticism, political idealism and cultural change? The trials and tribulations of growing up yield wisdom for all involved, both kids and parents. The young pose a constant challenge to the old, often an uncomfortable one, almost always an unexpected one, but meeting that challenge with hastily filled prescriptions may be bad medicine for everybody.

For teens who need medication just to function or lessen the real dangers they might pose to others or themselves, the new medications may truly be miraculous. I know from my own experience with clinical depression (contracted as an adult and treated with a combination of therapy and drugs) that such diseases are real and formidable, impossible to wish away. But for kids in the murky emotional borderlands described in books like *The Catcher in the Rye,* antidepressants, stimulants and sedatives aren't a substitute for books and records, heroes and antiheroes. "I get bored sometimes," Holden Caulfield says, "when people tell me to act my age. Sometimes I act a lot older than I am—I really do—but people never notice it. People never notice anything."

Maybe if people start noticing first and medicating second, more of today's confused young Caulfields will stand a chance of maturing into Salingers.

---

on Ritalin. "When he was 10 years old, he didn't want a birthday party because he just couldn't deal with it," she recalls. Then, his mother says, Nick "bottomed out and became suicidal, and one day I found him in a closet with a toy gun pointed at his head, and he said, 'If this was real, I'd use it.' " The next day she saw a psychologist who had recently evaluated Nick and was told, "If you don't get him help, next time he'll be successful." Nick was found to be suffering from clinical depression and took a series of antidepressants. "I was worried about my son's killing himself," says Susan, who was called by clinicians a "histrionic mother" and a "therapy junkie," as she spent $4,000 on drugs and therapy for her son. "I would have sold my house if that was what it would have taken."

Nick is better now, and has co-authored a book with his mom: *Kid Power Tactics for Dealing with Depression.* Susan is happy to have her son back safe—even though there is some stress. "It's so much fun to have an obnoxious 15-year-old," she says, "and I mean *normal* obnoxious."

—**Reported by Jodie Morse/New York, Alice Park/Washington and James Willwerth/ Los Angeles**

ADOLESCENT ATTRACTION TO CULTS

Eagan Hunter

ABSTRACT

This article details the reasons behind adolescents' attraction to cults. It is recommended that parents, teachers, and counselors familiarize themselves with the warning signs. Suggestions are offered on how to make adolescents less vulnerable to cult overtures.

Reprint requests to Brother Eagan Hunter, C.S.C., Professor of Education, St. Edward's University, School of Education, 3001 South Congress Avenue, Austin, Texas 78704.

Adolescence is the transitional period between the dependence of childhood and the assumption of the rights and responsibilities of adulthood. It is a time when young people attempt to understand who they are, what they can do, and why they are here. Their freedom to make decisions greatly increases, but, at the same time, certain adult privileges remain inaccessible. Their lives seem to be filled with possibilities, restrictions, and uncertainties.

New and unfamiliar situations quickly generate unrest and crisis, arising during an important period of identity development. To establish a coherent identity, adolescents draw from models and ideals found within their environment. They may seek out reliable standards to achieve a sense of security, only to find confusing, paradoxical social rules. They therefore may have difficulty distinguishing

From *Adolescence,* Fall 1998, pp. 709-714. © 1998 by Libra Publishers, Inc. Reprinted by permission.

between heroes and anti-heroes, and may end up seeing themselves only in negative terms, producing a severe identity crisis. Having sought independence, they find that they fear standing alone.

Thus, it is not surprising that adolescents, having encountered conflict, confusion, and frustration, often feel disoriented and anxious. Fearing rejection by a society that they do not understand, they may retreat into isolation, or demonstrate inappropriate emotional outbursts, aggression, and rebellion, and embrace radical causes. All of these are youthful cries of pain, cries for help and understanding.

Traditionally, young people have been critical of, and impatient with, the established values and behavior patterns of society. They desire change, and experience frustration when it does not occur. Their idealism leads them to believe that those in power, as well as established institutions, have failed to meet the legitimate needs of various groups. To them, social problems and their solutions stand out in stark clarity.

In addition, during adolescence higher-order thinking skills become engaged; it is a time of intellectual curiosity, of seeking truth. Youths are intellectually and spiritually open to new ideas. Unfortunately, they have not achieved the balance of experience and maturity that would enable them to sort truth from illusion and reality from fantasy in all situations. They have not gained sufficient sophistication to evaluate—critically and methodically—complex philosophies.

Many youth movements play upon this naive idealism and intellectual curiosity. The young person may be challenged to answer the clarion call to join a group that professes to offer a vision of a perfect society, one in which all injustices are rectified. After all, how could any self-respecting person, caring for the world and its people, not be willing to give this "new way" a try?

Group membership can lead to either positive or negative outcomes. For example, the Peace Corps and various forms of community service and mentor programs are excellent ways for youth to achieve self-actualization. On the other hand, gangs and cults suppress individuality and foster estrangement from society.

The personality profile of an adolescent susceptible to cult overtures might include identity confusion or crisis; alienation from family; weak cultural, religious, and community ties; and feelings of powerlessness in a seemingly out-of-control world. Studies have indicated that a surprising number of cult members come from democratic and egalitarian homes and upper socioeconomic levels, rather than overpermissive, overindulgent, dysfunctional, and poor families. In fact, Andron (1983) reports that many cults focus on the recruitment of gifted and creative adolescents. Therefore, it is extremely

difficult to delineate a precise portrait of potential adolescent cult members.

In a review of the literature, Wright and Piper (1986) reported that alienation from family relationships precedes cult membership. Youths are compensating for unfulfilled needs (e.g., love, sense of belonging), the lack of which hinders the development of self-esteem, social competence, and mastery of life tasks. In turn, this generates attempts to gain approval and recognition. Wright and Piper indicated that the attraction to cults is strengthened by the fact that a cult's rules often are better defined than those of the family. Adherence to the cult lifestyle often results in radical behavior changes, along with "a loss of identity" compensated by an "enslavement to cult leaders" and further estrangement from family.

Parents, teachers, and coaches sometimes place excessive demands on youth. Such pressures frequently lead to undesirable outcomes, such as physical or intellectual burnout, drug use, or escape to what appears to be the safety of a cult. Adults must remember that there is a time for everything—a time simply to enjoy being young, and later, after normal adolescent development has progressed, a time increasingly for admission into the competitive, success-oriented adult world.

There has been a marked decline in the influence of the family and traditional religious beliefs, with a concomitant liberalization of personal values. The social climate has nourished rejection of cultural and moral standards. This has left adults and especially adolescents with the dilemma of finding values with which to fill this vacuum, so as to be able to resolve old problems and discover new solutions. Mike Warnke (1972), a former drug addict and satanic high priest who became involved in the anti-occult counseling program Alpha Omega Outreach, explains that a person "is constructed like a triangle, with one side representing his physical needs, the second his mental needs, and the third his spiritual needs. A person fulfilling only his physical and mental needs is not complete . . . [and] is consciously or subconsciously undergoing a search for spiritual fulfillment, wherever he can find it—in drugs, the occult." The loss of society's religious and social moorings leaves many youths adrift. The desire to become a complete person—to complete the triangle of their being—leads many, Warnke warns, into dangerous ways.

In the absence of authentic, stabilizing standards upon which youth can depend and trust, self-destructive tendencies quickly emerge. Adolescents become vulnerable to academic failure, suicide, drug and alcohol abuse, pregnancy and sexually transmitted diseases, risk-taking behavior, violence, and gang and cult membership.

Zimbardo and Hartley (1985) reported that approximately 50% of the high school

students included in their survey had been approached to join a cult. Wright and Piper (1986) have indicated that cults are most successful in recruiting individuals between 18 and 23 years of age, when persons are most likely to be seeking "perfect" answers to life's questions and problems. Because of their immaturity, they fail to take into account the long-term consequences of cult membership.

Rudin (1990) defines cults as "groups or movements exhibiting an excessive devotion or dedication to some person, idea, or thing. Such cults employ unethically manipulative techniques of persuasion and control designed to advance the goals of the group's leaders to the determent of members, their families, or the community." Cults attract youths experiencing psychological stress, rootlessness, feelings of emptiness and of being disenfranchised, and identity diffusion and confusion. Such youths come from all walks of life and from all classes of society. Cults seem to offer confused and isolated adolescents a moratorium—a period of dropping-out, or a "time-out"—as well as a highly structured sense of belonging and a means of escape from being "normless."

The terms "church," "sect," and "cult" should be distinguished. Church usually is applied to specific religious organizations. A sect is an offshoot of a particular religious body, whose members prefer to follow doctrines or teachings that differ from the parent group. A cult exhibits many of the characteristics of a sect. However, it represents a major and abrupt break with the past. A cult is viewed by its members as the climax of history, and often emphasizes devotion to a single person. Legitimate movements withstand the test of time to prove their authenticity.

A distinguishing characteristic of cults is that they prey upon a person's fears through a systematic process of "brainwashing" and "programming." They recruit aggressively. Strong efforts are made to separate members from family and former associates—to cut them off from their past—in order to establish new values and standards requiring total dependence on, and devotion to, the cult itself. There is usually an all-powerful authoritarian leader. Members may be psychologically, physically, or sexually abused, with discipline maintained through fear. Rudin (1990) states that "what makes a group a cult is the deception and manipulation of its members and the harm done to them and to society, not its ideals or theology." Notable examples have been the mass suicide of the followers of Jim Jones in Guyana (1978), the holocaustic climax of the disciples of David Koresh in Waco, Texas (1993), and most recently the group suicide of the Heaven's Gate believers in San Diego (1997).

Davidowitz (1989) has stated that an increasing number of adolescents are falling under the influence of Satanism. Evidence includes the desecration of cemeteries and the theft of bodies; the appearance of satanic symbols and themes in contemporary literature, art, and music; and in an extreme case, the satanic, ritualistic murders in Matamoros, Mexico. Belitz and Schacht (1992) have indicated that male youths from abusive families are especially vulnerable to satanic cult recruitment. Adolescents seeking a sense of power over their own lives as well as over others are susceptible.

According to Rudin (1990), this process has several stages. Initially it begins as a fun experience, with adolescents involved in fantasy and role-playing games based on occult ideology and incorporating an obsession with violence. These adolescents are usually deeply involved in heavy metal rock music and, frequently, brag about their activities to boost their self-image. This type of involvement tends to make the individual receptive to satanic activities. A "dabbler" stage follows, in which satanic literature and paraphernalia are acquired. The transition from fun-and-games to serious interest opens the door to satanic recruitment through clubs, hangouts, and private parties. As involvement deepens, cruelty to animals, rape and molestation, drug use, and even murder may follow.

It is the responsibility of society in general and the family in particular to be alert to the danger signs, especially during the early stages of youth involvement. However, with society fractured and unable to fulfill this role, educators, social workers, and psychologists must rise to the occasion. In addition, the cooperation and support of religious institutions, civic organizations, and government agencies must be enlisted.

School and youth organizations can be particularly helpful. The sensitive teacher or counselor can be watchful for the warning signs—confusion, alienation, sudden changes in personality or behavior, withdrawal from home and social activities, the development of antisocial attitudes, a decline in academic achievement, the assumption of an unusual style of dress, and preference for music with satanic themes—and intervene in a timely fashion.

However, caring adults must be proactive rather than merely reactive. They can help adolescents to develop a strong self-concept, one that is not vulnerable to the harmful attractions of a cult. They can assist youths to formulate positive, realistic life goals, and ease the emotional impact of inevitable frustrations. Adults must be willing to discuss—knowledgeably, frankly, and honestly—the various personal and social issues confronting adolescents, such as substance abuse, AIDS, teenage pregnancy, as well as the insidiousness of cults.

Adolescents seek self-identity and acceptance as unique individuals. They search for standards and values upon which to model their behavior. Educational and social institutions must be made welcoming places in which young people feel a sense of belonging, places of understanding and trust, places of stability in a rapidly changing world. Adolescents should be shown ways to achieve a richer and more meaningful life, to attain their natural potential, and to become contributing members of society. The meeting of these challenges and opportunities is what education for life—not for death—is all about.

REFERENCES

Andron, S. (1983). Our gifted teens and the cults. *Gifted, Creative, Talented Children, 26,* 32–33.

Belitz, J., & Schacht, A. (1992). Satanism as a response to abuse: The dynamics and treatment of satanic involvement in male youths. *Adolescence, 27*(108), 855–872.

Davidowitz, E. (1989). Die mother father brother. *Redbook, 172,* 132–134.

Rudin, M. R. (1990). Cults and Satanism: Threats to teens. *National Association of Secondary School Principals Bulletin, 74,* 46–52.

Warnke, M. (1972). *The Satan seller.* South Plainfield, NJ: Bridge Publishers.

Wright, S. A., & Piper, E. S. (1986). Families and cults: Familial factors related to youth leaving or remaining in deviant religious groups. *Journal of Marriage and the Family, 48,* 15–25.

Zimbardo, P. G., & Hartley, C. (1985). Cults go to high school: A theoretical and empirical analysis of the initial steps in the recruitment process. *Cultic Studies Journal, 2,* 91–147.

Furlong, Mike, 213

Test Your Knowledge Form

We encourage you to photocopy and use this page as a tool to assess how the articles in **Annual Editions** expand on the information in your textbook. By reflecting on the articles you will gain enhanced text information. You can also access this useful form on a product's book support Web site at **http://www.dushkin.com/online/.**

NAME: DATE:

TITLE AND NUMBER OF ARTICLE:

BRIEFLY STATE THE MAIN IDEA OF THIS ARTICLE:

LIST THREE IMPORTANT FACTS THAT THE AUTHOR USES TO SUPPORT THE MAIN IDEA:

WHAT INFORMATION OR IDEAS DISCUSSED IN THIS ARTICLE ARE ALSO DISCUSSED IN YOUR TEXTBOOK OR OTHER READINGS THAT YOU HAVE DONE? LIST THE TEXTBOOK CHAPTERS AND PAGE NUMBERS:

LIST ANY EXAMPLES OF BIAS OR FAULTY REASONING THAT YOU FOUND IN THE ARTICLE:

LIST ANY NEW TERMS/CONCEPTS THAT WERE DISCUSSED IN THE ARTICLE, AND WRITE A SHORT DEFINITION:

We Want Your Advice

ANNUAL EDITIONS revisions depend on two major opinion sources: one is our Advisory Board, listed in the front of this volume, which works with us in scanning the thousands of articles published in the public press each year; the other is you—the person actually using the book. Please help us and the users of the next edition by completing the prepaid article rating form on this page and returning it to us. Thank you for your help!

ANNUAL EDITIONS: Adolescent Psychology 01/02

ARTICLE RATING FORM

Here is an opportunity for you to have direct input into the next revision of this volume. We would like you to rate each of the 46 articles listed below, using the following scale:

1. Excellent: should definitely be retained
2. Above average: should probably be retained
3. Below average: should probably be deleted
4. Poor: should definitely be deleted

Your ratings will play a vital part in the next revision. So please mail this prepaid form to us just as soon as you complete it. Thanks for your help!

RATING — ARTICLE

1. The Rise and Decline of the Teenager
2. The Way We Weren't: The Myth and Reality of the "Traditional" Family
3. Adolescence: Pathologizing a Normal Process
4. Inside the Teen Brain
5. Yesterday's Precocious Puberty Is Norm Today
6. The 1997 Body Image Survey Results
7. Adolescent Male Athletes: Body Image, Diet, and Exercise
8. A Study of White Middle-Class Adolescent Boys' Responses to "Semenarche" (The First Ejaculation)
9. The Consequences of Insufficient Sleep for Adolescents: Links between Sleep and Emotional Regulation
10. Musings in the Wake of Columbine: What Can Schools Do?
11. Mommy, What's a Classroom?
12. The LD Label for Relatively Well-Functioning Students: A Critical Analysis
13. Good Mentoring Keeps At-Risk Youth in School
14. Schools the Source of Rough Transitions
15. The Cheating Game
16. Gender Gap in Math Scores Is Closing
17. The Moral Development of Children
18. Raising Better Boys
19. Ethnicity, Identity Formation, and Risk Behavior among Adolescents of Mexican Descent
20. "I'm Just Who I Am"
21. The EQ Factor
22. Adolescence: Whose Hell Is It?

RATING — ARTICLE

23. How Teens Strain the Family
24. "Don't Talk Back!"
25. Effects of Paternal Absence on Male Adolescents' Peer Relations and Self-Image
26. Gay Families Come Out
27. The Truth about Tweens
28. Teen Jobs: How Much Is Too Much?
29. Inside the Crazy Culture of Kids Sports
30. Stop Blaming Kids and TV: Who Us?
31. The Secret Life of Teens
32. Teen Tobacco Wars
33. Too Young to Date?
34. A Clack of Tiny Sparks
35. The Neglected Heart: The Emotional Dangers of Premature Sexual Involvement
36. Boys Call Me Cow
37. Trends in Sexual Activity among Adolescent American Women: 1982–1995
38. Reflections on Two Decades of Research on Teen Sexual Behavior and Pregnancy
39. Key Skill for Teen Parents: Having Realistic Expectations
40. Young Adults and AIDS: 'It Can't Happen to Me'
41. Programs Go beyond "Just Saying No"
42. Courtroom Justice for Teens—by Teens
43. Looking for Trouble
44. Never Too Buff
45. Escaping from the Darkness
46. Adolescent Attraction to Cults

(Continued on next page)

ANNUAL EDITIONS: ADOLESCENT PSYCHOLOGY 01/02

BUSINESS REPLY MAIL
FIRST-CLASS MAIL PERMIT NO. 84 GUILFORD CT

POSTAGE WILL BE PAID BY ADDRESSEE

McGraw-Hill/Dushkin
530 Old Whitfield Street
Guilford, CT 06437-9989

Illmullmdudullmullldudldudadldudld

ABOUT YOU

Name   Date

Are you a teacher? ☐   A student? ☐
Your school's name

Department

Address   City   State   Zip

School telephone #

YOUR COMMENTS ARE IMPORTANT TO US!

Please fill in the following information:
For which course did you use this book?

Did you use a text with this *ANNUAL EDITION*? ☐ yes ☐ no
What was the title of the text?

What are your general reactions to the *Annual Editions* concept?

Have you read any particular articles recently that you think should be included in the next edition?

Are there any articles you feel should be replaced in the next edition? Why?

Are there any World Wide Web sites you feel should be included in the next edition? Please annotate.

May we contact you for editorial input? ☐ yes ☐ no
May we quote your comments? ☐ yes ☐ no